Lecture Notes in Computer Science　　8321

Commenced Publication in 1973
Founding and Former Series Editors:
Gerhard Goos, Juris Hartmanis, and Jan van Leeuwen

T0212839

Prosenjit Gupta   Christos Zaroliagis (Eds.)

Applied Algorithms

First International Conference, ICAA 2014
Kolkata, India, January 13-15, 2014
Proceedings

 Springer

Volume Editors

Prosenjit Gupta
Heritage Institute of Technology
Computer Science and Engineering
Chowbaga Road
Anandapur, Kolkata 700107, India
E-mail: prosenjit.gupta@heritageit.edu

Christos Zaroliagis
University of Patras
Department of Computer Engineering and Informatics
26500 Patras, Greece
E-mail: zaro@ceid.upatras.gr

ISSN 0302-9743   e-ISSN 1611-3349
ISBN 978-3-319-04125-4   e-ISBN 978-3-319-04126-1
DOI 10.1007/978-3-319-04126-1
Springer Cham Heidelberg New York Dordrecht London

Library of Congress Control Number: 2013956128

CR Subject Classification (1998): F.2, I.2, H.3-4, F.1, C.2, D.2, D.4.6

LNCS Sublibrary: SL 2 – Programming and Software Engineering

Typesetting: Camera-ready by author, data conversion by Scientific Publishing Services, Chennai, India

Printed on acid-free paper

Springer is part of Springer Science+Business Media (www.springer.com)

Preface

This volume contains papers accepted for presentation at the International Conference on Applied Algorithms (ICAA 2014) held at the Heritage Institute of Technology, Kolkata, India, during January 13–15, 2014, together with the extended or short abstracts of 7 invited lectures given by Susanne Albers (Technical University of Munich, Germany), Bhargab Bhattacharya (Indian Statistical Institute, Kolkata, India), Gautam Das (University of Texas at Arlington, USA), Dimitrios Gunopulos (University of Athens, Greece), Rina Panigrahy (Microsoft Research, Mountain View, USA), Assaf Schuster (Technion, Israel Institute of Technology, Haifa, Israel), and Christos Zaroliagis (CTI & University of Patras, Greece).

ICAA is a new conference series with a mission to provide a quality forum for researchers working in applied algorithms. Papers presenting original contributions related to the design, analysis, implementation, and experimental evaluation of efficient algorithms and data structures for problems with relevant real-world applications were sought, ideally bridging the gap between academia and industry. Papers were solicited describing original research in a variety of areas including (but not limited to):

- Algorithmic Microfluidics
- Algorithms for VLSI CAD
- Analysis of Algorithms
- Approximation Algorithms
- Big Data Algorithms
- Cloud Computing
- Computational Advertising
- Computational Biology
- Computational Geometry
- Computational Services Science
- Computational Transportation Science
- Cryptography and Security
- Databases
- Data Mining
- Data Structures
- Distributed Algorithms
- Energy Efficient Algorithms
- External Memory Algorithms
- Graph Algorithms
- Graph Drawing
- Hardware Accelerated Algorithms
- Heuristic Search
- Image Processing

- Information Retrieval
- Location Based Services
- Machine Learning
- Parallel Algorithms
- Pattern Recognition
- Railway Optimization
- Randomized Algorithms
- Recommender Systems
- Robotics
- Spatial Informatics
- Social Network Analysis
- Web Intelligence
- Web Mining
- Web Searching

In response to the call-for-papers, 122 submissions from 9 countries were received. The Program Committee (comprising of 31 members from 7 countries) selected 21 papers for presentation. The criteria for selection were perceived originality, quality, and relevance to the subject area of the conference. Considerable effort was devoted to the evaluation of the submissions and to providing authors with helpful feedback. Towards this end, the Program Committee was assisted by 45 external reviewers.

We thank all those who submitted papers for consideration, as well as the Program Committee members and external reviewers for their invaluable contribution. We thank the management of the Heritage Institute of Technology and the Kalyan Bharathi Trust and the entire Organizing Committee for the excellent arrangements leading up to and during the entire conference. Finally, we gratefully acknowledge the generous financial support received from the TEQIP grant which made this conference a possibility.

January 2014   Prosenjit Gupta
                                                     Christos Zaroliagis

Organizing Committee

Heritage Institute of Technology, Kolkata, India

Advisors

H.K. Chaudhary, Chairman	Kalyan Bharti Trust
P.K. Agarwal, CEO	Kalyan Bharti Trust
Probir Roy, Executive Director	Kalyan Bharti Trust
B.B. Paira, Advisor	Higher Education, Kalyan Bharti Trust
D.C. Ray, TEQIP-II Coordinator	Heritage Institute of Technology
S.N. Biswas, Deputy Director	Heritage Institute of Technology
Sukumar Ghosh, Professor	University of Iowa, USA

General Chairs

Pranay Chaudhuri, Principal	Heritage Institute of Technology
Amitava Bagchi, Professor	Department of Computer Science and Engineering

Organizing Chairs

Kalarab Ray
Tapan Chakraborty
Subhashis Majumder

Subcommittee Chairs

Satarupa Bagchi Biswas
Dinabandhu Bhandari
Arindam Chatterjee
Poulami Das
Aniruddha Dasgupta
Hemanta K. De
Anindita Kundu
Anindya Jyoti Pal
Shilpi Saha
Sujay Saha
Somenath Sengupta
Arvind Srivastava

Local Hospitality

All faculty members and technical assistants of
The Department of Computer Science and Engineering and
The Department of Information Technology,
Heritage Institute of Technology, Kolkata, India.

Program Committee

Bogdan Arsintescu	Google, Mountain View, USA
Mukul Bansal	MIT
Kostas Berberidis	University of Patras, Greece
Bhargab Bhattacharya	Indian Statistical Institute, India
Danny Chen	University of Notre Dame, France
Jinjun Chen	University of Technology, Australia
Anandaswarup Das	IBM Research
Gautam Das	University of Texas at Arlington, USA
Nabanita Das	Indian Statistical Institute, India
Aniruddha Dasgupta	Heritage Institute of Technology, India
Bhaskar Dasgupta	University of Illinois at Chicago, USA
Dimitrios Gunopulos	National and Kapodistrian University of Athens, Greece
Prosenjit Gupta	Heritage Institute of Technology, India
Ravi Janardan	University of Minnesota, USA
C.V. Jawahar	IIIT Hyderabad, India
Matthew Katz	Ben-Gurion University of the Negev, Israel
Spyros Kontogiannis	University of Ioannina
Vamsi Kundeti	Intel
Subhashis Majumder	Heritage Institute of Technology, India
Neeraj Mittal	University of Texas at Dallas, USA
Srihari Nelakuditi	University of South Carolina, USA
Nikos Nikolaidis	Aristotle University of Thessaloniki, Greece
Rina Panigrahy	Microsoft Research
Sudeshna Sarkar	IIT Kharagpur, India
Anup Sen	Indian Institute of Management, India
Michiel Smid	Carleton University, Canada
Jack Snoeyink	University of North Carolina at Chapel Hill, USA
Kannan Srinathan	IIIT Hyderabad, India
Kostas Tsichlas	Aristotle University of Thessaloniki, Greece
Dorothea Wagner	Karlsruhe Institute of Technology, Germany
Christos Zaroliagis	University of Patras, Greece

Additional Reviewers

Abu-Affash, A. Karim
Aschner, Rom
Bagchi, Amitava
Banerjee, Ansuman
Banerjee, Sabyasachee
Barash, Danny
Basu Chowdhuri, Partha
Basuchowdhuri, Partha
Baum, Moritz
Bläsius, Thomas
Carmi, Paz
Chatterjee, Arindam
Chen, Jianxu
Christodoulakis, Manolis
Das, Poulami
Fotakis, Dimitris
Freeman, Clinton
Fuchs, Fabian
Gallopoulos, Efstratios
Gounaris, Anastasios
Iakovidou, Nantia
Kappes, Andrea
Katsaros, Dimitrios

Kondapally, Ranganath
Konstantinou, Elisavet
Kosmatopoulos, Andreas
Kundu, Malay Kumar
Majumder, Prasenjit
Mchedlidze, Tamara
Mu, Jian
Nandy, Subhas
Nikoletseas, Sotiris
Nöllenburg, Martin
Papadopoulos, Apostolos
Prutkin, Roman
Ramachandran, Arunmoezhi
Rapti, Angeliki
Saha, Sujay
Segal, Michael
Sioutas, Spyros
Sur-Kolay, Susmita
Tefas, Anastasios
Tong, Yan
Wang, Jiazhuo
Xue, Yuan
Zhang, Yizhe

Abstracts of Invited Talks

Algorithmic Challenges in Digital Microfluidic Biochips: Protocols, Design, and Test*

Bhargab B. Bhattacharya[1,**], Sudip Roy[2,***], and Sukanta Bhattacharjee[1]

[1] Nanotechnology Research Triangle, Indian Statistical Institute,
Kolkata 700108, India
{bhargab,sukanta_r}@isical.ac.in
[2] Dept. of CSE, Indian Institute of Technology Kharagpur, Kharagpur 721302, India
sudipr@cse.iitkgp.ernet.in

Abstract. Recent emergence of microfluidic technology has imparted a profound impact on the implementation of miniaturized healthcare chips and systems. In this review article, we will elaborate on several algorithmic challenges that arise while realizing biochemical protocols on a digital microfluidic (DMF) lab-on-a-chip. In particular, we will focus on certain design automation issues of sample preparation, dilution gradient generation, layout planning, and testing of DMF biochips.

---

* Invited Paper.
** The work of B. B. Bhattacharya was supported by a special grant to Nanotechnology Research Triangle from Indian Statistical Institute, Kolkata, India.
*** This work of S. Roy was supported by Microsoft Corporation and Microsoft Research India under the Microsoft Research India PhD Fellowship Award (2010-2014).

Energy-Efficient Algorithms

Susanne Albers

Department of Computer Science
Technische Universität München
albers@in.tum.de

Abstract. We study algorithmic techniques for energy savings in computer systems. We consider power-down mechanisms that transition an idle system into low power stand-by or sleep states. Moreover, we address dynamic speed scaling, a relatively recent approach to save energy in modern, variable-speed microprocessors.

In the first part of the talk we survey important results in the area of energy-efficient algorithms. In the second part we investigate a setting where a variable-speed processor is equipped with an additional sleep state. This model integrates speed scaling and power-down mechanisms. We consider classical deadline-based scheduling and settle the complexity of the offline problem. As the main contribution we present an algorithmic framework that allows us to develop a number of significantly improved constant-factor approximation algorithms.

The material covered in this talk is contained in [1, 2].

References

1. S. Albers. Energy-efficient algorithms. *Communications of the ACM*, 53(5):86–96, 2010.
2. S. Albers and A. Antoniadis. Race to idle: New algorithms for speed scaling with a sleep state. *Proc. 23rd Annual ACM-SIAM Symposium on Discrete Algorithms*, 1266–1285, 2012.

Algorithms for Transport Optimization Theory and Practice

Christos Zaroliagis[1,2]

[1] Department of Computer Engineering & Informatics, University of Patras,
26504 Patras, Greece
[2] Computer Technology Institute & Press "Diophantus",
Patras University Campus, 26504 Patras, Greece
zaro@ceid.upatras.gr

Public or private transport gives rise to several optimization problems, which are typically characterized by high complexity and sheer size, while some of them pose, in addition, real-time response constraints. Efficient algorithms can make a great difference towards an efficient and effective solution of such problems. In this talk, a few important algorithmic approaches are surveyed that are theoretically sound and practically efficient for the transport optimization problems they solve.

In the first part of the talk, robustness issues are investigated for the line planning problem in public transport under a specific uncertainty setting, motivated by recent market regulations in the railway sector. In this setting, a potentially large number of line operators, operating as commercial organizations, offer services to customers, while a central (typically state) authority manages the railway network infrastructure. The line operators act as competing agents for the exploitation of the shared infrastructure and are unwilling to disclose their true incentives (utility functions). The network manager wishes to set up a fair cost sharing scheme for the usage of the shared resources and to ensure the maximum possible level of satisfaction of the competing agents. The challenge is to provide a solution that is robust to the unknown incentives of the line operators, which are neither predictable or quantifiable nor statically describable. Towards this goal, a decentralized incentive-compatible mechanism is presented [1,2] whose equilibrium point is (provably) the unknown social optimum. An accompanying experimental study of the aforementioned mechanism on both synthetic and real-world data shows fast convergence to the optimum. A wide range of scenarios is also explored, varying from an arbitrary initial state (to be solved) to small disruptions in a previously optimal solution (to be recovered). The experiments with the latter scenario show that the particular mechanism can be used as an online recovery scheme causing the system to re-converge to its optimum extremely fast.

In the second part of the talk, the route planning problem in large-scale road networks is investigated, focusing on two main issues: the efficient representation of such networks in a dynamic environment, and the computation (of not only a single optimal route but) of several source-to-destination alternative routes with specific quality characteristics.

To address the first issue, a new dynamic graph structure [3] is presented that is specifically suited for large-scale transportation networks providing simultaneously three unique features:

- *Compactness*: ability to efficiently access adjacent nodes or edges, a requirement set by all query algorithms in order to meet real-time response constraints.
- *Agility*: ability to change and reconfigure the graph's internal layout in order to improve the locality of the elements, according to a given algorithm.
- *Dynamicity*: ability to efficiently insert or delete nodes and edges.

The practicality and superiority of the new graph structure is demonstrated by an experimental study for shortest route planning in large-scale European and US road networks with a few dozen millions of nodes and edges. The particular structure is the first one that concerns the dynamic maintenance of a large-scale graph with ordered elements using a contiguous memory part, and which allows an arbitrary online reordering of its elements.

To address the second issue, improved methods are presented for computing a set of alternative source-to-destination routes in road networks in the form of an alternative graph [4]. The produced alternative graph is characterized by minimum path overlap, small stretch factor, as well as low size and complexity. Two existing approaches are surveyed and a new one is presented that improves upon those. An accompanying experimental study shows that the new approach can compute the entire alternative graph pretty fast even in continental size networks.

References

1. A. Bessas, S. Kontogiannis, and C. Zaroliagis. Incentive-Compatible Robust Line Planning. In *Robust and Online Large-Scale Optimization*, Chapter 4, Springer 2009, pp. 85–118.
2. A. Bessas, S. Kontogiannis, and C. Zaroliagis. Robust Line Planning in case of Multiple Pools and Disruptions. In *Theory and Practice of Algorithms in Computer Systems* – TAPAS 2011, Lecture Notes in Computer Science Vol. **6595** (Springer 2011), pp. 33-44.
3. G. Mali, P. Michail, A. Paraskevopoulos, and C. Zaroliagis. A New Dynamic Graph Structure for Large-scale Transportation Networks. In *Algorithms and Complexity* – CIAC 2013, LNCS Volume 7878, pp. 312–323. Springer, 2013.
4. A. Paraskevopoulos and C. Zaroliagis. Improved Alternative Route Planning. In *Proc. 13th Workshop on Algorithmic Approaches for Transportation Modeling, Optimization, and Systems* - ATMOS 2013, OASICS Vol. 33, pp. 108–122.

Mining and Analytics of Deep Web Repositories

Gautam Das

University of Texas at Arlington
gdas@uta.edu

Abstract. With the proliferation of deep web repositories (e.g., databases or document corpora) hidden behind proprietary web interfaces, e.g., keyword-/form-based search interfaces and hierarchical/graph-based browsing interfaces, efficient ways of exploring contents in such hidden repositories are of increasing importance in a wide variety of applications.

There are two key challenges: one on the proper understanding of interfaces, and the other on the efficient exploration, e.g., crawling, sampling and analytical processing, of very large repositories. In this talk, we focus on the fundamental algorithmic developments in the field, including web interface understanding, sampling, and data analytics over deep web repositories with various types of interfaces and containing structured or unstructured data. In the case of sampling, the objective is to draw sample tuples according to a pre-determined distribution over the repository. An example is simple random sampling which features uniform distribution over all documents/tuples in the deep web repository. The collected sample can be later used for analytical processing, mining, etc. In the case of analytics, the objective boils down to the ability to efficiently estimate aggregates (COUNT, SUM, MIN, MAX, etc.) over the deep web repository e.g., the total number of products in Amazons database, or the total number of documents indexed by Google. We shall discuss various recently developed efficient algorithms for sampling and aggregate estimation over such web repositories.

Efficient Distance Measures for Social Networks

Rina Panigrahy

Microsoft Corp.
Mountain View, CA
rina@microsoft.com

Abstract. A fundamental operation in large graphs such as social networks is computing the distance between two nodes. While the shortest path graph distance is one standard measure of distance, there may be other candidates such as s-t min cuts, effective resistance (or commute time), and Katz distance [2] that may better capture the similarity between the users represented by the nodes. This gives rise to two lines of questioning: first, what is a good distance measure between nodes that captures user similarity, and second, can it be computed efficiently in real time? Since the standard shortest path algorithms are expensive to run on large graphs in real time, we study an approach [1] that estimates it in real time by moving the time-consuming shortest-path computation offline, and looking up only the precomputed values at query time and performing simple and fast computations on these precomputed values. More specically, during the offline phase we compute and store a small sketch for each node in the graph, and at query-time we look up the sketches of the source and destination nodes and perform a simple computation using these two sketches to estimate the distance. The algorithm is a modification of distance oracles by Thorup and Zwick [4] that samples a small set of seed nodes and only stores the nearest few seeds from each node as its sketch. Our experiments show that this algorithm is able to estimate distances in large graphs within a small additive error. We also study alternate distance measures that are easy to compute in real time and looks not only the shortest path distance but also takes into account the number of such paths. We also compare these different distance measures and evaluate which correlates most to user similarity [3].

References

1. A. Das Sarma, S. Gollapudi, M. Najork, and R. Panigrahy. A sketch-based distance oracle for web-scale graphs. In *Proceedings of the third ACM international conference on Web search and data mining*, pages 401–410. ACM, 2010.
2. L. Katz. A new status index derived from sociometric analysis. *Psychometrika*, 18(1):39–43, 1953.
3. R. Panigrahy, M. Najork, and Y. Xie. How user behavior is related to social affinity. In *Proceedings of the fifth ACM international conference on Web search and data mining*, pages 713–722. ACM, 2012.
4. M. Thorup and U. Zwick. Approximate distance oracles. *Journal of the ACM (JACM)*, 52(1):1–24, 2005.

Monitoring Distributed, Heterogeneous Data Streams: The Emergence of Safe Zones

Daniel Keren[1], Guy Sagy[2], Amir Abboud[2], David Ben-David[2], Assaf Schuster[2], Izchak Sharfman[2], and Antonios Deligiannakis[3]

[1] Department of Computer Science, Haifa University
[2] Faculty of Computer Science, Israeli Institute of Technology
[3] Department of Electronic and Computer Engineering, Technical University of Crete

Abstract. In many emerging applications, the data to be monitored is of very high volume, dynamic, and distributed, making it infeasible to collect the distinct data streams to a central node and process them there. Often, the monitoring problem consists of determining whether the value of a global function, which depends on the union of all streams, crossed a certain threshold. A great deal of effort is directed at reducing communication overhead by transforming the monitoring of the global function to the testing of *local* constraints, checked independently at the nodes. Recently, *geometric monitoring* (GM) proved to be very useful for constructing such local constraints for general (non-linear, non-monotonic) functions. Alas, in all current variants of geometric monitoring, the constraints at all nodes share an identical structure and are, thus, unsuitable for handling heterogeneous streams, which obey different distributions at the distinct nodes. To remedy this, we propose a general approach for geometric monitoring of heterogeneous streams (HGM), which defines constraints tailored to fit the distinct data distributions at the nodes. While optimally selecting the constraints is an NP-hard problem, we provide a practical solution, which seeks to reduce running time by hierarchically clustering nodes with similar data distributions and then solving more, but simpler, optimization problems. Experiments are provided to support the validity of the proposed approach.

Exploiting Heterogeneous Data Sources: A Computing Paradigm for Live Web and Sustainability Applications

Dimitrios Gunopulos

Department of Informatics and Telecommunications
National and Kapodistrian University of Athens
kddlab.di.uoa.gr/dg.html
dg@di.uoa.gr

Abstract. Today we are witnessing advances in technology that are changing dramatically the way we live, work and interact with the physical environment. New revolutionary technologies are creating an explosion on the size and variety of information that is becoming available. Such technologies include the development and widespread adoption of networks of small and inexpensive embedded sensors that are being used to instrument the environment at an unprecedented scale. In addition, the last few years have brought forward the widespread adoption of social networking applications. Another trend with significant ramifications is the massive adoption of smartphones in the market. The rise of the social networking applications and the always-on functionality of the smartphones are driving the rise of a part of the web that is dedicated to recording, maintaining and sharing rapidly changing data which has been termed the Live Web. In this talk we present recent research work motivated by the trends we describe above. We also consider how such novel research results are enabling forms of computation. First, we focus on the specific problem of finding events or trends, including spatiotemporal patterns, when monitoring microblogging streams. Our work is mainly in the context of the INSIGHT FP7 project and we also consider data from sources as different as traffic sensors and Twitter streams. To put this research work in a general context, in the second part of the talk we consider the more general problem of developing applications and reasoning about the behavior of novel applications that exploit the new setting of the Live Web, and understanding the implications on the design, development and deployment of new applications in this setting. We describe initial work on the formulation of a new computing paradigm for this setting, and on describing how it can be applied for computational sustainability applications.

Table of Contents

Abstracts of Invited Talks

Invited Talks

Contributed Talks

Algorithmic Challenges in Digital Microfluidic Biochips: Protocols, Design, and Test*

Bhargab B. Bhattacharya[1,**], Sudip Roy[2,***], and Sukanta Bhattacharjee[1]

[1] Nanotechnology Research Triangle, Indian Statistical Institute,
Kolkata 700108, India
{bhargab,sukanta_r}@isical.ac.in
[2] Dept. of CSE, Indian Institute of Technology Kharagpur, Kharagpur 721302, India
sudipr@cse.iitkgp.ernet.in

Abstract. Recent emergence of microfluidic technology has imparted a profound impact on the implementation of miniaturized healthcare chips and systems. In this review article, we will elaborate on several algorithmic challenges that arise while realizing biochemical protocols on a digital microfluidic (DMF) lab-on-a-chip. In particular, we will focus on certain design automation issues of sample preparation, dilution gradient generation, layout planning, and testing of DMF biochips.

Keywords: Digital Microfluidics, Dilution, Mixing, Sample Preparation.

1 Introduction

In an attempt to mitigate the ever-increasing healthcare costs involved in timely diagnosis of cardiovascular diseases, cancer, diabetes, and global HIV crisis, a new field of interdisciplinary research called "Lab-on-a-Chip (LoC)", is emerging [1–4]. Typically, an LoC implements a bioprotocol on a single chip that is a few square centimeters in size, which provides a low-cost and fast diagnostic solutions to a variety of medical applications. For on-chip implementation of a bioassay, a fluidic algorithm is needed that will map the corresponding biochemical sequence of the assay to an LoC platform. Research in this new discipline of nanobiotechnology needs the integration of many disciplines, such as microelectronics, biochemistry, pathology, electronic design automation, and fabrication technology, among others. Compared to traditional bench-top procedures, biochips offer the advantages of low sample and reagent consumption, less likelihood of error due to minimal human intervention, high throughput and sensitivity [3, 4]. An ideal on-site biochemical analysis system should be inexpensive, sensitive, fully automated, integrated, and reliable. The emerging application areas of such biochips include, among others, clinical diagnostics,

---

* Invited Paper.
** The work of B. B. Bhattacharya was supported by a special grant to Nanotechnology Research Triangle from Indian Statistical Institute, Kolkata, India.
*** This work of S. Roy was supported by Microsoft Corporation and Microsoft Research India under the Microsoft Research India PhD Fellowship Award (2010-2014).

P. Gupta and C. Zaroliagis (Eds.): ICAA 2014, LNCS 8321, pp. 1–16, 2014.

especially, the immediate point-of-care diagnosis of diseases, enzymatic analysis (e.g., glucose and lactate assays), DNA analysis (e.g., polymerase chain reaction (PCR), nucleic acid sequence analysis), proteomic analysis involving proteins and peptides, immunoassay, and environmental toxicity monitoring. The continued growth in this emerging field will depend on the advances in algorithmic microfluidics and design automation tools customized for LoCs [4–14].

Microfluidic based biochips are of two kinds. In continuous-flow microfluidic (CMF) biochips, fluids can move through the microchannels fabricated on-chip with the help of the pressure-driven devices like micropumps and microvalves [15]. Digital microfluidic (DMF) biochips, on the other hand, use electrical actuation to manipulate (dispensing, navigation, merging, mixing, splitting, washing, sensing) discrete droplets of nanoliter volume of reactant fluids on a two-dimensional electrode array [4]. Recently, DMF biochips have gained wide acceptance in developing LoC applications.

Mixture preparation of several reactant fluids and dilution of a biochemical sample/reagent are two fundamental preprocessing steps in almost all biochemical assays, such as Blackburn Yeast Colony PCR, Splinkerette PCR, Touchdown PCR, Plant RNA Isolation, Yeast DNA Prep, One Step Miniprep, etc. [16–18]. In these bio-protocols, one may require a reactant fluid with a number of dilutions, or a mixture of several reagent fluids with a given volumetric ratio. For example, in "Yeast DNA Prep", a mixture requires 2% (v/v) Triton X-100 and 1% (w/v) SDS, where we need to dilute the Triton X-100 fluid to a concentration level as 2% and SDS to a concentration level as 1%. For another example bioassay "Blackburn Yeast Colony PCR", where a master-mixture is required to be prepared by mixing $2\mu L$ 5X Q-solution, $1\mu L$ PCR buffer, $0.2\mu L$ dNTPs, $0.2\mu L$ forward primer, $0.2\mu L$ reverse primer, $0.1\mu L$ Taq and $5.3\mu L$ water [17]. Thus, here the target ratio of these seven fluids is 20 : 10 : 2 : 2 : 2 : 1 : 53. Similarly, two target ratios of different set of fluids used in "Splinkerette PCR method" are 40 : 10 : 1 : 1 : 48 and 1 : 2 : 3 : 1 : 23 [17].

The basic idea of a microfluidic biochip is to integrate multiple bioassay operations such as detection, sample pre-treatment, and sample preparation on one chip [19]. Front-end functions for sample preparation — *mixing* of three or more different fluids and *dilution* of a fluid with the buffer solution (i.e., mixing of two different fluids), can be done on-chip or outside the chip during the preprocessing steps. Since off-chip sample preparation poses a significant hindrance to the overall bioassay completion time, for fast and high-throughput applications, sample preprocessing steps should also be automated on-chip, i.e., integrated and self-contained on the biochip itself. In this review article, we will discuss some design automation challenges and solutions of on-chip sample preparation, which will lead to an efficient architectural layout implementation of the biochip.

The remainder of the article is organized as follows: In Section 2, we describe the background of DMF biochips. A brief review of the existing techniques for automatic sample preparation protocols using such chips is provided in Section 3. Advances in dilution techniques and gradient generation methods are presented in Section 4. Some contemporary issues in mixing protocols and their layout design have been presented in Section 5. In Section 6 we briefly touch upon several testing issues in DMF biochips. Finally, in Section 7 we provide some concluding remarks.

2   Basics of Digital Microfluidic Biochips

A schematic diagram of the top view of a DMF biochip is shown in Fig. 1(a) and the cross-sectional view of a basic cell at a detection site of a DMF biochip is shown in Fig. 1(b). A unit cell in the array includes a pair of electrodes that acts as two parallel plates. The bottom plate contains a patterned array of individually controlled electrodes, and the top one consists of a single grounded electrode. The droplets are sandwiched between the two plates, and they rest on a hydrophobic surface over the bottom electrodes.

Droplet movement is achieved by controlling the wettability created due to the interfacial tension (surface tension) gradients between a conductive fluid and a solid electrode with an applied electric field between them. The droplet is moved to the activated electrode by applying a control voltage (above a threshold voltage) to an electrode adjacent to the droplet and, at the same time, deactivating the electrode just under the droplet. For liquids with high surface tension, a special phenomenon called electrowetting-on-dielectric (EWOD) effect [20, 21] is observed on DMF biochips [3]. A DMF biochip may contain several modules, like mixers, splitters, detectors, waste reservoirs, dispensers, and sensors. By varying the patterns of control voltage activation, many fluid-handling operations such as merging, splitting, mixing, and dispensing of droplets can be executed. In addition to electrodes, optical detectors such as LEDs and photodiodes are also integrated in microfluidic arrays to monitor colorimetric bioassays. Detailed descriptions of a DMF biochip and the four fundamental fluidic operations (dispensing, transporting, mixing and splitting) can be found in [1, 20, 22, 23]. For the control of DMF biochips, automation for the user, and technology exploitation, there is a pressing need for advances in computer-aided design algorithms and techniques.

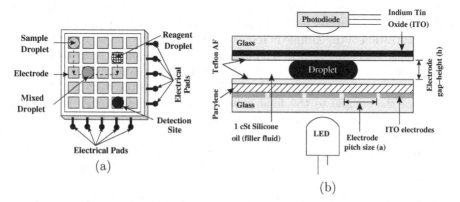

Fig. 1. (a) Top view of a DMF biochip and (b) Cross-sectional view of a cell at a detection site [4]

3   Protocols for Sample Preparation

3.1   Mixing Models

DMF biochips typically work with discrete droplets on a uniform two-dimensional array of equi-sized electrodes, hence their volumes are always integral multiples of one unit volume of a single droplet. A survey on such balanced mix/split modules can be found in [24, 25].

In *(k : ℓ) mixing model* (where k and ℓ are non-zero positive integers), k-unit volume of one fluid is mixed with ℓ-unit volume of another fluid to produce $(k+\ell)$-unit volume of resultant mixture fluid in a single mixing operation. Three different cases may be possible as follows: (i) $k = \ell = 1$, (ii) $k = \ell \neq 1$, and (iii) $k \neq \ell$. The first case, i.e., (1 : 1) mixing model is easy to implement.

In *(k : k) mixing model*, where $k \geq 1$, a DMF biochip needs a module that is capable of mixing two equal (one or more unit) volume fluid droplets or splitting a larger (two or more unit) volume droplet into two equal (one or more unit) volume droplets. Most of the prior work assumed the *(1 : 1) mixing model*, in which one unit-volume droplet of each of two type of fluids are mixed to produce two unit-volume mixture fluid. After each mix operation, the two unit-volume mixture can be split equally into two unit-volume droplets by a split operation. Next, one unit-volume droplet of the mixture is used in the next mixing step, while the other one is discarded as *waste droplets*. One mix operation and a subsequent split operation are together called a *mix-split cycle*.

In the *(k : ℓ) mixing model*, where $k \neq \ell$ and $k, \ell \geq 1$, k unit-volume droplet(s) of one fluid is (are) mixed with ℓ unit-volume droplet(s) of another fluid. After each mix operation, either the $(k + \ell)$-volume mixture can be split equally into two droplets or an one unit-volume droplet can be separated from that mixture by a split operation.

3.2   Dilution of a Fluid or Mixing of Two Fluids

The fluid with which the sample is mixed for dilution is called the diluent or buffer solution, e.g., water or other liquid that is neutral to the sample (i.e., with 0% concentration of the sample in it). Thus, dilution is the special case of mixing of two fluids, where one of them is a buffer (neutral) solution. In order to quantify the amount of raw sample (100% concentration) during sample preparation, we use the term *concentration factor (CF)*. It is defined as the ratio of the initial volume of the sample to the final volume of the diluted sample. In general, dilution of a sample to a CF C_1 can be achieved by mixing it with the same sample of CF C_2, where $C_2 < C_1$. The CF of the resultant sample will lie between C_1 and C_2 because, if the samples of CF C_1 and C_2 are mixed in a volumetric ratio of $k : \ell$, then the resulting $(k + \ell)$ unit volume fluid has a CF $C_r = \frac{k.C_1 + \ell.C_2}{k+\ell}$.

Dilutions are commonly used in biological studies to create a variety of concentration levels of the reactant fluids on a microfluidic device [26]. Concentrations can extend over a linear or non-linear range and they are generated by two types of dilution methods such as *linear* or *serial* dilution [26]. In the case of *linear dilution*, the stock solution and its diluent are mixed in different ratios, and this process can create linearly varying concentrations of the stock solution [26]. On the other hand, in *serial dilution*, a common example of which is the logarithmic method, a sample is repeatedly diluted using the same mixing ratio, e.g., 1 : 1. Three serial dilutions mixed at 1 : 1 yield the concentrations $\frac{1}{2}$, $\frac{1}{4}$ and $\frac{1}{8}$. Thus, the serial dilution creates discrete non-linear concentration values of the stock solution.

Recently, many dilution devices and schemes have been demonstrated in the literature for continuous-flow microfluidics (CMF) [27, 28], in order to generate various concentration gradients. However, in the case of DMF biochips, fluids can only be mixed using discrete volumes of droplets. Therefore, for DMF biochips, it is possible to carry out only serial dilution to achieve or approximate desired non-linear concentration levels. Thus, it is a challenge to achieve a desired concentration of the stock solution within a minimum number of mix-split steps with minimum error in target CF. However, only a few research articles were reported to date on automatic dilution in DMF biochips [15, 29–31]. An automated DMF-based protocol for extracting proteins from heterogeneous fluids by precipitation has been explained in [32]. This method requires several reagents with different concentration levels, such as 20% TCA (precipitant), 70/30 v/v chloroform/acetonitrile (rinse solution) and 100 mM borate buffer containing 1% SDS (resolubilizing buffer). Another example of a real assay is enzymatic glucose assay (Trinder's reaction); it uses a dilution factor of 200 or more [29].

Two basic kinds of dilution are: *exponential dilution* and *interpolated dilution*. If a sample is recursively diluted by the buffer solution taking equal volume of both of them for mixing, then the concentration of the sample changes exponentially by a factor of 2. That is, after d cycles of mixing and balanced splitting, the CF of the sample changes from C to $\frac{C}{2^d}$, i.e., the DF becomes 2^d. This type of dilution is called *exponential dilution*. If a sample of CF C_1 is diluted with its another CF C_2 taking equal volume of both of them for mixing, then the final CF of the sample becomes $\frac{C_1+C_2}{2}$. This is called *interpolated dilution*. Hence, for example, if two droplets of CFs $\frac{0}{1024}$ and $\frac{1024}{1024}$ are mixed, then the resultant CF after exponential dilution becomes $\frac{1}{2}$ (i.e., $DF = 2$). Again, if two droplets of CFs $\frac{1022}{1024}$ and $\frac{1024}{1024}$ are mixed, then the resultant CF after interpolated dilution becomes $\frac{1022+1024}{2.1024}$, i.e., $\frac{1023}{1024}$.

An (1 : 1)-*dilution tree* is the binary tree representation of the sequence of (1 : 1) mix-split steps required to achieve the desired CF of a fluid with the help of buffer fluid. Let T_{ms} be the total number of (1 : 1) mix-split steps in the dilution tree and W be the total number of waste droplets generated in producing two target droplets in the process. Given the desired CF C_t, the algorithm *twoWayMix* [15] converts C_t into a d-bit binary fraction and then scans the bits from right-to-left to construct the dilution tree of depth at most d. Each mix-split step combines two unit-volume fluids and outputs two units of their mixture. This algorithm has the advantage that it does not require any storage unit to store intermediate droplets; only the current droplet and the input fluids are required in the next step. However, this method works only

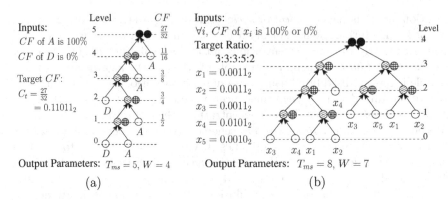

Fig. 2. (a) An $(1 : 1)$-dilution tree of depth $d = 5$ denoting the sequence of five $(1 : 1)$ mix-split steps for target CF $C_t = 84.375\%$ ($\approx \frac{27}{32} \equiv 0.11011_2$) obtained by *twoWayMix* [15] using fluid A (100% concentration) and buffer (0% concentration). (b) An $(1 : 1)$-mixing tree obtained by *MinMix* [15] and bit-representations of the example ratio $3 : 3 : 3 : 5 : 2$.

when the initial volumes are given with $CF = 0$ (buffer) and $CF = 1$ (100% concentration) sample. Dilution of a sample fluid from the supply of any two arbitrary CFs of that was left as a open problem in [15].

In the literature, a few articles have been reported on automatic dilution of a fluid using DMF biochips [29, 30]. Ren et al. [29] described an experimental study of on-chip dilution of a sample producing 38 integer dilution factors (in the range 2 to 64, given the constraint that only 64-fold exponential dilution and 16-fold interpolating dilution were available) in 10 mix-split steps by interpolating serial dilution method. However, no algorithmic scheme was presented for determining the mix-split steps to achieve the target CF from the input fluids. Griffith et al. [30] first proposed a dilution algorithm of $\mathcal{O}(d^3)$ time complexity, to determine a d-length sequence of mix-split steps for producing two target droplets, given an error tolerance of $\frac{1}{2^{d+1}}$ in the desired CF. It used a binary-search strategy to determine the required dilution steps as a directed graph. However, the design of a suitable architectural layout of electrodes for efficient implementation of the above-mentioned algorithm was left as an open problem.

3.3 Mixing of Three or More Fluids

In many bioprotocols, *mixture preparation* of three or more fluids with a desired ratio, is required. An $(1 : 1)$-*mixing tree* is a binary tree representation of the sequence of $(1 : 1)$ mix-split steps for the mixture preparation of several fluids. In an $(1 : 1)$-mixing tree, each leaf node corresponds to a unit-volume droplet and an internal (or non-leaf) node denotes the resultant mixture obtained by applying an $(1 : 1)$ mix-split step on two unit-volume fluid droplets corresponding to its two children. An internal node denotes one unit-volume droplet of the resultant mixture, which is used in the next mix operation denoted by the parent node of the considered internal node. The mixture denoted by an internal node can only be produced when the mixtures denoted by its child nodes are available or already produced. A post-order traversal of the mixing tree provides the sequence of $(1 : 1)$ mix-split steps required to produce the target mixture (of N fluids) denoted by the root of the tree. The total number of non-leaf nodes in a mixing tree, denoted by T_{ms}, is the total number of mix-split cycles required to produce the target mixture from the supplies and the depth of a mixing tree is denoted by d.

The well-known algorithm *MinMix* [15] determines a mixing protocol tree for a given ratio of several fluids. In this method, the required mixing tree, denoting a sequence of $(1 : 1)$ mix-split steps, is determined from the binary bit-representations of the target ratio (corresponding to all constituent fluids). This task graph is to be executed in order to produce the desired mixture droplets. An example $(1 : 1)$-mixing tree is shown in Fig. 2(b) for a target ratio $3 : 3 : 3 : 5 : 2$ of five fluids, and the corresponding binary representations used to construct the $(1 : 1)$-mixing tree are shown in Fig. 2(c). However, no architectural layout of electrodes was suggested for executing the mixing/dilution scheme on-chip, and the related design problems were left open.

4 Dilution/Mixing with Reduced Wastage

For an example of generating droplets of target CF $C_t = \frac{313}{1024} \simeq 0.30566_{10} \equiv 0.0100111001_2$ using *twoWayMix* [15], it is observed that five sample and six buffer droplets are required. In 10 mix-split steps, total nine waste droplets are generated. An algorithm called <u>D</u>ilution/<u>M</u>ixing with <u>R</u>educed <u>W</u>astage (*DMRW*) has been proposed by Roy et al. [33], which aims to reduce reactant wastage compared to *twoWayMix* [15]. The *DMRW* method uses a binary-search strategy to determine the dilution graph based on $(k : k)$ mixing model (where $k \geq 1$). For the example of generating droplets of target CFs $\frac{313}{1024}$, $\frac{127}{1024}$ and $\frac{513}{1024}$, the dilution graphs obtained by *DMRW* are shown in Figs. 3(a), 3(b) and 3(c), respectively.

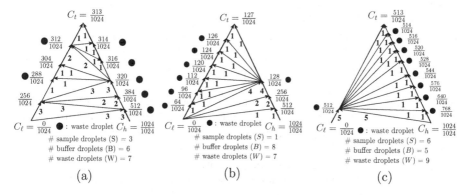

Fig. 3. Dilution graphs denoting the sequence of 10 $(k : k)$ mix-split steps to produce target CFs (a) $C_t = \frac{313}{1024}$, (b) $C_t = \frac{127}{1024}$ and (c) $C_t = \frac{513}{1024}$, obtained by *DMRW* [34]

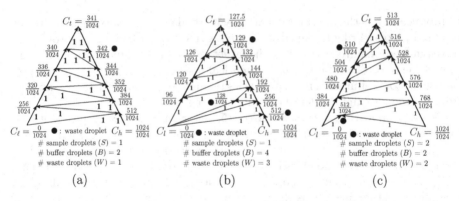

Fig. 4. Dilution graphs denoting the sequence of $(k : k)$ mix-split steps to produce target CFs (a) $C_t = \frac{341}{1024}$, (b) $C_t = \frac{127}{1024}$ and (c) $C_t = \frac{513}{1024}$, obtained by $IDMA$ [34]

Subsequently, an Improved Dilution/Mixing Algorithm ($IDMA$) was reported by Roy et al. [34] for further reduction of wastage in the dilution process. It is observed that the outdegree (skew) of a node with a certain intermediate CF value in the digraph obtained by $DMRW$ has a strong impact on waste droplet generation as well as on the number of (1 : 1) mix-split steps (e.g., see Figs. 3(b) and 3(c)). In the mix-split digraph obtained by $DMRW$, if the progression sequence towards the target CF alternates between the left(right) and right(left) arms, then the outdegree of each node can never exceed two (e.g., see Fig. 4(a)), and therefore, the waste is optimized and no additional demand of intermediate CFs is created. $IDMA$ perturbs the sequence of mix-split steps after a certain step by generating a new intermediate CF without following the binary-search strategy. It can reduce the requirement of input droplets to reduce W furthermore with reduced T_{ms} compared to $DMRW$. The procedure $IDMA$ terminates in $O(d)$ steps for producing a target CF with an accuracy of $\frac{1}{2^{d+1}}$. For example, $IDMA$ modifies the digraphs obtained by $DMRW$ for the two target CFs $C_t = \frac{127}{1024}$ and $C_t = \frac{513}{1024}$ as shown in Fig. 4(b) and 4(c), respectively, and reduces both the values of T_{ms} and W.

Detailed simulation results for $d = 10$, and an architectural layout with two rotary mixers of 16 electrodes, each (Fig. 5), were presented in [33, 34].

4.1 Generation of Dilution Gradients

In sample preparation, producing chemical and biomolecular concentration gradients is of particular interest. Dilution gradients play essential roles in in-vitro analysis of many biochemical phenomena including growth of pathogens and selection of drug concentration. For example, in drug design, it is important to determine the minimum amount of an antibiotic that inhibits the visible growth of bacteria isolate (defined as Minimum Inhibitory Concentration (MIC)). The drug with the least concentration factor (i.e., with highest dilution) that is capable of arresting the growth of bacteria, is considered as MIC. During the past decade, a variety of automated bacterial identification and antimicrobial

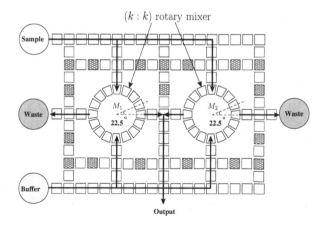

Fig. 5. Layout of electrodes with two DMF rotary mixers for $d = 10$ [33]

susceptibility test systems have been developed, which provide results in only few hours rather than days, compared to traditional overnight procedures [35]. Typical automated susceptibility methods use an exponential dilution gradient (e.g., $1\%, 2\%, 4\%, 8\%, 16\%$) in which CFs of the given sample are in geometric progression [36]. Linear dilution gradient (e.g., $15\%, 20\%, 25\%, 30\%, 35\%$), in which the CFs of the sample appear in arithmetic progression, offers more sensitive tests. Linear gradients are usually prepared by using continuous-flow microfluidic ladder networks [37], or by other networks of microchannels [38, 39]. Since the fluidic microchannels are hardwired, continuous-flow based diluters are designed to cater to only a pre-defined gradient, and thus they suffer from inflexibility and non-programmability. Also, these methods require a significant amount of costly stock solutions. In contrast, on a DMF biochip platform, a set of random dilution factors can be easily prepared.

4.2 Zero-Waste Linear Dilution Gradients

An algorithm for generating linear dilution gradients on a digital microfluidic platform was reported in [40], which can generate linear gradients without generating any waste droplets. In order to generate linear dilution gradients, this technique extends the target set by adding subsequent linear gradients (depends on the size of the target gradient set to be generated) so that the size of extended target gradient set becomes $2^k + 1$, for a minumim value of k. Next, a full binary search tree representing each gradient is constructed, denoted as Linear Dilution Tree (LDT) following which the required dilution gradient is produced in the postorder sequence of the LDT. The droplets with the concentration values corresponding to each internal node of LDT are used in subsequent mixing operations after their production and are regenerated later for replenishment. In this technique, it is assumed that the two boundary concentrations are available as input droplets. If boundary droplets are not available, they can be

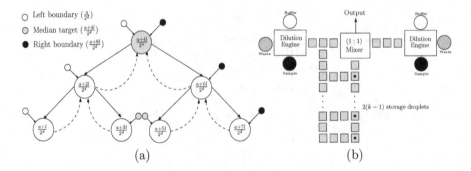

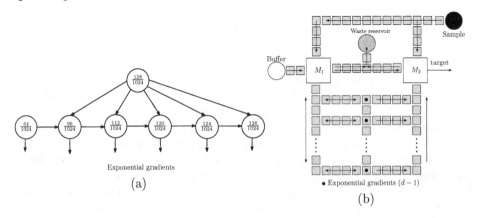

Fig. 6. (a) A linear dilution tree generating 9 linear dilutions $\{\frac{a}{2^d}, \frac{a+l}{2^d}, \ldots, \frac{a+8l}{2^d}\}$, where $\frac{a}{2^d}$ and $\frac{a+8l}{2^d}$ are left and right boundary respectively. (b) Architecture layout

Fig. 7. (a) Sequencing graph for an exponential dilution. (b) Architecture layout

efficiently generated using a dilution engine [41]. If the size of target gradient set is $2^k + 1$, then the proposed method can generate target gradients with no waste, otherwise a few waste droplets are generated during the process. The detailed performance analysis is given in [40]. An example generating 9 linear gradients is shown in Fig. 6(a), assuming the availability of two boundary droplets $\frac{a}{2^d}$ and $\frac{a+8l}{2^d}$, where a, l, d are the initial term, common difference and accuracy of the linear gradients respectively. An architectural layout is shown in Fig. 6(b), which uses $2(k-1)$ intermediate storage for generating any linear gradient target set of size at most $2^k + 1$. Moreover, two dilution engines [41] are used for supplying the two boundary droplets.

4.3 Exponential Dilution Gradients

The exponential dilution gradient also plays an important role in several biochemical protocols. Using the method REMIA [42], a wider class of exponential dilution gradient generation scheme is proposed recently [43]. An on-chip implementation of an exponential gradient generator on a DMF platform is shown in Fig. 7(b) [43].

5   Mixing Algorithms and Biochip Layout Design

A routing-aware mixing algorithm, known as R̲atio-ed M̲ixing A̲lgorithm (*RMA*) was described by Roy et al. [44]. This method identifies some disjoint *dilution subtrees* in a mixing tree based on top-down decomposition of the underlying algebraic expression of the given target ratio. The (1 : 1)-mixing model is used in this protocol to achieve the target mixture of several fluids. This technique yields a routing-aware layout design that reduces droplet transport time, which, in turn, expedites the execution of the mixing assay compared to the *MinMix* [15]. For the example target ratio 2 : 3 : 5 : 7 : 11 : 13 : 87, the mixing tree generated by *RMA* is shown in Fig. 8(a). The corresponding DMF biochip layout is shown in Fig. 8(b). The required mixing steps can be performed without any crossover among the routing paths of different fluid droplets (as shown in Fig. 8(b)). It is observed that when the mixing tree of *MinMix* is executed, the total number of crossovers among the routing paths becomes nine, whereas, for the mixing tree obtained by *RMA*, this number reduces to four.

Later, a routing-aware R̲esource (fluid-reservoirs and on-chip mixers) A̲llocation scheme for M̲ixture P̲reparation, referred to as *RAMP* was reported [45]. This algorithm outputs suitable placement of boundary reservoirs and on-chip mixers on a DMF biochip. It was observed that *RMA* along with *RAMP* can reduce the total crossovers among droplet routing paths for 74.6% cases of the total target ratios over *MinMix* along with *RAMP*. Thus, *RMA* along with *RAMP* can reduce the droplet transportation time during on-chip

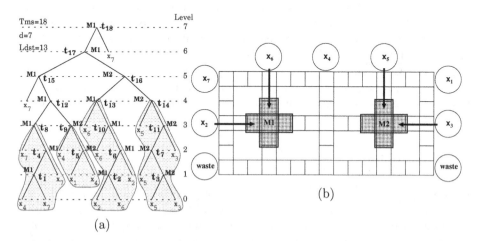

Fig. 8. For the example ratio 2 : 3 : 5 : 7 : 11 : 13 : 87, (a) (1 : 1)-mixing tree obtained by *RMA* [44], and (b) droplet routes for the mixing steps of the subtree rooted at t_{16} of the mixing tree.

mixture preparation. Subsequently, a few other dilution and mixing algorithms were reported with various optimization goals [13, 41, 42, 46–48].

6   Testing of DMF Biochips

Since microfluidic biochips are often used as life-critical devices, testing of them is very important in order to ensure reliability [49]. Some defects may lead to catastrophic failure of such chips, whereas, a few may cause parametric degradation leading to malfunctioning of certain modules.

Manufacturing test strategies can broadly be classified into two types: structural testing and functional testing [49, 50]. Structural testing targets detection of physical defects, such as, a short circuit between two adjacent electrodes, an open circuit between an electrode and the voltage source. Functional testing aims at identifying the presence of malfunctioning microfluidic functional modules, such as, dispensers, mixers, splitters. Structural testing may be performed for checking droplet movement between every adjacent pairs of electrodes. Such problems of optimal navigation of test droplets can be formulated in terms of Euler tour or Euler trail problems in an undirected graph representing the electrode adjacency structure [51–54]. A DMF biochip that has successfully passed the structural testing does not necessarily ensure correct operation of all of its functional modules such as mixers or splitters [55]. For example, a splitter block of such a DMF biochip may produce two unequal-sized droplets after splitting. Electrodes that support droplet transportation correctly may fail during droplet dispensing from the reservoirs. Several test procedures to detect such defects and malfunctions appear in [54–56]. On-line testing and error detection methods, which are suitable for in-field operation have been reported in the literature [10, 57–59].

Apart from defects and malfunctions, droplet contamination can pose a severe threat to the reliable execution of bioassays on a DMF biochip. For example, many biomedical assays involve on-chip transportation of substances containing macromolecules such as DNA, proteins, which may contaminate one or more electrodes [60]. Contamination may have serious erroneous effects on the outcome of the assay running on the chip. Therefore, efficient management and elimination of contamination is very important in order to ensure safe functioning of a biochip [12, 61–63].

7   Conclusions

In this review article, we have summarized the recent advances made in the area of droplet-based LoCs. Solutions to most of these problems require graph-theoretic formulations and optimization techniques. There are many open problems yet to be settled in the area of sample preparation, design, and testing of such chips.

References

[1] Fair, R.B.: Digital Microfluidics: Is a True Lab-on-a-Chip Possible? Microfluid. Nanofluid. 3, 245–281 (2007)

[2] Sista, R., Hua, Z., Thwar, P., Sudarsan, A., Srinivasan, V., Eckhardt, A., Pollack, M., Pamula, V.: Development of a Digital Microfluidic Platform for Point of Care Testing. Lab-on-a-Chip 8(12), 2091–2104 (2008)

[3] Abdelgawad, M., Wheeler, A.R.: The Digital Revolution: A New Paradigm for Microfluidics. Advanced Materials 21, 920–925 (2009)

[4] Chakrabarty, K., Xu, T.: Digital Microfluidic Biochips: Design and Optimization. CRC Press (2010)

[5] Bohringer, K.F.: Modeling and Controlling Parallel Tasks in Droplet-Based Microfluidic Systems. IEEE Transactions on COMPUTER-AIDED DESIGN of Integrated Circuits and Systems 25(2), 334–344 (2006)

[6] Yuh, P.H., Yang, C.L., Chang, Y.W.: BioRoute: A Network-Flow-Based Routing Algorithm for the Synthesis of Digital Microfluidic Biochips. IEEE Transactions on COMPUTER-AIDED DESIGN of Integrated Circuits and Systems 27(11), 1928–1941 (2008)

[7] Cho, M., Pan, D.Z.: A High-Performance Droplet Routing Algorithm for Digital Microfluidic Biochips. IEEE Transactions on COMPUTER-AIDED DESIGN of Integrated Circuits and Systems 27(10), 1714–1724 (2008)

[8] Maftei, E., Pop, P., Madsen, J.: Tabu Search-based Synthesis of Dynamically Reconfigurable Digital Microfluidic Biochips. In: Proc. of the CASES, pp. 195–204 (2009)

[9] Lin, C.C.Y., Chang, Y.W.: ILP-Based Pin-Count Aware Design Methodology for Microfluidic Biochips. In: Proc. of the DAC, pp. 258–263 (2009)

[10] Datta, S., Joshi, B., Ravindran, A., Mukherjee, A.: Efficient Parallel Testing and Diagnosis of Digital Microfluidic Biochips. ACM Journal on Emerging Technologies in Computing Systems 5(2), 1–17 (2009)

[11] Xiao, Z., Young, E.F.: Droplet-Routing-Aware Module Placement for Cross-Referencing Biochips. In: Proc. of the ISPD, pp. 193–199 (2010)

[12] Lin, C.C.Y., Chang, Y.W.: Cross-Contamination Aware Design Methodology for Pin-Constrained Digital Microfluidic Biochips. IEEE Transactions on COMPUTER-AIDED DESIGN of Integrated Circuits and Systems 30(6), 817–828 (2011)

[13] Hsieh, Y.L., Ho, T.Y., Chakrabarty, K.: A Reagent-Saving Mixing Algorithm for Preparing Multiple-Target Biochemical Samples Using Digital Microfluidics. IEEE Transactions on COMPUTER-AIDED DESIGN of Integrated Circuits and Systems 31(11), 1656–1669 (2012)

[14] Luo, Y., Chakrabarty, K., Ho, T.Y.: Error Recovery in Cyberphysical Digital Microfluidic Biochips. IEEE Transactions on COMPUTER-AIDED DESIGN of Integrated Circuits and Systems 32(1), 59–72 (2013)

[15] Thies, W., Urbanski, J.P., Thorsen, T., Amarasinghe, S.: Abstraction Layers for Scalable Microfluidic Biocomputing. Natural Computing 7(2), 255–275 (2008)

[16] OpenWetWare (October 2009), http://openwetware.org/wiki/Protocols

[17] BioCoder: A Programming Language for Biology Protocols, Microsoft Research India (December 2009),
http://research.microsoft.com/en-us/um/india/projects/biocoder/

[18] Bio-Protocols: http://www.bio-protocol.org/

[19] Fair, R.B., Srinivasan, V., Ren, H., Paik, P., Pamula, V.K., Pollack, M.G.: Electrowetting-Based On-Chip Sample Processing for Integrated Microfluidics. In: Technical Digest. IEEE International Electron Devices Meeting (IEDM 2003), pp. 32.5.1–32.5.4 (December 2003)

[20] Pollack, M.G., Fair, R.B., Shenderov, A.D.: Electrowetting-based Actuation of Liquid Droplets for Microfluidic Applications. Applied Physics Letters 77, 1725–1726 (2000)

[21] Brassard, D., Malic, L., Normandin, F., Tabrizian, M., Veres, T.: Water-oil Core-shell Droplets for Electrowetting-based Digital Microfluidic Devices. Lab-on-a-Chip 8, 1342–1349 (2008)

[22] Cho, S.K., Moon, H., Kim, C.J.: Creating, Transporting, Cutting, and Merging Liquid Droplets by Electrowetting-based Actuation for Digital Microfluidic Circuits. Journal of Microelectromechanical Systems 12(1), 70–80 (2003)

[23] Fouillet, Y., Jary, D., Chabrol, C., Claustre, P., Peponnet, C.: Digital Microfluidic Design and Optimization of Classic and New Fluidic Functions for Lab on a Chip Systems. Microfluidics and Nanofluidics 4(3), 159–165 (2008)

[24] Paik, P., Pamula, V.K., Fair, R.B.: Rapid Droplet Mixers for Digital Microfluidic Systems. Lab-on-a-Chip 3, 253–259 (2003)

[25] Paik, P., Pamula, V.K., Pollack, M.G., Fair, R.B.: Electrowetting-based Droplet Mixers for Microfluidic Systems. Lab-on-a-Chip 3, 28–33 (2003)

[26] Herold, K.E., Rasooly, A.: Lab-on-a-Chip Technology (vol. 1): Fabrication and Microfluidics. Caister Academic Press (August 2009)

[27] Kim, C., Lee, K., Kim, J.H., Shin, K.S., Lee, K.J., Kim, T.S., Kang, J.Y.: A Serial Dilution Microfluidic Device using a Ladder Network Generating Logarithmic or Linear Concentrations. Lab-on-a-Chip 8(3), 473–479 (2008)

[28] Lee, K., Kim, C., Ahn, B., Panchapakesan, R., Full, A.R., Nordee, L., Kang, J.Y., Oh, K.W.: Generalized Serial Dilution Module for Monotonic and Arbitrary Microfluidic Gradient Generators. Lab-on-a-Chip 9, 709–717 (2009)

[29] Ren, H., Srinivasan, V., Fair, R.B.: Design and Testing of an Interpolating Mixing Architecture for Electrowetting-Based Droplet-On-Chip Chemical Dilution. In: Proc. of the International Conference on Solid-State Sensors, Actuators and Microsystems (TRANSDUCERS), pp. 619–622 (2003)

[30] Griffith, E.J., Akella, S., Goldberg, M.K.: Performance Characterization of a Reconfigurable Planar-Array Digital Microfluidic System. IEEE Transactions on COMPUTER-AIDED DESIGN of Integrated Circuits and Systems 25(2), 345–357 (2006)

[31] Urbanski, J.P., Thies, W., Rhodes, C., Amarasinghe, S., Thorsen, T.: Digital Microfluidics using Soft Lithography. Lab-on-a-Chip 6(1), 96–104 (2006)

[32] Jebrail, M.J., Wheeler, A.R.: Digital Microfluidic Method for Protein Extraction by Precipitation. Journal of Analytical Chemistry 81, 330–335 (2009)

[33] Roy, S., Bhattacharya, B.B., Chakrabarty, K.: Optimization of Dilution and Mixing of Biochemical Samples using Digital Microfluidic Biochips. IEEE Transactions on COMPUTER-AIDED DESIGN of Integrated Circuits and Systems 29(11), 1696–1708 (2010)

[34] Roy, S., Bhattacharya, B.B., Chakrabarty, K.: Waste-Aware Dilution and Mixing of Biochemical Samples with Digital Microfluidic Biochips. In: Proc. of the IEEE/ACM Design, Automation and Test in Europe (DATE) Conference, pp. 1059–1064 (2011)

[35] Cira, N.J., Ho, J.Y., Dueck, M.E., Weibel, D.B.: A self-loading microfluidic device for determining the minimum inhibitory concentration of antibiotics. Lab Chip 12, 1052–1059 (2012)

[36] Sugiura, S., Hattori, K., Kanamori, T.: Microfluidic serial dilution cell-based assay for analyzing drug dose response over a wide concentration range. Analytical Chemistry 82(19), 8278–8282 (2010)

[37] Wang, S., Ji, N., Wang, W., Li, Z.: Effects of non-ideal fabrication on the dilution performance of serially functioned microfluidic concentration gradient generator. In: Nano/Micro Engineered and Molecular Systems (NEMS), pp. 169–172 (2010)

[38] Dertinger, S.K.W., Chiu, D.T., Jeon, N.L., Whitesides, G.M.: Generation of gradients having complex shapes using microfluidic networks. Analytical Chemistry 73(6), 1240–1246 (2001)

[39] Jang, Y.H., Hancock, M.J., Kim, S.B., Selimovic, S., Sim, W.Y., Bae, H., Khademhosseini, A.: An integrated microfluidic device for two-dimensional combinatorial dilution. Lab Chip 11, 3277–3286 (2011)

[40] Bhattacharjee, S., Banerjee, A., Ho, T.Y., Chakrabarty, K., Bhattacharya, B.B.: On producing linear dilution gradient of a sample with a digital microfluidic biochip. In: International Symposium on Electronic System Design, ISED (to appear, 2013)

[41] Roy, S., Bhattacharya, B.B., Ghoshal, S., Chakrabarty, K.: A High-Throughput Dilution Engine for Sample Preparation on Digital Microfluidic Biochips. IET Computers & Digital Techniques (IET-CDT), 9 pages (September 2013)

[42] Huang, J.D., Liu, C.H., Chiang, T.W.: Reactant Minimization during Sample Preparation on Digital Microfluidic Biochips using Skewed Mixing Trees. In: Proc. of IEEE/ACM ICCAD, pp. 377–384 (2012)

[43] Bhattacharjee, S., Banerjee, A., Ho, T.Y., Chakrabarty, K., Bhattacharya, B.B.: Eco-friendly sample preparation with concentration gradient on a digital microfluidic biochip. In: International Conference on Eco-friendly Computing and Communication Systems, ICECCS (to appear, 2013)

[44] Roy, S., Bhattacharya, B.B., Chakrabarti, P.P., Chakrabarty, K.: Layout-Aware Solution Preparation for Biochemical Analysis on a Digital Microfluidic Biochip. In: Proc. of the VLSID, pp. 171–176 (2011)

[45] Roy, S., Chakrabarti, P.P., Kumar, S., Bhattacharya, B.B., Chakrabarty, K.: Routing-Aware Resource Allocation for Mixture Preparation in Digital Microfluidic Biochips. In: IEEE ISVLSI, pp. 1–6 (2013)

[46] Bhattacharjee, S., Banerjee, A., Bhattacharya, B.B.: Sample preparation with multiple dilutions on digital microfluidic biochips. IET Computers & Digital Techniques (IET-CDT), 1–10 (2013)

[47] Mitra, D., Roy, S., Chakrabarty, K., Bhattacharya, B.B.: On-chip sample preparation with multiple dilutions using digital microfluidics. In: Proc. of the IEEE International Symposium on VLSI (ISVLSI), pp. 314–319 (August 2012)

[48] Chiang, T.W., Liu, C.H., Huang, J.D.: Graph-Based Optimal Reactant Minimization for Sample Preparation on Digital Microfluidic Biochips. In: Proc. of the IEEE VLSI-DAT, pp. 1–4 (2013)

[49] Mitra, D.: Studies in High-Throughput and Reliable Assay Operations on Digital Microfluidic Biochips. PhD thesis, Bengal Engineering and Science University, Shibpur, India (2012)

[50] Chakrabarty, K., Su, F.: Digital Microfluidic Biochips: Synthesis, Testing and Reconfiguration Techniques. CRC Press (2007)

[51] Mitra, D., Ghoshal, S., Rahaman, H., Chakrabarty, K., Bhattacharya, B.B.: Test planning in digital microfluidic biochips using improved eulerization techniques and the Chinese postman problem. In: IEEE Asian Test Symposium (ATS), pp. 111–116 (2010)

[52] Mitra, D., Ghoshal, S., Rahaman, H., Chakrabarty, K., Bhattacharya, B.B.: Test planning in digital microfluidic biochips using efficient eulerization techniques. Journal of Electronic Testing: Theory and Applications 27(5), 657–671 (2011)

[53] Su, F., Hwang, W., Mukherjee, A., Chakrabarty, K.: Testing and diagnosis of realistic defects in digital microfluidic biochips. Journal of Electronic Testing: Theory and Applications 23(2-3), 219–233 (2007)

[54] Xu, T., Chakrabarty, K.: Fault modeling and functional test methods for digital microfluidic biochips. IEEE Transactions on Biomedical Circuits and Systems 3(4), 241–253 (2009)

[55] Xu, T., Chakrabarty, K.: Functional testing of digital microfluidic biochips. In: International Test Conference (ITC), pp. 1–10 (2007)

[56] Mitra, D., Ghoshal, S., Rahaman, H., Bhattacharya, B.B., Majumder, D.D., Chakrabarty, K.: Accelerated functional testing of digital microfluidic biochips. In: IEEE Asian Test Symposium (ATS), pp. 295–300 (2008)

[57] Zhao, Y., Chakrabarty, K.: On-line testing of lab-on-chip using digital microfluidic compactors. In: IEEE International On-Line Testing Symposium, pp. 213–218 (2008)

[58] Zhao, Y., Chakrabarty, K.: Pin-count-aware online testing of digital microfluidic biochips. In: IEEE VLSI Test Symposium (VTS), pp. 111–116 (2010)

[59] Mitra, D., Ghoshal, S., Rahaman, H., Chakrabarty, K., Bhattacharya, B.B.: On-line error detection in digital microfluidic biochips. In: IEEE Asian Test Symposium (ATS), pp. 332–337 (2012)

[60] Fair, R.B., Khlystov, A., Tailor, T.D., Ivanov, V., Evans, R.D., Griffin, P.B., Srinivasan, V., Pamula, V.K., Pollack, M.G., Zhou, J.: Chemical and Biological Applications of Digital-Microfluidic Devices. IEEE Design & Test of Computers 24(1), 10–24 (2007)

[61] Zhao, Y., Chakrabarty, K.: Cross-contamination avoidance for droplet routing in digital microfluidic biochips. In: IEEE/ACM Design, Automation and Test in Europe (DATE), pp. 1290–1295 (2009)

[62] Mitra, D., Ghoshal, S., Rahaman, H., Chakrabarty, K., Bhattacharya, B.B.: On residue removal in digital microfluidic biochips. In: Great Lakes Symposium on VLSI (GLSVLSI), pp. 391–394 (2011)

[63] Mitra, D., Ghoshal, S., Rahaman, H., Chakrabarty, K., Bhattacharya, B.B.: Automated path planning for washing in digital microfluidic biochips. In: IEEE International Conference on Automation Science & Engineering (CASE), pp. 115–120 (2012)

Monitoring Distributed, Heterogeneous Data Streams: The Emergence of Safe Zones

Daniel Keren[1], Guy Sagy[2], Amir Abboud[2], David Ben-David[2],
Assaf Schuster[2], Izchak Sharfman[2], and Antonios Deligiannakis[3]

[1] Department of Computer Science, Haifa University
[2] Faculty of Computer Science, Israeli Institute of Technology
[3] Department of Electronic and Computer Engineering,
Technical University of Crete

Abstract. In many emerging applications, the data to be monitored is
of very high volume, dynamic, and distributed, making it infeasible to
collect the distinct data streams to a central node and process them there.
Often, the monitoring problem consists of determining whether the value
of a global function, which depends on the union of all streams, crossed
a certain threshold. A great deal of effort is directed at reducing communication overhead by transforming the monitoring of the global function
to the testing of *local* constraints, checked independently at the nodes.
Recently, *geometric monitoring* (GM) proved to be very useful for constructing such local constraints for general (non-linear, non-monotonic)
functions. Alas, in all current variants of geometric monitoring, the constraints at all nodes share an identical structure and are, thus, unsuitable
for handling heterogeneous streams, which obey different distributions at
the distinct nodes. To remedy this, we propose a general approach for geometric monitoring of heterogeneous streams (HGM), which defines constraints tailored to fit the distinct data distributions at the nodes. While
optimally selecting the constraints is an NP-hard problem, we provide
a practical solution, which seeks to reduce running time by hierarchically clustering nodes with similar data distributions and then solving
more, but simpler, optimization problems. Experiments are provided to
support the validity of the proposed approach.

1 Introduction

For a few years now, processing and monitoring of distributed streams has been
emerging as a major effort in data management, with dedicated systems being
developed for the task [4]. This paper deals with *threshold queries* over distributed streams, which are defined as "retrieve all items x for which $f(x) \leq T$",
where $f()$ is a scoring function and T some threshold. Such queries are the building block for many algorithms, such as top-k queries, anomaly detection, and
system monitoring. They are also applied in important data processing and data
mining tools, including feature selection, decision tree construction, association
rule mining, and computing correlations.

P. Gupta and C. Zaroliagis (Eds.): ICAA 2014, LNCS 8321, pp. 17–28, 2014.

Geometric monitoring (GM) [22,5,11,15] has been recently proposed for handling such threshold queries over distributed data. While a more detailed presentation is deferred until Section 2, we note that GM can be applied to the important case of scoring functions $f()$ evaluated at the average of dynamic data vectors $v_1(t), \ldots, v_n(t)$, maintained at n distributed nodes. Here, $v_i(t)$ is an m-dimensional data vector, often denoted as *local vector*, at the i-th node N_i at time t (often t will be suppressed). In a nutshell, each node monitors a convex subset, often referred to as the node's *safe-zone*, of the *domain* of these data vectors, as opposed to their *range*. What is guaranteed in GM is that the global function $f()$ will not cross its specified threshold as long as all data vectors lie within their corresponding safe-zones. Thus, each node remains silent as long as its data vector lies within its safe zone. Otherwise, in case of a safe-zone breach, communication needs to take place in order to check if the function has truly crossed the given threshold.

The geometric technique can support any scoring function $f()$, evaluated at the average of the data vectors.

A crucial component for reducing the communication required by the geometric method is the design of the safe-zone in each node. Nodes remain silent as long as their local vectors remain within their safe-zone. Thus, good safe-zones increase the probability that nodes will remain silent, while also guaranteeing correctness: a global threshold violation cannot occur unless at least one node's local vector lies outside the corresponding node's safe-zone.

However, prior work on geometric monitoring has failed to take into account the nature of heterogeneous data streams, in which the data distribution of the local vectors at different nodes may vary significantly. This has led to a uniform treatment of all nodes, independently of their characteristics, and the assignment of identical safe-zones (i.e., of the same shape and size) to all nodes.

As we demonstrate in this paper, designing safe-zones that take into account the data distribution of nodes can lead to efficiently monitoring threshold queries at a fraction (requiring an order of magnitude fewer messages) of what prior techniques achieve. However, designing different safe-zones for the nodes is by no means an easy task. In fact, the problem is NP-hard (proof omitted due to lack of space). We thus propose a more practical solution that hierarchically clusters nodes, based on the similarity of their data distributions, and then seeks to solve many small (and easier) optimization problems.

Hereafter we denote our proposed method for geometric monitoring of heterogeneous streams as **HGM**, in contrast to prior work on geometric monitoring that is denoted **GM**.

2   Related Work

Space limitations allow us to only survey previous work on geometric monitoring (GM). We now describe some basic ideas and concepts of the GM technique, which was introduced and applied to monitor distributed data streams in [22,23].

As described in Section 1, each node N_i maintains a local vector v_i, while the monitoring function $f()$ is evaluated at the average v of the v_i vectors. Before the monitoring process, each node N_i is assigned a subset of the data space, denoted as S_i – its *safe-zone* – such that, as long as the local vectors are inside their respective safe-zones, it is guaranteed that the global function's value did not cross the threshold; thus the node remains silent as long as its local vector v_i is inside S_i. If $v_i \notin S_i$ (local violation), a violation recovery ("balancing") algorithm [22] can be applied.

For details and scope of GM see [15] and the survey in [6]. Recently, GM was successfully applied to detecting outliers in sensor networks [5], extended to prediction-based monitoring [11], and applied to other monitoring problems [16,18,10].

Basic Definitions Relating to GM. A basic construct is the *admissible region*, defined by $A \triangleq \{v | f(v) \leq T\}$. Since the value we wish to monitor is $f\left(\frac{v_1 + \ldots + v_n}{n}\right)$, any viable assignment of safe-zones must satisfy

$\bigwedge_{i=1}^{n} (v_i \in S_i) \rightarrow v = (v_1 + \ldots + v_n)/n \in A$. This guarantees that as long as all nodes are silent, the average of the v_i vectors remains in A and, therefore, the function has not crossed the threshold. The question is, of course, how to determine the safe-zone S_i of each node N_i; in a sense to be made precise in Section 2.1, it is desirable for the safe-zones to be as large as possible.

In [15] it was proved that all existing variants of GM share the following property: each of them defines some convex subset C of A (different methods induce different C's), such that each safe-zone S_i is a translation of C – that is, there exist vectors u_i $(1 \leq i \leq n)$ such that $S_i = \{u_i + c | c \in C\}$ and $\sum_{i=1}^{n} u_i = 0$. This observation unifies the distinct variants of GM, and also allows to easily see why $\bigwedge_{i=1}^{n} (v_i \in S_i)$ implies that $v \in C \subseteq A$ – it follows immediately from the fact that convex subsets are closed under taking averages and from the fact that the u_i vectors sum to zero.

Here we assume that C is given; it can be provided by any of the abovementioned methods. We propose to extend previous work in a more general direction. Our goal here is to handle a basic problem which haunts all the existing GM variants: *the shapes of the safe-zones at different nodes are identical.* Thus, if the data is heterogeneous across the distinct streams (an example is depicted in Figure 1), meaning that the data at different nodes obeys different distributions, existing GM algorithms will perform poorly, causing many local violations that do not correspond to global threshold crossing ("false alarms").

2.1   Safe-Zone Design

In this paper, we present a more general approach that allows to assign *differently shaped* safe-zones to different nodes. Our approach requires tackling a difficult optimization problem, for which practical solutions need to be devised. We now

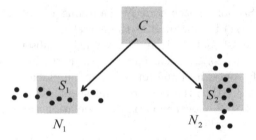

Fig. 1. Why GM may fail for heterogeneous streams. Here C is equal to a square, and the data distribution at the two nodes is schematically represented by samples. In GM, the safe-zones at both nodes are restricted to be a translation of C, and thus cannot cover the data; HGM will allow much better safe-zones (see Section 2.1, and Figure 2).

seek to formulate an optimization problem, whose solution defines the safe-zones at all nodes. The safe-zones should satisfy the following properties:

Correctness: If S_i denotes the safe-zone at node N_i, we must have: $\bigwedge_{i=1}^{n} (v_i \in S_i) \to (v_1 + \ldots + v_n)/n \in C$. This ensures that every threshold crossing by $f(v)$ will result in a safe-zone breach in at least one node.

Expansiveness: Every safe-zone breach (local violation) triggers communication, so the safe-zones should be as "large" as possible. We measure the "size" of a safe-zone S_i by its probability volume, defined as $\int_{S_i} p_i(v)dv$ where p_i is the pdf of the data at node N_i. Probabilistic models have proved useful in predicting missing and future stream values in various monitoring and processing tasks [7,24,13], including previous geometric methods [15], and their incorporation in our algorithms proved useful in monitoring real data (Section 4). To handle these two requirements, we formulate a constrained optimization problem as follows:

> **Given** (1) probability distribution functions $p_1, \ldots, p_n$ at n nodes
> (2) A convex subset C of the admissible region A
>
> Maximize $\int_{S_1} p_1 dv_1 \cdot \ldots \cdot \int_{S_n} p_n dv_n$ (expansiveness)
>
> Subject to $\frac{S_1 \oplus \cdots \oplus S_n}{n} \subseteq C$ (correctness)

where $\frac{S_1 \oplus \cdots \oplus S_n}{n} = \left\{ \frac{v_1 + \cdots + v_n}{n} \mid v_1 \in S_1, \ldots, v_n \in S_n \right\}$, or the *Minkowski sum* [20] of $S_1, \ldots, S_n$, in which every element is divided by n (the *Minkowski average*). Introducing the Minkowski average is necessary in order to guarantee correctness, since v_i must be able to range over the entire safe-zone S_i. Note that instead of using the constraint $\frac{S_1 \oplus \cdots \oplus S_n}{n} \subseteq A$, we use $\frac{S_1 \oplus \cdots \oplus S_n}{n} \subseteq C$. This preserves correctness, since $C \subseteq A$. The reason we chose to use C is that typically it's much easier to check the constraint for the Minkowski average containment in a convex set; this is discussed in Section 3.4.

To derive the target function $\int_{S_1} p_1 dv_1 \cdot \ldots \cdot \int_{S_n} p_n dv_n$, which estimates the probability that the local vectors of all nodes will remain in their safe-zones, we assumed that the data is not correlated between nodes (hence we multiply the individual probabilities), as it was the case in the experiments in Section 4 (see also [24] and the discussion therein). If the data is correlated, the algorithm is essentially the same, with the expression for the probability that data at some node breaches its safe-zone modified accordingly.

Note that correctness and expansiveness have to reach a "compromise": figuratively speaking, the correctness constraint restricts the size of the safe-zones, while the probability volume increases as the safe-zones become larger. This trade-off is central in the solution of the optimization problem.

The advantage of the resulting safe-zones is demonstrated by a schematic example (Figure 2), in which C and the stream pdfs are identical to those in Figure 1. In HGM, however, the individual safe-zones can be shaped very differently from C, allowing a much better coverage of the pdfs, while adhering to the correctness constraint. Intuitively speaking, nodes can trade "geometric slack" between them; here S_1 trades "vertical slack" for "horizontal slack".

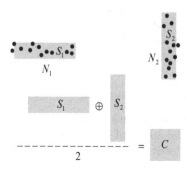

Fig. 2. Schematic example of HGM safe-zone assignment for two nodes, which also demonstrates the advantage over previous work. The convex set C is a square, and the pdf at the left (right) node is uniform over a rectangle elongated along the horizontal (vertical) direction. HGM can handle this case by assigning the two rectangles S_1, S_2 as safe-zones, which satisfies the correctness requirement (since their Minkowski average is equal to C). GM (Figure 1) will perform poorly in this case.

3   Constructing the Safe-Zones

We now briefly describe the overall operation of the distributed nodes. The computation of the safe-zones is initially performed by a coordinator node, using a process described in this section. This process is performed infrequently, since there is no need to change the safe-zones of a node unless a global threshold violation occurs. As described in Section 2.1, the input to the algorithm is: (1) The probability distribution functions $p_1, \ldots, p_n$ at the n nodes. These pdfs can be of any kind (e.g., Gaussian [23], random walk [21], uniform, etc). (2) A convex subset C of the admissible region A.

Given this input, the coordinator applies the algorithm described in Sections 3.1 to 3.5 to compute $S_1 \ldots S_n$ which solve the optimization problem defined in Section 2.1. Then, node N_k is assigned S_k.

3.1   Solving the Optimization Problem

In order to efficiently solve our optimization problem, we need to answer several questions:

- What kinds of shapes to consider for candidate safe-zones?
- The target function is defined as the product of integrals of the respective pdfs on the candidate safe-zones. Given candidate safe-zones, how do we efficiently compute the target function?
- Given candidate safe-zones, how do we efficiently test if their Minkowski average lies in C?
- As we will point out, the number of variables to optimize over is very large, with this number increasing with the number of nodes. It is well-known that the computational cost of general optimization routines increases at a super-linear rate with the number of variables. To remedy this issue, we propose in Section 3.5 a hierarchical clustering approach, which uses a divide-and-conquer algorithm to reduce the problem to that of recursively computing safe-zones for small numbers of nodes.

3.2   Shape of Safe-Zones to Consider

The first step in solving an optimization problem is determining the parameters to optimize over. Here, the space of parameters is huge – *all* subsets of the Euclidean space are candidates for safe-zones. For one-dimensional (scalar) data, intervals provide a reasonable choice for safe-zones, but for higher dimensions no clear candidate exists.

To achieve a practical solution, we choose the safe-zones from a parametric family of shapes, denoted by S. This family of shapes should satisfy the following requirements:

- It should be broad enough so that its members can reasonably approximate every subset which is a viable candidate for a safe-zone.
- The members of S should have a relatively simple shape. In practice, this means that they are polytopes with a restricted number of vertices, or can be defined by a small number of implicit equations (e.g., polynomials [14]).
- It should not be too difficult to compute the integral of the various pdfs over members of S (Section 3.3).
- It should not be too difficult to compute, or bound, the Minkowski average of members of S (Section 3.4).

The last two conditions allow efficient optimization. If computing the integrals of the pdf or the Minkowski average are time consuming, the optimization process may be lengthy. We thus considered and applied in our algorithms various polytopes (such as triangles, boxes, or more general polytope) as safe-zones; this yielded good results in [15].

The choices of S applied here have provided good results in terms of safe-zone simplicity and effectiveness. However, the challenge of choosing the best shape for arbitrary functions and data distributions is quite formidable, and we plan to continue studying it in the future.

3.3   Computing the Target Function

The target function is defined as the product of integrals of the respective pdfs on the candidate safe-zones. Typically, data is provided as discrete samples. The integral can be computed by first approximating the discrete samples by a continuous pdf, and then integrating it over the safe-zone. We used this approach, fitting a GMM (Gaussian Mixture Model) to the discrete data and integrating it over the safe-zones, which were defined as polytopes. To accelerate the computation of the integral, we used Green's Theorem to reduce a double integral to a one-dimensional integral over the polygon's boundary, for the two-dimensional data sets in the experiments. For higher dimensions, the integral can also be reduced to integrals of lower dimensions, or computed using Monte-Carlo methods.

3.4   Checking the Constraints

A simple method to test the Minkowski sum constraint relies on the following result [9]:

Lemma 1. *If P and Q are convex polytopes with vertices $\{P_i\}$, $\{Q_j\}$, then $P \oplus Q$ is equal to the convex hull of the set $\{P_i + Q_j\}$.*

Now, assume we wish to test whether the Minkowski average of P and Q is contained in C. Since C is convex, it contains the convex hull of every of its subsets; hence it suffices to test whether the points $(P_i + Q_j)/2$ are in C, for all i, j. If not all points are inside C, then the constraint violation can be measured by the maximal distance of a point $(P_i + Q_j)/2$ from C's boundary. The method easily generalizes to more polytopes: for three polytopes it is required to test the average of all triplets of vertices, etc.

3.5   Hierarchical Clustering

While the algorithms presented in Sections 3.3-3.4 reduce the running time for computing the safe-zones, our optimization problem still poses a formidable difficulty. For example, fitting octagonal safe-zones [15] to 100 nodes with two-dimensional data requires to optimize over 1,600 variables (800 vertices in total, each having two coordinates), which is quite high. To alleviate this problem, we first organize the nodes in a hierarchical structure, which allows us to then solve the problem recursively (top-down) by reducing it to sub-problems, each containing a much smaller number of nodes.

We first perform a bottom-up hierarchical clustering of the nodes. To achieve this, a distance measure between nodes needs to be defined. Since a node is represented by its data vectors, a distance measure should be defined between subsets of the Euclidean space. We apply the method in [8], which defines the distance between sets by the L^2 distance between their moment vectors (vectors whose coordinates are low-order moments of the set). The moments have to be computed only once, in the initialization stage. The leaves of the cluster tree are individual nodes, and the inner vertices can be thought of as "super nodes", each containing the union (Minkowski average) of the data of nodes in the respective sub-tree. Since the moments of a union of sets are simply the sum of the individual sets' moments, the computation of the moment for the inner nodes is very fast.

After the hierarchical clustering is completed, the safe-zones are assigned top-down: first, the children of the root are assigned safe-zones under the constraint that their
Minkowski average is contained in C. In the next level, the grandchildren of the root are assigned safe-zones under the constraint that their Minkowski average is contained in their parent nodes' safe-zones, etc. The leaves are either individual nodes, or clusters which are uniform enough and can all be assigned safe-zones with identical shapes.

4   Experiments

HGM was implemented and compared with the GM method, as described in [15], which is the most recent variant of previous work on geometric monitoring that we know of. We are not aware of other algorithms which can be applied to monitor the functions treated here (the ratio queries in [12] deal with accumulative ratios and not instantaneous ones as in our experiments).

4.1   Data, Setup and Monitored Functions

Data and Monitored Functions. Our data consists of air pollutant measurements taken from "AirBase – The European Air Quality Database" [3], measured in micrograms per cubic meter. Nodes correspond to sensors at different geographical locations. The data at different nodes greatly varies in size and shape and is irregular as a function of time. The monitored functions were chosen due to their practical importance, and also as they are non-linear and non-monotonic and, thus, cannot be handled by most existing methods. In Section 4.2 results are presented for monitoring the ratio of NO to NO_2, which is known to be an important indicator in air quality analysis [17]. An example of monitoring a quadratic function in three variables is also presented (Section 4.3);

quadratic functions are important in numerous applications (e.g., the variance is a quadratic function in the variables, and a normal distribution is the exponent of a quadratic function, hence thresholding it is equivalent to thresholding the quadratic).

Choosing the Family of Safe-Zones. To solve the optimization problem, it is necessary to define a parametric family of shapes S from which the safe-zones will be chosen. Section 3.2 discusses the properties this family should satisfy. In [15], the suitability of some families of polytopes is studied for the simpler, but related, problem of finding a safe-zone common to all nodes. The motivations for choosing S here were:

- Ratio queries (Section 4.2) – the triangular safe-zones (Figure 3) have the same structure, but not size or location, as C, and are very simple to define and apply.

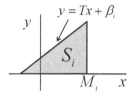

Fig. 3. Triangular safe-zones used for ratio monitoring

- Quadratic function (Section 4.3) – here we allowed general polytopes, and tested the results for increasing numbers of vertices. The model selected was with 12 vertices, in which the target function to optimize was "saturated" (i.e. adding more vertices increased the value by less than 0.1%).

Optimization Parameters and Tools. The triangular safe-zones (Section 4.2) have two degrees of freedom each (M_i and β_i, see Figure 3), hence for n nodes we have $2n$ parameters to optimize over. The safe-zones in Section 4.3 require 36 parameters each. In all cases we used the Matlab routine fmincon to solve the optimization problem [1]. To compute the integral of the pdf on the safe-zones, data was approximated by a Gaussian Mixture Model (GMM), using a Matlab routine [2].

4.2   Ratio Queries

This set of experiments concerned monitoring the ratio between two pollutants, NO and NO_2, measured in distinct sensors. Each of the n nodes holds a vector (x_i, y_i) (the two concentrations), and the monitored function is $\frac{\sum y_i}{\sum x_i}$ (in [12] ratio is monitored but over aggregates over time, while here we monitor the instantaneous ratio for the current readings). An alert must be sent whenever this function is above a threshold T (taken as 4 in the experiments), and/or when the NO_2 concentration is above 250. The admissible region A is a triangle, therefore convex, so $C = A$. The safe-zones tested were triangles of the form depicted in Figure 3, a choice motivated by the shape of C. The half-planes method (Section 3.4) was used to test the constraints. An example with four nodes, which demonstrates the advantage of allowing different safe-zones at the distinct nodes, is depicted in Figure 4.

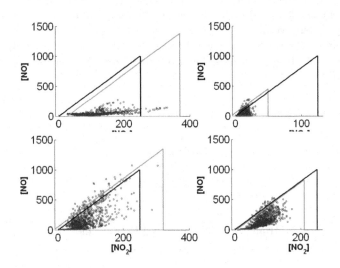

Fig. 4. Example of safe-zones with four nodes. The convex set C is the triangle outlined in black, safe-zones are outlined in green. Nodes with more compact distributions are assigned smaller safe-zones, and nodes with high values of the monitored function (NO/NO_2 ratio) are assigned safe-zones which are translated to the left in order to cover more data. This is especially evident in the top right node, in which the safe-zone is shifted to the left so it can cover almost all the data points. In order to satisfy the Minkowski sum constraint, the safe-zone of top left node is shifted to the right, which in that node hardly sacrifices any data points; also, the larger safe-zones are balanced by the smaller ones. Note that HGM allows safe-zones which are *larger* than the admissible region A, as opposed to previous work, in which the safe-zones are subsets of A.

Improvement over Previous GM Work. We compared HGM with GM in terms of the number of produced local violations. In Figure 5, the number of safe-zone violations is compared for various numbers of nodes. HGM results in significantly fewer local violations, even for a small number of nodes. As the number of nodes increases, the benefits of HGM over GM increase. For a modest network size of 10 nodes, HGM requires less than an order of magnitude fewer messages than GM.

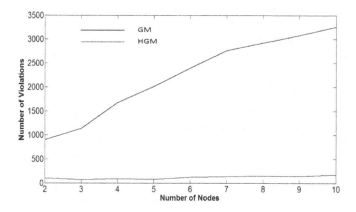

Fig. 5. Comparison of our HGM (green) to GM [15] (blue) in terms of number of violations, up to 10 nodes

4.3 Monitoring a Quadratic Function

Another example consists of monitoring a quadratic function with more general polyhedral safe-zones in three variables (Figure 6). The data consists of measurements of three pollutants (NO, NO_2, SO_2), and the safe-zones are polyhedra with 12 vertices. The admissible region A is the ellipsoid depicted in pink; since it is convex, $C = A$. As the extent of the data is far larger than A, the safe-zones surround the regions in which the data is denser. Here we did not compare to previous methods.

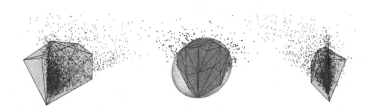

Fig. 6. Monitoring a quadratic function. The set C is the pink ellipsoid, the safe-zones are polyhedra with 12 vertices each (in pale blue), and their Minkowski average is in green.

References

1. http://tinyurl.com/kxssfgl
2. DCPR (Data Clustering and Pattern Recognition) Toolbox, http://tinyurl.com/nxospq2
3. The European air quality database, http://tinyurl.com/ct9bh7x

4. Abadi, D.J., Ahmad, Y., Balazinska, M., Çetintemel, U., Cherniack, M., Hwang, J.-H., Lindner, W., Maskey, A., Rasin, A., Ryvkina, E., Tatbul, N., Xing, Y., Zdonik, S.B.: The design of the borealis stream processing engine. In: CIDR (2005)
5. Burdakis, S., Deligiannakis, A.: Detecting outliers in sensor networks using the geometric approach. In: ICDE (2012)
6. Cormode, G.: Algorithms for continuous distributing monitoring: A survey. In: AlMoDEP (2011)
7. Deshpande, A., Guestrin, C., Madden, S., Hellerstein, J.M., Hong, W.: Model-driven data acquisition in sensor networks. In: VLDB (2004)
8. Elad, M., Tal, A., Ar, S.: Content based retrieval of vrml objects: an iterative and interactive approach. In: Proceedings of the Sixth Eurographics Workshop on Multimedia 2001 (2002)
9. Fogel, E., Halperin, D.: Exact and efficient construction of minkowski sums of convex polyhedra with applications. Computer-Aided Design 39(11) (2007)
10. Garofalakis, M.N., Keren, D., Samoladas, V.: Sketch-based geometric monitoring of distributed stream queries. PVLDB (2013)
11. Giatrakos, N., Deligiannakis, A., Garofalakis, M.N., Sharfman, I., Schuster, A.: Prediction-based geometric monitoring over distributed data streams. In: SIGMOD (2012)
12. Gupta, R., Ramamritham, K., Mohania, M.K.: Ratio threshold queries over distributed data sources. In: ICDE (2010)
13. Kanagal, B., Deshpande, A.: Online filtering, smoothing and probabilistic modeling of streaming data. In: ICDE (2008)
14. Keren, D., Cooper, D.B., Subrahmonia, J.: Describing complicated objects by implicit polynomials. IEEE Trans. Pattern Anal. Mach. Intell. 16(1) (1994)
15. Keren, D., Sharfman, I., Schuster, A., Livne, A.: Shape sensitive geometric monitoring. IEEE Trans. Knowl. Data Eng. 24(8) (2012)
16. Kogan, J.: Feature selection over distributed data streams through optimization. In: SDM (2012)
17. Kurpius, M.R., Goldstein, A.H.: Gas-phase chemistry dominates o3 loss to a forest, implying a source of aerosols and hydroxyl radicals to the atmosphere. Geophysical Research Letters 30(7) (2007)
18. Papapetrou, O., Garofalakis, M.N., Deligiannakis, A.: Sketch-based querying of distributed sliding-window data streams. PVLDB 5(10) (2012)
19. Sagy, G., Keren, D., Sharfman, I., Schuster, A.: Distributed threshold querying of general functions by a difference of monotonic representation. PVLDB 4(2) (2010)
20. Serra, J.P.: Image analysis and mathematical morphology. Academic Press, London (1982)
21. Shah, S., Ramamritham, K.: Handling non-linear polynomial queries over dynamic data. In: ICDE (2008)
22. Sharfman, I., Schuster, A., Keren, D.: A geometric approach to monitoring threshold functions over distributed data streams. ACM Trans. Database Syst. 32(4) (2007)
23. Sharfman, I., Schuster, A., Keren, D.: Shape sensitive geometric monitoring. In: PODS (2008)
24. Tang, M., Li, F., Phillips, J.M., Jestes, J.: Efficient threshold monitoring for distributed probabilistic data. In: ICDE (2012)

Exploiting Heterogeneous Data Sources: A Computing Paradigm for Live Web and Sustainability Applications

Dimitrios Gunopulos

Department of Informatics and Telecommunications
National and Kapodistrian University of Athens
kddlab.di.uoa.gr/dg.html
dg@di.uoa.gr

Abstract. Today we are witnessing advances in technology that are changing dramatically the way we live, work and interact with the physical environment. New revolutionary technologies are creating an explosion on the size and variety of information that is becoming available. Such technologies include the development and widespread adoption of networks of small and inexpensive embedded sensors that are being used to instrument the environment at an unprecedented scale. In addition, the last few years have brought forward the widespread adoption of social networking applications. Another trend with significant ramifications is the massive adoption of smartphones in the market. The rise of the social networking applications and the always-on functionality of the smartphones are driving the rise of a part of the web that is dedicated to recording, maintaining and sharing rapidly changing data which has been termed the Live Web. In this talk we present recent research work motivated by the trends we describe above. We also consider how such novel research results are enabling forms of computation. First, we focus on the specific problem of finding events or trends, including spatiotemporal patterns, when monitoring microblogging streams. Our work is mainly in the context of the INSIGHT FP7 project and we also consider data from sources as different as traffic sensors and Twitter streams. To put this research work in a general context, in the second part of the talk we consider the more general problem of developing applications and reasoning about the behavior of novel applications that exploit the new setting of the Live Web, and understanding the implications on the design, development and deployment of new applications in this setting. We describe initial work on the formulation of a new computing paradigm for this setting, and on describing how it can be applied for computational sustainability applications.

1 Introduction

Today we are witnessing advances in technology that are changing dramatically the way we live, work and interact with the physical environment. New revolutionary technologies are creating an explosion on the size and variety of information that is becoming available. Such technologies include the development

P. Gupta and C. Zaroliagis (Eds.): ICAA 2014, LNCS 8321, pp. 29–36, 2014.

and widespread adoption of networks of small and inexpensive embedded sensors that are being used to instrument the environment at an unprecedented scale. In addition, the last few years have brought forward the widespread adoption of social networking applications. Another trend with significant ramifications is the massive adoption of smartphones in the market. The rise of the social networking applications and the always-on functionality of the smartphones are driving the rise of a part of the web that is dedicated to recording, maintaining and sharing rapidly changing data which has been termed the Live Web.

In this environment we will see the emergence of novel, complex, mobile cyberphysical systems where people actively participate through personal mobile phones, in the process of sensing, instrumenting and analyzing live data. Applications may be as simple as providing alternative routing paths in a transportation application, to more sophisticated examples such as planning common carpool routes or optimizing routes in future public transportation systems, to applications with hard real-time constraints such as emergency response systems to natural or man-caused disasters. In fact new applications are moving beyond the entertainment and information sharing domains and into the emergency response and resource allocation domains, where more robust solutions are required.

In this talk we present recent research work along the trends we describe above. We also consider how such novel research results are enabling forms of computation. First, we focus on the specific problem of finding events or trends, including spatiotemporal patterns, when monitoring microblogging streams. Our work is mainly in the context of the INSIGHT FP7 project [INS], and we also consider data from sources as different as traffic sensors and Twitter streams. To put this research work in a general context, in the second part of the talk we consider the more general problem of developing applications and reasoning about the behavior of novel applications that exploit the new setting of the Live Web, and understanding the implications on the design, development and deployment of new applications in this setting. We describe initial work on the formulation of a new computing paradigm for this setting, and on describing how it can be applied for computational sustainability applications.

2   A New Computing Paradigm for the Live Web Setting

We maintain that a new computing paradigm is developing and it is worthwhile to explore in more detail the changing nature of computational resources, and understand the characteristics, advantages and constraints they bring forth. We focus specifically on the development and the impact of current trends such as the Live Web, the availability and the ability to handle massive data, the advent of human computing, and the impact of this paradigm to sustainability applications.

The Live Web: The rise of the social networking applications and the always-on functionality of the smartphones are driving the rise of an ever increasing part of the web that is dedicated to recording, maintaining and sharing rapidly changing data which has been termed **Live web**. The **Live Web** phenmenon goes back to the development and extensive use of RSS feeds and publish-subscribe applications on the web, which allowed the distribution of information in real time. The popularity of blogging and microblogging has showcased the problems present in searching such live data, where freshness of the information is very important in addition to the content.

Think about this: I read about the earthquake on Twitter seconds before I felt it. Oh, times... how you've changed.

Today the Live Web comprises these parts of the web that are dedicated and used by the users to document their lives, exchange and share information with colleagues and friends, but also connect their online presence with real life considerations. The technologies of today are ushering a new era where the live web becomes the canvas where people not only can share instantaneously and continuously aspects of their lives, but also create virtual communities with direct connections to the real world, and become both data producers and data consumers at the same time. The Live Web encompasses social networking sites, as exemplified by Twitter or Facebook, but also other sites that the users use to post information, experiences, and so on, including blogs, review sites that serve as a combined repository of knowledge on several topics, and which are becoming very influential on how people make decisions on several everyday problems. The important characteristics of the Live Web are:

Fig. 1. Live Web examples

(i) data in the Live web typically have temporal information associated with them. The data themselves may be changing continuously (for example, the location of the user), or their relevance to a query or a task may change continually (for example, blogging about current events). For example, consider twitter: only the latest twits are easily accessible from the interface, and if a person does not respond or retransmit a twit soon after receiving it, it is very unlikely that this action will take place later.

(ii) It is important to stress that very frequently these data have **spatial** information as well, and this information is crucial in evaluating the data. Space is becoming extremely important as well, and will become even more so in the future, as shown by the adoption of location services and location based ad placement applications. Spatial and temporal data permeate peoples lives and describe how people perform several activities. The term spatial capital refers to how peoples location can impact, influence etc their lives, chances of success, etc [BMM+12].

(iii) One of the most important uses of the Live Web is for building networks and enabling collaborations. This is a major contrast with the static web, as exemplified by the traditional search engine interface, where users search static information using different queries.

Big Data: Recently, and in parallel with the Live Web development, we are witnessing the emergence of prominent technologies such as the Cloud infrastructure [CLOUD] and the MapReduce framework [DG04] that have enabled data collection, storage, and analysis at an unprecedented level. Advances in sensor networking and the availability of low-cost sensor-enabled devices has led to the integration of sensors into vital sectors of transportation, healthcare, and emergency response. These sensors give us an unprecedented monitoring capability over our environment, leading to the collection of very large datasets, but analyzing such large datasets is not an easy task. The popularity of the MapReduce framework in particular is attributed to its simplicity, portability and powerful functional abstractions. The MapReduce framework's support for the weak connectivity model of computations across open networks makes it very appropriate for a mobile network setting [DKG+10].

Human Computing Paradigm: the trends we describe above are enabling forms of computation that were not possible before. Several initiatives aim to harness human input via crowdsourcing to process queries that neither database systems nor search engines can adequately answer. Several proposals have been made to develop languages for posing complex queries and to model data, with SQL being a widespread and straightforward answer to the problem. The paradigm is forcing us to rethink long-help assumptions, such as the closed-world assumption typically made in the databases area for query processing, which does not hold when humans can answer queries as well. It is important to note that data analysis is an inherently human process, involving creative collaborations over time and distances. Crowdsourcing techniques are being developed to allow such analysis to be incorporated to a computer system. Solutions are interdisciplinary, drawing from databases, data mining, statistics and systems.

Computational Sustainability: The sustainable use of resources is rapidly becoming a priority for societies, as the demand for resources increases at a fast pace. Sustainability is already a major consideration in the management of all resources at the urban level, both physical resources such as energy, the environment, water, but also social resources, such as healthcare or public transportation. The notion of sustainability was introduced in Our Common Future, the seminal report of the United Nations World Commission on Environment and Development, published in 1987 [UN]. While sustainability is a fundamental capability for any society, achieving sustainability and resource optimization represents a very complex problem because of the many factors involved: the possible solutions are severely constrained by the available resources (i.e., computational, human, infrastructure), advance planning, the impacts on the environment and society, and the inherent unreliability in understanding and managing the dynamics of social solutions. Computation takes a major role in the development of successful sustainability applications. In fact, Computational Sustainability [SUST] is a new, and currently rapidly developing research area that is focusing on this exact point. Several sustainability problems revolve around optimized use of resources, and such problems naturally lead to formalizations that are amenable to combinatorial optimization solutions, with energy conservation problems a particular case in point. Therefore the traditional approach is to treat such problems as optimization problems. Such solutions are certainly very useful, but do not take into account the entire picture. We propose not only to use traditional computational resources, but to fully exploit the changing landscape of the current computational environment, where connectivity is a commodity, and human computing is at our grasp. The scope of the problems certainly makes it clear that we need to fully bring to bear todays advanced and powerful computational resources in order to make significant headway in hard sustainability problems.

To summarize, we are moving towards a new, live-web enabled and human-assisted computing environment which will exhibit the following characteristics:

1. Always on connectivity through a mobile device,
2. Merging of virtual and real life (e.g. most twitter or facebook users use their real identities when using social media)
3. Availability of massively distributed and human computing components
4. Necessity to develop always very complicated mechanisms, where grass-routes development and optimization are the most general and effective approaches

The applications that will be developed in the future, will be developed and deployed in this environment, and these characteristics must be taken into account during their design. In fact, the development of tools that to support this process is an extremely important stepping stone for the development of successful applications.

3   Current and Future Work

Searching in the Live Web: The live web is an important social computing tool, where trends can be dynamically analyzed and events can be identified. For example, by tracking the popularity of terms across space and time, a news portal can determine which articles to present to each user, based on their respective vocabulary, location and timeframe. A user living in region that is being affected by a major event is more likely to be interested in reading relevant articles than someone who lives thousands of miles away.

We have developed recently ranking mechanisms to rank the results of keyword searches when retrieving time-stamped documents (e.g. tweets on Twitter, news articles, blog-posts), or documents with spatiotemporal signatures. We expect that such information is particularly useful when discussing events with a strong spatiotemporal impact. These are influential events that affect multiple places in the world for extended timeframes (Figure 2). Thus, they are more likely to be of interest to users. Our work is a natural extension of approaches that are limited to the temporal and spatial dimension of burstiness, including our recent work that has appeared in [LAP+09] and [LVG+12]. Spatiotemporal patterns are a natural way to detect trends. For example, given the set of terms that describe an item (e.g. a person or product), we can identify when and where it was popular [Figure 2. This information can help the user who is interested in trendy topics and can also be used as input to campaigns.

In more recent work [VG13] we show how to identify events in microblogging streams: we exploit notions from emotional theories, combined with spatiotemporal information and employ online event detection mechanisms to solve the problem at large scale in a distributed fashion [Figure 3].

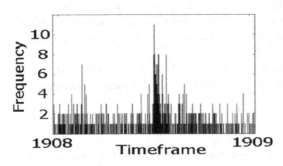

Fig. 2. A historical example: using the frequency of appearance of the word earthquake in press of the period we can pinpoint the time that the 1909 San Fransisco Earthquake took place

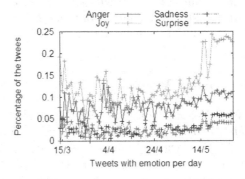

Fig. 3. An example of a timeseries of daily emotions from Twitter: March 15 to May 24 2012

Social Computing: SmartCity and Sustainability Applications

The main objective of the typical SmartCity application is the successful integration of intelligent services and new technologies that can help people modify their behavior to be more sustainable. Data collection and analysis will play an important role in enabling intelligent and adaptable management of the entire system.

Consider for example the problem of minimizing peak energy consumption in a city or a neighborhood; the benefits will be energy efficiency and energy efficiency and savings to be achieved in the residents (e.g, using smart meters at appliances), as well as in the management of the overall electricity distribution in an optimized and controlled manner [CDW+11].

Other examples include initiatives aiming to reduce energy demand and improve environmental sustainability of urban transportation. Urban transportation is facing a grand challenge that is often called sustainable accessibility: providing access to goods, services and opportunities necessary to enable human development, while preserving and restoring the environment [BFF+10]. As an illustrative example, consider a transit authority that plans its bus routes and wants to know whether a specific route is taken by at least K users between 8:00-9:00am. In such a scenario, one is interested in asking a crowd of users in some target area to participate with their local trace history through an open call. In particular, the users can passively participate in the resolution of the query for monetary benefit or intellectual satisfaction, without disclosing their traces to the authority or the querying node (Figure 4). Such a privacy-respecting property makes it easier and simpler for people to participate in collaborative efforts. It is also important to stress here that the

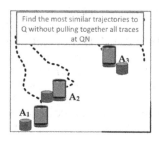

Fig. 4. In a distributed environment we must be able to answer nearest neighbor queries without compromising user privacy

tools we propose to build will allow every user to initiate an activity and build a community around it, again making the process not dependent to a global server or authority.

In our recent work [BKG13][ZLC+13] we describe how to use crowdsourcing techniques to collect traffic and mobility data from users, to use subsequently in order to optimize the public transportation rooting or improve traffic flow in a city. One of the important points of our work is to improve privacy for the users by using a local (in the mobile device) storage model for the data. As a result, efficient distributed indexing mechanisms for complex data have to be developed, to make the approach practical. Figure 4 shows an example of a mechanism that searches for similar objects (trajectory pieces in the example) in a set of mobile devices.

Acknowledgments. This work has been co-financed by EU and Greek National funds through the Operational Program "Education and Lifelong Learning" of the National Strategic Reference Framework (NSRF) - Research Funding Programs THALIS - GeomComp, THALIS - DISFER, ARISTEIA - MMD" and the EU FP7 funded project INSIGHT (www.insight-ict.eu).

References

[BKG13]   Boutsis, I., Kalogeraki, V., Gunopulos, D.: Efficient event detection by exploiting crowds. In: DEBS 2013, pp. 123–134 (2013)

[BMM+12]   Batty, M., Morphet, R., Massuci, P., Stanilov, K.: Entropy, complexity and Spatial Information, CASA Working Paper 185, UCL (Publication Date: May 24, 2012)

[CDW+11]   Chen, F., Dai, J., Wang, B., Sahu, S., Naphade, M., Lu, C.T.: Activity Analysis Based on Low Sample Rate Smart Meters. In: ACM KDD 2011 (2011)

[CLOUD]   http://en.wikipedia.org/wiki/Cloud_computing

[COMS]   http://www.comscore.com/Insights/Press_Releases/2012/10/ comScore_Reports_August_2012_U.S._Mobile_Subscriber_Market_Share

[DG04]   Dean, J., Ghemawat, S.: MapReduce: Simplified Data Processing on Large Clusters. In: OSDI 2004, San Fransisco, CA, pp. 137–150 (2004)

[DKG+11a] Dou, A.J., Kalogeraki, V., Gunopulos, D., Mielikäinen, T., Tuulos, V.H.: Scheduling for real-time mobile MapReduce systems. In: DEBS 2011, pp. 347–358 (2011)

[DKG+11b] Dou, A.J., Kalogeraki, V., Gunopulos, D., Mielikäinen, T., Tuulos, V.H., Foley, S., Yu, C.: Data Clustering on a Network of Mobile Smartphones

[INS]   The INSIGHT Project: http://www.insight-ict.eu

[LAP+09]   Lappas, T., Arai, B., Platakis, M., Kotsakos, D., Gunopulos, D.: On burstiness-aware search for document sequences. In: KDD 2009, pp. 477–486 (2009)

[LVG+12]   Lappas, T., Vieira, M.R., Gunopulos, D., Tsotras, V.J.: On the Spatiotemporal Burstiness of Terms. PVLDB 5(9), 836–847 (2012)

[SUST]   http://www.computational-sustainability.org/

[UN]   http://www.un-documents.net/wced-ocf.htm

[VG13]   Valkanas, G., Gunopulos, D.: How the Live Web feels about Events. In: ACM CIKM 2013 (2013)

[ZLC+13]   Zeinalipour-Yazti, D., Laoudias, C., Costa, C., Vlachos, M., Andreou, M.I., Gunopulos, D.: Crowdsourced Trace Similarity with Smartphones. IEEE Trans. Knowl. Data Eng. 25(6), 1240–1253 (2013)

Constructing an n-dimensional Cell Complex from a Soup of $(n − 1)$-Dimensional Faces

Ken Arroyo Ohori[1], Guillaume Damiand[2], and Hugo Ledoux[1]

[1] Delft University of Technology, The Netherlands
[2] Université de Lyon, CNRS, UMR 5205, LIRIS, F-69622, France

Abstract. There is substantial value in the use of higher-dimensional (>3D) digital objects in GIS that are built from complex real-world data. This use is however hampered by the difficulty of constructing such objects. In this paper, we present a dimension independent algorithm to build an n-dimensional cellular complex with linear geometries from its isolated $(n − 1)$-dimensional faces represented as combinatorial maps. It does so by efficiently finding the common $(n − 2)$-cells (ridges) along which they need to be linked. This process can then be iteratively applied in increasing dimension to construct objects of any dimension. We briefly describe combinatorial maps, present our algorithm using them as a base, and show an example using 2D, 3D and 4D objects which was verified to be correct, both manually and using automated methods.

1 Introduction

Higher-dimensional digital objects represent well-defined extents of space in arbitrary dimensions. In geographic information systems (GIS), these can be generated when 2D/3D space, time [1], scale [2], semantics [3], or others are all treated as independent axes of a coordinate system. An example of such an object is presented in Fig. 1. This form of representation offers interesting advantages compared to traditional ones where multiple representations of the same object are stored separately and linked in an ad hoc fashion, such as conceptual simplicity, immediate access to all existing topological relationships, the possibility to represent complex events like motion and the ease of maintaining consistency between objects [5].

However, creating higher dimensional digital objects from real-world data is inherently difficult on multiple levels. Since we are usually only familiar with up to 3D physical space, describing such objects might be straightforward mathematically, but it is nonetheless unintuitive. Higher dimensional data models are also complex, and thus realising even very simple objects requires a large number of operations on abstract elements. Finally, manipulating the related data structures while ensuring that all its required references are correctly kept is already non-trivial in 3D [6], and increasingly difficult in higher dimensions.

Nonetheless, it is possible to use the concepts behind boundary representation to significantly reduce the difficulty of the problem. In boundary representation (b-rep or BREP), an n-dimensional closed object can be unambiguously

P. Gupta and C. Zaroliagis (Eds.): ICAA 2014, LNCS 8321, pp. 37–48, 2014.
© Springer International Publishing Switzerland 2014

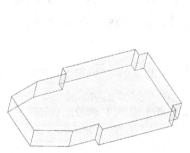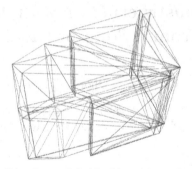

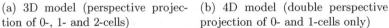

(a) 3D model (perspective projection of 0-, 1- and 2-cells)   (b) 4D model (double perspective projection of 0- and 1-cells only)

Fig. 1. The Aula Congress Centre in the TU Delft campus represented as extruded 3D and 4D models

described by the $(n-1)$-dimensional boundary that encloses it, as originally defined by Baumgart [7] and Braid [8] for a (3D) solid with a (2D) surface boundary composed of flat polygonal patches. This concept is valid in higher dimensions as well, and is related to the concept of a cell complex [9] in topology, where an n-dimensional cell (n-cell) in the complex has a number of $(n-1)$-cells (faces) as its boundary, and these faces are also part of the complex. An n-cell is an abstract object which is considered to be homeomorphic to an n-ball (e.g. point, segment, disk, ball, etc.). In this paper we use combinatorial maps to represent a cell complex, which are described in Sec. 2.

The $(n-1)$-dimensional boundary of an n-cell is much easier to conceive than the original n-cell, since the $(n-1)$-cells that it is composed of can be themselves described individually. However, this requires the existence of an algorithm that is able to connect these separate $(n-1)$-cells to form the n-cell in an efficient manner, abstracting such issues as incompatible orientations in the model, the handling of duplicate cells and the identification of common boundaries. This operation, fully dimension independent, presented in Sec. 3 and the focus of the present paper, can be performed recursively in increasing dimension to generate arbitrary cell complexes in any dimension, and thus we refer to it as incremental construction.

Another possible use of incremental construction is to generate the topological information, i.e. incidence and adjacency, between a set of existing objects. This is in fact simply a subset of what the problem incremental construction is meant to solve—the identification of common boundaries—, and fits very well within the frame of GIS, where data models tend to contain very limited topological information but topological queries are of great importance [10]. Some GIS models, like the OGC Simple Features Specification [11] have no topology in their structure, even repeating the coordinates of individual points when these appear in multiple line segments or polygons. Others, such as CityGML [12], only have implicit topological information (e.g. these surfaces should form a closed shell) which is often unenforced in their geometry.

We have implemented our algorithm based on the CGAL Combinatorial Maps and Linear Cell Complex packages, which are described in Sec. 4 together with the details of our implementation, including a discussion of the computational complexity of our approach. In Sec. 5, we present an example in 4D that shows this approach in practice, comparing its output with correct results which have been generated by the Linear Cell Complex package and verifying it analytically. We finish with conclusions and discussion in Sec. 6.

2   Combinatorial Maps

Combinatorial maps (or simply maps) are an ordered topological model originally proposed by Edmonds [13] to describe the 2D surfaces of 3D objects. Their extension to arbitrary dimensions is described by Lienhardt [14] for objects without boundaries and extended by Poudret et al. [15] to objects with boundaries. They are able to describe subdivisions of orientable quasi-manifolds[1].

Intuitively, a combinatorial map is composed of two elements: *darts* and relations between them (β). The precise definition of a dart is related to an underlying simplicial decomposition of the object, each dart being equivalent to a simplex in it. However, intuitively it can be seen as an oriented edge on the boundary of a facet, which itself is on the boundary of a solid, which itself is on the boundary of a 4-cell, and so on. It is therefore equivalent to the half-edge data structure in 2D, but extends naturally to higher dimensions. Meanwhile, the relations are functions connecting darts that are related along a certain dimension. In this manner, β_1 joins consecutive oriented edges within a facet forming a loop, β_2 joins adjacent facets within a solid, β_3 joins adjacent solids within a 4-cell, and so on. As in other models based on directed elements, β_i-joined darts for $i > 1$ have opposite orientations.

More formally, an n-dimensional combinatorial map (or n-map) is defined by an $(n+1)$-tuple $M = (D, \beta_1, \ldots, \beta_n)$ where D is a finite and non-empty set of darts, β_1 is a partial permutation on D (a function $f : D \cup \{\varnothing\} \to D \cup \{\varnothing\}$ such that $\forall d_1 \in D$, $\forall d_2 \neq d_1 \in D$, $f(d_1) \neq \varnothing$ and $f(d_2) \neq \varnothing \Rightarrow f(d_1) \neq f(d_2)$), $\forall 2 \leq i \leq n$, β_i is a partial involution (a partial permutation f such that $\forall d \in D$, $f(d) \neq \varnothing \Rightarrow f(f(d)) = d$), and $\forall 1 \leq i < i+2 \leq j \leq n$, $\beta_i \circ \beta_j$ is also a partial involution (see an example in Fig. 2).

Here, $\varnothing$ is a special value used to indicate that a given dart d has no other dart in relation by a given β_i. In such a case we have $\beta_i(d) = \varnothing$ and that means that d belongs to the i-boundary of the described object (it belongs to only one i-cell). A dart d is said to be i-free when $\beta_i(d) = \varnothing$. Otherwise it is i-sewn with a second dart d' and we have $\beta_i(d) = d' \neq \varnothing$.

In order to traverse an n-map, the orbit operator $< A > (d) = < \beta_{a1}, \ldots, \beta_{ak} > (d)$ obtains all the darts that can be reached from dart d by successive applications of the links $\beta_{a1}, \ldots, \beta_{ak} \in A$. Certain orbits are particularly interesting: for any $1 \leq i \leq n$, $< \hat{\beta_i} > (d) = < \beta_1, \ldots, \beta_{i-1}, \beta_{i+1}, \ldots, \beta_n > (d)$ contains all

---

[1] A specific combinatorial interpretation of the concept of a manifold. See Lienhardt [14] for details.

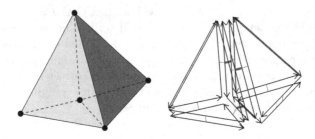

Fig. 2. (Left) A 3D cellular complex composed with two tetrahedra sharing a common face. There are 2 3-cells, 7 2-cells, 9 1-cells and 5 0-cells. (Right) The corresponding 3D combinatorial map having 48 darts.

the darts in the i-cell of d, while $< \{\beta_i \circ \beta_j | \forall i, j\, 1 \leq i < j \leq n\} > (d)$ contains all the darts in the 0-cell (vertex) of d. As two darts linked by a β_i have opposite directions (for $2 \leq i \leq n$), they belong to the two vertices of a same edge. Thus by combining two β, we obtain a dart of the same vertex than d.

When the relations in an orbit are applied in a well-defined order, these orbits are generated in a consistent manner. This makes it possible to generate a canonical representation of (a subset of) the darts in a map, which combined with labelled darts can be used to test combinatorial map isomorphism in quadratic time, as shown by Gosselin et al. [16] and demonstrated by searching for patterns in images.

The incremental construction of cells in a combinatorial map is based on the sewing operator, which joins two i-cells along an $(i - 1)$-cell which after the operation lies in their common boundary. Intuitively, given two i-free darts d_1 and d_2, the i-sew operation between d_1 and d_2 will pairwise link the orbits of these two darts by β_i so that we will obtain $\beta_i(d_1) = d_2$.

We can see in Fig. 3 an example of the 3-sew operation. Starting from a 3D combinatorial map describing two isolated tetrahedra, we identify two faces by using the 3-sew operations on darts d and d'. This operation puts in relation all the darts of the two initial faces by pairs so that we obtain a valid combinatorial map (i.e. the constraint that $\beta_1 \circ \beta_3$ is a partial involution is still satisfied).

A combinatorial map only describes the topological part of an object in term of a cell complex, i.e. the set of cells in all dimensions and all the incidence and adjacency relations. Applications often require adding information associated with specific cells (e.g. to associate a colour to each vertex, or a normal to each face). This is possible thanks to the attribute notion. An i-attribute is the information associated with i-cells. As cells are implicitly represented by sets of darts in combinatorial maps, links between i-attributes and i-cells are done through the darts of the i-cells: all the darts belonging to a same i-cell are linked to the same i-attribute.

These attributes are very useful as they allow to associate any information to any cell, and given a dart, we have a direct access to all of its associated attributes. Moreover, these attributes can be used to describe the geometry of

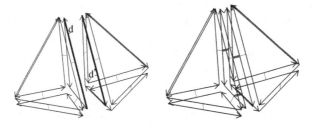

Fig. 3. (Left) A 3D combinatorial map describing 2 isolated tetrahedra. (Right) The 3D combinatorial map obtained after 3-sewing darts d and d'. All the darts of the two initial faces are 3-sewed by pairs.

the objects. Indeed, we can associate to each vertex of a combinatorial map a point in $\mathbb{R}^{d2}$ by using 0-attributes. A combinatorial map with this type of embedding gives a linear cell complex. Indeed, in this case, the geometry of each edge is a segment, the geometry of each face is a planar polygon, and so on. $d2$ is the dimension of the geometry, i.e. the dimension of the ambient space. Generally we have $d2 \geq d$ (d being the combinatorial dimension). For example we can use $d = d2 = 2$ to describe a planar graph embedded in a plane or $d = 2$ and $d2 = 3$ to describe a polyhedral mesh embedded in $\mathbb{R}^3$.

Now given two i-cells in a linear cell complex, we can test if these two cells are identical, i.e. if they have both the same topology and the same embedding information. To test if they have the same topology, we use the technique introduced above for combinatorial map isomorphism, by considering only the two i-cells instead of two whole combinatorial maps. Testing if the two cells have the same embedding can be done during the isomorphism test, simply by testing if two darts d and d' considered by the isomorphism function are linked with two points with the same coordinates. Note that we have to consider the two possible orientations of one of the two i-cells in order to detect also if the two cells are identical but with reverse orientations. We make use of this technique to efficiently test for the identity of two cells in Sec. 3.

3   Incremental Construction

Since an n-cell in a cell complex can be described by the $(n - 1)$-cells on its boundary, the same thinking can be applied in reverse: a yet unbuilt n-cell can be constructed based on a set of $(n-1)$-cells which are known to form its complete (closed) boundary.

The algorithm is applied object by object in increasing dimension, constructing isolated 0-cells first, and continuing through 2-cells, 3-cells and further. Our explanation follows the construction of *single cell* of a certain dimension, starting with unique isolated vertices in Sec. 3.1. 1-cells are skipped since 2-cells can be easily described as a succession of 0-cells. 2-cells are then built from an ordered sequence of 0-cells, as covered in Sec. 3.2. Finally, for n-cells ($n > 2$), the method receives an unordered set (soup) of $(n-1)$-cells, the geometries of which are used as faces of the finished n-cell that is returned, as explained in Sec. 3.3. These individual cell creation algorithms are applied object by object in order of increasing dimension, so that the lower dimensional cells generated as the output of earlier stages can be used as the input of latter stages.

The incremental construction algorithm as a whole keeps track of already built cells by maintaining a reference to one of their darts, making sure that no identical cells (with equal geometry and topology) are ever created. For efficiency reasons, it is convenient to use darts which are embedded into the lexicographically smallest points of each cell, which combined with smallest point indices for all existing n- and $(n-1)$-cells, and the $(n-2)$-cells on the boundary of the $(n-1)$-cells to be used, greatly accelerates this process.

3.1 Vertices (0D)

A single point, as defined by a unique tuple of coordinates, can be present in multiple higher dimensional cells and thus described multiple times. However, to ensure the correct generation of topology and enforce the orientable quasi-manifold criterion, it should only be created once. When doing so, a new point embedding at that location should be created, and a new free dart representing the 0-cell should be created and linked to it. Every new instance of the same point should then link to this original dart.

The output of this step is thus a map from each input point to a 0-cell (dart embedded into a point) at that location (see an example in Fig. 4(a)).

3.2 Facets (2D)

In order to create a 2-cell from a sequence of 0-cells, three general steps are needed:

1. The unique 0-cells, as resulting from the evaluation of the 0-cells' point embeddings in the map obtained when processing all 0-cells, are obtained. The result of this evaluation might be the same 0-cell as provided, or an already existing 0-cell at that location. Each of these 0-cells might be a single 1-free dart, in which case it can be used directly (see an example in Fig. 4(b)), or it can be a non 1-free group of darts, in which case it has already been used as part of a different 1-cell (and possibly other higher dimensional cells). These darts used in 1-cells can be reused only when they would become part of the 2-cell that will be built and are not part of any 2-cell. If the darts cannot be reused, a copy of them *with opposite orientation* has to be created, linking it to the same embedding as the original (see examples in Fig. 4(c) to (h). In all these cases, there is at least one dart which is duplicated). The opposite orientation ensures that the two (old and new) can then be 2-sewn when constructing a 3-cell in a subsequent step.

2. The darts obtained in the previous step are 1-sewn sequentially, and the last is 1-sewn to the first, forming a closed loop.

3. Just as in the creation of 0-cells, a 2-cell can be on the boundary of multiple higher dimensional cells (or simply described multiple times in the input), and as such, it is necessary to check if the 2-cell has already been created. If any comparison returns that the 2-cell already exists, the newly created darts are deleted[2] and the existing one is returned, otherwise the new 2-cell is returned.

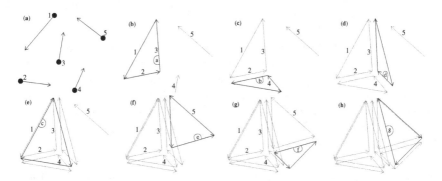

Fig. 4. Illustration of the different steps of the reconstruction of 2-cells. (a) Initial configuration: one dart per vertex. (b) After $a = $ make_2_cell$(1, 2, 3)$. (c) After $b = $ make_2_cell$(2, 4, 3)$. (d) After $d = $ make_2_cell$(1, 4, 3)$. (e) After $c = $ make_2_cell$(1, 4, 2)$. (f) After $e = $ make_2_cell$(1, 3, 5)$. (g) After $f = $ make_2_cell$(5, 3, 4)$. (h) Final result, after $g = $ make_2_cell$(4, 5, 1)$.

3.3   3-Cells and Higher (Dimension Independent)

The method to create n-cells from their $(n-1)$-cell boundaries is identical for all $n > 2$, allowing a dimension-independent function to be created. As with the creation of 2-cells from 0-cells, it consists of three general steps:

1. First of all, whether each $(n-1)$-cell has already been created beforehand is checked. This is meant so that multiple identical $(n-1)$-cells are never created in the final cell complex, even when they are given as input. If an $(n-1)$-cell already exists and it is $(n-1)$-free, it is reused as part of the n-cell (see an example in Fig. 5(a)). If it exists but is already part of a different n-cell, it is duplicated with reverse orientation (see an example in Fig. 5(b) for face labeled d). As in the case of 2-cells, this is done so that it has the same geometric embeddings and attributes, but its opposite orientation ensures that the two (old and new) can be directly n-sewn together.
2. The $(n-1)$-cells (faces) are $(n-1)$-sewn along their common $(n-2)$-dimensional boundaries (ridges). If two groups of connected $(n-1)$-cells with incompatible orientations would be joined by this operation (i.e. the

---

[2] Since the 2-cell already exists, all the used darts are copies of existing ones. This deletion thus does not erase any unique instance of a 0- or 1-cell.

pair of two corresponding ridges have the same orientation), the orientation of one of the groups is reversed before the link is created. If more than one match for a ridge is found, the object being represented is not a quasi-cellular manifold, and thus cannot be represented using combinatorial maps.

3. The newly constructed n-cell is finally compared to other n-cells to check if it already exists. If an n-cell is found to exist, the algorithm should delete the darts that are part of the newly created n-cell and instead return the existing cell. This ensures that only a single instance of an n-cell is created.

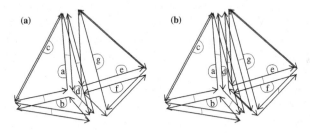

Fig. 5. Illustration of the two steps of the reconstruction of 3-cells. We start from the combinatorial map given in Fig. 4(h) which is the result of the reconstruction of 2-cells. (a) After `make_3_cell`(a, b, c, d). (b) Final result, after `make_3_cell`(d, e, f, g).

4   Implementation and Complexity

We have implemented the incremental construction algorithm in C++ using the Combinatorial Maps and Linear Cell Complex packages in CGAL[3]. In order to improve the performance of the incremental construction algorithm, we use some indices that map the lexicographically smallest point embedding of some cells of a given dimension to a dart embedded at that location. These indices are implemented as C++ Standard Library[4] maps with point embeddings as keys and lists of darts as values, using a custom compare function so that the points are internally sorted in lexicographical order. Because std::map is normally implemented as a self-balancing binary search tree, $O(\log n)$ search, insertion and deletion times and $O(n)$ space can be expected.

Since we create objects dimension by dimension, it is not necessary to maintain indices for all the cells of all dimensions at the same time. The only ones used are: all n- and $(n-1)$-cells, and the $(n-2)$-cells on the boundary of the $(n-1)$-cells for that step. Most of these can be built incrementally, adding new cells as they are created in $O(\log c)$, with c the number of cells of that dimension, assuming that the smallest vertex and a dart embedded there are kept during its construction. The complexity of building any index of cells of any dimension is thus $O(c \log c)$ and it uses $O(c)$ space. Note that this also gives the computational complexity of creating a map of all unique 0-cells in the cell complex.

---

[3] The Computational Geometry Algorithms Library: http://www.cgal.org

[4] For instance, the GNU Standard C++ Library: http://gcc.gnu.org/libstdc++/

Checking whether a given cell already exists in the cell complex is more complex. Finding a list of cells that have a certain smallest vertex is done in $O(\log c)$. Theoretically, all existing cells in the complex could have the same smallest vertex, leading to up to c quadratic time cell-to-cell comparisons just to find whether one cell exists. However, every dart is only part of *a single* cell of any given dimension, so while every dart could conceivably be a starting point for the identity comparison, a single dart cannot be used as a starting point in more than one comparison, and thus a maximum of d_{complex} identity comparisons will be made for *all* cells, with d_{complex} the total number of darts in the cell complex. From these d_{complex} darts, two identity comparisons are started, one assuming that the two cells (new and existing) have the same orientation, and one assuming opposite orientations. Each of these involves a number of dart-to-dart comparisons in the canonical representations that *cannot* be higher than the number of darts in the smallest of the two cells. The number of darts in the existing cell is unknown, but starting from the number of darts in the newly created cell (d_{cell}), it is safe to say that no more than d_{cell} dart-to-dart comparisons will be made in each identity test, leading to a worst-case time complexity of $O(d_{\text{complex}}d_{\text{cell}})$. Note that this is similar to an isomorphism test starting at every dart of the complex.

Finally, creating an n-cell from a set of $(n-1)$-cells on its boundary is more expensive, since the $(n-2)$-cell (ridge) index needs to be computed for every n-cell. Following the same reasoning as above, it can be created in $O(r \log r)$ with r the number of ridges in the n-cell, and uses $O(r)$ space. Checking whether a single ridge has a corresponding match in the index is done in $O(d_{\text{cell}}d_{\text{ridge}})$, with d_{cell} the number of darts in the n-cell and d_{ridge} the number of darts in the ridge to be tested. Since this is done for all the ridges in an n-cell, the total complexity of this step, which dominates the running time of the algorithm, is

$$\sum_{\text{ridges}} O(d_{\text{cell}}d_{\text{ridge}}) = O(d_{\text{cell}}^2).$$

The analyses given above give an indication of the computational and space complexity of the incremental algorithm as a whole. However, it is worth noting that in realistic cases the algorithm fares far better than in these worst-case scenarios: the number of cells that have a certain smallest vertex is normally far lower than the total number of cells in the complex, most of their darts are not embedded at the smallest vertex, and from these darts most identity comparisons will fail long before reaching the end of their canonical representation.

Finally, one more nuance can affect the performance of this approach. We have discussed that when two groups of darts with incompatible orientations have to be joined, the orientation of one of these has to be reversed. This is easily done by obtaining all the connected darts of one of the groups, preferably the one that is expected to be smaller, and reversing their orientation 2-cell by 2-cell. Every dart d in a 2-cell is then 1-sewn to the previous dart in the polygonal curve of the 2-cell ($\beta_1^{-1}(d)$). A group of n darts can then have its orientation reversed in $O(n)$ time. This is not a problem in practice since GIS datasets generally store nearby objects close together, but if a cell complex is incrementally constructed in the worst possible way, i.e. creating as many disconnected groups as possible, this could have to be repeated for every cell of every dimension.

5   Example

The CGAL Linear Cell Complex package provides functions to generate a series of primitives which are known to be created with correct geometry and topology, and can then be sewn together to generate more complex models. We have therefore created various 2D, 3D and 4D cell complexes using both these functions and our approach. In this manner it was possible to test the validity of our models using the identity comparison described in Sec. 2, as well as manually verifying all β-links.

In the following we show an interesting case, how a tesseract (see Fig. 6) can be generated using our approach. A tesseract is the 4D analogue of a cube, and is a 4-cell bounded by 8 cubical 3-cells, each of which is bounded by 6 square 2-cells. It thus consists of one 4-cell, 8 3-cells, 24 2-cells, 32 1-cells and 16 0-cells.

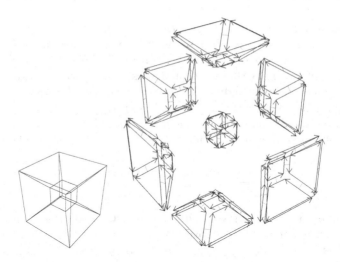

Fig. 6. (Left) A tesseract (edges only). (Right) A combinatorial maps representation of a tesseract, β_3 and the "external" cube are omitted for clarity.

Using our approach, an empty 0-cell index is first created. Then, the 16 vertices of the tesseract, each vertex p_i described by a tuple of coordinates $(x_i, y_i, z_i, w_i,$ can be created as $p_i = \texttt{make\_0\_cell}(x_i, y_i, z_i, w_i)$, which returns a unique dart embedded at each location, and added to the 0-cell index. At this point, the algorithm would have built an unconnected cell complex consisting solely of 16 completely free darts.

An empty index of 2-cells is then created. Each of its 24 square facets can be built based on its vertices as $f_i = \texttt{make\_2\_cell}(p_j, p_k, p_l, p_m)$, which 1-sews (copies of) these darts in a loop and returns the dart embedded at the smallest vertex of the facet. These are added to the index of 2-cells. Since every vertex is used in 6 different 2-cells, each dart would be copied 5 times. The cell complex at this point thus consists of 24 disconnected groups of 4 darts each.

Next, an empty index of 3-cells is created and the index of 0-cells can be deleted. For each of the 8 cubical 3-cells, a function call of the form $v_i = $ make_3_cell$(f_j, f_k, f_l, f_m, f_n, f_o)$ is made. At this point, an index of the 1D ridges of each face is built, which is used to find the 12 pairs of corresponding ridges that are then be 2-sewn together. When a 3-cell is created, it is added to the index. Since every facet bounds two 3-cells, each dart is duplicated once again, resulting in a cell complex of 8 disconnected groups of 24 darts each.

Finally, the tesseract is created with the function $t = $ make_4_cell$(v_1, v_2, \ldots, v_8)$. This can use the index of 2-cells to find the 24 corresponding pairs of facets that are then 3-sewn to generate the final cell complex.

We tested the validity of this object by performing a series of tests on the structure (complete and symmetric sewing), testing whether each cube was identical to the expected outcome, and manually verified the β-links of its 192 darts.

6   Conclusions and Future Work

We have shown that it is possible to apply the fundamental concept of boundary representation, describing an n-cell by its $(n-1)$-dimensional faces, to incrementally construct cell complexes of any dimension. To the best of our knowledge, this technique is the only one that has been described and/or implemented for 4D cell complexes or higher. Using a variety of indices is efficient, generating an n-cell in $O(d^2)$ in the worst case, with d the total number of darts in the cell, and our algorithm should fare markedly better in realistic datasets.

We intend to use this approach, supplemented with techniques under development that generate the required $(n-1)$-dimensional faces, to generate objects for higher dimensional geographic information systems, as well as other applications. This will allow us to take real-world 3D city models and incorporate additional dimensions to them, such as time and scale, to create 4D/5D objects to which higher dimensional analyses can be performed.

Acknowledgments. This research is supported by the Dutch Technology Foundation STW, which is part of the Netherlands Organisation for Scientific Research (NWO), and which is partly funded by the Ministry of Economic Affairs (Project code: 11300).

References

[1] Peuquet, D.J.: Representations of Space and Time. Guilford Press (2002)
[2] van Oosterom, P., Meijers, M.: Towards a true vario-scale structure supporting smooth-zoom. In: Proceedings of the 14th ICA/ISPRS Workshop on Generalisation and Multiple Representation, Paris (2011)

[3] Baglatzi, A., Kuhn, W.: On the formulation of conceptual spaces for land cover classification systems. In: Vandenbroucke, D., Bucher, B., Crompvoets, J. (eds.) Geographic Information Science at the Heart of Europe. Lecture Notes in Geoinformation and Cartography, pp. 173–188. Springer (2013)

[4] Raper, J.: Multidimensional geographic information science. Taylor & Francis (2000)

[5] Stoter, J., Ledoux, H., Meijers, M., Arroyo Ohori, K., van Oosterom, P.: 5D modeling - applications and advantages. In: Proceedings of the Geospatial World Forum 2012, p. 9 (2012)

[6] Mäntylä, M.: An introduction to solid modeling. Computer Science Press, New York (1988)

[7] Baumgart, B.G.: A polyhedron representation for computer vision. In: Proceedings of the National Computer Conference and Exposition, May 19-22, pp. 589–596 (1975)

[8] Braid, I.: The synthesis of solids bounded by many faces. Communications of the ACM 18(4), 209–216 (1975)

[9] Hatcher, A.: Algebraic Topology. Cambridge University Press (2002)

[10] Egenhofer, M.J., Franzosa, R.D.: Point-set topological spatial relations. International Journal of Geographical Information Systems 5(2), 161–174 (1991)

[11] OGC: OpenGIS Implementation Specification for Geographic Information - Simple Feature Access - Part 1: Common Architecture. Open Geospatial Consortium, 1.2.1 edn. (May 2011)

[12] Open Geospatial Consortium: OGC City Geography Markup Language (CityGML) Encoding Standard, 2.0.0 edn. (April 2012)

[13] Edmonds, J.: A combinatorial representation of polyhedral surfaces. Notices of the American Mathematical Society 7 (1960)

[14] Lienhardt, P.: N-dimensional generalized combinatorial maps and cellular quasi-manifolds. International Journal of Computational Geometry and Applications 4(3), 275–324 (1994)

[15] Poudret, M., Arnould, A., Bertrand, Y., Lienhardt, P.: Cartes combinatoires ouvertes. Technical Report 2007-01, Laboratoire SIC, UFR SFA, Université de Poitiers (October 2007)

[16] Gosselin, S., Damiand, G., Solnon, C.: Efficient search of combinatorial maps using signatures. Theoretical Computer Science 412(15), 1392–1405 (2011)

A Digital-Geometric Algorithm for Generating a Complete Spherical Surface in $\mathbb{Z}^3$

Sahadev Bera[1], Partha Bhowmick[2], and Bhargab B. Bhattacharya[1]

[1] Advanced Computing and Microelectronics Unit,
Indian Statistical Institute, Kolkata, India
[2] Department of Computer Science and Engineering,
Indian Institute of Technology, Kharagpur, India
{sahadevbera,bhowmick}@gmail.com, bhargab@isical.ac.in

Abstract. We show that the construction of a digital sphere by circularly sweeping a digital semicircle (generatrix) around its diameter results in appearance of some holes (absentee voxels) in its spherical surface of revolution. This incompleteness calls for a proper characterization of the absentee voxels whose restoration in the surface of revolution can ensure the required completeness. In this paper, we present a characterization of the absentee voxels using certain techniques of digital geometry and show that their count varies quadratically with the radius of the semicircular generatrix. Next, we design an algorithm to fill up the absentee voxels so as to generate a spherical surface of revolution, which is complete and realistic from the viewpoint of visual perception. Test results have also been furnished to substantiate our theoretical findings. The proposed technique will find many potential applications in computer graphics and 3D imaging.

Keywords: Digital circle, Digital sphere, Digital geometry, Geometry of numbers, Number theory.

1 Introduction

Over the last two decades, works related with geometric primitives in 2D and 3D digital space have gained much momentum due to their numerous applications in computer graphics, image processing, and computer vision. Apart from straight lines and planes [1–4], several theoretical works have come up in recent time, which are mostly on the characterization of digital spheres and hyperspheres. A majority of these works in 3D digital space are extended manifestations of similar works on characterization and generation of circles, rings, discs, and circular arcs in the digital plane [5–12]. The reason of reconceptualization of these geometric primitives in the digital space is that their properties in the Euclidean/real space are often inadequate and inappropriate to efficiently solve the related problems in the digital space. Hence, with the emergence of new paradigms, such as digital calculus [13], digital geometry [14], theory of words and numbers [15, 16], etc., proper characterization is required to enrich our understanding and hence enhance these paradigms as well.

P. Gupta and C. Zaroliagis (Eds.): ICAA 2014, LNCS 8321, pp. 49–61, 2014.

Our problem is on finding a *closed digital surface* defined by a set of points in $\mathbb{Z}^3$ such that they optimally approximate a real sphere with integer radius. Some of the existing works closely resemble our work, but they deal with spheres having real radius. For example, several works exist in the literature for finding lattice points on or inside a real sphere of a given radius [17–24], and also on finding a real sphere that passes through a given set of lattice points [25]. These works are closely related to finding lattice points on circles [26, 27], ellipsoids [28, 29], and surfaces of revolution [30]. For hypersphere generation, characterization of a discrete analytical hypersphere has been done in [31] to develop an algorithm, which is an extension of the algorithm for generating discrete analytical circles. The algorithm is, however, quite expensive owing to complex operations in the real space. An extension of the idea used in [31] has been done in [32] based on a non-constant thickness function [33], but no algorithm for generation of a digital sphere or hypersphere has been proposed. To the best of our knowledge, the only algorithm for digitization of a real sphere with integer radius has been proposed in [34]. It constructs the sphere as a sequence of contiguous digital circles by using Bresenham's circle drawing algorithm. Such an approach fails to ensure the completeness of the generated digital sphere, since it gives rise to absentee (missing) voxels, as shown in this paper. The digital sphere generated by our algorithm, on the contrary, does not have any absentee voxel, since it fixes these absentees based on a digital-geometric characterization.

The work proposed in this paper is focused on finding and fixing the absentee voxels (3D points with integer coordinates) in the digital spherical surface of revolution. Covering such a spherical surface of revolution by coaxial digital circles (with integer radius and integer center) in $\mathbb{Z}^3$ cannot produce the desired completeness of the surface owing to absentee voxels. Interestingly, the occurrence of absentees in such a cover is possibly a lesser fact. The greater fact is that the absentees occur in multitude—an observation that motivates the requirement of their proper characterization, which subsequently aids in designing a proven algorithm to generate a complete spherical surface in $\mathbb{Z}^3$.

We have organized the paper as follows. In Sec. 2, we introduce few definitions and important properties related with digital circles, digital discs, and digital spheres considered in our work. In Sec. 3, we derive the necessary and sufficient condition for a voxel to be an absentee in a sphere of revolution. In Sec. 3.1, we use this condition to prove that the absentee count while covering a digital sphere of radius r by coaxial digital circles—generated by the circular sweep of a digitally circular arc of radius r (digital generatrix)—varies quadratically with r. In Sec. 3.2, we explain the algorithm to locate and fix these absentee voxels. In Sec. 4, we present some test results that substantiate our theoretical findings, and draw our concluding notes.

2   Preliminaries

There exist several definitions of digital circles (and discs, spheres, etc.) in the literature, depending on whether the radius and the center coordinates are real

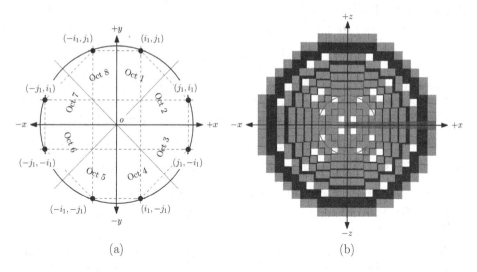

Fig. 1. (a) 8-symmetric points $\{(i,j) : \{|i|\} \cup \{|j|\} = \{i_1, j_1\}\}$ in eight respective octants of a digital circle $\mathcal{C}^{\mathbb{Z}}(r)$. (b) $\mathcal{H}_{\cup}^{\mathbb{Z}}(r)$ for $r = 10$, with the $+y$ axis pointing inwards w.r.t. the plane of the paper.

or integer values. Irrespective of these definitions, a digital circle (sphere) is essentially a set of points with integer coordinates, which are called *digital points* or *pixels* (*voxels*) [14]. In this paper, we consider the *grid intersection digitization* [14, 35] of a real circle with integer radius and having center with integer coordinates. Such a digitization produces a digital circle, which can be generated by the well-known *midpoint circle algorithm* or the *Bresenham circle algorithm* [36], and its definition is as follows.

Definition 1 (Digital circle). *A digital circle with radius $r \in \mathbb{Z}^+$ and center $o(0,0)$ is given by* $\mathcal{C}^{\mathbb{Z}}(r) = \left\{ (i,j) \in \mathbb{Z}^2 : \left| \max(|i|,|j|) - \sqrt{r^2 - (\min(|i|,|j|))^2} \right| < \frac{1}{2} \right\}$.

The points in $\mathcal{C}^{\mathbb{Z}}(r)$ are connected in 8-neighborhood. The points defining its *interior* are connected in 4-neighborhood, and hence separated by $\mathcal{C}^{\mathbb{Z}}(r)$ from its *exterior* points, which are also connected in 4-neighborhood [14].

All the results in this paper are valid for any non-negative integer radius and any center with integer coordinates. So, for sake of simplicity, henceforth we consider the center as o and use the notation $\mathcal{C}^{\mathbb{Z}}(r)$ instead of $\mathcal{C}^{\mathbb{Z}}(o,r)$, where $r \in \mathbb{Z}^+ \cup \{0\}$. We specify it explicitly when the center is not o.

A real point or a pixel (x,y) is said to be lying in Octant 1 if and only if $0 \leqslant x \leqslant y$ (Figure 1(a)). We use the notation $\mathcal{C}_1^{\mathbb{Z}}(r)$ to denote Octant 1 of $\mathcal{C}^{\mathbb{Z}}(r)$, and $\mathbb{Z}_1^2$ to denote all points in Octant 1 of $\mathbb{Z}^2$.

Definition 2 (Digital disc). *A digital disc of radius r consists of all digital points in $\mathcal{C}^{\mathbb{Z}}(r)$ and its interior, and is given by $\mathcal{D}^{\mathbb{Z}}(r) = \{(i, j_c) \in \mathbb{Z}^2 : 0 \leq i \cdot i_c \leq i_c^2 \wedge \left| \max(|i_c|, |j_c|) - \sqrt{r^2 - (\min(|i_c|, |j_c|))^2} \right| < \frac{1}{2} \}.$*

Note that in Def. 2, the condition $0 \leq i \cdot i_c \leq i_c^2$ relates a disc pixel (i, j_c) to a circle pixel (i_c, j_c), as $0 \leq i_c$ implies $0 \leq i \leq i_c$ and $i_c \leq 0$ implies $i_c \leq i \leq 0$. If we consider the union of all digital circles centered at o and radius in $\{0, 1, 2, \ldots, r\}$, then the resultant set $\mathcal{D}_{\cup}^{\mathbb{Z}}(r) := \bigcup_{s=1}^{r} \mathcal{C}^{\mathbb{Z}}(s)$ is not identical with the digital disc of radius r. The set $\mathcal{D}_{\cup}^{\mathbb{Z}}(r)$ contains absentee pixels, as defined below.

Definition 3 (Disc absentee). *A pixel p is a disc absentee if and only if there exists some $r' \in \{1, 2, \ldots, r\}$ such that p is a point in the interior of $\mathcal{C}^{\mathbb{Z}}(r')$ and in the exterior of $\mathcal{C}^{\mathbb{Z}}(r' - 1)$.*

The above definition implies that if p is any disc absentee, then p does not belong to any digital circle, i.e., $p \in \mathcal{D}^{\mathbb{Z}}(r)$ and $p \notin \mathcal{D}_{\cup}^{\mathbb{Z}}(r)$. Hence, the set of disc absentees is given by $\mathcal{A}^{\mathbb{Z}^2}(r) = \mathcal{D}^{\mathbb{Z}}(r) \setminus \mathcal{D}_{\cup}^{\mathbb{Z}}(r)$. The above definition of disc absentee is used in the following definitions related to *spherical surfaces of revolution* in $\mathbb{Z}^3$. However, henceforth we do not use the term "*of revolution*" for sake of simplicity. We also drop the term "*digital*" from any digital surface in $\mathbb{Z}^3$.

Let $\mathcal{C}_{1,2}^{\mathbb{Z}}(r)$ denote the first quadrant (comprising the first and the second octants) of $\mathcal{C}^{\mathbb{Z}}(r)$, which is used as the *generatrix*. When we rotate $\mathcal{C}_{1,2}^{\mathbb{Z}}(r)$ about y-axis through $360°$, we get a stack (sequence) of circles representing a *hemisphere*, namely $\mathcal{H}_{\cup}^{\mathbb{Z}}(r) := \bigcup_{(i,j) \in \mathcal{C}_{1,2}^{\mathbb{Z}}(r)} \mathcal{C}^{\mathbb{Z}}(c, i)$, where $c = (0, j, 0)$ denotes the center of $\mathcal{C}^{\mathbb{Z}}(c, i)$, as shown in Figure 1(b). Each circle $\mathcal{C}^{\mathbb{Z}}(c, i)$ in this stack is generated by rotating a pixel $(i, j) \in \mathcal{C}_{1,2}^{\mathbb{Z}}(r)$ about y-axis. The previous circle in the stack is either $\mathcal{C}^{\mathbb{Z}}(c', i - 1)$ or $\mathcal{C}^{\mathbb{Z}}(c'', i)$, where $c' = (0, j', 0)$ with $j' \in \{j, j + 1\}$, and $c'' = (0, j + 1, 0)$. There is no absentee between $\mathcal{C}^{\mathbb{Z}}(c, i)$ and $\mathcal{C}^{\mathbb{Z}}(c'', i)$, as they have the same radius. But as the radii of $\mathcal{C}^{\mathbb{Z}}(c, i)$ and $\mathcal{C}^{\mathbb{Z}}(c', i - 1)$ differ by unity, there would be absentees (Definition 4) between them in $\mathcal{H}_{\cup}^{\mathbb{Z}}(r)$. Each such absentee p would lie on the plane of $\mathcal{C}^{\mathbb{Z}}(c, i)$ in the exterior of $\mathcal{C}^{\mathbb{Z}}(c, i - 1)$, since p did not appear in the part of $\mathcal{H}_{\cup}^{\mathbb{Z}}(r)$ constructed up to $\mathcal{C}^{\mathbb{Z}}(c', i - 1)$ and appeared only after constructing $\mathcal{C}^{\mathbb{Z}}(c, i)$. Hence, we have the following definition.

Definition 4 (Sphere absentee). *A voxel p is a sphere absentee lying on the plane $y = j$ if and only if there exist two consecutive points (i, j) and $(i - 1, j')$ in $\mathcal{C}_{1,2}^{\mathbb{Z}}(r)$, $j' \in \{j, j + 1\}$, such that p lies in the interior of $\mathcal{C}^{\mathbb{Z}}(c, i)$ and in the exterior of $\mathcal{C}^{\mathbb{Z}}(c, i - 1)$, where $c = (0, j, 0)$.*

On inclusion of the sphere absentees (lying above zx-plane) with $\mathcal{H}_{\cup}^{\mathbb{Z}}(r)$, we get the *complete hemisphere*, namely $\mathcal{H}^{\mathbb{Z}}(r)$. On taking $\mathcal{H}_{\cup}^{\mathbb{Z}}(r)$ and its reflection on zx-plane, we get the *sphere*, namely $\mathcal{S}_{\cup}^{\mathbb{Z}}(r)$. Similarly, the union of $\mathcal{H}^{\mathbb{Z}}(r)$ and its reflection on zx-plane gives the *complete sphere* in $\mathbb{Z}^3$. Let $\mathcal{A}^{\mathbb{Z}^3}(r)$ be the set of sphere absentees. The number of points in $\mathcal{A}^{\mathbb{Z}^3}(r)$ is double the absentee count in $\mathcal{H}^{\mathbb{Z}}_{\cup}(r)$. We have the following definitions on spheres and their absentees.

Definition 5 (Complete sphere). *A complete (hollow) sphere of radius r is given by* $\mathcal{S}^{\mathbb{Z}}(r) = \mathcal{S}^{\mathbb{Z}}_{\cup}(r) \cup \mathcal{A}^{\mathbb{Z}^3}(r)$.

2.1   Previous Results

We need the following results from [37] to count and fix the absentees in the surface of revolution.

Theorem 1. *The total count of disc absentees lying in $\mathcal{D}^{\mathbb{Z}}_{\cup}(r)$ is given by*

$$|\mathcal{A}^{\mathbb{Z}^2}(r)| = 8 \sum_{k=0}^{m_r - 1} |\mathcal{A}^{\mathbb{Z}^2}_k(r)|,$$

where $|\mathcal{A}^{\mathbb{Z}^2}_k(r)| = \left\lceil \sqrt{(2k+1)r - k(k+1)} \right\rceil - \left\lceil 2k + 1 + \frac{1}{2}\sqrt{(8k^2 + 4k + 1)} \right\rceil$
and $m_r = r - \lceil r/\sqrt{2} \rceil + 1$.

Theorem 2. $|\mathcal{A}^{\mathbb{Z}^2}(r)| = \Theta(r^2)$.

3   Absentee Voxels in Digital Sphere of Revolution

As mentioned earlier in Sec. 2, the digital hemisphere and the digital sphere of revolution have absentee voxels, which can be characterized based on their unique correspondence with the absentee pixels of $\mathcal{D}^{\mathbb{Z}}_{\cup}(r)$. To establish this correspondence, we consider two consecutive pixels $p_i(x_i, y_i)$ and $p_{i+1}(x_{i+1}, y_{i+1})$ of the generating curve $\mathcal{C}^{\mathbb{Z}}_{1,2}(r)$ corresponding to $\mathcal{H}^{\mathbb{Z}}_{\cup}(r)$. We have three possible cases as follows.

1. $(x_{i+1}, y_{i+1}) = (x_i + 1, y_i)$ (Octant 1)
2. $(x_{i+1}, y_{i+1}) = (x_i + 1, y_i - 1)$ (Octant 1 or Octant 2)
3. $(x_{i+1}, y_{i+1}) = (x_i, y_i - 1)$ (Octant 2)

For Case 1, we get two concentric circles of radii differing by unity and lying on the same plane; the radii of the circles corresponding to p_i and p_{i+1} are x_i and $(x_{i+1} =)x_i + 1$. Hence, for Case 1, the absentee voxels between two consecutive circles easily correspond to the absentee pixels between $\mathcal{C}^{\mathbb{Z}}(o, x_i)$ and $\mathcal{C}^{\mathbb{Z}}(o, x_i+1)$.

For Case 2, the circle generated by p_{i+1} has radius $x_{i+1} = x_i + 1$ and its plane lies one voxel apart w.r.t. the plane of the circle generated by p_i. Hence, if these two are circles are projected on zx-plane, then the absentee pixels lying between the projected circles have a correspondence with the absentee voxels between the original circles.

For Case 3, we do not have an absentee, as the circles generated by p_i and p_{i+1} have the same radius ($x_i = x_{i+1}$).

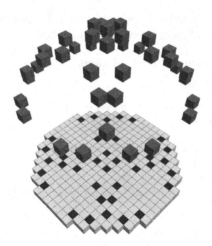

Fig. 2. One-to-one correspondence for $r = 10$ between absentee voxels (shown in red) in $\mathcal{H}_\cup^{\mathbb{Z}}(r)$ and absentee pixels (shown in blue) in $\mathcal{D}_\cup^{\mathbb{Z}}(r)$

Hence, the count of absentee voxels in $\mathcal{H}_\cup^{\mathbb{Z}}(r)$ is same as the count of absentee pixels in $\mathcal{D}_\cup^{\mathbb{Z}}(r)$. However, it may be noted that the count of voxels present in $\mathcal{H}_\cup^{\mathbb{Z}}(r)$ would be greater than the count of pixels present in $\mathcal{D}_\cup^{\mathbb{Z}}(r)$, since for each digital circle of a particular radius $s \in \{0, 1, 2, \ldots, r\}$ in $\mathcal{D}_\cup^{\mathbb{Z}}(r)$, there would be one or more digital circles of radius s (in succession) in $\mathcal{H}_\cup^{\mathbb{Z}}(r)$. We have the lemma on the correspondence of absentee count in $\mathcal{H}_\cup^{\mathbb{Z}}(r)$ with that in $\mathcal{D}_\cup^{\mathbb{Z}}(r)$.

Lemma 1. *If $p(i, j, k)$ is an absentee voxel in $\mathcal{H}_\cup^{\mathbb{Z}}(r)$, then the pixel (i, k) obtained by projecting p on xz-plane is an absentee pixel in $\mathcal{D}_\cup^{\mathbb{Z}}(r)$.*

The above one-to-one correspondence between the absentees in the hemispherical surface of revolution for radius $r = 10$ and the absentees related to the digital disc of radius $r = 10$ is shown in Figure 2. This one-to-one correspondence between the absentee set in $\mathcal{H}_\cup^{\mathbb{Z}}(r)$ and that in $\mathcal{D}_\cup^{\mathbb{Z}}(r)$ leads to the following theorem.

Theorem 3. *The total count of absentee voxels in $\mathcal{H}_\cup^{\mathbb{Z}}(r)$ is $|\mathcal{A}^{\mathbb{Z}^2}(r)| = \Theta(r^2)$.*

Proof. Follows from Lemma 1 and Theorem 2.

On taking the reflection of $\mathcal{H}^{\mathbb{Z}}(r)$ about the zx-plane, we get the complementary digital hemisphere of revolution, namely $\mathcal{H}'^{\mathbb{Z}}(r)$. The set $\mathcal{H}^{\mathbb{Z}}(r) \cup \mathcal{H}'^{\mathbb{Z}}(r)$ is the digital sphere of revolution, $\mathcal{S}^{\mathbb{Z}}(r)$, corresponding to which we get double the count of absentee voxels compared to that in $\mathcal{H}^{\mathbb{Z}}(r)$. Hence, we have the following theorem.

Theorem 4. *The total count of absentee voxels lying on $\mathcal{S}^{\mathbb{Z}}(r)$ is given by*

$$|\mathcal{A}^{\mathbb{Z}^3}(r)| = 2|\mathcal{A}^{\mathbb{Z}^2}(r)| = 16 \sum_{k=0}^{m_r-1} |\mathcal{A}_k^{\mathbb{Z}^2}(r)| = \Theta(r^2).$$

Proof. Follows from Theorem 1 and Theorem 3.

3.1   Necessity and Sufficiency for an Absentee Voxel

We use the following lemmas from [37, 38] for deriving the necessary and sufficient conditions to decide whether a given voxel is an absentee or not.

Lemma 2. *The squares of abscissae of the pixels with ordinate j in $\mathcal{C}_1^{\mathbb{Z}}(r)$ lie in the interval $I_{r-j}^{(r)} := \left[u_{r-j}^{(r)}, v_{r-j}^{(r)}\right)$, where $u_{r-j}^{(r)} = r^2 - j^2 - j$ and $v_{r-j}^{(r)} = r^2 - j^2 + j$.*

Lemma 3. *A pixel (i, j) is an absentee if and only if i^2 lies in the integer interval $J_{r-j}^{(r)} := \left[v_{r-j}^{(r)}, u_{r+1-j}^{(r+1)}\right)$ for some $r \in \mathbb{Z}^+$.*

We have now the following theorem on the necessity and sufficiency for an absentee voxel in $\mathcal{D}_{\cup}^{\mathbb{Z}}(r)$.

Theorem 5. *A voxel $p(i, j, k)$ is an absentee if and only if $i^2 \in J_{r'-k}^{(r')}$ for some $r' \in \mathbb{Z}^+$ and $r'^2 \in I_{r-j}^{(r)}$.*

Proof. Lemma 1 implies that when $p(i, j, k)$ is an absentee voxel in $\mathcal{H}_{\cup}^{\mathbb{Z}}(r)$, then its projection pixel $p'(i, k)$ on zx-plane is absentee pixel in $\mathcal{D}_{\cup}^{\mathbb{Z}}(r)$. Hence, by Lemma 3, i^2 lies in $J_{r'-k}^{(r')}$ for some $r' \in \mathbb{Z}^+$. What now remains to check is the condition for y-coordinate of p. Observe that there exists a digital circle $\mathcal{C}^{\mathbb{Z}}(c, r')$ centered at $c = (0, j, 0)$ on the hemisphere of revolution such that the the projection of $\mathcal{C}^{\mathbb{Z}}(c, r')$ on zx-plane is the digital circle of radius r' in $\mathcal{D}_{\cup}^{\mathbb{Z}}(r)$. Again $p(i, j, k)$ and $\mathcal{C}^{\mathbb{Z}}(c, r')$ lie on the same plane, i.e., $y = j$. Hence, the pixel (r', j) must lie on the generating circular arc, $\mathcal{C}_{1,2}^{\mathbb{Z}}(r)$, and so by Lemma 2, we have $r'^2 \in I_{r-j}^{(r)}$.

Conversely, if $i^2 \in J_{r'-k}^{(r')}$, then $p \notin \mathcal{H}_{\cup}^{\mathbb{Z}}(r)$; and if $r'^2 \in I_{r-j}^{(r)}$ for some $r' \in \{0, 1, 2, \ldots, r\}$, then $p \in \mathcal{H}^{\mathbb{Z}}(r)$, wherefore p is an absentee.

An example of absentee voxel is $(2, 50, 4)$ in hemisphere of revolution of radius $r = 50$ (Figure 3), since for $k = 4$, we have $r' = 4$ for which $v_{r'-k}^{(r')} = r'^2 - k^2 + k = 16 - 16 + 4 = 4$, $u_{r'+1-k}^{(r'+1)} = (r' + 1)^2 - k^2 - k = 25 - 16 - 4 = 5$, thus giving $J_0^{(4)} = [4, 5) = [4, 4]$ in which lies the square number $4 = i^2$ and $u_{r-j}^{(r)} = r^2 - j^2 - j = 50^2 - 50^2 - 50 = -50$, $v_{r-j}^{(r)} = r^2 - j^2 + j = 50^2 - 50^2 + 50 = 50$, thus giving $I_0^{(50)} = [-50, 50)$ which contains $16 = r'^2$.

On the contrary, $(3, 50, 4)$ is not an absentee voxel, as for $k = 4$, there is no such r' for which $J_{r'-4}^{(r')}$ contains 3^2; in fact, for $k = 4$, we get the interval $I_{5-4}^{(5)} = [5^2 - 4^2 - 4, 5^2 - 4^4 + 4) = [5, 12]$ with $r' = 5$, which contains 3^2, thereby making $(3, 50, 4)$ a point on hemisphere of revolution of radius $r = 50$ at the plane $y = 50$.

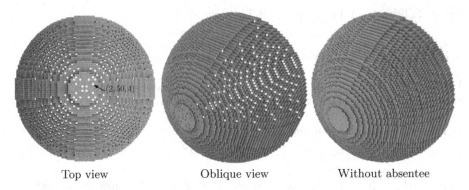

| Top view | Oblique view | Without absentee |

Fig. 3. Left, middle: Incomplete digital hemisphere with absentee voxels for $r = 50$.
Right: Complete hemisphere without any absentee generated by Algorithm 1.

3.2   Algorithm for Fixing the Absentee Voxels

Algorithm 1 (AVH) shows the steps for fixing the absentee voxels corresponding
to the hemisphere $\mathcal{H}_\cup^{\mathbb{Z}}(r)$ having radius r. The generating curve, which is an input
to this algorithm, is the circular arc, $\mathcal{C}_{1,2}^{\mathbb{Z}}(r)$. This circular arc is a (ordered)
sequence of points, $\{p_t(i_t, j_t, 0) \in \mathbb{Z}^3 : t = 1, 2, \ldots, n_r\}$, whose first point is
$p_1(0, r, 0)$ and last point is $p_{n_r}(r, 0, 0)$. The point p_{t+1} can have i_{t+1} either same
as i_t of the previous point p_t or greater than i_t by unity. For the former case,
there is no absentee between the two circles generated by p_t and p_{t+1}. For the
latter, the absentees are computed by invoking the procedure ACC, as shown in
Step 4 of Algorithm 1.

The procedure ACC finds the absentee voxels between two concentric circles,
$\mathcal{C}_{y=j}^{\mathbb{Z}}(c, i)$ and $\mathcal{C}_{y=j}^{\mathbb{Z}}(c, i+1)$ of radii i and $i+1$, each centered at $(0, j, 0)$ on $y = j$
plane. The set of all absentees between these two circles is denoted by A. As an
absentee lies just after the end of a *voxel-run* corresponding to the interval $I_{r-j}^{(r)}$
(Lemma 2), the procedure ACC first computes the voxel-run in the plane $y = j$
(Steps 5–8). Then, in Step 9, it determines whether the next voxel is an absentee
in Octant 1, using Lemma 3. For each absentee voxel in Octant 1, the absentees
in all other octants are included in A, as shown in Step 10. Figure 2(a) shows
the hemisphere for $r = 10$, whose absentees (shown in red) have been fixed by
Algorithm 1.

4   Test Results and Conclusion

We have implemented Algorithm 1 to compute the count of absentee voxels and
circle voxels for increasing radii. Table 1 shows these counts for r varying from
0 to 10,000. As derived analytically, we observe that as the radius increases, all
the three values increase with a quadratic dependency on r, which is reflected in

---

Algorithm 1. (AVH) Fixing absentee voxels in the hemisphere

Input: Generating circular arc, $\mathcal{C}_{1,2}^{\mathbb{Z}}(r) := \{p_1, p_2, \ldots, p_{n_r}\}$
Output: Absentee voxels in $\mathcal{H}_{\cup}^{\mathbb{Z}}(r)$

1 $\mathcal{A}^{\mathbb{Z}^3}(r) \leftarrow \emptyset$
2 **for** $t = 1, 2, \ldots, n_r - 1$ **do**
3   **if** $i_{t+1} > i_t$ **then**
4         $\mathcal{A}^{\mathbb{Z}^3}(r) \leftarrow \mathcal{A}^{\mathbb{Z}^3}(r) \cup \text{ACC}(\mathcal{C}_{1,2}^{\mathbb{Z}}(r), t)$

5 **return** $\mathcal{A}^{\mathbb{Z}^3}(r)$

Procedure $\text{ACC}(\mathcal{C}_{1,2}^{\mathbb{Z}}(r), t)$

---

1 $A \leftarrow \emptyset, r \leftarrow i_t$
2 **int** $i \leftarrow 0, k \leftarrow r, s \leftarrow 0, w \leftarrow r - 1$
3 **int** $l \leftarrow 2w$
4 **while** $k \geq i$ **do**
5   **repeat**
6        $s \leftarrow s + 2i + 1$
7        $i \leftarrow i + 1$
8   **until** $s \leq w$
9   **if** $i^2 \in J_{r-k}^{(r)}$ and $k \geq i$ **then**
10       $A \leftarrow A \cup \{(i', j_t, k') : \{|i'|\} \cup \{|k'|\} = \{i, k\}\}$
11    $w \leftarrow w + l, l \leftarrow l - 2, k \leftarrow k - 1$

12 **return** A

---

their corresponding plots shown in Figure 4. Figure 5 shows the relative count of absentee voxels w.r.t. the total number of voxels. Notice that, as the radius increases, the approximate value of this relative count tends to a constant (0.058). In Figure 3, we have shown an instance of the hemispherical surface generated by Algorithm 1 for radius 50.

The above test results and their theoretical analysis indicate that the ratio of the absentee voxels to the total number of voxels tends to a constant for large radius. Knowledge of geometric distributions of absentee voxels is shown to be useful for algorithmic generation of a digital sphere of revolution. An asymptotic tight bound for the count of absentees is given, but finding a closed-form solution on the exact count of absentees for a given radius still remains an open problem. Characterization of these absentees requires further in-depth analysis, especially if we want to generate a solid digital sphere with concentric digital spheres. Apart from spheres, generation of various other types of surfaces of revolution, which should be free of any absentee voxels, has also many applications in 3D imaging and graphics, such as creation of interesting pottery designs, as shown recently in [39].

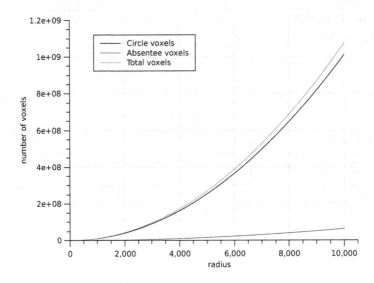

Fig. 4. Number of circle voxels, absentee voxels, and total voxels versus radius in the digital sphere of revolution

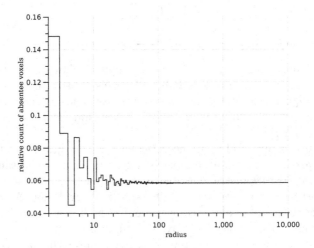

Fig. 5. Relative percentage of absentees vs.radius in digital sphere of revolution

Table 1. Number of absentee voxels in the sphere of revolution for radius from 0 to 10,000

r	$\lvert \mathcal{S}_\cup^Z(r) \rvert$	$2\lvert \mathcal{A}^{Z^3}(r) \rvert$	$\lvert \mathcal{S}^Z(r) \rvert$	r	$\lvert \mathcal{S}_\cup^Z(r) \rvert$	$2\lvert \mathcal{A}^{Z^3}(r) \rvert$	$\lvert \mathcal{S}^Z(r) \rvert$
0	1	0	1	1200	14543190	902056	15445246
1	6	0	6	1300	17063386	1058408	18121794
2	46	8	54	1400	19796562	1227664	21024226
3	82	8	90	1500	22720358	1409144	24129502
4	170	8	178	1600	25858590	1603424	27462014
5	254	24	278	1700	29186106	1810216	30996322
6	330	24	354	1800	32729258	2029288	34758546
7	498	40	538	1900	36460174	2261192	38721366
8	614	40	654	2000	40391978	2505328	42897306
9	830	48	878	2100	44542482	2762328	47304810
10	1002	80	1082	2200	48877878	3031440	51909318
20	3978	256	4234	2300	53433334	3313344	56746678
30	8962	560	9522	2400	58172210	3607600	61779810
40	16310	1016	17326	2500	63132842	3914608	67047450
50	25374	1592	26966	2600	68275238	4234008	72509246
60	36438	2296	38734	3000	90906366	5637120	96543486
70	49510	3080	52590	3500	123729002	7672616	131401618
80	64526	3992	68518	4000	161600518	10021480	171621998
90	81582	5080	86662	4500	204521258	12683288	217204546
100	100622	6248	106870	5000	252490950	15658504	268149454
200	404262	25104	429366	5500	305509450	18946648	324456098
300	908250	56320	964570	6000	363576838	22548008	386124846
400	1617026	100304	1717330	6500	426693594	26462560	453156154
500	2524486	156608	2681094	7000	494859006	30690136	525549142
600	3638230	225456	3863686	7500	568134414	35231256	603365670
700	4949282	307064	5256346	8000	646401914	40085200	686487114
800	6461350	400768	6862118	8500	729718814	45252704	774971518
900	8182310	507392	8689702	9000	818084450	50732656	868817106
1000	10097978	626304	10724282	9500	911499582	56526944	968026526
1100	12223938	757888	12981826	10000	1009962778	62620784	1072583562

References

1. Brimkov, V.E., Barneva, R.P., Brimkov, B., de Vieilleville, F.: Offset approach to defining 3D digital lines. In: Bebis, G., et al. (eds.) ISVC 2008, Part I. LNCS, vol. 5358, pp. 678–687. Springer, Heidelberg (2008)
2. Feschet, F., Reveillès, J.-P.: A Generic Approach for n-Dimensional Digital Lines. In: Kuba, A., Nyúl, L.G., Palágyi, K. (eds.) DGCI 2006. LNCS, vol. 4245, pp. 29–40. Springer, Heidelberg (2006)
3. Kenmochi, Y., Buzer, L., Sugimoto, A., Shimizu, I.: Digital planar surface segmentation using local geometric patterns. In: Coeurjolly, D., Sivignon, I., Tougne, L., Dupont, F. (eds.) DGCI 2008. LNCS, vol. 4992, pp. 322–333. Springer, Heidelberg (2008)

4. Woo, D.M., Han, S.S., Park, D.C., Nguyen, Q.D.: Extraction of 3D Line Segment Using Digital Elevation Data. In: Proceedings of the 2008 Congress on Image and Signal Processing, CISP 2008, vol. 2, pp. 734–738. IEEE Computer Society, Washington, DC (2008)

5. Chan, Y.T., Thomas, S.M.: Cramer-Rao lower bounds for estimation of a circular arc center and its radius. Graphical Models and Image Processing 57, 527–532 (1995)

6. Davies, E.R.: A hybrid sequential-parallel approach to accurate circle centre location. Pattern Recognition Letters 7, 279–290 (1988)

7. Doros, M.: On some properties of the generation of discrete circular arcs on a square grid. Computer Vision, Graphics, and Image Processing 28, 377–383 (1984)

8. Haralick, R.M.: A measure for circularity of digital figures. IEEE Trans. Sys., Man & Cybern. 4, 394–396 (1974)

9. Nagy, B.: Characterization of digital circles in triangular grid. Pattern Recognition Letters 25, 1231–1242 (2004)

10. Pal, S., Bhowmick, P.: Determining digital circularity using integer intervals. Journal of Mathematical Imaging and Vision 42, 1–24 (2012)

11. Thomas, S.M., Chan, Y.T.: A simple approach for the estimation of circular arc center and its radius. Computer Vision, Graphics, and Image Processing 45, 362–370 (1989)

12. Yuen, P.C., Feng, G.C.: A novel method for parameter estimation of digital arc. Pattern Recognition Letters 17, 929–938 (1996)

13. Nakamura, A., Aizawa, K.: Digital circles. Computer Vision, Graphics, and Image Processing 26, 242–255 (1984)

14. Klette, R., Rosenfeld, A.: Digital Geometry: Geometric Methods for Digital Picture Analysis. Morgan Kaufmann Series in Computer Graphics and Geometric Modeling. Morgan Kaufmann, San Francisco (2004)

15. Klette, R., Rosenfeld, A.: Digital straightness: A review. Discrete Applied Mathematics 139, 197–230 (2004)

16. Mignosi, F.: On the number of factors of Sturmian words. Theoretical Computer Science 82, 71–84 (1991)

17. Brimkov, V.E., Barneva, R.P.: On the polyhedral complexity of the integer points in a hyperball. Theoretical Computer Science 406, 24–30 (2008)

18. Heath-Brown, D.R.: Lattice points in the sphere. Number theory in progress, vol. II, pp. 883–892. Walter de Gruyter, Berlin (1999)

19. Chamizo, F., Cristóbal, E., Ubis, A.: Visible lattice points in the sphere. Journal of Number Theory 126, 200–211 (2007)

20. Chamizo, F., Cristobal, E.: The sphere problem and the L-functions. Acta Mathematica Hungarica 135, 97–115 (2012)

21. Fomenko, O.: Distribution of lattice points over the four-dimensional sphere. Journal of Mathematical Sciences 110, 3164–3170 (2002)

22. Magyar, A.: On the distribution of lattice points on spheres and level surfaces of polynomials. Journal of Number Theory 122, 69–83 (2007)

23. Ewell, J.A.: Counting lattice points on spheres. The Mathematical Intelligencer 22, 51–53 (2000)

24. Tsang, K.M.: Counting lattice points in the sphere. Bulletin of the London Mathematical Society 32, 679–688 (2000)

25. Maehara, H.: On a sphere that passes through n lattice points. European Journal of Combinatorics 31, 617–621 (2010)

26. Cappell, S.E., Shaneson, J.L.: Some Problems in Number Theory I: The Circle Problem (2007), http://arxiv.org/abs/math.NT/0702613

27. Honsberger, R.: Circles, Squares, and Lattice Points. Mathematical Gems I, 117–127 (1973)
28. Kühleitner, M.: On lattice points in rational ellipsoids: An omega estimate for the error term. Abhandlungen Aus Dem Mathematischen Seminar Der Universitat Hamburg 70, 105–111 (2000)
29. Chamizo, F., Cristbal, E., Ubis, A.: Lattice points in rational ellipsoids. Journal of Mathematical Analysis and Applications 350, 283–289 (2009)
30. Chamizo, F.: Lattice points in bodies of revolution. Acta Arithmetica 85, 265–277 (1998)
31. Andres, E., Jacob, M.: The discrete analytical hyperspheres. IEEE Trans. Visualization and Computer Graphics 3, 75–86 (1997)
32. Fiorio, C., Jamet, D., Toutant, J.L.: Discrete circles: an arithmetical approach with non-constant thickness. In: Latecki, L.J., Mount, D.M., Wu, A.Y. (eds.) Vision Geometry XIV, Electronic Imaging, San Jose (CA), USA. SPIE, vol. 6066, p. 60660C (2006)
33. Fiorio, C., Toutant, J.-L.: Arithmetic discrete hyperspheres and separatingness. In: Kuba, A., Nyúl, L.G., Palágyi, K. (eds.) DGCI 2006. LNCS, vol. 4245, pp. 425–436. Springer, Heidelberg (2006)
34. Montani, C., Scopigno, R.: Spheres-to-voxels conversion. In: Glassner, A.S. (ed.) Graphics Gems, pp. 327–334. Academic Press Professional, Inc., San Diego (1990)
35. Stelldinger, P.: Image Digitization and its Influence on Shape Properties in Finite Dimensions. IOS Press (2007)
36. Foley, J.D., van Dam, A., Feiner, S.K., Hughes, J.F.: Computer Graphics — Principles and Practice. Addison-Wesley, Reading (1993)
37. Bera, S., Bhowmick, P., Stelldinger, P., Bhattacharya, B.B.: On covering a digital disc with concentric circles in $\mathbb{Z}^2$. Theoretical Computer Science 506, 1–16 (2013)
38. Bhowmick, P., Bhattacharya, B.B.: Number theoretic interpretation and construction of a digital circle. Discrete Applied Mathematics 156, 2381–2399 (2008)
39. Kumar, G., Sharma, N., Bhowmick, P.: Wheel-throwing in digital space using number-theoretic approach. International Journal of Arts and Technology 4, 196–215 (2011)

Bar 1-Visibility Drawings of 1-Planar Graphs

Shaheena Sultana, Md. Saidur Rahman, Arpita Roy, and Suraiya Tairin

Graph Drawing and Information Visualization Laboratory,
Department of Computer Science and Engineering,
Bangladesh University of Engineering and Technology (BUET),
Dhaka-1000, Bangladesh
{shaheenaasbd,arpita116,suraiya_pakhi}@yahoo.com,
saidurrahman@cse.buet.ac.bd

Abstract. A bar 1-visibility drawing of a graph G is a drawing of G where each vertex is drawn as a horizontal line segment called a bar, each edge is drawn as a vertical line segment between its incident vertices such that each edge crosses at most one bar. A graph G is bar 1-visible if G has a bar 1-visibility drawing. A graph G is 1-planar if G can be drawn in the plane such that each edge has at most one crossing. In this paper we give $O(n)$ time algorithms to find bar 1-visibility drawings of diagonal grid graphs, maximal outer 1-planar graphs, recursive quadrangle 1-planar graphs and pseudo double wheel 1-planar graphs, where n is the number of vertices in the input graph.

1 Introduction

A 1-*planar drawing* of a graph G is a drawing of G on a two dimensional plane where each edge can be crossed by at most one other edge. A graph G is 1-*planar* if G has a 1-planar drawing. A *straight-line drawing* of a graph G is a drawing of G such that every edge of G is drawn as a straight-line segment. A *right angle crossing drawing* or *RAC drawing* is a straight-line drawing where any two crossing edges form right angles at their intersection point. A *RAC graph* is a graph that has a RAC drawing. A *bar 1-visibility drawing* of a graph G is a drawing of G where each vertex is drawn as a horizontal line segment called a bar, each edge is drawn as a vertical line segment between its incident vertices such that each edge crosses at most one bar. A graph G is *bar 1-visible* if G has a bar 1-visibility drawing. A bar 1-visible graph and a bar 1-visibility drawing of the same graph is shown in Figures 1(a) and (b), respectively.

RAC graphs and 1-planar graphs have been extensively studied [2,8,10,16]. Pach and Tóth proved that 1-planar graphs with n vertices have at most $4n - 8$ edges [14], whereas Didimo *et al.* showed that a RAC graph with $n > 3$ vertices has at most $4n - 10$ edges [7]. Recognizing both of the classes of graphs is NP-hard [1,11]. Recently Eades and Liotta studied the relationship between RAC graphs with maximum edge density and 1-planar graphs [9].

The concept of bar visibility drawing came up in the early 1980s when many new problems in visibility theory arose, originally inspired by applications dealing with determining visibilities between different electrical components in VLSI

P. Gupta and C. Zaroliagis (Eds.): ICAA 2014, LNCS 8321, pp. 62–76, 2014.
© Springer International Publishing Switzerland 2014

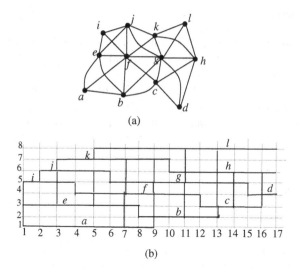

(a)

(b)

Fig. 1. (a) A bar 1-visible graph, and (b) a bar 1-visibility drawing of the same graph

design. Other applications arise when large graphs are to be displayed in a transparent way, and in the rapidly developing field of computer graphics. A *bar visibility drawing* of a planar graph G is a drawing of G where each vertex is drawn as a horizontal line segment and each edge is drawn as a vertical line segment where the vertical line segment representing an edge must connect the horizontal line segments representing the end vertices. Otten and Wijk [13] have shown that every planar graph admits a visibility drawing, and Tamassia and Tollis [17] have given $O(n)$ time algorithm for constructing a visibility drawing of a planar graph of n vertices. Dean *et al.* have introduced a generalization of visibility drawing for a non-planar graph which is called bar k-visibility drawing [3]. In a *bar k-visibility drawing* of a graph, the vertical line segment corresponding to an edge intersects at most k bars which are not end points of the edge. Thus a visibility drawing is a bar k-visibility drawing for $k = 0$.

In this paper we give $O(n)$ time algorithms to find bar 1-visibility drawings of diagonal grid graphs and maximal outer 1-plane graphs which are RAC graphs. We also give algorithms to find bar 1-visibility drawings of recursive quadrangle 1-planar graphs and pseudo double wheel 1-planar graphs which are not RAC graphs.

The rest of the paper is organized as follows. In Section 2 we describe some of the definitions that we have used in our paper. In Sections 3 we present $O(n)$ time algorithms for finding bar 1-visibility drawings of diagonal grid graphs and maximal outer 1-plane graphs and in Section 4 we present algorithms for finding bar 1-visibility drawings of recursive quadrangle 1-planar graphs and pseudo double wheel 1-planar graphs. Finally, in Section 5 we conclude our paper with a list of open problems.

2   Preliminaries

In this section we introduce some terminologies and definitions which will be used throughout the paper. For the graph theoretic definitions which have not been described here, see [5,12].

A graph is *planar* if it can be embedded in the plane without edge crossing except at the vertices where the edges are incident. A *plane graph* is a planar graph with a fixed planar embedding. A plane graph divides the plane into some connected regions called the *faces*. The unbounded region is called the *outer face* and all the other faces are called the *inner faces*. The vertices on the outer face are called the *outer vertices* and all the other vertices are called *inner vertices*. A $p \times q$-*grid graph* is a graph whose vertices correspond to the grid points of a $p \times q$-grid in the plane and edges correspond to the grid lines between two consecutive grid points. A *diagonal grid graph* $G_{p,q}$ is a $p \times q$-grid graph with diagonal edges in each cell. Figure 2(a) shows the 3×3-grid graph and Figure 2(b) shows a diagonal grid graph $G_{3,3}$. Let $abcd$ be a cell of a diagonal grid graph, as illustrated in Figure 2(c). The edge connecting the bottom-left corner to the top-right corner is called *right-diagonal edge* and The edge connecting the bottom-right corner to the top-left corner is called *left-diagonal edge* of the cell.

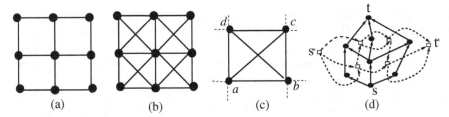

(a)   (b)   (c)   (d)

Fig. 2. (a) A grid graph, (b) a diagonal grid graph, (c) one cell of a diagonal grid graph and (d) construction of the dual-like graph G^* of a planar st-graph

The following terminologies and definitions are described as in [5]. An acyclic digraph with a single source s and a single sink t is called an st-*graph*. A *plane st-graph* is an st-graph that is planar and embedded with vertices s and t on the boundary of the outer face. Let G be a plane st-graph and F be its set of faces. F contains two representatives of the outer face: the "left outer face" s^*, which is incident to the edges on the left boundary of G and the "right outer face" t^*, which is incident to the edges on the right boundary of G. Additionally, for each $e = (u, v)$ we define $orig(e) = u$ and $dest(e) = v$. Also, we define $left(e)$ (respectively $right(e)$) to be the face to the left (respectively right) of e. We now define a dual-like graph G^* of G as follows. The vertex set of G^* is the set F of faces of G, and G^* has an edge $e^* = (f, g)$ for each edge $e \neq (s, t)$ of G, where $f = left(e)$ and $g = right(e)$. In Figure 2(d) the vertices and edges of G are drawn by black circles and solid lines respectively, and the vertices and edges of G^* are drawn by white rectangles and dotted lines respectively.

Let G be a digraph with n vertices and m edges. A *topological numbering* of G is an assignment of numbers to the vertices of G, such that, for every edge

(u, v) of G, the number assigned to v is greater than the one assigned to u. If the edges of digraph G have nonnegative weights associated with them, a *weighted topological numbering* is a topological numbering of G, such that, for every edge (u, v) of G, the number assigned to v is greater than or equal to the number assigned to u plus the weight of (u, v). The numbering is *optimal* if the range of numbers assigned to the vertices is minimized. Let G be a plane st-graph with n vertices. Two paths π_1 and π_2 of G are said to be non-intersecting if they are edge disjoint. They do not cross at common vertices but can touch at vertices. Let Π be a collection of non-intersecting paths of G. In the visibility drawing of G, for every path π of Π, if the edges of π are vertically aligned then the drawing is called *constrained visibility drawing*. The following result on constrained visibility drawing is known [6]. But in our result it is not necessary to cover all the edges of G by non-intersecting paths of G.

Lemma 1. *Let G be a plane st-graph of n vertices, and let Π be a set of non-intersecting paths of G. Then one can find a constrained visibility drawing of G in $O(n)$ time with $O(n^2)$ area, where the edges of every path π in Π are vertically aligned.*

A 1-planar graph G is optimal if no edges can be added to G without losing 1-planarity. That is, an *optimal 1-planar graph* of n vertices has the highest number of edges among all 1-planar graphs of n vertices [16]. An *outer 1-plane graph* is a plane embedding of a graph such that all vertices lie on the outer face and there is at most one crossing on each edge. An outer 1-plane graph $G = (V, E)$ is a *maximal outer 1-plane graph* if for each pair u, v of vertices where (u, v) is not an edge, adding the edge (u, v) to G makes it not outer 1-plane; that is, $G' = (V, E \cup (u, v))$ is not outer-1-plane for every drawing of the edge (u, v) [4].

3   Bar 1-Visibility Drawings of 1-Planar RAC Graphs

Some interesting labeling properties of diagonal grid graphs have been studied recently by Selvaraju and Pricilla [15]. Recently Dehkordi showed that outer 1-plane graphs are RAC graphs [4]. In Section 3.1 we develop an $O(n)$ time algorithm for finding a bar 1-visibility drawing of a diagonal grid graph and in Section 3.2 we develop an algorithm for finding a bar 1-visibility drawing of a maximal outer 1-plane graph.

3.1   Diagonal Grid Graphs

In this section we prove the following theorem.

Theorem 1. *A diagonal grid graph $G_{p,q}$ admits a bar 1-visibility drawing Γ on a grid of size $(q + 2p - 2) \times (3(p + q) - 3)$. Furthermore, Γ can be found in $O(n)$ time, where $n(= pq)$ is the number of vertices in $G_{p,q}$.*

Proof. We construct a bar 1-visibility drawing Γ of a diagonal grid graph $G_{p,q}$ as follows. Let $G_{p,q}$ be a diagonal grid graph, as illustrated in Figure 3(a).

Clearly $G_{p,q}$ is RAC drawable and 1-planar. We first obtain a graph G from $G_{p,q}$ by deleting the left-diagonal edge of each cell. Clearly G is a plane graph, as illustrated in Figure 3(b). Let v_{ij}, $1 \leq i \leq p$ and $1 \leq j \leq q$, be the vertex corresponding to the grid point on the ith row and jth column of the $p \times q$ grid. We now assign a number $Y(v_{ij})$ to each vertex v_{ij} as follows. We set $Y(v_{1,j}) = j$ for $1 \leq j \leq q$, and for $1 < i \leq p$ we set $Y(v_{ij}) = Y(v_{(i-1)j}) + 2$. We now construct a directed graph from G by assigning direction to each edge from lower number to higher number. We add a vertex s below the first row and a vertex t above the last row. We also add directed edges $(s, v_{1,j})$ and $(v_{p,j}, t)$ for $1 \leq j \leq q$. Let G_{st} be the resulting digraph, as illustrated in Figure 3(c). From the construction one can observe that G_{st} is an st-graph. We now construct a visibility drawing of G_{st} as follows. This construction proceeds similarly to [17].

We now construct G_{st}^* of G_{st} and assign unit weights to the edges of G_{st}^* and compute an optimal weighted topological numbering X of G_{st}^* according to [5], as illustrated in Figure 3(d). We then draw each vertex v as a horizontal line segment $\Gamma(v)$ at y-coordinate $Y(v)$ and between x-coordinate $X(left(v))$ and $X(right(v) - 1)$. We call $X(left(v))$ the start of $\Gamma(v)$ and $X(right(v) - 1)$ the end of $\Gamma(v)$. For each edge e, we draw the vertical line segment $\Gamma(e)$ at x-coordinate $X(left(e))$, between y-coordinate $Y(orig(e))$ and $Y(dest(e))$. Let u be the top-left vertex and v be the bottom-right vertex of a cell in a diagonal grid graph. Then one can observe from the drawing algorithm that $X(left(v) - X(right(u) - 1)) = 2$.

We now obtain a bar 1-visibility drawing of G from the visibility drawing Γ of G_{st} as follows. We first delete $\Gamma(s)$ and $\Gamma(t)$ from the drawing together with the drawings of the edges incident to s and t. The visibility drawing Γ of G_{st} is illustrated in Figure 3(e). We insert one vertical grid line (column) between the two consecutive vertical grid lines i and j if $i = left(e)$ and $j = right(e)$ for some right-diagonal edge e by expanding the drawing towards $+x$ direction. We perform this insertion operation for every i, j. After this insertion operation the difference of x-coordinate of end of $\Gamma(u)$ and start of $\Gamma(v)$ will be three, where u is the top-left vertex and v is the bottom-right vertex of a cell in a diagonal grid graph. We thus extend the end of $\Gamma(u)$ by 2 units in $+x$-direction and the end of $\Gamma(v)$ by one unit to the $-x$-direction. We can place the deleted left-diagonal edges in the vertical segment which will be placed between starting point of the horizontal bar corresponding to bottom-right vertex and end point of the extended horizontal segment corresponding to top-left vertex in each cell. By extending these bars, the right-diagonal edge in each cell crosses horizontal bar corresponding to top-left vertex in the drawing. Since all edges including left- diagonal edges can be placed at end point and start point of the horizontal bars then only right-diagonal edges always pass through one horizontal bar corresponding to the vertex, the drawing becomes a bar 1-visibility drawing Γ. The bar 1-visibility drawing of $G_{p,q}$ is illustrated in Figure 3(f). In this figure the solid thick lines are left-diagonal edges of each cell and the dotted thick lines are right-diagonal edges which intersect the horizontal bar of each cell.

From the above bar 1-visibility drawing we now calculate the grid size in the following way. The height of the drawing is $Y(v_{pq}) = q + 2p - 2$. The width of the drawing is the length of the longest path in G_{st}^*. Since each cell of G contains two faces, the longest path of G_{st}^* is at most $2(p+q)$. We now compute the size of bar 1-visibility drawing. One can observe that at most $(p-1) + (q-1) - 1 = p + q - 3$ new columns are inserted for constructing bar 1-visibility drawing of $G_{p,q}$ from the visibility drawing of G. Thus the width of the bar 1-visibility drawing is $(3(p+q) - 3)$. Thus we obtain a bar 1-visibility drawing on a grid of size $(q + 2p - 2) \times (3(p+q) - 3)$.

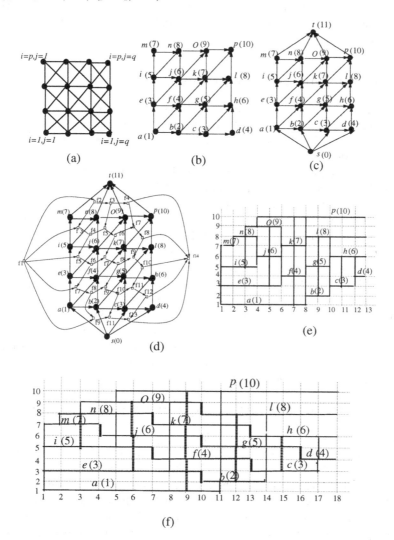

Fig. 3. (a) A diagonal grid graph $G_{p,q}$, (b) graph G with a numbering of vertices, (c) a digraph G_{st}, (d) a dual-like graph G_{st}^*, (e) a bar visibility drawing of G and (f) a bar 1-visibility drawing of a diagonal grid graph $G_{p,q}$

G_{st} from G can be constructed in $O(n)$ time. Then a visibility drawing Γ of G_{st} can be obtained in $O(n)$ time [5]. Next a bar 1-visibility drawing of G from the visibility drawing Γ of G_{st} can be constructed by inserting vertical grid line, placing left-diagonal edges and extending some bars in $O(n)$ time. Thus a bar 1-visibility drawing Γ of a diagonal grid graph $G_{p,q}$ can be found in $O(n)$ time.   □

A diagonal grid graph G has $n = pq$ vertices. If $p > q$ then the area of the bar 1-visibility drawing is $O(p^2)$ and if $p < q$ then the area is $O(q^2)$. When $p \cong q$ then the area of the bar 1-visibility drawing is $O(pq) = O(n)$. The bar 1-visibility drawing obtained by our algorithm is "compact" in a sense that there is at least one line segment for every vertical and horizontal grid line except the last vertical grid line.

3.2   Maximal Outer 1-Planar Graphs

In this Section we give an algorithm for obtaining a bar 1-visibility drawing of a maximal outer 1-plane graph. This problem has an interesting correlation with a constrained visibility drawing of a planar st-graph. To describe the algorithm, we need some definitions.

Let G be a maximal outer 1-plane graph. In a maximal outer 1-plane graph, each edge crossing is surrounded by a cycle of length 4 and no edge in this cycle has a crossing [4]. We call such a cycle of length four a *quadrangle*. An edge e of an outer-1-plane graph is called a *crossing edge* if e has a crossing; otherwise e is called a *non-crossing edge*. In the Figure 4(a), a, b, c, d is a quadrangle. In quadrangle a, b, c, d, edges (a, c) and (b, d) are crossing edges and edges (a, b), (b, c), (c, d) , (d, a) are non-crossing edges. Each crossing edge of a quadrangle is called a *diagonal*. We call a labeling of vertices of a maximal outer 1-plane graph by integers 1 to n (where n is the number of vertices in the graph) a *diagonal labeling* when every quadrangle has one diagonal whose endpoints receive the lowest and highest labels among the labels assigned to the quadrangle. For example, Figure 4(a) shows a maximal outer 1-plane graph G and Figure 4(b) shows a diagonal labeling of G. We can introduce diagonal labeling on the maximal outer 1-plane graph. We have the following lemma.

Lemma 2. *Every maximal outer 1-plane graph admits diagonal labeling.*

Proof. Let G be a maximal outer 1-plane graph. We will prove that G has a diagonal labeling. Let v be a vertex in G. Then assign 1 to v. After that we will give next numbers to those vertices which are incident to non-crossing edges from v in counterclockwise order. Then assign numbers to the vertices which are incident to crossing edges from v. We then consider the vertex labeled by 2 and assign next numbers to the vertices in the same way. Since the labeling has been done always in increasing order and the vertices incident to crossing edges are labeled later, the diagonal of a quadrangle got the highest and lowest numbers among the numbers of four vertices of the quadrangle. Figure 4(b) illustrates a diagonal labeling of the maximal outer 1-plane graph in Figure 4(a).   □

Using this diagonal labeling, we can construct a bar 1-visibility drawing of a maximal outer 1-plane graph as proved by the following theorem.

Theorem 2. *A bar 1-visibility drawing of a maximal outer 1-plane graph G of n vertices can be computed in $O(n)$ time.*

Proof. Let G be a maximal outer 1-plane graph, as illustrated in Figure 4(a). By Lemma 2, G has a diagonal labeling, as illustrated in Figure 4(b). We first orient every edge from lower number to higher number, as illustrated in Figure 4(b). We next identify the crossing edge containing the highest number and the lowest number in each quadrangle. Then we construct a planar graph G' from G by passing the crossing edge containing the highest number and the lowest number through the vertex which are right side of the edge in each quadrangle, as illustrated in Figure 4(c). The crossing edge which is passed through the vertex is identified as a non-intersecting path. Since we pass all the crossing edges through the vertices which are right side of the edges, these satisfies the conditions of non-intersecting paths stated in the result on constrained visibility drawing [6]. More than one sink vertex is found in the graph, as illustrated in Figure 4(c). We thus construct planar st-graph by adding dummy edges between the sink vertices to the highest labeled sink vertex, as illustrated in Figure 4(d). Since the graph is outer planar, the obtained graph remains planar after adding dummy edges. Then we construct a constrained visibility drawing of this planar st-graph according to Lemma 1 [6]. All edges can be placed at end point and start point of the horizontal bars. Since crossing edges containing the highest number and the lowest number for all quadrangles always pass through one horizontal bar corresponding to the vertex, the drawing becomes a bar 1-visibility drawing. The bar 1-visibility drawing of G is illustrated in Figure 4(e). In this figure the dotted lines are crossing edges containing the highest number and the lowest number for all quadrangles.

Diagonal labeling of G can be obtained in $O(n)$ time. Then G' from G and planar st-graph can be constructed in $O(n)$ time. Next a constrained visibility drawing of this planar st-graph can be done in $O(n)$ time [6]. Thus a bar 1-visibility drawing of a maximal outer 1-plane graph can be computed in $O(n)$ time. □

4   Bar 1-Visibility Drawings of 1-Planar Non-RAC Graphs

In the previous section, we showed that diagonal grid graphs and maximal outer 1-planar graphs are two classes of 1-planar graphs that have bar 1-visibility drawings. Recently Eades and Liotta showed that every maximally dense RAC graph is 1-planar [9]; on the other hand, they introduced a class of 1-planar graphs which is not RAC drawable. We call this class of graphs recursive quadrangle 1-planar graphs. Suzuki studied the combinatorial properties of the optimal 1-planar graphs having $4n - 8$ edges [16] which we will define as "pseudo double wheel 1-planar graphs". Since a RAC graph with $n > 3$ vertices has at most

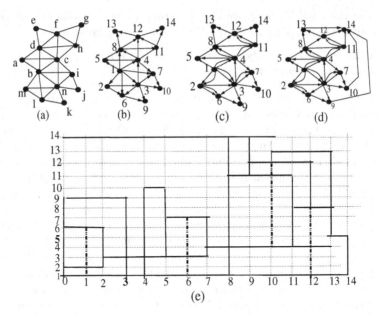

Fig. 4. (a) A maximal outer 1-plane graph G, (b) a diagonal labeling of G, (c) planar graph G', (d) a planar st-graph and (e) a bar 1-visibility drawing of G

$4n - 10$ edges [7], pseudo double wheel 1-planar graphs are not RAC graphs. In Section 4.1 we develop a recursive way to find a bar 1-visibility drawing of a recursive quadrangle 1-planar graph and in Section 4.2 we develop a procedure to find a bar 1-visibility drawing of a pseudo double wheel 1-planar graph.

4.1 Recursive Quadrangle 1-Planar Graphs

The class *recursive quadrangle 1-planar graph* is defined recursively as follows. G_0 is a 1-planar graph of eight vertices. G_0 has an 1-planar drawing, as illustrated in Figure 5(a) where the cycle $abcd$ is drawn as the outer rectangle and none of the four edges on the outer rectangle has a crossing. Let $abcd$ be the outer rectangle of G_i, $i \geq 0$. Graph G_{i+1} is obtained from G_i by adding a new outer rectangle $a'b'c'd'$ and 16 new edges as described in Figure 5(c) and (e), where the four edges on the the outer face do not have any crossing. Let G be a 1-planar graph and x be a vertex of G and (x, y) be an edge of G. We denote by $\Gamma(G)$, $\Gamma(x)$, $\Gamma(x, y)$ a bar 1-visibility drawing of G, the drawing of a vertex x as a horizontal bar in $\Gamma(G)$, and the drawing of an edge (x, y) as a vertical line segment in $\Gamma(G)$, respectively. For a vertex x in G, let a and b be the x-coordinates of the two ends of $\Gamma(x)$ such that $a < b$. We call a and b the *start* and the *end* of $\Gamma(x)$, respectively. We now have the following theorem.

Theorem 3. *Every recursive quadrangle 1-planar graph $G_i, i \geq 0$ is a bar 1-visible graph. Furthermore, a bar 1-visibility drawing $\Gamma(G)$ of a recursive quadrangle 1-planar graph G of n vertices can be computed in $O(n)$ time.*

Proof. We prove every recursive quadrangle 1-planar graph $G_i, i \geq 0$ is a bar 1-visible graph by induction on i. Let $abcd$ be the outer rectangle of G_0, as illustrated in Figure 5(a). Then G_0 has a bar 1-visibility drawing, as illustrated in Figure 5(b) where (i) $\Gamma(a)$ is the bottommost bar, $\Gamma(c)$ is the topmost bar, $\Gamma(d)$ is the second bottommost bar and $\Gamma(b)$ is the second topmost bar; (ii) starts of $\Gamma(c)$ and $\Gamma(d)$ have the smallest x-coordinate of the drawing and starts of $\Gamma(a)$ and $\Gamma(b)$ have the second smallest x-coordinate of the drawing; and (iii) $\Gamma(a, b)$ crosses $\Gamma(d)$. We assume that $i > 0$ and G_j, for $j < i$, has a bar visibility drawing satisfying (i)-(iii) above. We now show that G_i has a bar 1-visibility drawing satisfying (i)-(iii) above. Let $a'b'c'd'$ be the outer rectangle of G_i. We obtain a graph G_{i-1} by deleting the four vertices on the outer rectangle of G_i. Let $abcd$ be the outer rectangle of G_{i-1}. By the inductive hypothesis, G_{i-1} has a bar 1-visibility drawing satisfying (i)-(iii), as illustrated in Figure 5(d). We now obtain a bar 1-visibility drawing of G_i from the visibility drawing of G_{i-1} as follows. Extend the start of $\Gamma(a)$, $\Gamma(d)$ and $\Gamma(b)$ by four, four and two units, respectively, to the $-x$-direction. Extend the end of $\Gamma(c)$ and $\Gamma(b)$ by five unit each to the $+x$-direction. Draw $\Gamma(a'), \Gamma(d'), \Gamma(b')$ and $\Gamma(c')$ as the bottommost, 2nd bottommost, 2nd topmost and topmost bars outside $\Gamma(G_{i-1})$ and draw the new edges as vertical line segments such that (i)-(iii) are satisfied in $\Gamma(G_i)$, as illustrated in Figure 5(f).

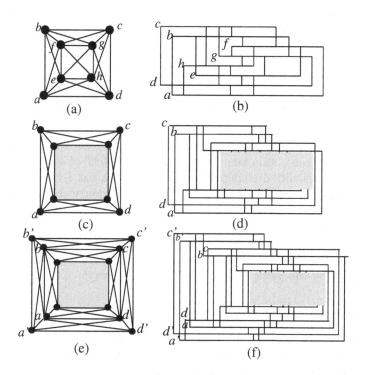

Fig. 5. Illustration for the proof of Theorem 3

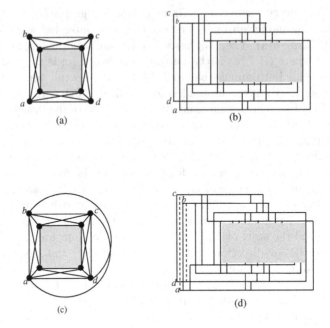

Fig. 6. (a) A recursive quadrangle 1-planar graph G, (b) a bar 1-visibility drawing of G, (c) an optimal 1-planar graph G' obtained from G by adding two edges and (d) a bar 1-visibility drawing of G'

One can develop a recursive algorithm for finding a bar 1-visibility drawing of a recursive quadrangle 1-planar graph from the induction proof above. Since a bar 1-visibility drawing of G_i can be obtained in constant time from the bar 1-visibility drawing of G_{i-1}, the algorithm takes $O(n)$ time, in total.   □

By adding two more edges to recursive quadrangle 1-planar graph G of $4p$, $p \geq 2$ vertices, we can obtain an optimal 1-planar graph G' of $4p$, $p \geq 2$ vertices. From the bar 1-visibility drawing of G we can obtain a bar 1-visibility drawing of G' by adding the drawing of additional two edges as vertical line segments as illustrated in Figure 6.

Thus the following theorem holds.

Theorem 4. *Every optimal 1-planar graph obtained from recursive quadrangle 1-planar graph by adding two edges is a bar 1-visible graph.*

4.2 Pseudo Double Wheel 1-Planar Graphs

We begin with the formal definition of even pseudo double wheel 1-planar graph. Let C be a cycle $v_1u_1v_2u_2...v_nu_n$ of even number of vertices embedded on a plane. Let x and y be two vertices outside and inside of C, respectively. We connect

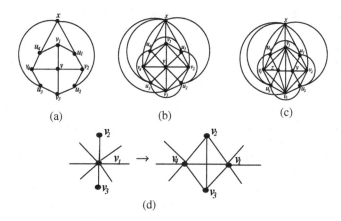

(a)   (b)   (c)

(d)

Fig. 7. (a) A pseudo double wheel, (b) an even pseudo double wheel 1-planar graph G, (c) an odd pseudo double wheel 1-planar graph G' and (d) Q_v splitting

x with u_i and y with v_i for $i = 1...n$. Let H be the resulting plane graph, as illustrated in Figure 7(a). We add a pair of crossing edges to each face of H, as illustrated in Figure 7(b). The resulting graph is an optimal 1-planar graph, as introduced by Suzuki [16]. We call this optimal 1-planar graph *even pseudo double wheel 1-planar graph*.

Q_v *splitting* is an expansion operation at v_1 defined as follows : (i) Identify v_2 and v_3 such that there are v_1v_2 and v_1v_3 edges but no v_2v_3 edge. (ii) Split $v_1v_2v_3$ path (iii) Rename one copy of v_1 as v_4. (iv) Join v_1 , v_4 and v_2 , v_3. Splitting is illustrated in Figure 7(d). An optimal 1-planar graph obtained from even pseudo double wheel 1-planar graph by one splitting operation is called *odd pseudo double wheel 1-planar graph*, as illustrated in Figure 7(c).

We now have the following theorem.

Theorem 5. *A bar 1-visibility drawing of a pseudo double wheel 1-planar graph G of n vertices can be found in $O(n)$ time.*

Proof. We will construct a bar 1-visibility drawing of an even pseudo double wheel 1-planar graph and an odd pseudo double wheel 1-planar graph.

Let G be an even pseudo double wheel 1-planar graph. We first draw n bars where $1st$ topmost bar is y, $2nd$ topmost bar is x and other n-2 bars starting from $3rd$ topmost bar are $v_1, u_1, v_2, u_2...v_n, u_n$ respectively. We next draw $n-2$ vertical lines from $v_1, u_1, v_2, u_2...v_n, u_n$ to y each crossing x and another $n-2$ vertical lines from $v_1, u_1, v_2, u_2...v_n, u_n$ to x without crossing any bar. We next join each of the $v_2, u_2, v_3, u_3...v_{n-1}, u_{n-1}$ bars to 4 bars 1 and 2 unit up and below itself. We next consider v_1, u_1, v_n and u_n. We next join v_1 to u_1, v_1 to v_n, v_1 to u_n and v_n to u_n by vertical lines without crossing any bar. At last we draw a vertical line from u_1 to u_n crossing v_n. Since each vertical line crosses at most one bar, the drawing becomes bar 1-visibility drawing. The bar 1-visibility drawing of G is illustrated in Figure 8(a).

Let G' be an odd pseudo double wheel 1-planar graph of n vertices. We first find v_i and v_j on C such that v_i and v_j have degree 8. We next draw n bars where 1st topmost bar is z, 2nd topmost bar is y, 3rd topmost bar is x and other $n-3$ bars starting from 4th topmost bar are v_1, u_1, v_2, $u_2...v_n$, u_n respectively. We next draw $n-3$ vertical lines from v_1, u_1, v_2, $u_2...v_n$, u_n to x without crossing any bar. Then join y to v_i,u_i, v_{i+1}, $u_{i+1}...v_j$ by vertical lines. These lines cross bar x. We next draw vertical lines from z to v_j,u_j, v_{j+1}, $u_{j+1}...v_n$, u_n, v_1, $u_1...v_j$ crossing bar x. We next join each of the v_2, u_2, v_3, $u_3...v_{n-1}$, u_{n-1} bars to 4 bars 1 and 2 unit up and below itself. Now we consider v_1, u_1, v_n and u_n. We next join v_1 to u_1, v_1 to v_n, v_1 to u_n and v_n to u_n, y to z by vertical lines without crossing any bar. We next draw a vertical line from u_1 to u_n crossing v_n. At last we join v_i to v_j. Since each vertical line crosses at most one bar, the drawing becomes bar 1-visibility drawing. The bar 1-visibility drawing of G' is illustrated in Figure 8(b).

Since in the algorithm drawing of each bar at different places and joining those bars can be done in constant time, a bar 1-visibility drawing of an even pseudo double wheel 1-planar graph and an odd pseudo double wheel 1-planar graph drawing can be found in $O(n)$ time.   □

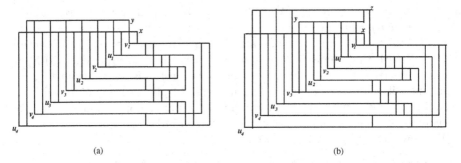

(a)   (b)

Fig. 8. (a) A bar 1-visibility drawing of an even pseudo double wheel 1-planar graph and (b) a bar 1-visibility drawing of an odd pseudo double wheel 1-planar graph

5   Conclusion

In this paper we have given $O(n)$ time algorithms to find bar 1-visibility drawings of diagonal grid graphs and maximal outer 1-planar graphs which are RAC graphs. We have also presented algorithms for finding bar 1-visibility drawings of recursive quadrangle 1-planar graphs and pseudo double wheel 1-planar graphs in $O(n)$ time.

Pach and Tóth [14] proved that a 1-planar graph of n vertices can have at most $4n-8$ edges whereas Dean et al. [3] showed that a bar 1-visible graph can have at most $6n-20$ edges. The bound for bar 1-visible graph is tight since for each $n \geq 8$ there exists a bar 1-visible graph with exactly $6n-20$ edges [3]. Thus not all bar 1-visible graphs are 1-planar graphs. This can be well illustrated by the following example. A bar 1-visibility drawing of an optimal 1-planar graph G of eight vertices in Figure 9(a), is shown in Figure 9(b), but Figure 9(c) shows a bar 1-visibility drawing of a graph of eight vertices which has more edges. Suzuki [16] proved that every optimal 1-planar graph can be obtained from an even pseudo double wheel 1-planar graph by a sequence of Q_v splittings and "Q_4 additions". We were able to construct bar 1-visibility drawing of every 1-planar graph that we considered as an example, but yet to find a formal proof. We thus conjecture as follows.

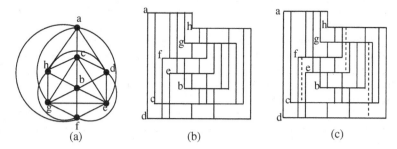

Fig. 9. (a) An optimal 1-planar graph G, (b) a bar 1-visibility drawing of G and (c) a bar 1-visibility drawing of G' obtained by adding some edges to G

Conjecture 1. Every 1-planar graph is a bar 1-visible graph.

Following interesting open problems have come out from this work.

1. Recognition of both RAC graphs and 1-planar graphs are NP-complete problems. It is interesting to know the complexity of recognizing a bar 1-visible graph. Finding a complete characterization of bar 1-visible graph is also an interesting open problem.
2. How to find a 1-planar embedding of a 1-planar graph?
3. Can we find a complete characterization of bar k-visibility drawing?

References

1. Argyriou, E.N., Bekos, M.A., Symvonis, A.: The straight-line RAC drawing problem is NP-hard. In: Černá, I., Gyimóthy, T., Hromkovič, J., Jefferey, K., Králović, R., Vukolić, M., Wolf, S. (eds.) SOFSEM 2011. LNCS, vol. 6543, pp. 74–85. Springer, Heidelberg (2011)
2. Arikushi, K., Fulek, R., Keszegh, B., Morić, F., Tóth, C.D.: Graphs that admits right angle crossing drawing. In: Thilikos, D.M. (ed.) WG 2010. LNCS, vol. 6410, pp. 135–146. Springer, Heidelberg (2010)
3. Dean, A.M., Evans, W., Gethner, E., Laison, J.D., Safari, M.: Bar k-visibility graphs. Journal of Graph Algorithms and Applications 11(1), 45–59 (2007)
4. Dehkordi, H., Eades, P.: On algorithmic right angle crossing graph drawing. Int. J. Comput. Geometry 22(6), 543–557 (2012)

5. Di Battista, G., Eades, P., Tamassia, R., Tollis, I.G.: Graph Drawing: Algorithms for the Visualization of Graphs. Prentice-Hall Inc. (1999)
6. Di Battista, G., Tamassia, R., Tollis, I.G.: Constrained visibility representation of graphs. Inform. Process. Letters 41, 1–7 (1992)
7. Didimo, W., Eades, P., Liotta, G.: Drawing graphs with right angle crossings. In: Dehne, F., Gavrilova, M., Sack, J.-R., Tóth, C.D. (eds.) WADS 2009. LNCS, vol. 5664, pp. 206–217. Springer, Heidelberg (2009)
8. Didimo, W., Eades, P., Liotta, G.: A characterization of complete bipartite RAC graphs. Information Processing Letters 110(16), 687–691 (2010)
9. Eades, P., Liotta, G.: Right angle crossing graphs and 1-planarity. In: Speckmann, B. (ed.) GD 2011. LNCS, vol. 7034, pp. 148–153. Springer, Heidelberg (2011)
10. Fabrici, I., Madaras, T.: The structure of 1-planar graphs. Discrete Mathematics 307(7-8), 854–865 (2007)
11. Korzhik, V.P., Mohar, B.: Minimal obstructions for 1-immersions and hardness of 1-planarity testing. In: Tollis, I.G., Patrignani, M. (eds.) GD 2008. LNCS, vol. 5417, pp. 302–312. Springer, Heidelberg (2009)
12. Nishizeki, T., Rahman, M.S.: Planar Graph Drawing. Lecture notes series on computing. World Scientific (2004)
13. Otten, J., Van Wijk, J.G.: Graph representation in interactive layout design. In: The Proceedings of IEEE International Symposium on Circuits and Systems, pp. 914–918 (1978)
14. Pach, J., Tóth, G.: Graphs drawn with few crossings per edge. Combinatorica 17(3), 427–439 (1997)
15. Selvaraju, P., Pricilla, B.: On cordial labeling: The grid, diagonal grid, structured web graphs. International Journal of Algorithms, Computing and Mathematics 2(1), 5–14 (2009)
16. Suzuki, Y.: Optimal 1-planar graphs which triangulate other surfaces. Discrete Mathematics 310(1), 6–11 (2010)
17. Tamassia, R., Tollis, I.G.: A unified approach to visibility representations of planar graphs. Discrete and Computational Geometry 1, 321–341 (1986)

Search Strategies for Subgraph Isomorphism Algorithms

Uroš Čibej and Jurij Mihelič

University of Ljubljana, Ljubljana, Slovenia
{uros.cibej,jurij.mihelic}@fri.uni-lj.si

Abstract. Searching for subgraph isomorphisms is an essential problem in pattern matching. Most of the algorithms use a branch-and-bound method to sequentially assign pattern nodes to compatible nodes in the target graph. It is well known that the order in which nodes are assigned, a so-called search strategy, influences drastically the size of the search space. In this article we investigate the impact of various search strategies on the efficiency of two algorithms, the first being the Ullmann's algorithm and the second one the recently proposed improvement of Ullmann's algorithm. From the large set of proposed orders we find the most successful ones by thorough testing on a large database of graphs.

Keywords: subgraph isomorphism, Ullmann's algorithm, search strategy.

1 Introduction

Graphs are an essential form of data organization and are emerging in the most surprising applications from chemistry [1], neurology [10], social sciences [2], linguistics [11], and many more. One of the frequent tasks when analyzing graphs is the search for different patterns. The problem of finding instances of a given graph in a larger graph is called *subgraph isomorphism problem*. Due to the ubiquity of this problem it has been studied extensively, both from a purely theoretical point of view as well as from a more practical point of view.

From a theoretical point the problem is very difficult, as it has been shown to be NP-complete and the counting version of the problem is #P complete [8]. Many different approaches were developed for solving the problem. One approach is to reduce the complexity of the problem by imposing a restriction on input graphs. Polynomial time exact algorithms exist for trees [16] and some classes of graphs with a bounded treewidth [9]. However, in many cases such restrictions are not an acceptable option, so we still have to resort to exponential-time algorithms, which work on all graphs.

From a practical point of view, Ullmann [15] gave a search algorithm which is unfeasible in theory but works great in practice. Since the introduction of this algorithm new algorithms have been introduced [3, 14, 12], which are considered to be superior to Ullmann's. But recently, we managed to devise [13] a set of improvements of Ullmann's algorithm which demonstrate that Ullmann's

P. Gupta and C. Zaroliagis (Eds.): ICAA 2014, LNCS 8321, pp. 77–88, 2014.

algorithm is still very competitive, in many cases even better than the above mentioned newer solutions.

The main scope of the paper is to investigate the possibilities of improving Ullmann's algorithm even further, since there are still many aspects that have not yet been systematically tested. We focus on the pattern-node selection order, called the *search strategy*, which is the part of the algorithm that has a very large impact on the running time. Several search strategies have been proposed since the original article was published, our goal is to devise a common framework for all this strategies which will serve as a foundation for testing already known orders and designing new ones.

The remainder of the article is organized as follows. In the next section we give the problem definition. In Section 3 we describe the Ullmann's algorithm. In Section 4 we describe a large set of possible sorting orders, Section 5 shows the results of a large empirical evaluation of the described orders, and finally Section 6 concludes the paper and gives ideas for future work.

2   Preliminaries

First let us define basic notions from the graph theory since graphs represent the main object of our discussion. We use the notation most widely used in the literature, namely, a graph $G = \langle V, E \rangle$ is represented by two sets: the set V of nodes and a set $E \subseteq V \times V$ of edges between these nodes. Graph can be directed, if the pairs representing edges are ordered, otherwise they are undirected. In this paper we mostly consider undirected graphs, but all the findings can easily be adapted to deal with directed graphs.

The following definitions are required for the remainder of the article. Two nodes are called *adjacent* if they share a common edge. A *neighborhood* of a node $i \in V$ (sometimes called *open neighborhood*) is the set of all the nodes that are adjacent to i, i.e., $\mathcal{N}_G(i) = \{j \in V \mid (i, j) \in E\}$. A *closed neighborhood* of a node contains also the node itself, i.e., $\mathcal{N}[i] = \mathcal{N}(i) \cup \{i\}$. Additionally, we define the degree $\delta_G(i)$ of the node i as the number of nodes in its neighborhood, i.e., $\delta_G(i) = |\mathcal{N}_G(i)|$.

The input to the subgraph isomorphism problem consists of two graphs : a *pattern graph* $G = \langle V, E \rangle$, and a *target graph* $H = \langle U, F \rangle$. Without any loss of generality we use $V = \{1, \ldots, n\}$ and $U = \{1, \ldots, m\}$ where $n \leq m$.

A (ordinary) *subgraph isomorphism* between a pattern $G = \langle V, E \rangle$ and a target $H = \langle U, F \rangle$ is an injective function $f : V \longrightarrow U$ satisfying the condition $(i, j) \in E \Rightarrow (f(i), f(j)) \in F$. Similarly an *induced subgraph isomorphism* between a pattern $G = \langle V, E \rangle$ and a target $H = \langle U, F \rangle$ is an injective function $f : V \longrightarrow U$ satisfying the condition $(i, j) \in E \Leftrightarrow (f(i), f(j)) \in F$. The difference between the ordinary and the induced subgraph isomorphism is demonstrated with an example in Fig. 1.

The subgraph isomorphism problem is, given a pattern graph G and a target graph H, to find a subgraph isomorphism between G and H, or to decide that none exists. Another option is to find all the subgraph isomorphisms between G and H. The algorithms discussed in the paper may be used to find one or all

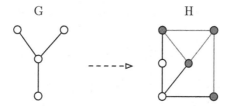

Fig. 1. Subgraph isomorphism that is not an induced isomorphism. The pattern G is a subgraph of the target H. However, the red edge of H is missing in G in order to be an induced subgraph isomorphism.

subgraph isomorphisms as well as ordinary or induced subgraph isomorphisms between directed or undirected graphs.

3   Ullmann's Algorithm and Modifications

In this section we describe Ullmann's algorithm [15] for the subgraph isomorphism problem. In the original article the algorithm was given in a sort of assembly language, which makes it difficult to read by modern standards. In what follows, we give a brief and high-level overview of the algorithm in a more readable fashion, in order to provide a suitable context for the further discussion of search strategies.

The main idea of the algorithm is very simple: sequentially try to map pattern nodes to the target nodes, and during the process check for any inconsistencies in the structure of the mapped graph, i.e., the mapped nodes should retain the same connectivity as the nodes in the pattern graph.

To check for such inconsistencies a binary matrix M of size $n \times m$ is used. We call M a *compatibility matrix*, for obvious reasons. The rows of the matrix M correspond to the vertices $i \in V$ of the pattern G, and the columns of M correspond to the vertices $j \in U$ of the target H. In particular, the element in the i-th row and the j-th column of the matrix M equals 1 if and only if the pattern node $i \in V$ is compatible with the target node $j \in U$. *Compatible* in this context means that in the process of the search no constraint was found that would prevent the pattern node to be mapped unto the corresponding target node. All the other values in the matrix are equal to 0. The trace of the algorithm is a list of matrices $M^0, M^1, M^2, \ldots$, where the matrix M^{i+1} is a reduced versions of M^i, since new constraints were imposed by mapping the node $i + 1$ to a new node of H.

If the algorithm manages to construct the matrix M^n a subgraph isomorphism has been found. If, on the other hand, cannot map a node i, than it backtracks and tries a new mapping for the node $i - 1$.

The *initial compatibility matrix* M^0 is built using a simple criterion, which checks whether a node $i \in V$ has at most the same degree as $j \in U$. More formally, we define M^0 as

$$m_{i,j}^0 = \begin{cases} 1 & \delta_G(i) \le \delta_H(j) \\ 0 & \text{otherwise.} \end{cases}$$

Algorithm 1 gives an overview of how Ullman's algorithm counts all the subgraph isomorphisms.

Algorithm 1. countIso() - counting subgraph isomorphisms with Ullman's algorithm

---

1 **Function** countIso(G,H, order, M^{depth}, depth);
   Input: graphs G and H, an ordering of pattern nodes *order*, current
         compatibility matrix M^{depth}, current *depth*
   Output: number of subgraph isomorphisms $G \to H$
2 nIso = 0;
3 i = order(depth);   // search strategy
4 **forall the** $j \in H$ **do**
5 │ **if** $M^{depth}(i,j) = 1$ **then**
6 │ │ **if** *depth* = n **then** all nodes mapped
7 │ │ │ nIso+=1;   // isomorphism found
8 │ │ **end**
9 │ │ **else**
10 │ │ │ $M^{depth+1}$ = refine(i,j,M^{depth});
11 │ │ │ nIso+=countIso(G,H,order, $M^{depth+1}$, depth+1);
12 │ │ **end**
13 │ **end**
14 **end**
15 **return** *nIso*

The crucial part of Ullmann's algorithm is the refinement of the compatibility matrix, which is shown in line 10. This function checks the entire matrix and tries to reduce the number of ones in the matrix by checking the neighborhoods of each pair of vertices. For two nodes, i and j, to stay compatible each node in the neighborhood of i must have at least one compatible node in the neighborhood of j. More formally, $m_{i,j} = 1$ if and only if

$$\forall x \in \mathcal{N}_G(i) \exists y \in \mathcal{N}_H(j) : m_{x,y} = 1.$$

The refinement checks this condition for each pair, and the pairs that are not compliant with this restriction are also not compatible anymore. Each refinement repeatedly sweeps the compatibility matrix until no more ones can be changed to zero. Notice that the refinement is quite a costly operation, i.e., $O(d_G nm\Delta_G \Delta_H)$, where d_G is the diameter of G, and Δ_G and Δ_H are the maximum degrees in G and H, respectively.

Due to this high complexity of the refinement procedure, a set of improvements were recently devised [13] that greatly improve its computational costs. We will call this algorithm UI (short for Ullmann improved). The main improvements of UI can be summarized in three points:

- Improved filtering - when a node i is assigned to another node j, they become incompatible with all the other nodes. This can be propagated into the

neighborhood of i, since nodes in $\mathcal{N}(i)$ are incompatible with the nodes not in $\mathcal{N}(j)$.
- Improved refinement - the complete refinement sweeps the entire matrix to check for any changes. The partial refinement checks only the neighborhood of the last changes in the matrix, resulting in a large spedup of the algorithm.
- Lowered space requirements - using a history of changes in the compatibility matrix, the space is reduced from $O(n^3)$ to $O(n^2)$.

These two algorithms will be used in the experimental evaluation of the described search strategies.

4   Search Strategies

Line 3 of Algorithm 1 defines a function which sorts the nodes of the pattern graph based on some criteria. We call that order the *search strategy*, we will sometimes use *node order* or simply order.

Concerning the correctness of the algorithm, the search strategy may be arbitrary, but concerning the efficiency it has a profound impact. The intuition for a good search strategy is to place the pattern nodes that are the least compatible with any target node high in the search strategy. This will prune the search tree as soon as possible, thus cutting the most branches and reducing the search space significantly.

In this sections we will explore various possibilities for the search strategies. Graph theory provides an abundance of features that can be taken into account when sorting the nodes. Our first goal is to devise a generalized framework into which these features can be plugged in.

The general sorting algorithm is composed of two criteria, which will iteratively select the next node in the search strategy:

1. The primary criterion will build a set of candidate nodes and
2. the secondary criterion will be used to select one node from the candidate set.

These two criteria are then interchanged until all the nodes of the pattern graph are in the search strategy. This idea is described in more detail in Algorithm 2.

Algorithm 2. Generalized sorting order algorithm

Data: pattern graph $G = \langle V, E \rangle$
Result: search strategy $ord : \mathbb{N} \to V$

1 $i = 0$;
2 $Vis = \emptyset$;   // visited nodes
3 **while** $i < |G|$ **do**
4 | $A =$ nodes in $V \setminus Vis$ by primary criterion;   // candidate set
5 | $v =$ choose node from A by secondary criterion;
6 | $ord(i) = v$;
7 | $Vis = Vis \cup \{v\}$;
8 | $i = i+1$;
9 **end**

This generalized algorithm represents a suitable framework for a variety of different approaches which can be used to find suitable search strategies. In what follows, we first describe a set of possible primary criteria and then a set of secondary criteria, which can be independently combined together to form a concrete instance of the sorting algorithm.

4.1   Primary Criteria

The primary criterion is used to select a candidate set of nodes, from which a single node will be selected based on the secondary criterion. In our case we will use this criterion to include some topological information into the search strategy, but it can also be used to get a set of candidates based on various other features of the graph.

All Nodes. This criterion is applied when we want to ignore any topology in the graph and use all the nodes as the candidates for the selection. In this case the secondary criterion is used as the only feature for ordering the nodes.

Depth. The candidate set in this case is the entire level of a breadth-first search, i.e. we start at an arbitrary node v and first sort all the nodes at distance 1, then all the nodes at distance 2, etc.

Neighborhood. This rule chooses the neighbors of the already visited nodes Vis. In the beginning when the set Vis is empty all the nodes of the graph are candidates for the selection. This means that the secondary criterion chooses the first node, and the order 'grows' from that node. The guiding force for this growth is the secondary criterion.

Maximum Subdegree. We define the *subdegree* of a node to be the number of edges from the node to the nodes in the set Vis:

$$d_{Vis}(v) = |\{u \in Vis | (v, u) \in E\}|$$

In this case the candidate set A is the set of all the nodes that have the maximum subdegree.

4.2   Secondary Criteria

We will use the secondary criteria to include some intuitive measures that prune the search tree as soon as possible.

Random. For comparison purpose we use a random selection from the candidate set A.

Degree. The order which was already proposed by Ullmann in [15] is the ordering of the pattern vertices by their degree (descending). The intuition behind this ordering is that the nodes with the highest degree can usually be mapped to the fewest target nodes, which reduces the search space already at the top levels of the search tree.

Open-Neighborhood Clustering. Another criterion which can be used for ordering the pattern nodes is the number of edges in the neighborhood of a node, i.e.

$$|\{e_{jk} : e_{jk} \in E \wedge v_j, v_k \in \mathcal{N}(i)\}|$$

This measure is sometimes called clustering, and this is the term we will use henceforth. Choosing nodes with higher clustering also reduces the search space, because more edges in the neighbourhood means more restrictions to the compatibility matrix.

Closed-Neighborhood Clustering. This criterion is the same as the open-neighborhood clustering, but instead of the open neighborhood, all the edges in the closed neighborhood $\mathcal{N}[i]$ are considered.

Eccentricity. The fourth criterion we are going to use is the eccentricity of a node. The eccentricity is simply the greatest distance from the node to any other node in the graph. With this measure we are preferring the nodes with lower eccentricity. The intuition behind this criterion is that we would like to start the search in the center of the graph, this means that the graph will be fixed in the target graph faster, resulting in a smaller search space.

We described four possibilities for the primary criterion and five possibilities for the secondary criterion. In the following we will abbreviate the primary criteria as: ALL (all nodes), DEPTH (depth), NEIGH (neighborhood), SUBD (maximal subdegree); and secondary criteria as: RND (random), DEG (degree), ONC (open-neighborhood clustering), CNC (closed-neighborhood clustering), and ECC (eccentricity). We can combine any primary criterion with any secondary criterion, so altogether we have 20 possible search strategies, a concrete instance will be denoted by the abbreviations of the primary and the secondary criteria used, e.g. DEPTH-ONC for depth primary criterion used with open-neighborhood clustering for secondary criterion.

4.3   Example

To demonstrate how this combinations work in practice, let us give an example of the NEIGH-DEG search strategy and SUBD-DEG criteria. Fig. 2 shows the graph and the two search strategies. The labels at the nodes represent the order of the nodes.

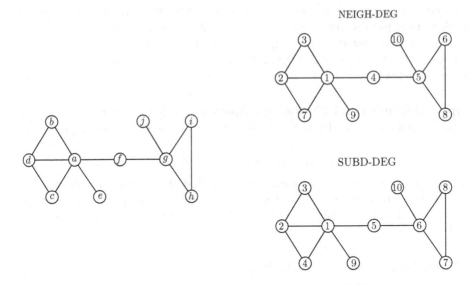

Fig. 2. The example graph labeled (left) with NEIGH-DEG (right-top) and SUBD-DEG (right-bottom) search strategies

How this ordering was obtained can easily be seen if we write down the candidate set A at each iteration of the algorithm, this shows the action of the primary criterion.

NEIGH-DEG	SUBD-DEG
1. $A = V$, $v = a$	1. $A = V$, $v = a$
2. $A = \{b, c, d, e, f\}$, $v = d$	2. $A = \{b, c, d, e, f\}$, $v = d$
3. $A = \{b, c, e, f\}$, $v = b$	3. $A = \{b, c\}$, $v = b$
4. $A = \{c, e, f\}$, $v = f$	4. $A = \{c\}$, $v = c$
5. $A = \{c, e, g\}$, $v = g$	5. $A = \{e, f\}$, $v = f$
6. $A = \{c, e, h, i, j\}$, $v = i$	6. $A = \{e, g\}$, $v = g$
7. ...	7. ...

5   Experimental Evaluation

The experiments were conducted on a well-known test-case library [4], which was used to evaluate several algorithms, e.g. [5–7, 14, 12]. For our evaluation we used the test-set of Erdős-Rényi random graphs of various sizes and various densities.

More specifically, we took 6300 test cases altogether. Graphs were generated with different features, one of them being the edge probability of 0.01, 0.05, and 0.1, the second one the sizes target graphs 20, 40, 60, 80, 100, 200, and 400. And the patterns were 20%, 40%, and 60% of the target graph.

To investigate the impact of the size of the problem instance on the running time we grouped these test cases into three groups: small graph (20, 40, 60 nodes

- 2700 test cases), medium graph (80, 100 nodes - 1800 test cases), and large graphs (200, 400 nodes - 1800 test cases).

All the tests were run on a 2.8-GHz iMac with an Intel Core i7 processor and 4 GB of memory running Mac OS X 10.6 Snow Leopard. The goal for the algorithm was to find all the subgraph ismorphisms.

The results are shown in the following manner. The x-axis shows the execution time (log-scale) and the y-axis shows the number of test cases that were solved in time $\leq x$.

For comparison reasons, let us look at a completely random search strategy, to demonstrate the impact that a search strategy has on the overall running time. Figure 3 shows a comparison between ALL-RND and ALL-DEG. Ullmann's algorithm with ALL-DEG managed to solve all the instances in under 10 seconds time, whereas with ALL-RND it solved less than 1000. We exclude the RND criterion from the further tests, since it is clearly non-competitive.

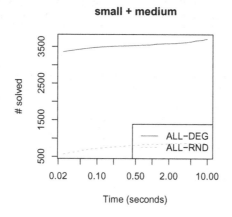

Fig. 3. The random search strategy vs. a simple degree strategy

5.1   Tests with Ullmann's Algorithm

Next we wil have a look at the results with of the testing of the classical Ullmann's algorithm with all the 16 remaining strategies. Figure 5 shows the results with the best search strategies for each of the primary criteria. In all cases the simplest DEG criterion was the best, and surprisingly there are almost no differences between primary criteria. This is a surprising result, since other criteria use more information about the graph and should thus obtain a better search strategy. It seems that the main reason (as it will be seen in the UI tests shortly) is the Ullmann's refinement procedure which finds all this information implicitly, so additionally incorporating it into the search strategy does not improve the running times.

From the strategies that are not shown in the results we can highlight the eccentricity, which performed quite bad in combination with all primary criteria.

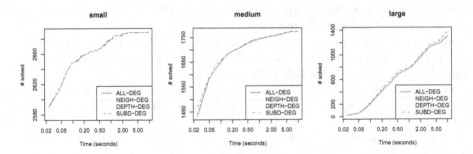

Fig. 4. The best search strategies for Ullman's algorithm

5.2 Tests with UI

The improved Ullmann's algorithm showed much more variety in the results. The best strategies are summarized in the graphs of Figure 5. The two best primary criteria are SUBD and NEIGH, while the best secondary criterion is CNC, closely followed by DEG.

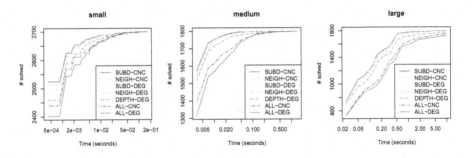

Fig. 5. The best sorting strategies for UI

Again, from the orders not shown in the results, eccentricity is not a good criteria to use as a UI search strategy, since it performed bad with all the primary criteria.

6   Conclusions

The main focus of this article are the possibilities to improve the exact algorithms for the subgraph isomorphism problem. Branch-and-bound algorithms use a so-called search strategy, i.e. an ordering of pattern nodes which guides the search for suitable mappings between pattern and target nodes. Search strategies have a large impact on the size of the search space so devising new ones is a promising aspect for speeding up current algorithms.

In this article we presented a systematic exploration and testing of search strategies in Ullmann's algorithm and an improved version called UI. We presented a two-criteria sorting algorithm for finding search strategies. This presents a framework which can used to systematically test many more criteria that can be taken from the rich set of features that can be found in graph theory.

We used 4 primary criteria and 5 secondary criteria to devise 20 possible search strategies.All these strategies were empirically evaluated on large test set of random graphs.

For the Ullmann's algorithm we demonstrated that, surprisingly,the basic search strategy ALL-DEG is still the most competitive since there were no significant speedups when compared to more complicated search strategies. We speculate that the main reason is the full refinement procedure used in Ullmann's algorithm that does not take into account any topological features of the graph, so also the search strategies that use this information do not help much. An open question for the future work is what are the features that could potentially improve the search strategy in this algorithm.

The algorithm UI shows much more diverse results, since its refinement and filtering procedures are highly dependent on the graph topology. The tests demonstrate that the primary criterion that works the best is maximum subdegree (SUBD) and the best secondary criterion is closed neighborhood clustering (CNC).

Even though we focused only on two algorithms, the general framework with two criteria sorting algorithm could be used also in VF2 or other algorithms that use a branch-and-bound paradigm. In our future work we will investigate the impact of search strategies in these algorithms as well as devise new criteria which could improve all the algorithms even further.

References

1. Balaban, A.T.: Applications of graph theory in chemistry. Journal of Chemical Information and Computer Sciences 25(3), 334–343 (1985)
2. Carrington, P.J., Scott, J., Wasserman, S.: Models and methods in social network analysis. Cambridge University Press (2005)
3. Cordella, L.P., Foggia, P., Sansone, C., Vento, M.: A (sub)graph isomorphism algorithm for matching large graphs. IEEE Trans. Pattern Analysis and Machine Intelligence 26(10), 1367–1372 (2004)
4. De Santo, M., Foggia, P., Sansone, C., Vento, M.: A large database of graphs and its use for benchmarking graph isomorphism algorithms. Pattern Recognition Letters 24(8), 1067–1079 (2003)
5. Foggia, P., Sansone, C.: A performance comparison of five algorithms for graph isomorphism. In: TC-15 Workshop on Graph-based Representations in Pattern Recognition (2001)
6. Foggia, P., Sansone, C., Vento, M.: A database of graphs for isomorphism and subgraph isomorphism benchmarking. In: Proc. of the 3rd IAPR TC-15 International Workshop on Graph-based Representations (2001)
7. Foggia, P., Sansone, C., Vento, M.: A Performance Comparison of Five Algorithm for Graph Isomorphism. In: 3rd IAPR-TC15 Workshop on Graph-based Representations in Pattern Recognition (2001)

8. Fürer, M., Prasad Kasiviswanathan, S.: Approximately counting embeddings into random graphs. In: Goel, A., Jansen, K., Rolim, J.D.P., Rubinfeld, R. (eds.) APPROX and RANDOM 2008. LNCS, vol. 5171, pp. 416–429. Springer, Heidelberg (2008)
9. Gupta, A., Nishimura, N.: The complexity of subgraph isomorphism for classes of partial k-trees. Theoretical Computer Science 164(1), 287–298 (1996)
10. He, Y., Evans, A.: Graph theoretical modeling of brain connectivity. Current Opinion in Neurology 23(4), 341–350 (2010)
11. Krahmer, E., Van Erk, S., Verleg, A.: Graph-based generation of referring expressions. Computational Linguistics 29(1), 53–72 (2003)
12. Lipets, V., Vanetik, N., Gudes, E.: Subsea: an efficient heuristic algorithm for subgraph isomorphism. Data Mining and Knowledge Discovery 19(3), 320–350 (2009)
13. Mihelič, J., Čibej, U.: Improvements of ullmann's algorithm for subgraph isomorphism (submitted for publication, 2013)
14. Solnon, C.: All Different-based filtering for subgraph isomorphism. Artificial Intelligence 174(12-13), 850–864 (2010)
15. Ullmann, J.R.: An Algorithm for Subgraph Isomorphism. J. Assoc. for Computing Machinery 23, 31–42 (1976)
16. Valiente, G.: Algorithms on Trees and Graphs. Springer (2002)

Analysis of Concentration Errors in Sample Dilution Algorithms on a Digital Microfluidic Biochip

Nilina Bera[1], Subhashis Majumder[1], and Bhargab B. Bhattacharya[2]

[1] Department of Computer Science and Engineering,
Heritage Institute of Technology, Kolkata, West Bengal 700 107, India
{nilina.bera,subhashis.majumder}@heritageit.edu
[2] Advanced Computing and Microelectronics Unit,
Indian Statistical Institute, Kolkata 700 108, India
bhargab@isical.ac.in

Abstract. Sample preparation is an important step in any biochemical protocol, and several algorithms are known for automating them on a digital microfluidic (DMF) lab-on-a-chip (LoC). On-chip dilution of a sample on a DMF biochip involves several mix-split steps, which often suffer from the inaccuracies caused by unbalanced splitting of micro-fluid droplets. Also, error minimization is essential because of the limited availability of the stock solutions and costly reagents. In this work, we analyze the performance of two dilution algorithms Min-Mix (Thies et al., 2008) and DMRW (Roy et al., 2010) in the presence of volumetric errors that may occur during the splitting process. Our analysis exposes many interesting error behaviors and indicates possible solutions to correct them in a cyber-physical microfluidic platform.

1 Introduction

Recent years have seen a surge in interest in designing automation methods for digital microfluidic (*DMF*) lab-on-chip (*LoC*) [1]. The emerging application areas include clinical diagnostics, enzymatic analysis, deoxyribonucleic acid (*DNA*) analysis, proteomic analysis, immunoassay and environmental toxicity analysis [1,2].

A DMF LoC is inexpensive, sensitive, fully automated, integrated, reliable and compatible with a broad range of samples. The DMF LoC technology offers the advantage of on-site chemical/bio-chemical analysis and detection. It also offers many other conveniences like portability, reduction of reactant usage, faster analysis times, increased automation, low power consumption and high throughput [3].

An LoC implements biochemical laboratory protocols or assays on a single chip that is around a few square centimeters in size. Research in this new discipline of nanobiotechnology needs the integration of many disciplines, such as, microelectronics, biochemistry, computer-aided design and optimization to name

P. Gupta and C. Zaroliagis (Eds.): ICAA 2014, LNCS 8321, pp. 89–100, 2014.

a few. Compared to traditional bench-top procedures, biochips offer the advantages of low sample and reagent consumption and less likelihood of errors due to minimal human intervention [1].

Electrowetting is one of the several techniques that is used to actuate microdroplets [4]. The use of electrowetting for droplet dispensing, transport, merging, mixing and splitting has been investigated [4][5]. More recently, an enzymatic glucose assay has also been demonstrated on an electrowetting based microfluidic device [6].

2   Concentration Error Control with Corrective Measures

In this work, we focus on the analysis of volumetric errors (ϵ) which are often introduced while diluting a sample on-chip. Analysis of concentration errors of the droplets is carried out during dispensing and splitting on-chip. A volumetric error is caused by an unbalanced splitting of a microfluid droplet. A volumetric error, in turn, may result in an unacceptable error in the target concentration of the sample. Dilution of a sample is an important step in almost all bio-analytical systems requiring sample preparation (pre-reaction).

An investigation of the concentration errors on a DMF platform has not yet been conducted to the best of our knowledge. It is therefore necessary to develop a scheme for the sample preparation step in a fully functional droplet-based microfluidic device. The primary sources of concentration error are: 1) droplet volume variation in dispensing and splitting operations; 2) inadequate mixing and 3) the presence of insoluble chemicals or contaminants in the droplets.

For our study we consider two dilution algorithms designed for DMF biochips: (i) TwoWayMix (TWM) based on bit scanning [7] and (ii) Dilution and Mixing with Reduced Wastage ($DMRW$) [8] based on a gradual convergence method.

To begin with, let us consider the generation of four target concentration factors (C_t): 1) $C_t = \frac{313}{1024} = 0.30566_{10} = 0.0100111001_2$; 2) $C_t = \frac{341}{1024} = 0.33301_{10} = 0.0101010100_2$; 3) $C_t = \frac{555}{1024} = 0.54199_{10} = 0.1000101010_2$; 4) $C_t = \frac{899}{1024} = 0.87793_{10} = 0.1110000011_2$; We assume 10 mix-split steps, so that the maximum concentration error is $\frac{1}{2^{11}}$.

In TWM method, the number of the waste droplets is always fixed. In general, DMRW produces fewer waste droplets than the TWM method[7]. The lower the wastage, the less is the concentration error and this relation is consistent over a wide range of errors introduced in the rotary mixers. Based on an error model, we now study the performance of these two algorithms.

Our proposed concentration error control model involving both TWM and DMRW algorithms introduces volumetric errors to the generated droplets during the dispensing and splitting phase. In (1:1) mix/split model, we assume that splitting of $2x$ volume droplet causes two resulting droplets of volume $(1 + \epsilon)x$ or $(1 - \epsilon)x$ respectively where the volumetric error ϵ is randomly chosen.

In addition, we have investigated if the volumetric error can be generated in a deterministic way based on the polarity of the rotary mixer. If the electrode in the reservoir is positively polarized, then, the electrode is activated to retract the liquid and pinch off a droplet with an additional volume (ϵ) always getting added to the unit volume droplet generated to create $(1+\epsilon)$. For a negatively polarized electrode, the pinched off droplet will not be one unit volume in measurement but will be always less than the unit volume. This means, ϵ will be always subtracted from the unit volume of the droplet producing resulting volume $(1 - \epsilon)$.

The on-chip experiment to generate droplets, one at a time, with volumetric error (ϵ) utilizing the TWM and DMRW schemes designed to execute both in random and deterministic fashions can definitely improve the scope of analysis and tracking of concentration error of droplets on DMF platform.

2.1 Extended TWM Scheme

The foundation of the extended TWM scheme is the original TWM method for mixing two or more fluids (sample/reagents) at any given ratio considering (1:1) mixing model. The algorithm converts C_t into its binary representation where the length of the binary bit stream represents the total number of mix/split operations. The TWM method scans the bits from right-to-left to generate droplets of intermediate CF ($C_{intermediate}$) with a goal to reach C_t [7].

In the extended TWM scheme, we consider two different ways by which volumetric error gets introduced in the process, one randomized and the other polarized. In the former case, the volumetric errors are introduced randomly with positive and negative signs as and when a bigger droplet is being split into unit droplets. However, in the polarized case, it is assumed that there may be a permanent error in the polarization of a pair of electrodes of the DMF rotary mixer, so that whenever they are used to split two unit droplets, one of them consistently draws a larger droplet $(v + \epsilon)$ towards it, so that the other droplet becomes smaller $(v - \epsilon)$ consistently. It is assumed that the rotary mixers are designed to randomly dispense the ϵ along with the unit volume droplets to create $C_{intermediate}$.

The deterministic generation of droplet is based on the assumption that for the positively polarized electrodes, ϵ is always added to and for the negatively polarized electrodes, ϵ is always subtracted from the number of droplets demanded for the mix/split operation to compute $C_{intermediate}$.

2.2 Extended DMRW Scheme

The extended DMRW scheme is designed to generate, analyze and investigate concentration errors associated with dilution control applying both random and deterministic techniques as explained in subsection 2.1.

The DMRW algorithm [8] starts with the two initial CFs. At every mix/split step, the algorithm requires only two CFs, called the boundary CFs, one lower and one higher than the C_t. The volumes of the droplets and $C_{intermediate}$ are calculated purely based on the volumes of the lower and higher sides of the resultant CF to be produced.

The wastage is nothing but pinching-off an extra volume (ϵ) that is either added to or subtracted from the required unit droplet volume (v) depending on the polarity of the electrode array of the DMF rotary mixer. For the deterministic condition with positively polarized electrodes, the result of the split operation would always produce $(v+\epsilon)$ and balance the leftover with $(v-\epsilon)$. This means, to utilize 3 droplets for successive mix/split operations, the required volume would be $(3v + 3\epsilon)$ and the leftover would be $(1v - 3\epsilon)$ considering the total volume of droplets produced in the earlier mixing operation is $4v$. For negative polarity, the resulting volume produced would be $(v - \epsilon)$ and the leftover would be $(v + \epsilon)$.

It was observed that at the final step, the deviations of the resultant CF from the target CF and the differential errors computed to reach the target CF are much more consistent in the DMRW scheme than in the TWM scheme.

2.3   Analysis of Concentration Errors for the DMRW Scheme

Let us consider an example when the target CF is $\frac{313}{1024}$ and $\epsilon = .001$. In the Extended DMRW scheme, step 3 (shown in Table 1) generates 6 volumes of $\frac{320.09595}{1024}$ as a result of mix/split operation. Out of this, 5 volumes of the $C_{intermediate}$ would be utilized in the successive iterations producing a waste droplet of volume $(1 - 5 * 0.001)$.

$$\frac{320.09595}{1024} = \frac{\frac{256.12793}{1024}.(3 + 3 * 0.0010) + \frac{384.06396}{1024}.(3 + 3 * 0.0010)}{6 + 6 * 0.0010} \tag{1}$$

Table 1. Extended DMRW with polarized error to reach Target CF : $\frac{313}{1024}$ with Positive Error 0.001

Step	Lower CF	Higher CF	Resultant CF	Volume at Lower Side	Volume at Higher Side	Total Droplets	Wastage
9	312.09995/1024	314.09894/1024	313.09943/1024	1 + 1*0.0010	1 + 1*0.0010	2	0
8	312.09995/1024	316.09796/1024	314.09894/1024	1 + 1*0.0010	1 + 1*0.0010	2	1 - 1*0.0010
7	312.09995/1024	320.09595/1024	316.09796/1024	1 + 1*0.0010	1 + 1*0.0010	2	1 - 1*0.0010
6	304.10394/1024	320.09595/1024	312.09995/1024	2 + 2*0.0010	2 + 2*0.0010	4	1 - 3*0.0010
5	288.11194/1024	320.09595/1024	304.10394/1024	1 + 1*0.0010	1 + 1*0.0010	2	0
4	256.12793/1024	320.09595/1024	288.11194/1024	1 + 1*0.0010	1 + 1*0.0010	2	1 - 1*0.0010
3	256.12793/1024	384.06396/1024	320.09595/1024	3 + 3*0.0010	3 + 3*0.0010	6	1 - 5*0.0010
2	256.12793/1024	512.0/1024	384.06396/1024	2 + 2*0.0010	2 + 2*0.0010	4	1 - 3*0.0010
1	0.0/1024	512.0/1024	256.12793/1024	3 +/- 0.0	3 + 3*0.0010	6	0
0	0.0/1024	1024.0/1024	512.0/1024	3 +/- 0.0	3 +/- 0.0	6	1 - 5*0.0010

Differential Error = 3.1765582E-4

During the dispensing of droplets, one at a time, from the DMF rotary mixer, we assume that the electrodes are positively polarized. Thus, instead of unit volume dispensing, the resulting volume of the droplet dispensed will be always $(1 + 1 * 0.001)$ (shown in Table 1). This means, from a mixer of 6 unit volume droplets with intermediate CF $\frac{512}{1024}$ (Step 0), if we want to utilize 3 unit volumes to create a set of droplets with intermediate CF $\frac{256.12793}{1024}$ (Step 1) and 2 unit volumes to create another set of droplets with intermediate CF $\frac{384.06396}{1024}$ (Step 2), then the desired volumes of droplets required for mix/split operations will be $(3 + 3 * 0.001)$ and $(2 + 2 * 0.001)$ respectively with a remaining $(1 - 5 * 0.001)$ left in the waste storage (Step 0).

In this example, we have applied ϵ as 0.001, the additional amount that is dispensed from the positively polarized electrodes along with the unit volume droplet. We have analyzed 20 different cases of variable amounts of volumetric error (ϵ) getting dispensed from the rotary mixer and being added to the unit volume droplet dispensed from the mixer.

Additionally, we have assumed that the DMF rotary mixer can be charged with negatively polarized electrodes. In this situation, the volumetric errors produced will be subtracted from the dispensed unit volume droplets. Thus, the resulting volume of the droplet dispensed will be always $(1 - 1 * 0.0010)$. This means, from a mixer of 6 unit volume droplets with $C_{intermediate}$ $\frac{255.87195}{1024}$, if we want to utilize 2 unit volumes to create a set of droplets with $C_{intermediate}$ $\frac{383.93597}{1024}$, 3 unit volumes to create set of droplets with $C_{intermediate}$ $\frac{319.90396}{1024}$ and the rest unit volume to create a set of droplets with $C_{intermediate}$ $\frac{287.88794}{1024}$ then the desired volumes of droplets required for mix/split operations will be $(2 - 2 * 0.001), (3 - 3 * 0.001)$ and $(1 - 1 * 0.001)$ respectively with 0.006 volume of wastage reported.

We tried both positive and negative polarities with rigorous trial conditions to make sure extended DMRW can handle concentration errors and waste minimization consistently and efficiently. To reach the target CF $\frac{313}{1024}$, if the differential error is $3.1765582E - 4$ (as shown in Table 1 footer) with the application of positive polarity, then the differential error will be the opposite $-3.1794832E - 4$ with the application of negative polarity.

2.4   Droplet Demand Calculation with Concentration Errors

During per execution step of the extended DMRW algorithm, the demand for the total number of unit volume droplets of the resultant $C_{intermediate}$ is calculated as follows: 1) If p be the total number of unit volume droplets of a resultant CF to be utilized in the successive steps of the mix/split sequence, then the total demand for the particular droplet is computed as $2 * \lceil \frac{p}{2} \rceil$. 2) For example, consider the 3rd step of the mix/split sequence as shown in Table 1. To determine the total demand for the droplets with resultant CF $\frac{320.09595}{1024}$, we sum up the number of unit volume droplets with CF $\frac{320.09595}{1024}$ needed in the subsequent mixing steps toward reaching the target CF $\frac{313}{1024}$. It is observed that a total of 6 unit volume droplets of $C_{intermediate}$ $\frac{320.09595}{1024}$ is required to generate new resultant CFs in subsequent 4 steps. 3) In this way, the complete mix/split sequence is scanned bottom-up to obtain the droplet demands of different $C_{intermediate}$ as shown in Volume at Lower Side, Volume at Higher Side and Total Droplets columns of Table 1.

2.5   Comparative Error Analysis of TWM and DMRW

We have carried out a performance analysis of the extended TWM and DMRW schemes with the introduction of volumetric errors. The lab-on-chip (LoC) experiment is performed not only with just one kind of volumetric error, i,e, ϵ is not just a constant volume additionally getting pinched off from the polarized electrode. The performance of the mixing/dilution algorithms have been studied against twenty different trial volumetric errors in the range (0.001 to 0.10) to generate four different target CF(s) as mentioned in section 2.

Table 2. Polarized Performance of TWM and DMRW algorithms to reach $C(t) = \frac{313}{1024}$ for polarized error

Trial	Volumetric Error	Bit Scanning (Polarized)			DMRW (Polarized)		
		Final Volume	Deviation	Target Error	Final Volume	Deviation	Target Error
1	0.001	313.1045	0.10449219	3.34E-04	313.09943	0.09942627	3.18E-04
2	0.002	313.20886	0.2088623	6.67E-04	313.1988	0.1987915	6.35E-04
3	0.003	313.31302	0.3130188	0.00100006	313.29803	0.29803467	9.52E-04
4	0.004	313.41714	0.41714478	0.001332731	313.39722	0.3972168	0.001269063
5	0.005	313.52112	0.52111816	0.001664914	313.49625	0.49624634	0.001585452
6	0.006000001	313.6251	0.62509155	0.001997098	313.5952	0.59521484	0.001901645
7	0.007000001	313.72885	0.7288513	0.002328598	313.6941	0.6940918	0.002217546
8	0.008	313.83267	0.8326721	0.002660294	313.79282	0.79281616	0.002532959
9	0.009000001	313.93625	0.9362488	0.00299121	313.89145	0.891449	0.00284808
10	0.010000001	314.0397	1.0397034	0.003321736	313.99008	0.9900818	0.003163201
11	0.02	315.06894	2.0689392	0.006610029	312.99008	-0.009918213	-3.17E-05
12	0.03	316.088	3.0880127	0.009865855	313.97043	0.97042847	0.00310041
13	0.04	317.09695	4.0969543	0.013089311	312.98038	-0.019622803	-6.27E-05
14	0.049999997	318.09598	5.095978	0.01628108	313.95123	0.9512329	0.003039083
15	0.059999995	319.08542	6.0854187	0.019442232	312.97092	-0.029083252	-9.29E-05
16	0.06999999	320.06525	7.0652466	0.022572672	313.93234	0.9323425	0.00297873
17	0.07999999	321.0358	8.035797	0.025673473	312.96155	-0.03845215	-1.23E-04
18	0.08999999	321.99698	8.996979	0.028744342	313.91388	0.9138794	0.002919742
19	0.09999999	322.94937	9.949371	0.031787127	312.95236	-0.04763794	-1.52E-04
20	0.109999985	323.89264	10.892639	0.034800764	313.89575	0.89575195	0.002861827

Simulation data for the polarized performance of TWM and DMRW schemes to reach $C(t) = \frac{313}{1024}$ is listed in the Table 2. We have computed the Final Volume after 10 mix/split operations to achieve the target CF. Measurement of the Deviation $((313 - FinalVolume))$ and the Target Error $(\frac{Deviation}{313})$ was carried out for 20 trials with volumetric errors ranging from 0.001 to 0.109999985.

Figure 1 to Figure 3 represent the performance plots of differential errors against trials to reach $C(t)$ $\frac{313}{1024}$, $\frac{341}{1024}$ and $\frac{555}{1024}$ respectively.

2.6   Corrective Measures for Extended DMRW Scheme

The extended DMRW scheme is designed to generate, analyze and investigate concentration errors associated with dilution control applying both random and polarized techniques as explained earlier.

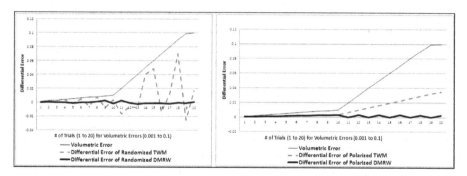

Fig. 1. Performance plot of TWM and DMRW algorithms to reach Target CF $\frac{313}{1024}$ displaying Differential Error

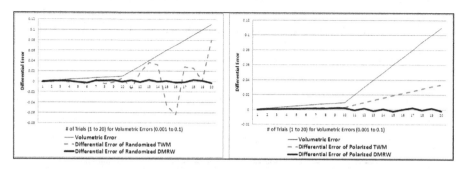

Fig. 2. Performance plot of TWM and DMRW algorithms to reach Target CF $\frac{341}{1024}$ displaying Differential Error

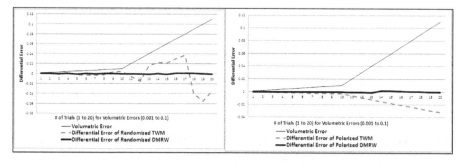

Fig. 3. Performance plot of TWM and DMRW algorithms to reach Target CF $\frac{555}{1024}$ displaying Differential Error

The Steps we have taken to introduce the corrective measures are:

•Dilution Step 1: Mix $v*\frac{0}{1024}$ with $v*\frac{1024}{1024}$ to produce the first $C_{intermediate}$ $(2v*\frac{512}{1024})$.

•Dilution Step 2: Mix $C_{intermediate}$ (as obtained from Step 1) without introducing ϵ with the lower or the upper bound of the concentration factor (*CFs*) as determined from the target *CFs*.

•Dilution Step 3 to the final step: Mix lower and upper bounds of the CF with ϵ as designed for the respective schemes, such as, DMRW-Positively-Polarized, DMRW-Negatively-Polarized or DMRW-Randomly-Polarized.

Only in the dilution step 2, we have avoided adding (subtracting) ϵ to (from) v as the corrective measure to use only the pure droplet volume without any ϵ. While progressing through the dilution steps to reach the final Target CF, the $C_{intermediate}$ being generated for the respective dilution steps is not affected by the mix/split operation with $(v + \epsilon)$ or $(v - \epsilon)$ as desired.

In the several experiments conducted to reach target CFs ($\frac{341}{1024}, \frac{555}{1024}, \frac{899}{1024}, \frac{313}{1024}$), our proposed scheme of error correction actually reduces the effect of concentration errors in the final concentration to be achieved. Figure 4 represents the Deviation of $C_{intermediate}$ from Target CF $\frac{341}{1024}$ with and without Corrective Measures.

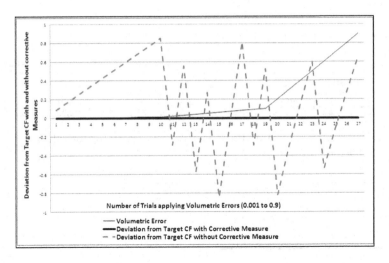

Fig. 4. Concentration Error Control with Corrective Measure : Tracking Deviation of $C_{intermediate}$ from Target CF $\frac{341}{1024}$

From the experiments, it is observed that if the dilution step 2 is made accurate then the other volumetric errors will have insignificant impact on the accuracy of the target concentration. Hence, by using a sensor-based checkpoint, the outcome of dilution step 2 can be tested and the re-mix and re-split strategy can be adopted to correct the error in cyber-physical systems.

3   Weighted Dilution

In this section, we present how weighted dilution can help us in the process of sample preparation and error analysis. We look forward to devise a generalized scheme for sample preparation on LoC, error computation and monitoring to achieve a user-defined C_t in case of weighted dilution.

DMF biochips work with discrete droplets, i.e., their volumes are always integral multiples of that of a single droplet (unit volume). In $(k : l)$ mixing model, k-unit volume of one substance is mixed with l-unit volume of another substance to produce $(k + l)$ unit volumes of the resultant mixture in a single mixing operation. Our proposed scheme is designed to create droplets with a target concentration C_t, converting the input droplets given in percentage of the sample.

The problem faced in case of weighted dilution scheme is that the technology is not quite ready yet to handle any general $(k : l)$ mixing or splitting case. Hence for our analysis, we have worked with the simplest case of $((1 : 2)$ or $(2 : 1))$ mixing along with $(1 : 1)$ mixing and splitting operations.

3.1 Motivation

In order to justify the usage of weighted dilution, we give below the different ways to create a typical sample of 37% (say) from a given 100% sample and 0% buffer solution. We use a number of (1:1) and (1:2) mixing steps to create the sample but note that the total number of steps in each case is 10. Table 3 represents the 11 alternative ways to create a sample of 37%.

Table 3. 11 Alternative Ways to create 37% Sample in exactly 10 Steps

Dilution Method	Number of 1:1 Steps	Number of 1:2 Steps	Denominator	37%=	Closest Integral Numerator	Fractional Error	Error in Concentration
0	10	0	$2^{10}=1024$	378.88/1024	379	0.12/1024	1.1718E-04
1	9	1	$2^{10}*3^1=1536$	568.32/1536	568	0.32/1536	2.08E-04
2	8	2	$2^8*3^2 = 2304$	852.48/2304	852	0.48/2304	2.08E-04
3	7	3	$2^7*3^3 = 3456$	1278.72/3456	1279	0.28/3456	8.1018E-05
4	6	4	$2^6*3^4 = 5184$	1918.08/5184	1918	0.08/5184	1.5432E-05
5	5	5	$2^5*3^5 = 7776$	2877.12/7776	2877	0.12/7776	1.5432E-05
6	4	6	$2^4*3^6 = 11664$	4315.68/11664	4316	0.32/11664	2.7434E-05
7	3	7	$2^3*3^7 = 17496$	6473.52/17496	6474	0.48/17496	2.7434E-05
8	2	8	$2^2*3^8 = 26244$	9710.28/26244	9710	0.28/26244	1.0669E-05
9	1	9	$2^1*3^9 = 39366$	14565.42/39366	14565	0.42/39366	1.0669E-05
10	0	10	$3^{10} = 59049$	21848.13/59049	21848	0.13/59049	2.2015E-06

For every alternative method, we present the 1) type of mixing model (number of 1 : 1 and 1 : 2 mixing steps); 2) denominator for the specified mixing method; 3) equivalent fraction for 37% sample; 4) closest integral numerator; 5) fractional error and 6) error in concentration. Note that, though we have used the same number of steps in all the alternatives, the error in the target concentration reduces with increasing number of weighted steps, which may be one of the motivations to study the weighted dilution methodology.

3.2   Overview of Weighted Dilution Algorithm

We propose to start the algorithm with two initial *CFs*. Like DMRW algorithm, at every mix/split step, the algorithm requires only the two initial CFs, called the boundary CFs, one lower and one higher than the C_t. Based on the proximity of C_t to the lower (left) or higher (right) boundaries, we would apply the weighted mix model ((2:1) or (1:2) respectively). If C_t is inclined more towards the lower CF, then the lower CF is mixed more to generate the intermediate CF, i.e., we can generate the $C_{intermediate}$ by making the mixture using (2 : 1) ratio. Otherwise, the upper CF is mixed more to generate the $C_{intermediate}$ using (1 : 2) mix ratio. However, to achieve the target in minimum number of steps, sometimes a deviation from the above general rule is required. The step creation is totally dynamic and the target can be reached either with just one dilution step or in several steps subjected to a maximum number. It can be proved by induction that, we can achieve any target numerator (C_t) on top of a pre-computed denominator. The denominator depends on the number of 1 : 1 and 1 : 2 (or 2 : 1) steps allowed. For lack of space, we omit the details of the proof.

As for example, our proposed weighted dilution scheme is able to reach any target numerator (1 to 431) on top of a pre-computed denominator ($2^4*3^3 = 432$) that can be obtained by mixing of 4 steps of balanced (1 : 1) mixing and 3 steps of weighted ((1 : 2) or (2 : 1)) mixing. The target C_t may be achieved either with just 1 step of (1:1) mixing or by using a maximum of 7 mix/split steps.

We cite some more examples to show the working procedure of our algorithm,

1) $C_t = \frac{216}{432}$: Use just one step of mixing $\frac{0}{432}$ with $\frac{432}{432}$ using (1:1) mix-model.
2) $C_t = \frac{217}{432}$: Need all possible 7 steps; first 4 steps with balanced (1 : 1) dilution and the next 3 steps with weighted (2 : 1) dilution.
3) $C_t = \frac{405}{432}$: Use 4 balanced (1 : 1) steps.
4) $C_t = \frac{399}{432}$: 6 steps need 4 balanced (1 : 1) and two weighted mix/split steps.
In Table 4, we show in detail how to achieve $C_t = \frac{399}{432}$.

Table 4. Dilution steps obtained to reach Target $= \frac{399}{432}$

Step 1: Mix 0/432 with 432/432 to obtain 216/432 using (1:1) mix-model.
Step 2: Mix 216/432 with 432/432 to obtain 324/432 using (1:1) mix-model.
Step 3: Mix 324/432 with 432/432 to obtain 378/432 using (1:1) mix-model.
Step 4: Mix 378/432 with 432/432 to obtain 405/432 using (1:1) mix-model.
Step 5: Mix 378/432 with 405/432 to obtain 396/432 using (1:2) mix-model.
Step 6: Mix 396/432 with 405/432 to obtain 399/432 using (2:1) mix-model.

Note that in Table 4, since 396 is closer to 405 than 378 we use 1:2 in Step 5, whereas 399 is closer to 396 than 405, we use 2:1 in Step 6.

3.3   Wastage Minimization

Our proposed algorithm in case of Weighted Dilution is designed to reduce the number of dilution steps thereby reducing the wastage of droplets, implying consumption of smaller volume of samples and reagents as compared to earlier methods using only (1:1) mix models. In other words, the scheme will ensure an efficient and faster operation with minimal error and thus will be time and cost effective.

Table 5. Comparison Measurement of Weighted and Balanced Dilutions

S. No.	Number of Dilution Steps	Denom.	Avg # of Dilution Steps over all fractions	Avg # of Waste Droplets	Avg # of Droplets of Total Input (Sample+Buffer)	% of Wastage
1	6 (1:1) + 2 (1:2) Steps	576	7.46	4.18	7.07	59.12
	9 (1:1) Steps	512	8.02	4.49	6.49	69.18
2	5 (1:1) + 3 (1:2) Steps	864	7.49	4.78	7.75	61.68
	9 (1:1) Steps	512	8.02	4.49	6.49	69.18
3	5 (1:1) + 3 (1:2) Steps	864	7.49	4.78	7.75	61.68
	10 (1:1) Steps	1024	9.01	5.02	7.02	71.51
4	7 (1:1) + 2 (1:2) Steps	1152	8.45	4.71	7.6	61.97
	10 (1:1) Steps	1024	9.01	5.02	7.02	71.51
5	7 (1:1) + 3 (1:2) Steps	3456	9.48	5.86	8.82	66.44
	12 (1:1) Steps	4096	11	6.12	8.12	75.37
6	9 (1:1) + 2 (1:2) Steps	4608	10.45	5.82	8.71	66.82
	12 (1:1) Steps	4096	11	6.12	8.12	75.37

Since, a (2:1) mixing step is considered more costly than a (1:1) mixing step in present day technology, it is not fully justified to compare two alternative methods having the same number of steps as done in subsection 3.1. So, in Table 5, we compare a fully balanced mixing procedure with a composite procedure (with some weighted steps), whose denominators are close to one another. We have compared the average value of important parameters, such as, the number of total input droplets, the number of waste droplets and the number of dilution steps. We have used several balanced procedures with denominators (512, 1024, 4096) and several weighted procedures with denominators (576, 864, 1152, 3456, 3888, 4608). Note that in all the six comparisons the percentage of wastage in case of the corresponding Weighted Scheme was about 10% less than its Balanced counterpart, as listed in the last column of Table 5. This fact was true, irrespective of whether its denominator was more or less than the balanced procedure.

4   Conclusion

A thorough and critical analysis of the DMRW scheme versus the TWM algorithm was undertaken to assess their tolerance for concentration errors over a wide range of concentration factors (CF) for DMF Biochips. Our proposed concentration error control model including corrective measures to reach C_t, enables us to compute the error in terms of the deviations of the resultant CFs from the target CFs. Comparing the concentration errors obtained from the DMRW method in differential and percentile modes with those obtained from the TWM method, it is observed that for a given C_t, the results from DMRW method are more precise, reproducible and reliable and therefore, the DMRW method is more efficient and consistent relative to the TWM method in terms of error control.

We further investigated a weighted dilution scheme where we have worked with the simplest case of (2 : 1) mixing along with (1 : 1) mixing and splitting operations. Our analysis shows that if technology permits, introducing some (2 : 1) steps along the traditional (1 : 1) steps actually reduces the effect of concentration errors in the final concentration achieved. In other words, the scheme will ensure an efficient and faster operation with minimal error and thus will be time and cost effective.

References

1. Chakrabarty, K., Xu, T.: Digital Microfluidic Biochips: Design and Optimization. CRC Press (2010)
2. Ren, H., Srinivasan, V., Fair, R.B.: Design and testing of an interpolating mixing architecture for electro wetting-based droplet-on-chip chemical dilution. In: Proc. Int. Conf. Solid-state Sensors, Actuators Microsyst. (Tranducers), pp. 619–622 (2003)
3. Fair, R.B., Srinivasan, V., Ren, H., Paik, P., Pamula, V.K., Pollack, M.G.: Electrowetting-based on-chip Sample processing for integrated microfluidics. In: Proc. IEEE IEDM Tech. Dig., pp. 32.5.1–32.5.4 (2003)
4. Pollack, M.G., Shendorov, A.D., Fair, R.B.: Electrowetting-based actuation of droplets for integrated microfluidics. Lab on a Chip 2(1), 96–101 (2002)
5. Paik, P., Pamula, V.K., Pollack, M.G., Fair, R.B.: Electrowetting-based droplet mixers for microfluidic systems. Lab on a Chip 3(1), 28–33 (2003)
6. Srinivasan, V., Pamula, V., Pollack, M.G., Fair, R.B.: A digital microfluidic biosensor for multianalyte detection. In: Technical Digest MEMS 2003, pp. 327–330 (2003)
7. Theis, W., Urbanski, J.P., Thorsen, T., Amarasinghe, S.: Abstraction layers for scalable microfluidic biocomputing. Nat. Comput. 7(2), 255–275 (2008)
8. Roy, S., Bhattacharya, B.B., Chakrabarty, K.: Optimization of Dilution and Mixing of Biochips. IEEE TCAD 29(11), 1696–1708 (2010)

Choosing and Working of an Anonymous Leader

M.R. Rajeevalochana and Kannan Srinathan

International Institute of Information Technology

Abstract. We revisit the problem of anonymous communication where nodes communicate without revealing their identity. We propose its use in the choosing of a node as an anonymous leader and subsequent communication to and from this leader such that its identity is not revealed. We give indistinguishability definitions for anonymous leader and prove it to be secure in an arbitrary reliable network.

Keywords: Anonymous channels, Leader, Secure Multi-party computation, Trusted third party.

1 Introduction

1.1 Anonymous Communication

Anonymity in communication can be either sender anonymity or receiver anonymity or both. Anonymity is maintained if by sending a message a node's identity of being sender/receiver isn't revealed to other nodes.

Chaum introduced the concept of anonymous communication in his seminal paper [1] with the idea of mix nets. Messages while traversing through intermediate routers are mixed with other messages such that any relation to the original sender is lost. Much research has since gone into optimising and and strengthening this idea. Onion routing [2] , for example, is a popular practical approach used in anonymous mailing and browsing. DC nets, also proposed by Chaum [3], allow the broadcasting of messages without revealing the sender. An advantage of the DC net is its non-interactivity, in the sense that after an initial key exchange, players can broadcast messages without any further player to player communications. A drawback however is that an adversary can corrupt or block messages without being traced. Detecting such an adversary often comes at a cost to computation, communication or increase in rounds [4].

Hevia and Micciancio [5] give strong mathematical and yet intuitive formal definitions of anonymity of the sender and receiver, where the adversary (and other nodes) do not gain any information beyond that leaked by the channel. They measure anonymity as the indistinguishability of the sender (or receiver) from other nodes by looking at the transcript of all messages received by each node. In our paper, we shall use a modified definition of anonymity such that not all nodes can communicate anonymously. Indeed, we want only the leader (more on this below) to do so.

Waidner, in [6], builds on the DC net by Chaum. His protocol called the DC+ net makes use of collision resolving protocols to enable the DC net to

P. Gupta and C. Zaroliagis (Eds.): ICAA 2014, LNCS 8321, pp. 101–109, 2014.

avoid honest collisions in communication. However, it is not secure against an active adversary, such as deliberate collisions or modifying messages.

1.2 Leader

A leader in general is one who takes decisions and/or directs the flow of work. In computer science however, the concept of a leader is looser. The leader can be one who actively has power and control in the protocol, or only takes some special action different from other nodes in the protocol, such as the one to initiate the protocol. Some examples of nodes performing special actions include firewalls, routers, key generators, servers, etc.

1.3 Our Contribution

Anonymous Leader. Due to its special nature, the leader is often the focus of adversarial attack. For example, a server maintaining the session keys of the other nodes is the weak point of security in the network, and hence more likely to being attacked. We propose the use of anonymous communication to hide the leader from the other nodes, and hence make it harder for the adversary to specifically attack it. We give a formal definition of anonymous leader, where one node is chosen as the leader uniformly at random, and give protocols to enable this chosen leader to communicate with the other nodes while maintaining anonymity. At no time must the adversary or other nodes realise which node is the leader. The node elected as leader is subverted independent of the protocol if it is already under adversarial control.

Applications. We propose 1 possible way to make use of the anonymous leader protocol. The program to be run on a simulated TTP can suffer delay due to the computation required to simulate it. We propose that only a few nodes take part in simulating the TTP so that the computation requirements on the other nodes is decreased so is the network traffic. But to ensure that the adversary does not target these nodes, we propose to make them anonymous, so that it is not known which nodes are part of the simulation and which are not. This ensures that the adversary cannot do better than assume that all the nodes are part of the simulation and attack indiscriminately. But, this method is only efficient if the computation cost of simulating the program by all the nodes is significantly higher than simulating it only only a few nodes and the added cost of keeping them anonymous. Other possible applications of anonymous leader is left as future work.

2 Preliminaries

2.1 Network

The network in this paper is considered to be a set of nodes connected by point to point channels with leakage. The channels are reliable, i.e. messages cannot be modified within a channel. Each node also acts as a router between nodes on opposite sides of it, i.e. each node knows the network layout and participates in routing messages. The leak is of the form : (a) Total network flow is public: all messages sent in the system are known to all nodes. (b) Traffic per party: the messages sent or received by a particular node are also known to all nodes. Such a leak implies that all communication is public knowledge, and hidden, private communication are not allowed.

2.2 Adversary

The nodes in the network are semi honest in that they will execute the protocol given to them but will try to gain information in the background. In addition, some nodes might be under adversarial control. The adversary is modelled as a Byzantine adversary i.e. adversarial nodes can arbitrarily diverge from the protocol, can send wrong messages or even actively try to sabotage the network. But the adversary is constrained to behave in such a manner that it is not caught. Adversarial nodes cannot take actions that reveal themselves to be subverted. The variable t represents the total number of adversarial nodes in the network, while n represents the total number of nodes. This model captures both the fact that the honest nodes do not trust each other and the presence of the adversary.

2.3 Trusted Third Party

Trusted third party (TTP) is a node that is unanimously trusted by all nodes in the network. This also means that the TTP cannot be subverted by an adversary. In practice, this is not possible and hence TTP cannot exist. But, all the nodes together can simulate such a trusted third party with the help of security primitives such as the one way function. This immediately puts a restriction on the nodes as well as the adversary to be bound by probabilistic polynomial time. The simulated trusted third party can then be used to securely solve multi-party problems. By secure, we mean that no node gains any information beyond that which they gain from the simulated third party's program output as well as the program code itself, since the program must be known to all the nodes to be able to simulate it. If the Universal Turing Machine (UTM) is run on the simulated TTP with the actual program as input to it, the nodes will not know this actual program code, and hence will be unable to derive information from it. Unfortunately, simulating the UTM is extremely expensive computationally, and a driving force is to find efficient multi-party protocols. The simulation of a TTP is quite involved [7] [8] [9] [10]and reduced to simulation of the XOR and AND gates, which are proven secure, using which we can simulate any program as a combination of XOR and NAND securely, such as arithmetic and logical operations. In this paper, we will consider the Simulated third party as a black box with secure channels between it and the various nodes as well as secure protocols to execute operations on $(+, *, GF_{2^n})$ and $(+, *, Z_P)$ finite fields, although this can be generalised to other fields. $+$ on GF2 is equivalent to the XOR boolean operation. Let a black box secure protocol for logical operation be given too, defined as a function $f(x, y)$ where $x, y \in GF2^n$ or Z_P and mapped to $\{0, 1\}$ such that $f(x, y) = 1$ if $x = y$, else 0. These protocols are built on the XOR and AND gates.

2.4 Verifiable Secret Sharing

Each memory block of the simulated TTP is stored as a block on each node, such that the XOR of all these blocks gives the actual memory block to be stored, i.e. each node stores an XOR copy or share. Sending data to the TTP is simulated as first getting n XOR shares of that data, and sending one share to each node. Faster protocols use Shamir secret sharing rather than XOR shares. Since a node under adversarial control can deviate arbitrarily, it might corrupt its share and hence corrupt a memory block of the TTP. To prevent this, we will use Verifiable Secret Sharing (VSS). Given t adversarial nodes, each share must have copies to detect if any of the copies get corrupted. Optimal and efficient protocols for this have been designed already, for example [11]. Unfortunately, VSS puts a bound on the number of adversaries tolerable (fault tolerance), more precisely it requires that $n > 3t + 1$.

2.5 Anonymous Communication

Hevia and Micciancio [5] give an indistinguishability based definition for anonymous communication. The variants of sender and receiver anonymity are modelled as part of the leak in the network. The indistinguishability game has the adversary produce two message matrices (of the form $M_{(i,j)}$ = message set of all messages sent from node i to node j), is allowed to observe the anonymous communication protocol on the network passively under one of these message matrices, and is then required to have a non-negligible advantage in determining under which matrix the protocol was executed. The two message matrices must have the same leak information, i.e. if $f(M)$ is the leak, then $f(M_1) = f(M_2)$ for the message matrices M_1 and M_2 given by the adversary. Since the adversary can freely choose the values and destinations of all messages in the protocol (i.e. the message matrix), it follows that a protocol anonymous under this definition must hide all partial information on the message matrix M except for what is implied by the known information $f(M)$. In particular, sources and destinations of the messages are hidden up to the extent that they do not follow from the known information. However, we modify this definition to account for two changes:

- The adversary in their model is passive, while we allow an active adversary in the network.
- Our protocol must allow only the leader node to be able to communicate anonymously and not all nodes.

We shall define the anonymous leader in terms of anonymous communication as an indistinguishability game and give protocols that satisfy this definition.

2.6 Model, Notation and Assumptions

Define the network (n, t) as follows: Let n be the total number of nodes, each of which is indexed by x in $[0, n-1]$, and define N as the set of the nodes. Let A be the set of adversarial nodes and t be the number of adversarial nodes. Let $V = \{0, 1\}^l$ be the message space with $l = l(k)$ being the message length for some polynomial l in parameter k. Let $X = \{X_n\}_{n \in N}$ be a Probability ensemble such that X_n is a distribution on the parameter n. Define the execution of protocol π with input $I = I(x)$ for $x \in [0, n]$ under adversary A as the process where each node x follows the instructions of protocol π using $I(x)$ as input . Let M be the message matrix such that $m_{i,j}$ is the (multi)set of messages from node i to node j at the end of the protocol. Define the notation for the given protocols on the simulated TTP as:

- $a + b$, $a * b$, where $a, b \in GF_{2^n}$ and $+$, $*$ are the operations defined as such on this group. The operations are securely implemented by black box protocols.
- XOR(a, b) is equivalent to $a + b$ in GF_2, and bitwise $a + b$ in GF_{2^n}, i.e. $s[i] = a[i] + b[i]$ on all bit positions i, where $+$ is on GF_2.
- if_equal(a, b) stands for the logical equality comparison protocol, it returns 1 if $a = b$ and 0 otherwise. $a = b$ if $a - b = 0$, where $-$ is the negation of the $+$ operation on the group.

3 Anonymous Leader

3.1 Definition 1: Anonymous Leader

Given a network (n, t) with n total nodes, t of which are adversarial. Let node i be the anonymous leader and P_n the prior probability distribution of the adversary, where $P_n(x)$ is the probability estimate of the node x being the leader. For any input $I = I(x)$ for $x \in [0, n - 1]$ and message matrix M, where $M_{a,b}$ is the (multi)set of messages from node a to node b at the end of the protocol, given by the adversary, protocol run on input I and sending messages exactly as given by message matrix M maintains leader anonymity iff the posterior probability $Pr_n(x)$ the probability of node x being the leader is indistinguishable from the prior probability.

$|P_n(x) - Pr_n(x \text{ given } M)| < \mu(x)$,for some negligible function $\mu(x)$

This definition can be reduced to being secure over message set of messages sent to and from the anonymous leader. Intuitively, any communication with the anonymous leader must not reveal any information of which node is the anonymous leader. If node i, the leader, is already subverted, then $P_n(i) = 1$, and maintains this probability independent of protocol, and hence satisfies the definition. The adversary wins the game if he comes up with an input I and message matrix M such that the posterior probability becomes distinguishable from the prior probability, and hence gains information on the leader.

3.2 Choosing the Anonymous Leader

Choosing the anonymous leader is simply letting a particular node know that it is legitimate leader, without revealing it to other nodes.

Theorem 1. There can be no valid choosing of an anonymous leader without the existence of a trusted third party or bystander.

Proof. Any choosing or election protocol executed internally within the network reveals as output the node elected, and hence fails. Since, before the protocol, every node has equal chance of being chosen as the leader, no prior information can be used to selectively gain information. Hence, no choosing is possible. Solution with existence of a trusted vote collector or third party can be seen easily as follows: the TTP randomly chooses a node as leader and sends a bit $b_n(x)$ to each node x securely, where $b_n(x)$ is 1 if x is the leader and 0 else. Since a bit is sent to each node, adversary cannot know which node got bit 1 unless that node is already adversarial.

Protocol 1 Choosing the Leader. Since, a true trusted third party does not exist, we simulate one (as explained in introduction above). Define the protocol P on the network running a simulated third party as:

- Each node $x \in N$ generates a $log(n)$ bit string uniformly at random, say r_x and sends it to the simulated TTP.
- The simulated TTP does XOR of all these bit strings, i = XOR(r_x for all $x \in N$)
- Let i be the node chosen as leader.
- Simulated TTP sends if_equal(x,i) to every node x in the network, and re-members i for future communication.

Correctness. Only node i gets the bit 1 securely, while all other nodes get the bits 0. Since XOR and if_equal are known to be secure simulations, protocol P is secure too. Further, the probability of node x being selected is uniformly random and hence does not reveal any information to the adversary.

3.3 Communication with the Chosen Anonymous Leader: Leader as the Anonymous Receiver

Assume Protocol 1 has been executed to choose node i as the leader. Now, we want the node i as the leader to be able to receive messages from other nodes without revealing to other nodes that it is the leader, i.e. satisfy definition 1 above.

Protocol 2 Leader as Anonymous Receiver. Let node S be the sender and leader be the receiver. The protocol is quite simple. Node S sends the message m $\in$ M as a multi cast to all the other nodes. Hashing schemes or secure protocols can be used to ensure the message m is not modified en route by the adversary. Although, only the leader node needs to receive the correct un-modified message m.

Correctness. Since, message is being received by all the nodes, adversary has no way to gain information on the leader. His probability estimate remains same, and hence satisfies Definition 1 above and is secure.

3.4   Communication with the Chosen Anonymous Leader: Leader as the Anonymous Sender

Theorem 2. Anonymous communication while satisfying Definition of anonymous leader above is impossible without the existence of a trusted bystander or third party which actively helps in the protocol.

Proof. Anonymous channel by definition implies any node can potentially communicate through it. But, we want only the anonymous leader to communicate anonymously, and hence require a sort of filter. But, we want the filter to be trusted as it should not reveal who the leader is. Any filtering within the network fails as other nodes have no knowledge of who the leader is, and hence cannot distinguish legitimate leader from communicating and an adversarial node pretending to be the leader. Hence, the filter must be a trusted outside person, or third party.

Protocol 3 Leader as Anonymous Sender. Since, a true trusted third party does not exist, we simulate one within the network. Let leader be the sender and R be the receiver. Simulate a TTP on the network such that it knows already who the leader is, and let Protocol P be defined as:

- Each node $x \in N$ not the leader, generates a random message m_x and sends to simulated TTP. Node i, the leader, sends its original intended message m to simulated TTP.
- Simulated TTP computes the sum S = $\displaystyle\sum_{\text{each node } x \in N} m_x * if\_equal(x, i)$, where i is the random node selected in Protocol 1 as the anonymous leader.
- Simulated TTP sends this sum S to the receiver R.

Correctness. Since all nodes send some message to the simulated TTP, step 1 is secure. Since multiplication and if_equal are securely executed with sub protocols, the computation of sum S is also secure. Furthermore, the sum S is exactly equal to the message m that the leader wants to send, as if_equal(x,i) will be 1 only when x=i, which is the case for the leader only. Hence, the receiver receives the message m as the sum S securely without revealing the leader's identity. The adversary gains no information after completion of the protocol, and hence the protocol satisfies Definition 1 above and is secure.

4   Applications

4.1   Optimised Simulation of TTP

In an (n, t) network having n total nodes, t of which are adversarial, a secure TTP is simulated by all the nodes in the network. Depending on the complexity of the program running on the simulated TTP, this results in a huge amount of computation at each node (a lot of the nodes performing the same computation to ensure adversary cannot corrupt the memory) as well as network traffic. We propose the use of our protocols with some modification to select not 1 but k (a small constant) number of anonymous leaders and to simulate the TTP over these anonymous leaders, with the driving focus being reduction in computation. Only the nodes chosen as anonymous leaders have to simulate the TTP and execute the program given to it. The other nodes only have to contribute in maintaining the anonymous leader protocol. This would be effective if the complexity of the program to be run on a TTP simulated by all the nodes is much more than the complexity to run the same program on a TTP simulated by only k nodes plus the complexity of the anonymous leader protocol to keep these k nodes anonymous. The anonymous leader protocol must thus allow selecting k leaders, each of which can talk anonymously not just with the other nodes but with each other as well. Note that the anonymous leader protocol simulates a TTP as well, and we will distinguish by calling the actual TTP simulation and program as Original-TTP and Original-Program respectively.

Protocol 4 Selecting k Anonymous Leaders. Slight modification to Protocol 1. Define the protocol P on the network running the simulated third party as:

- Each node x $\in$ N generates k number of $log(n)$ bit strings uniformly at random, say $r_{x_i}, i \in [0, k-1]$ and sends it to the simulated TTP.
- The simulated TTP does XOR of all these bit strings, $l_i = XOR(r_{x_i}, x \in N), i \in [0, k-1]$
- Let l_i be the k nodes chosen as leaders.
- Simulated TTP sends $OR(if\_equal(x, l_i)$ for all $i \in [0, k-1]$)to every node x in the network, and remembers l_i for future communication.

Protocol 5 Leader as Anonymous Sender and Receiver. For the sender to be anonymous, all the nodes must talk, and for the receiver to be anonymous, all the nodes must listen. Let leader a be the sender and leader b be the receiver. Simulate a TTP on the network such that it knows already who the leaders are i.e $l_i, i \in [0, k-1]$, and let Protocol P be defined as:

- Each node x $\in$ N not the leader a, generates a random message m_x and sends to simulated TTP. Node a, the leader, sends its original intended message m to simulated TTP.
- Simulated TTP computes the sum S $= \displaystyle\sum_{\text{each node } x \in N} m_x * OR(if\_equal(x, l_i),$ $i \in [0, k-1])$.
- Simulated TTP broadcasts this sum S to all the nodes.

Protocol 6 the Optimised TTP

- Select/elect k anonymous leaders.
- Simulate the Original-TTP on these k nodes, and run the Original-Program on the Original-TTP.

5   Conclusion

The security of the Protocols 2 and 3 enable the working and communicating of 1 or more nodes chosen uniformly at random as the leader. Although one application has been discussed, it is our strong belief that its applications can be far reaching and not entirely explored and left as future work. The simulation of the TTP, specifically the AND gate, and consecutively the logical and arithmetic operations are costly operations that require communication between the various nodes. The protocols above are neither proven optimal nor are they proven to depend on simulating the TTP. Indeed, optimal solutions might not directly require a simulated TTP and our solution is in some sense an ideal solution. The focus is only to prove existence, and optimal protocols are beyond the scope of this paper.

References

1. Chaum, D., Rivest, R., Chaum, D.L.: Untraceable electronic mail, return addresses, and digital pseudonyms. Communications of the ACM 24, 84–88 (1981)
2. Reed, M.G., Syverson, P.F., Goldschlag, D.M.: Anonymous connections and onion routing. IEEE Journal on Selected Areas in Communications 16, 482–494 (1998)
3. Chaum, D.: The dining cryptographers problem: Unconditional sender and recipient untraceability. Journal of Cryptology 1, 65–75 (1988)
4. Golle, P., Juels, A.: Dining cryptographers revisited. In: Cachin, C., Camenisch, J.L. (eds.) EUROCRYPT 2004. LNCS, vol. 3027, pp. 456–473. Springer, Heidelberg (2004)
5. Hevia, A., Micciancio, D.: An indistinguishability-based characterization of anonymous channels. In: Borisov, N., Goldberg, I. (eds.) PETS 2008. LNCS, vol. 5134, pp. 24–43. Springer, Heidelberg (2008)
6. Waidner, M.: Unconditional sender and recipient untraceability in spite of active attacks. In: Quisquater, J.-J., Vandewalle, J. (eds.) EUROCRYPT 1989. LNCS, vol. 434, pp. 302–319. Springer, Heidelberg (1990)
7. Michael, B.-O., Shafi, G., Avi, W.: Completeness theorems for non-cryptographic fault-tolerant distributed computation. In: Proceedings of the Twentieth Annual ACM Symposium on Theory of Computing, STOC 1988, pp. 1–10. ACM, New York (1988)
8. Damgard, I., Geisler, M., Kroigaard, M., Nielsen, J.: Asynchronous multiparty computation. Theory and implementation IACR e-print eprint.iacr.org/2008/415
9. Goldreich, O., Micali, S., Wigderson, A.: How to play any mental game. In: Symposium on Theory of Computing, STOC, pp. 218–229 (1987)
10. Yao, A.: How to generate and exchange secrets. In: Foundations of Computer Science, FOCS, pp. 162–167 (1986)
11. Gennaro, R., Micali, S.: Verifiable secret sharing as secure computation. In: Guillou, L.C., Quisquater, J.-J. (eds.) EUROCRYPT 1995. LNCS, vol. 921, pp. 168–182. Springer, Heidelberg (1995)

An Efficient ID Based Security Algorithm for Mutual Node Authentication and Key Management: An Elliptic Curve Cryptography Based Approach

Nilanjan Sen

Department of Computer Application,
Pailan College of Management and Technology, Kolkata 700 104, India
nilanjansenin@yahoo.co.in

Abstract. The biggest challenge in the field of networking is the secured communication between the nodes within the network system; therefore it has become one of the major and attractive fields of research in computer network. The importance of Elliptic Curve Cryptography (ECC) in this field is increasing rapidly because of its smaller key size compare to other known public-key algorithms. Several user authentication and key management algorithms or schemes have been developed so far but most of them contain complex computations. Not only that, most of the schemes also rely on remote server for node authentication as well as node communication. In this paper, an ECC based algorithm has been proposed to overcome these kinds of complexities. The proposed work will do mutual authentication and session key management for node communication efficiently without putting extra burden on any server but with lesser computation time.

Keywords: Elliptic Curve Cryptography, Public-key Cryptography, Mutual authentication, Session Key management.

1 Introduction

Whenever we think about communication between two nodes in the computer network system, a few questions come into our mind related to secured communication. The first question is obviously related with node authentication, that is how the two communicating nodes validate each other and secondly, how they will communicate securely through the non-trusted communication channel. The security key plays the most important role in this regard. The researchers have developed several algorithms for secured communication based on symmetric key and asymmetric or public key, among which one technique, based on Elliptic Curve computation, has gained immense popularity within a short period of time. The use of Elliptic Curve Cryptography (ECC) in public-key cryptosystem is increasing day by day due to its unique features over other existing public-key cryptography techniques. Proposed by Victor Miller and Neal Koblitz separately in 1985, ECC has gradually become most popular technique among the

P. Gupta and C. Zaroliagis (Eds.): ICAA 2014, LNCS 8321, pp. 110–121, 2014.

researchers due to several reasons. Though sounds alike, it has no relation with the geometrical figure ellipse. It is named so because the cubic equation which represents elliptic curve (commonly known as Weierstrass equation) is similar to the equation used to calculate the circumference of an ellipse [1].

Previously, the public key cryptosystem were based on either multiplicative group or the multiplicative group of finite field. Later on, the researchers studied the utility of group of points of Elliptic curve in public key cryptosystem over a large finite field [2]. The feature which makes ECC more efficient than other public-key algorithms is that, fully exponential time is required by the best known algorithm to solve Elliptic Curve Discrete Logarithm problem (ECDLP) which is the hard mathematical problem in ECC, whereas the hard mathematical problems in other non-ECC based public-key algorithms like RSA or DSA can be solved in sub-exponential time [3]. Secondly, the key size in ECC is much smaller compare to others. Like other public-key algorithms e.g. RSA, DSA etc. ECC is also used for secure data communication which includes encryption/ decryption operation, node authentication, key management etc. In this paper, I have proposed an algorithm which deals with node registration by the Central Server for authorizing a new node, as well as node authentication and generation of session key for secure data communication. Plain text encryption/ decryption operation using ECC is not the subject of discussion in this paper, readers may view [4] for the same. The main aim of this work is to develop an efficient algorithm for node registration, node authentication as well as session key management using ECC.

The remaining portion of this paper is organized as follows. Section 2 provides an overview of Elliptic curve and ECC. In Section 3, some existing works on this field have been discussed. Section 4 discusses the proposed algorithm. In Section 5, security analysis of the proposed algorithm has been done, especially how it can prevent different kinds of attacks. Section 6 contains a comparison table, where different schemes are compared with the proposed scheme. Finally, in Section 7 the conclusion is provided.

2   Preliminaries

2.1   Elliptic Curve (EC)

An Elliptic curve E over a field K is represented by a cubic equation of the form $y^2 + axy + by = x^3 + cx^2 + dx + e$. This equation is known as Weierstrass equation. In this equation, the coefficients a, b, c, d and e are real numbers and belong to K and discriminant of E, $\Delta \neq 0$ [5].

The two basic EC operations are point addition and point doubling [3]. The addition of two points over E yields another point on the curve E. This can be represented as $P + Q = R$ where P, Q and R are the points over E. The set of points forms an abelian group [5]. This group has a lot of importance in Elliptic curve cryptography. On the other hand, point doubling means addition of same point. For instance, $P + P = 2P$, where P is a point over E. Another operation, known as scalar point multiplication over E is done by repeated addition of the same point for n number of times. For example $n.P = P + P + P + n - \text{times}$ [3]. The same operation can be done by applying a combination of point addition and point doubling also. For instance, $5.P$ can be obtained by two consecutive point doubling, and one point addition operations, e.g., $P + P = 2P$, $2P + 2P = 4P$, $4P + P = 5P$. This scalar point multiplication operation has huge importance in elliptic curve cryptography.

2.2   Elliptic Curve Cryptography (ECC)

In ECC, we can use either a prime curve over Z_p (a set of non-negative integer and p is a prime number) where a cubic equation is used, all the variables and coefficients of that equation take the values between 0 and $p - 1$ and modulo p calculations are performed, or we can use a binary curve over $GF(2^m)$ where the values of all variables and coefficients are taken from $GF(2^m)$ [1]. A very common form of EC equation, $y^2 = x^3 + ax + b(mod\ p)$ is used for ECC over Z_p, p is a prime and $p > 3$. This equation is denoted as $E_p(a, b)$ where a and b are coefficients of the equation. For certain values of a and b, a group can be defined on $E_p(a, b)$ if and only if $(4a^3 + 27b^2)mod\ p \neq 0\ mod\ p$ [1]. $(4a^3 + 27b^2)$ is known as the discriminant of the curve.

Some of the problems of Elliptic Curve are described below which are believed to be unsolvable [6] so far.

- **Elliptic Curve Discrete Logarithm problem (ECDLP):** If we choose two points P and Q over $E_p(a, b)$, then it is extremely hard to find the value of r, $r \in Z_p$ from the equation $Q = r.P$ for very large r.
- **Computational Diffie-Hellman problem (CDHP):** If we choose two integer values m and n; m, $n \in Z_p$ and a point P over $E_p(a, b)$, then given $P, m.P$ and $n.P$, it is extremely hard to find the point $(m.n).P$ over $E_p(a, b)$.
- **Elliptic Curve Factorization Problem (ECFP):** If we choose two integer values m and n; m, $n \in Z_p$ and a point P over $E_p(a, b)$ and calculate $Q = m.P + n.P$ where $Q \in E_p(a, b)$, it is extremely hard to find $m.P$ and $n.P$ over $E_p(a, b)$.

In addition to that, one unique property of EC is, if we choose two integer values m and n, m, $n \in Z_p$ and calculate R and S as $R = m.P$ and $S = n.P$, $P \in E_p(a, b)$, then

$$m \cdot S = n \cdot R \tag{1}$$

because $m.S = m.n.P = n.R$. In ECC, from the combination of $< m,\ R >$, m is considered as private key and R, the public key [1].

My proposed algorithm is based on the difficulties of ECDLP, ECFP mentioned above and the property of EC as in equation (1).

3   Related Work

Authentication of the valid user as well as key management for data encryption/ decryption is the most essential part of any cryptosystem. Different researchers are working on these topics using either the conventional techniques like RSA, DSA or using ECC. A very popular approach used now-a-days is identity based scheme [7,6]. In this kind of approach, user can not repudiate its identity. On the other hand, less storage space is required in this scheme. In the current section we will discuss some of the related works, there pros and cons, and in the next section we will see how the proposed algorithm tries to solve these problems.

Some ID-based authentication schemes on ECC, proposed by Choie, Jeong and Lee in 2005 [8] or Wu, Chiu and Chieu [9] in the same year, used bilinear pairings which required complex and lengthy computations. On the other hand, some of the schemes proposed by Chen and Song; Jiang, Li and Xu in 2007 ; Cao, Kou, Dang and Zhao in 2008 lacked either mutual authentication or the session key agreement between the node and the server [7].

The scheme proposed by Tian, Wong and Zhu in 2005 [10] [which was an improved version of Huang et als AKA protocol (2003)] contained two phases viz. certificate generation phase and authentication and key agreement phase. The scheme worked with a Certificate Authority and a set of communicating nodes. The responsibilities of Certificate Authority were not only to certify the nodes, but also to store the certificates and public keys of the nodes. The calculations for certificate generation and key agreement were also very complex. In addition to that, total 4 rounds of communication were required which was a time consuming process.

Wu, Chiu and Chieu in 2005 proposed an ID-based scheme where remote authentication was done using smart card [9]. Its password authentication phase was either timestamp based or nonce based. On the other hand, Jia et al in 2006 proposed the scheme which also had a password change phase [11]. Both the schemes used bilinear pairing for the authentication phases which increased the computational cost of the schemes.

The scheme proposed by Abi-Char, Mhamed and El-Hassan in 2007 contained the features of mutual authentication and key agreement but required 3 rounds of communication for the authentication [12]. Another scheme proposed by Yang and Chang in 2009 also contained mutual authentication and a session key agreement between the node and the server [7]. In their paper, they discussed about the unsuitability of Tian, Wong and Zhus scheme for mobile devices, and proposed an ID-based remote mutual authentication scheme along with key agreement, which could be suitable for mobile devices.

4   Proposed Work

The schemes discussed so far in the previous section either require a Certificate Authority or a server as well as some complex, time consuming calculations like bilinear pairing for the key authentication and session key agreement. Some algorithms permit the nodes to directly communicate to each other without session key leading to several possibilities of attacks like Man-in-the-middle or Replay attack. But most of the schemes have one common feature, i.e. the use of hash function.

Apart from elliptic curve point multiplication and addition, the above mentioned schemes use one or more than one one-way hash functions for registration of the node, mutual authentication or session key management. The use of hash function requires extra calculations. In mobile devices like laptop, tablet, PCs or cellular phones, any operation requires consumption of energy, and one of the important aspects of mobile devices is energy efficiency. Damasevicius, Ziberkas, Stuikys and Toldinas analyzed the energy efficiency versus quality characteristics of 17 well known hash algorithms in a mobile device [13]. Moreover, hash functions are vulnerable, for example, if we take two popular hash functions into consideration, namely MD5 and SHA-1, it has been proved from the works of Wang et al. and other researchers that they are quite vulnerable to collision [14,15,16]. By considering the above factors, I have not used hash function in my proposed algorithm so that it can be implemented in both wired as well as wireless devices.

The goal of my proposed algorithm is to perform node authentication and key management using lesser computation compare to other related schemes without compromising the security of the network system. The proposed scheme has the following characteristics:

- The Central Server is required only to register the valid nodes, not for authentication.
- No node needs to store others key.
- No hash function is used.
- Two communicating nodes will authenticate each other during communication.
- One session key will be used for each session.
- In the proposed scheme, communication can be carried over even through an unsecured channel without any security glitch.
- The number of elliptic curve multiplication and addition must be lesser than the other schemes without compromising the security of the system.

The principle feature of the algorithm is that, first of all, if any node 'A' wants to be the part of the system, it needs to register itself in to the system with the help of a Central Server. After the successful registration, if 'A' wants to communicate with another node 'B', it will send a message to 'B'. The message will be used to check the authentication of 'A' as well 'B' will generate the session key using it. So that will minimize the number of calculation and hence will save the time and energy of the nodes.

The algorithm chooses an elliptic curve equation

$$y^2 = x^3 + ax + b \tag{2}$$

represented as $E_p(a,\ b)$ over $GF(p)$, p is a prime number greater than 3 and a and b are integer modulo p. The discriminant of equation (2), Δ is not equal to zero [5], i.e.

$$4a^3 + 27b^2 \neq 0 \tag{3}$$

It also chooses a point P over the chosen elliptic curve $E_p(a,\ b)$. This algorithm works in two phases:

4.1 Registration Phase

a. The 'Central Server' (CS) of the system randomly chooses a large number $Pr_{CS} \in Z_p^*$ and calculate Pub_{CS} as

$$Pub_{CS} = Pr_{CS} \cdot P \tag{4}$$

Z_p^* is the set of non-negative integers less than p and are co-prime to p. The Pub_{CS} and Pr_{CS} are the public and private key respectively for the CS. According to the Discrete Logarithm problem, it is very hard to find Pr_{CS} from equation (4) for very large Pr_{CS} [1]. $Pub_{CS} \in E_p(a, b)$.

b. Node A first generates its own identification number ID_A randomly and sends that number to Central Server through a secured channel. $ID_A \in Z_p^*$.

c. Central Server calculates ID_A' as follows:

$$ID_A' = ID_A \cdot Pr_{CS} \tag{5}$$

and then sends ID_A' to A through the secured channel.

d. After receiving ID_A', 'A' checks whether $ID_A'.P = ID_A.Pub_{CS}$ or not. If it is matched, then 'A' sends acknowledgment to CS. Otherwise it rejects ID_A', generates new ID_A, and sends it to CS with proper message. This step continues until and unless 'A' gets valid ID_A'.

e. After getting the "successful" acknowledgment from 'A', CS publishes ID_A' as registered identification number of 'A'.

f. Node A picks a random number $Pr_A \in Z_p^*$ and calculate Pub_A as

$$Pub_A = Pr_A \cdot P \tag{6}$$

$Pub_A \in E_p(a, b)$. 'A' publishes its public key Pub_A.

g. Like 'A', node B also generates its pair of public and private key i.e., Pub_B and Pr_B and publishes Pub_B.

The entire registration process is depicted in figure 1.

4.2 Node Authentication and Session Key Generation through Agreement

a. Node A picks a large random number N, $N \in Z_p^*$.
b. 'A' does the following calculations:

$$E = ID_A' \cdot Pr_A \cdot Pub_B \tag{7}$$

$$Q = ID_A \cdot N \cdot Pub_{CS} \tag{8}$$

$$E' = Q + E \tag{9}$$

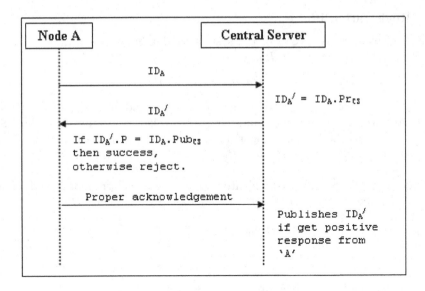

Fig. 1. Node registration by Central Server

c. After that, 'A' takes timestamp T_1 which represents current time and sends the message $< E^/, N, T_1 >$ to node B.

d. After receiving $< E^/, N, T_1 >$, 'B' first checks that whether the timestamp T_1 is valid or not. If it is invalid then 'B' rejects the packet otherwise it checks the validity of the sender. At first, 'B' computes E (which is a point on $E_p(a, b)$) as $ID^/_A.Pr_B.Pub_A$ because $ID^/_A.Pr_B.Pub_A = ID^/_A.Pr_B.Pr_A.P = ID^/_A.Pr_A.Pub_B$. Then 'B' subtracts E from $E^/$ to get $Q^/$.

$$E = ID^/_A . Pr_B . Pub_A \tag{10}$$

$$Q^/ = E^/ - E \tag{11}$$

Then 'B' computes $F = ID^/_A.N.P$ and checks it with $Q^/$, because $F = ID^/_A.N.P = ID_A.Pr_{CS}.N.P = ID_A.N.Pub_{CS}$. This is equivalent to Q.

$$F = ID^/_A . N . P \tag{12}$$

Next, 'B' will check whether $F = Q^/$ or not. If both are equal, it proves the validity of the sender and B takes the x-coordinate of point E, otherwise 'B' rejects the message $< E^/, N, T_1 >$.

e. 'B' takes a large random number $R \in Z_p^*$. Then x is multiplied by R to get the session key S. Multiplication is done to get the bigger key.

$$S = x . R \tag{13}$$

f. 'B' does a point multiplication operation as below

$$M = S \cdot Pr_B \cdot Pub_A \tag{14}$$

g. Lastly 'B' takes the timestamp T_2 which represents current time and sends $< M, R, T_2 >$ to node A.

h. After receiving the message from 'B', 'A' first checks the timestamp T_2. If it is valid, then 'A' calculates S by multiplying x (which is the x-coordinate of E) by R. Then it multiplies S, Pr_A and Pub_B to calculate M' as (15)[1] and checks whether $M' = M$ or not. If they are equal, then it proves the validity of 'B'. 'A' and 'B' then choose S as their session key.

$$M' = S \cdot Pr_A \cdot Pub_B \tag{15}$$

The entire operation of the algorithm is depicted in the figure 2.

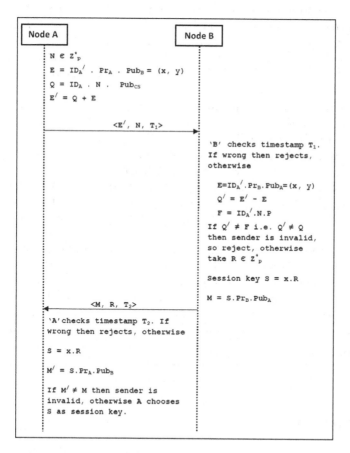

Fig. 2. Node authentication and generation of Session key

---

[1] Computation is same as equation (10).

The session key S is generated by multiplying the x-coordinate of the point E i.e. x by a large random number R. The reason behind this is, as a value, x is comparatively small. Multiplying x by R will yield a large key. For every new session, a new point E and the new random numbers R will be taken to generate the new session key.

5   Security Analysis

The prime features of my algorithm are that, two nodes can directly communicate with each other without the help of any trusted third party. They authenticate each other and at the same time generate the session key with limited number of computations compare to other algorithms. This proposed algorithm is invulnerable to following attacks:

- **Man-in-the-middle attack:** If any adversary 'D' intercepts $< E', N, T_1 >$ and changes E' to E'' by calculating $E'' = Q + ID'_A.Pr_D.Pub_B$, where Pr_D is the private key of the adversary and then send $< E'', N, T_1 >$ to B, receiver B will try to decrypt E'' using As public key Pub_A. So when B will subtract newly computed E from E'', the result will not be same as F. So B will reject it.

   The adversary can generate Q from ID'_A, N and P, but Q is used to validate the sender only. Only receiver can properly compute E as it is encrypted by its own public key.
- **Replay attack:** If any adversary intercepts the message and resends it to receiver at either of the two ends, i.e. either to 'A' or to 'B', then either of the receivers checks the timestamp of its corresponding message i.e., T_1 or T_2. If it gets the same value of corresponding timestamp, then it will reject the packet, because different values of T_1 and T_2 are being used for different sessions in this scheme.
- **Unauthorized user attack:** If any unauthorized, outside node tries to communicate with the authorized nodes within the network, this attempt can be easily exposed when the receiver will calculate the equations (10), (11) and (12), and check Q' with F. For example, if any unauthorized node 'D' generates its ID say ID'_D and calculate E as $ID'_D.Pr_D.Pub_B$ and sends it to B, then after doing the computation as equations (10), (11) and (12), the value of Q' will not match with F, because ID'_D is not published by Central Server. Moreover, it is not possible for B to know the public key of D as D is not a valid node. So, B will reject the request.

6   Comparison

The comparisons of proposed scheme with the other schemes discussed in Section 3 are presented in Table 1. The table is, to some extent, based on the comparison table in [7], but several modifications are made here. One new field "Hash operation" is introduced. Apart from that, computational cost is calculated based on the registration phase, mutual authentication and key agreement phases, but excluding the system initialization phase. The mutual authentication and key agreement phases using bilinear pairing are not considered here, though the bilinear pairing computation costs a lot in terms of efficiency of an algorithm. From the comparison table, it is clear that proposed scheme is more efficient than the other schemes in terms of computational cost and other aspects.

Table 1. Comparison of efficiency between the proposed scheme and other schemes

Properties	Tian et al.	Wu et al.	Jia et al.	Abi-char et al.	Yang & Chang	Proposed scheme
Mutual authentication	$\checkmark$	X	X	$\checkmark$	$\checkmark$	$\checkmark$
Key agreement	$\checkmark$	X	X	$\checkmark$	$\checkmark$	$\checkmark$
Hash operation	$\checkmark$	$\checkmark$	$\checkmark$	$\checkmark$	$\checkmark$	X
Certificate generation/ Smart card	$\checkmark$	$\checkmark$	$\checkmark$	X	X	X
Bilinear Pairings computations	X	$\checkmark$	$\checkmark$	X	X	X
Computation costs (excluding system initialization phase and bilinear pairing computation)	11M+ 5A+ 6H+ 1D	a) Time-stamp based: 5M + 1A + 2H b) Nonce based: 8M+ 1A+ 1H	6M+ 3A + 4H	7M+ 5A+ 1MM+ 5H	11M+ 4A+ 10H	9M+ 2A
Communication rounds	4	2	2	3	2	2

M: Elliptic curve scalar multiplication; A: Elliptic curve point addition; D: Symmetric key decryption; MM: Modular multiplication; H: Hash operation

7   Conclusion

In this paper, I have proposed an Identity based security algorithm for mutual node authentication and session key management for communicating nodes in a conventional network system. This scheme can be used in mobile communication system also. Unlike the other schemes, in this scheme, Central Server is used only for registering the nodes. The authentication and session key management is done by the communicating nodes themselves with lesser computations compare to other existing schemes. The detail comparison is given in the comparison table in Section 6. This work can be continued in future for further improvement. The improved version of the proposed scheme can be applied to other related fields of security like message authentication.

Acknowledgement. I would like to express my profound and deep sense of gratitude to my colleagues Prof. Manojit Chattopadhyay and Dr. Surajit Chattopadhyay for their invaluable help, guidance and suggestions, and my wife Ms. Rinku Sen for her immense support without which my work would not have been successful.

References

1. Stallings, W.: Cryptography and Network Security, Principles and Practice, 5th edn. Prentice Hall
2. Koblitz, N.: Elliptic Curve Cryptosystems. Mathematics of Computation, American Mathematical Society 48(177), 203–209 (1987)
3. Lopez, J., Dahab, R.: An Overview of Elliptic Curve Cryptography. Technical Report IC-00-10,
   http://citeseerx.ist.psu.edu/viewdoc/summary?doi=10.1.1.37.2771
4. Vigila, S.M.C., Muneeswaran, K.: Implementation of Text based Cryptosystem using Elliptic Curve Cryptography. In: First International Conference on Advanced Computing, December 13-15, pp. 82–85 (2009)
5. Hankerson, D., Menezes, A., Vanstone, S.: Guide to Elliptic Curve Cryptography. Springer (2004)
6. Li, F., Xin, X., Hu, Y.: Identity-based broadcast signcryption. Computer Standard and Interfaces 30, 89–94 (2008)
7. Yang, J., Chang, C.: An ID-based remote mutual authentication with key agreement scheme for mobile devices on elliptic curve cryptosystem. Computer & Security, 138–143 (2009)
8. Choie, Y.J., Jeong, E., Lee, E.: Efficient identity-based authenticated key agreement protocol from pairings. Applied Mathematics and Computation 162(1), 179–188 (2005)
9. Wu, S., Chiu, J., Chieu, B.: ID-based remote authentication with smart cards on open distributed system from Elliptic curve cryptography. In: IEEE International Conference on Electro Information Technology (May 2005)
10. Tian, X., Wong, D.S., Zhu, R.W.: Analysis and Improvement of Authenticated Key Exchange Protocol for Sensor Networks. IEEE Communication Letters 9(11), 970–972 (2005)
11. Jia, Z., Zhang, Y., Shao, H., Lin, Y., Wang, J.: A Remote User Authentication Scheme Using Bilinear Pairings and ECC. In: Proceedings of the Sixth International Conference on Intelligent Systems Design and Applications (ISDA 2006), vol. 2, pp. 1091–1094 (October 2006)
12. Abi-Char, P.E., Mhamed, A., El-Hassan, B.A.: A Fast and Secure Elliptic Curve Based Authenticated Key Agreement Protocol For Low Power Mobile Communications. In: The 2007 International Conference on Next Generation Mobile Applications, Services and Technologies (September 2007)

13. Damasevicius, R., Ziberkas, G., Stuikys, V., Toldinas, J.: Energy Consumption of Hash Functions. Elektronika Ir Elektrotechnika 18(10) (2012) ISSN 1392-1215

14. Wang, X., Yu, H.: How to break MD5 and other hash functions. In: Cramer, R. (ed.) EUROCRYPT 2005. LNCS, vol. 3494, pp. 19–35. Springer, Heidelberg (2005)

15. Wang, X., Yin, Y.L., Yu, H.: Finding Collisions in the Full SHA-1. In: Shoup, V. (ed.) CRYPTO 2005. LNCS, vol. 3621, pp. 17–36. Springer, Heidelberg (2005)

16. Stevens, M.: Fast Collision Attack on MD5. IACR ePrint archive report (2006)

Automata for Modeling the Distributed Probabilistic Reversible Processes

Arpit[1], Afza Shafie[2], and Wan Fatimah Wan Ahmad[1]

[1] Computer and Information Sciences Department, Universiti Teknologi
PETRONAS, Bandar Seri Iskandar, 31750, Tronoh, Perak, Malaysia
[2] Fundamental and Applied Sciences Department, Universiti Teknologi PETRONAS,
Bandar Seri Iskandar, 31750, Tronoh, Perak, Malaysia

Abstract. This paper presents the construction of an automaton termed
the *Concurrent Probabilistic Reversible Automata* (*CPRA*). It models the
distributed systems which exhibit probabilistic behaviour and also relies
on backtracking as the basis to make a system fault tolerant. Here, the
basic concepts of non-probabilistic automata have been extended by introducing the discrete probabilities on the set of transitions for modelling
the probabilistic nature of computing environment. In addition, concurrency has been implemented by defining *parallel joint*(ˆ) operator dealing
with the odds of shared transitions. A memory structure has also been
defined to keep track of past transitions in order to facilitate the backtracking without losing the initial computations, which may result in inconsis-
tent states as well. The major contribution of this work can be seen in
three aspects: first, defining an automaton to model *full non-determinism*
along with probabilistic characterisation without making any distinctions
between states and actions by which some of the previous formalism suffers; second, association of memory with the automata that preserves concurrency during backtracking; third, the implementation of the *parallel
joint* operator to facilitate the concurrency. Although, the full probabilistic analysis of *CPRA* can be performed by applying the principles of *measure theory* on the traces of *CPRA* but it is reported as future work.

1 Introduction

Today, distributed computing in a probabilistic environment is dominant where
the choices over the next set of actions are governed probabilistically and determined by a scheduler, some expert systems or a random number generator
machine. Some examples of such systems are the *Binary Exponential Back Off
protocol* [1], various cryptographic protocols, such as the *Elliptic Cryptographic
protocol* [2], various network probabilistic communication protocols, such as the
Root Contention protocol [3] etc. Concurrency and synchronisation among several sub-systems of a system rule out traditional testing to ensure the quality
of the system. Moreover, in a probabilistic environment, one may also be interested in investigating the odds of a system to be in a certain state, e.g. by
what probability the system will be in deadlock; or want to quantify the various

P. Gupta and C. Zaroliagis (Eds.): ICAA 2014, LNCS 8321, pp. 122–136, 2014.
© Springer International Publishing Switzerland 2014

properties of the system, such as fairness, invariance etc. Moreover, backtracking or roll back which is the basic of all fault tolerant strategies makes the testing of system much harder. Generally, testing assesses the system code against certain requirements; therefore, it only gives confidence about the final system, whereas, verification authenticates the correctness of the system against its formal description. Moreover, analysis is also required to quantitatively answer the questions regarding the properties of a system and this requires behaviour of the system to be specified formally. Hence, the formal specification of a system is vital for verification and analysis purposes [4].

Formal specification or formal modeling means an axiomatic approach towards the representation of systems behaviour. Formal modeling by the state machine (automaton) is one of the oldest techniques and even dominant today. In this sequence, the classical automata theory has been extended in several dimensions to reflect the changes in computing environment, e.g. parallel composition operator has been introduced to model the concurrency; or *PA* (*Probabilistic Automata*) have been proposed to model the probabilistic processes [5,6]. The scope of the state machines is not limited up to the modelling but it also provides the semantics to various process algebras, e.g. $\lambda - calculus$ [7] is based on the classical automata theory, and the *Calculus of Communicating Systems* (*CCS*) [8] relies on *Labelled Transition System* (*LTS*)[8] for its semantics.

The main contribution of this article is to propose an automaton capable of modelling reversible concurrent probabilistic processes. Concurrency is the basic of all distributed systems therefore terms, concurrent process and distributed process, are used interchangeably throughout this text. Literature review as summarised in Section 2 provides the necessary motivations behind this work. Also, Section 2 informs that no single formalism has been proposed yet to model reversibility, concurrency, and probabilistic behaviour, simultaneously.

Proposed automaton makes a clear distinction between the nondeterministic and probabilistic choices. For the analysis purpose, non-deterministic choices can be further resolved by a scheduler which schedules the next transition among the set of transitions; odds on next transitions scheduled by the scheduler provides the space for full probabilistic reasoning of such systems. Here, the term "full" implies the system where all choices are governed by some probability distribution. The full probabilistic analysis of *CPRA* has been proposed as future work. The proposed definition also takes care of providing the facility to represent *internal* and *external* non-deterministic choices. Concurrency has been implemented by the proposed parallel composition operator named the *parallel joint* (^) operator. The novelty of the proposed automata also lies in making no distinctions among the states and actions while composing two automata by which previous formalism suffers. Reversibility, on the other side, has been implemented by associating a memory structure with the automata. The memories should not be maximally flexible, alone, but also be consistent. This is in the sense that memories should not allow a system to reach any previously non-assessable states during backtracking, simultaneously, not introduce the fake casual dependencies on the reversible actions of a system. In this respect, the memories of *CPRA* are consistent and the intuitions behind the consistencies of the memories are presented in this paper but the formal proof is deferred for future.

2 Background

This section is organised into two subsections based on the state machines capable of modelling probabilistic processes and reversible processes, respectively.

2.1 Probabilistic Automata (PA)

Under this category, various automata have been proposed each of which is capable of modelling the concurrent stochastic processes but not reversibility. The key variances among the proposed models are summarised below.

1. *Fully probabilistic vs. fully non-deterministic.* In fully probabilistic automata, all of the choices are governed by the probability distributions later called the probabilistic choices. Probability distribution captures the uncertainty of the behaviour of the system. However, sometimes it is impossible to identify the exact probability distribution over choices due to the lack of information. The only one known is the upper bound and lower bound, in such cases, one has to incorporate all of the possible choices and this brings about non-determinism. The requisites of non-determinism for modelling various phenomena have been mentioned in [9]. Further, non-determinism is classified into *external* and *internal* non-determinism [5,6], respectively. *External* non-deterministic choices are governed by the environment by specifying several transitions with different labels leaving from the same state. Whereas, *internal* non-deterministic choices are specified by several transitions having the same labels leaving from the same or different states. The term of *full non-determinism* includes both *internal* and *external* non-determinism. This diagonal requirement of incorporating non-deterministic along with probabilistic choices is one of the causes of divergence among different proposed *PA*.

2. *Reactive vs. Generative.* Most of the *PA* have adopted one of these two styles to implement its transition function while a few of them have used both styles to define the transition function over different sets of actions. The categorisation of the actions is a part of the definition of such automata, one of which is *I/O probabilistic automata* [9]. The *reactive* style of the transition function defines the probability distribution over the set of states while the *generative* style defines on tuples of state and actions [5].

3. *Distinctions among states and actions.* To implement an appropriate composition operator, some of the *PA* [9,6] have made a number of distinctions among their actions and states. This is the reflection of the attempts of including non-determinism in *PA*. In this attempt, more formalisms have been proposed but some of them are based on constrain functions and others

use a biased factor to implement a parallel composition operator. Further, they have a high complexity in terms of usability. Some of the dominant techniques, used with some variations by most of the proposed PAs to implement their respective parallel composition operators, include CCS [8], CSP[6] and ACP [6]. All of these three styles have two variations: *synchronous* and *asynchronous*. *Synchronous* forces its operands to synchronise whenever possible. In contrast, *asynchronous* provides the freedom to either synchronise or to act independently [6,8]. Various composition styles adopted by some PA are summarised in Table 1.

Here, some PA are summarised in Table 2 with their pros and cons, which are important for providing theoretical backgrounds and motivations for proposing new models.

Table 1. Composition styles of some PA (*t: total communication function*)

Abbreviations	Synchronous	Asynchronous
I/O probabilistic automata [9]	-	-
Stratified probabilistic automata [5]	*CCS, CSP, ACP*	-
Vardi Probabilistic automata [6]	ACP^t	-
Segla probabilistic automata [10]	*CCS, CSP, ACP*	*CCS, CSP, ACP*
Simple Segla probabilistic automata [10]	*ACP*	-
Pnueli-Zuck probabilistic automata [6]	-	-
General probabilistic automata [6]	-	-
Abstract probabilistic automata [11]	ACP^t	*ACP*

2.2 Probabilistic Reversible Automata (PRA)

Reversibility means rewinding computational steps. It is generally introduced by the fault tolerant strategies implemented by the software systems. In a distributed setting, synchronisation in backward computation refers to a key factor for the system consistency, therefore, it must be modelled and verified. But PA are not capable of modelling the reversibility, moreover, no formalism has been found in literatures to do so. Although, there are some automata in the field of quantum computing, model reversibility of stochastic processes; but still lack in concurrency. These automata belong under the category are known as *Probabilistic Reversible Automata*(PRA); *Doubly stochastic automata* [12] and *Probabilistic Reversible Decide and Halt Automata* (*DH-PRA*) [13] are most dominant in this category. *DH-PRA* is the most general one and it has close links with the *Quantum Finite Automata* (*QFA*). *DH-PRA* with some restrictions can be considered as a special case of the *Nayaks quantum automata*[13]. One more formalism, termed as $RCCS$[14], models reversibility and concurrency. $RCCS$ is an instance of the process algebras.

Table 2. Summary of PA [∼: Not, A (Distinctions among actions), S (Distinctions among states), T (Transitions), I (Input actions), O (Output Actions), P (Probabilistic states), N (Nondeterministic states), D (Deterministic states), G (*Generative* type), R (*Reactive* Type), FN (*Full non-determinism*), IN (*Internal* non-determinism), EN (External non-determinism), FP (Full probabilistic), Attribute[argument] (Attributes applied to that argument)]

Abbreviations	Probability Distribution	Distinctions	Modeling Characteristics	Drawbacks
I/O probabilistic automata [9]	R[I], G[O]	∼S, I, O	EN[I], FP[O]	Distinctions among actions
Stratified probabilistic automata [5]	G	∼A, P, D	FP[P]	Distinctions among states
Vardi probabilistic automata [6]	R	∼A, P, N	EN[P]	Distinctions among states
Segla probabilistic automata [10]	G[T]	∼S, ∼A	FN, FP	Parallel composition makes probabilistic analysis difficult
Simple Segla probabilistic automata [10]	R[T]	∼ S, ∼A	FN, ∼S, ∼FP	Not full probabilistic
Pnueli-Zuck probabilistic automata [6]	G[G[T]]	∼ S, ∼A	FN, ∼S, ∼FP	Complex and no equivalence theory defined
General probabilistic automata [6]	G[G[T]], G[R[S]]	∼ S, ∼A	FN, ∼S, ∼FP	Complex and no equivalence theory defined

3   Proposed Work

Here, a state machine *CPRA* has been proposed on the ground of the research issues identified in Section 2. It is capable of modelling, reversibility; concurrency; and probabilistic behaviour, of software processes but before proceeding towards it, let's take a look on nomenclatures which will be used throughout this section.

Nomenclatures

1. $\mathbb{N}$ denotes the set of natural numbers.
2. Let θ be a set then $\wp(\theta)$ is the power set of θ.
3. Let θ be a finite set and $\alpha \in \mathbf{Ord}$ is an ordinal then a sequence u is a mapping from α into θ, where, $\mathbf{Ord}$ is the set of ordinals. u is represented by $(u_n)_{n \leq \alpha}$ and it's length by $|u| = \alpha$.
4. Let θ be a finite set, and u and v are the two sequences over θ, then *concatenation* operation $u \circ v$ is a mapping from ordinal $|u| + |v|$ to θ and it is defined as follows:

$$(u \circ v)_i = \begin{cases} u_i, & \text{if } i < |u| \\ v_j, & \text{if } i = |u| + j, j < |v| \end{cases} .$$

5. Let μ be a probability distribution on a set θ then it is represented by $\mu[\theta] = 1$.
6. Let μ be a probability distribution on a finite set $\{s_1, s_2, \ldots, s_n\}$ then this finite distribution is represented by $\{s_1 \mapsto \mu(s_1), s_2 \mapsto \mu(s_2), \ldots, s_n \mapsto \mu(s_n)\}$. Here, the probability of an event which doesn't exist is assumed to be 0.

3.1   Definition of *CPRA*

Definition 1. *A CPRA* $C = \langle S_C, \Sigma_C, s_c, \Gamma_C, m_C, Z_C, \{\uparrow, \downarrow\}, \delta_C, push_C, pop_C, conf_C, \partial_C \rangle$ *is an ordered 12-tuple defined as follows:*

1. S_C *represents a finite set of states.*
2. Σ_C *represents a finite set of actions called as* input symbols.
3. s_C^0 *refers to an initial state of C.*
4. Γ_C *is a set of* memory *elements such that if* $z \in \Gamma_C$ *then* $z = (z_n)_{n \leq 5}$ *or* $z = Z_C$.
5. *Let* $\alpha \in$ **Ord** *then memory* $m_C^0 = (m_n^0)_{n \leq \alpha}$ *is a sequence over* Γ_C. *It is organised in the form of a stack with* $push_C$ *and* pop_C *operations. However, if* $\alpha = \phi$ *then* $m_C^0 = (Z_C)$.
6. $Z_C \in \Gamma_C$ *is an initial element of* memory *also act as a demiliter of the memory.*
7. $\{\uparrow, \downarrow\}$ *is a set of commands such that* $\uparrow$ *and* $\downarrow$ *implies forward and backward move, respectively.*
8. $\delta_C : S_C \longrightarrow \wp\{\mu | \exists \theta[\theta \subseteq (S_C \times \Sigma_C) \wedge \mu[\theta] = 1]\}$ *is called* state function.
9. *If* $z \in \Gamma_C$ *and* $m \in conf_C$ *then* $push_C(z, m) = z \circ m$.
10. *Let* $\alpha \in$ **Ord** *and* $m = (m_n)_{n \leq \alpha}$ *such that* $m \in conf_C$ *then* $pop_C(m) = (m_n)_{n < \alpha}$.
11. $conf_C = \{m | \exists z \exists m'[z \in \Gamma_C \wedge m' \in conf_C \wedge (m = push_C(z, m') \vee m = pop_C(m') \vee m = m_C^0)]\}$.
12. *Trasition function* ∂_C *is given by:*

$$\partial_C : S_C \times \{\uparrow, \downarrow\} \times conf_C \longrightarrow \wp \left(\bigcup_{\exists s[s \in S_C \wedge \mu \in \delta_C(s)]} (\mu \times conf_C) \right).$$

Let $s \in S_C$, $cd \in \{\uparrow, \downarrow\}$ *and* $m \in conf_C$ *then*
CASE 1: $cd = \uparrow$

$$\partial_C(s, cd, m) = \{\langle \mu(\langle s', \alpha \rangle), m' \rangle | \mu \in \delta_C(s) \wedge \mu(\langle s', \alpha \rangle) > 0 \wedge$$
$$m' = push_C(z, m)\},$$
$$z = (*, \mu(\langle s', \alpha \rangle), \alpha, \mu - \mu(\langle s', \alpha \rangle), \delta_C(s) - \mu).$$

CASE 2: $cd = \downarrow$

$$\partial_C(s, cd, m) = \{\langle \langle s', \alpha \rangle \mapsto 1, m' \rangle | \delta_C(s') = m_{15} \cup (\{m_{12}\} \cup m_{14}) \wedge$$
$$m_{13} = \alpha \wedge m' = pop_C(m)\}.$$

The proposed automaton remains in one of the states in S during its life time. Let $s \in S$ be the current state of the proposed automata then it has a choice to move forward or backtrack. These choices are specified by $\uparrow$ and $\downarrow$, respectively. The transition from the state s also depends upon the current configuration of the *memory* m^0. The collection of different configurations of m is represented by *conf*. Let $m' \in conf$ is the present configuration of m^0 and if there is a forward transition from s (represented by $\uparrow$) then the proposed automaton has the probabilistic choices in $S \times \Sigma$ in terms of transition; m' is also pushed accordingly. Let $\langle \mu(\langle s', \alpha \rangle), n \rangle \in \partial(s, \uparrow, m')$ such that $\langle s', \alpha \rangle \in S \times \Sigma$ and $n = push(z, m')$, where $z = (*, \mu(\langle s', \alpha \rangle), \alpha, \mu - \mu(\langle s', \alpha \rangle), \delta(s) - \mu)$ then $\mu(\langle s', \alpha \rangle)$ is the probability of the transition, and $\mu \in \delta(s)$ represents non-deterministic choice on a set mapped by $\delta(s)$. All the information required to backtrack from s' to s is pushed in the memory, in particular, $*$ signifies no synchronization has been made; $\mu(\langle s', \alpha \rangle)$ tells the probability of the transition made; α refers the *input symbol* visited during the transition; and $\mu(\langle s', \alpha \rangle)$ together with $\mu - \mu(\langle s', \alpha \rangle)$ and $\delta(s) - \mu$ depict the state which must be reached during backtracking from s' (it is s in this case).

3.2   Definition of Parallel Joint Operator ($\hat{\ }$)

Parallel joint ($\hat{\ }$) operator is a binary operator which implements the concurrency by composing two *CPRA*. Before defining *parallel joint* operation, one more definition is presented here which shows how the probabilities are distributed when two *CPRA* are composed. The definition is divided into cases based on the fact that the transitions of both *CPRA* share the same *input symbol* or not. Here, the natural phenomenon; the odds for an input symbol to synchronize or to act independently are same (an analogy can be understood by the experiment of tossing a fair coin), has been exploited to distribute probabilities among transitions of two *CPRA*.

Let, C and D be two *CPRAs* with their respective sets of *input* symbols Σ_C and Σ_D then $sync_{C,D} = \{\tau_\alpha | \alpha \in \Sigma_c \wedge \alpha \in \Sigma_c\}$ denotes the set of possible synchronisations by C and D. Here, τ_α is called *sysnchronisation action* on shared *input symbol* α.

Definition 2. *Let A and B be two CPRA associated with two probability distributions μ and λ such that for a state $a \in S_A$; $\mu \in \delta_A(a)$, and $\lambda \in \delta_B(b)$ for a state $b \in S_B$, then $\mu \| \lambda$ is defined as a probability distribution on $(S_A \times S_B) \times (\Sigma_A \cup \Sigma_B \cup syn_{A,B})$, and*

$$\mu \| \lambda(\langle \langle a', b' \rangle, \tau_\alpha \rangle) = \frac{1}{2} \times \mu(\langle a', \alpha \rangle) \times \frac{1}{2} \times \lambda(\langle b', \alpha \rangle); \text{ for all } \alpha \in \Sigma_A \cap \Sigma_B \tag{1}$$

and $\langle a', b' \rangle \in S_A \times S_B$,

$$\mu \| \lambda(\langle \langle a', b \rangle, \beta \rangle) = \frac{1}{2} \times \mu(\langle a', \beta \rangle) \times \left(1 - \sum_{s \in S_A \times S_B \wedge \tau_\alpha \in syn_{A,B}} \mu \| \lambda(\langle s, \tau_\alpha \rangle) \right);$$

for all $\beta \in \Sigma_A$ and $a' \in S_A$, and

$$\tag{2}$$

$$\mu\|\lambda(\langle\langle a,b'\rangle,\beta\rangle) = \frac{1}{2} \times \left(1 - \sum_{s\in\ S_A\times S_B\wedge\tau_\alpha\in syn_{A,B}} \mu\|\lambda\left(\langle s,\tau_\alpha\rangle\right)\right) \times \lambda(\langle b',\beta\rangle);$$

for all $\beta \in \Sigma_B$ and $b' \in S_B$.

$$(3)$$

Definition 3. *Let A and B be two CPRA then parallel joint $P = C\,\hat{}\,D$ is a CPRA defined as follows:*

1. $S_P = S_A \times S_B$.
2. $\Sigma_P = \Sigma_A \bigcup \Sigma_B \bigcup syn_{A,B}$.
3. $s_P^0 = \langle s_A^0, s_B^0\rangle$.
4. $\Gamma_P = \Gamma_A \times \Gamma_B$.
5. $m_P^0 = \langle m_A^0, m_B^0\rangle$.
6. $Z_P = \langle Z_A, Z_B\rangle$.
7. $\{\uparrow,\downarrow\}$ *is set of commands having the usual meanings as in A or B.*
8. δ_P *takes a state $\langle a,b\rangle \in S_P$ and returns a set of probability distributions on $S_P \times \Sigma_P$, i.e. $\delta_P(\langle a,b\rangle) = \{\mu\|\lambda \mid \mu \in \delta_A(a) \wedge \lambda \in \delta_B(b)\}$.*
9. $push_P(\langle y,z\rangle, \langle m,n\rangle) = \langle push_A(y,m), push_B(z,n)\rangle$, *where $\langle y,z\rangle \in \Gamma_P$ and $\langle m,n\rangle \in conf_P$.*
10. $pop_P(\langle m,n\rangle) = \langle pop_A(m), pop_B(n)\rangle$, *where $\langle m,n\rangle \in conf_P$.*
11. $conf_P = conf_A \times conf_B$.
12. *Trasition function ∂_P is given by:*

$$\partial_P : S_P \times \{\uparrow,\downarrow\} \times conf_P \longrightarrow \wp\left(\bigcup_{\exists s[s\in S_P \wedge \mu\in\delta_P(s)]} (\mu \times conf_P)\right).$$

Let $s = \langle a,b\rangle \in S_P$ and $m = \langle n,p\rangle \in conf_P$ then
CASE 1: $cd = \uparrow$

$$\partial_P(s,cd,m) = \{\langle\nu(\langle s',\alpha\rangle),m'\rangle \mid \exists\langle c',d'\rangle[\langle c',d'\rangle \in S_P \wedge s' = \langle c',d'\rangle\wedge$$
$$\nu \in \delta_P(s) \wedge \nu(\langle s',\alpha\rangle) > 0 \wedge m' = push_P(z,\langle n,p\rangle)] \wedge \alpha \in \Sigma_P\}.$$

Let $\exists\mu[\mu \in \delta_A(a)]$ and $\exists\lambda[\lambda \in \delta_B(b)]$ such that $\nu = \mu\|\lambda$ then z is given by
SUBCASE 1: $\alpha = \tau_\beta \wedge \beta \in \Sigma_A \cap \Sigma_B$

$$z = \langle(p,\mu(\langle a',\alpha\rangle),\alpha,\mu - \mu(\langle a',\alpha\rangle),\delta_A(a) - \mu),$$
$$(n,\lambda(\langle b',\alpha\rangle),\alpha,\lambda - \lambda(\langle b',\alpha\rangle),\delta_B(d) - \lambda)\rangle.$$

SUBCASE 2: $\alpha \neq \tau_\beta \wedge \beta \in \Sigma_A \cap \Sigma_B \wedge b' = b$

$$z = \langle(*,\mu(\langle a',\alpha\rangle),\alpha,\mu - \mu(\langle a',\alpha\rangle),\partial_A(a) - \mu),\phi\rangle.$$

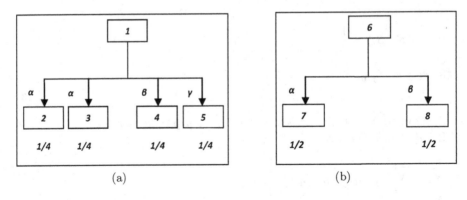

Fig. 1. (a) Probability distribution μ (b) Probability distribution λ

SUBCASE 3: $\alpha \neq \tau_\beta \wedge \beta \in \Sigma_A \cap \Sigma_B \wedge c' = c$

$$z = \langle \phi, (*, \lambda(\langle b', \alpha \rangle), \alpha, \lambda - \lambda(\langle b', \alpha \rangle), \partial_B(b) - \lambda) \rangle.$$

CASE 2: $cd = \downarrow$

$$\partial_P(s, cd, m) = \{ \langle \langle s', \alpha \rangle \mapsto 1, m' \rangle | s' \in S_P \wedge \alpha \in \Sigma_P \wedge m' = pop_P(m) \wedge$$
$$\forall \mu \forall \lambda [\mu \in n_{1_5} \cup (\{n_{1_2}\} \cup n_{1_4}) \wedge \lambda \in p_{1_5} \cup (\{p_{1_2}\} \cup p_{1_4} \Leftrightarrow \mu \| \lambda \in \delta_P(s'). \quad (4)$$

SUBCASE 1: $n_{1_2} = p_{1_2} = \alpha$, $n_{1_1} = pop_A(p)$ and $p_{1_1} = pop_B(n)$

$$z = \langle n, p \rangle.$$

SUBCASE 2: $\alpha = n_{1_2}$ and $p_{1_1} = n_{1_1} = *$

$$z = \langle n, \phi \rangle.$$

SUBCASE 3: $\alpha = p_{1_2}$ and $p_{1_1} = n_{1_1} = *$

$$z = \langle \phi, p \rangle.$$

The *parallel joint* operator is an *asynchronous* type and defines probabilities over a choice to synchronize or to act independently.

Example 1. This example insulates how the probabilities are distributed two *CPRA*s are composed by the *parallel joint* operator. Figure 1 (a) and Figure 1 (b) represent two probability distributions; μ and λ, associated with state functions of *CPRA*; C and D, respectively. Figure 2 shows the probability distribution $\mu \| \lambda$.

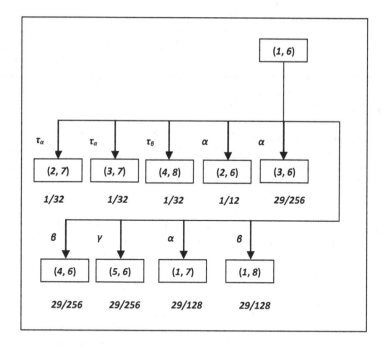

Fig. 2. Probability distribution $\mu \parallel \lambda$

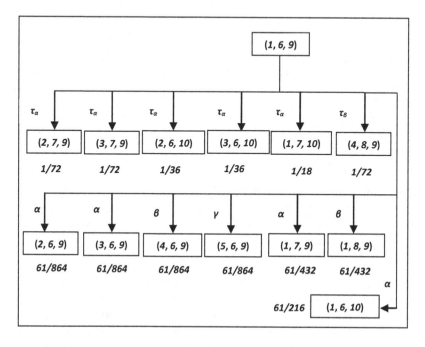

Fig. 3. Probability distribution $\mu \parallel \lambda \parallel \vartheta$

3.3   Properties of the CPRA

Here, two propositions are proposed which show that the *parallel joint* operation is invariant of the order in which two *CPRA* are composed. These propositions will be helpful in proving the *structural congruence* on the *parallel joint* operator. *Structural congruence* relation along with the equivalence theory of *CPRA* is deferred for the future.

Proposition 1. *Let A and B be two CPRA associated with two probability distributions μ and λ such that for a state $a \in S_A$; $\mu \in \delta_A(a)$, and $\lambda \in \delta_B(b)$ for a state $b \in S_B$, then $\forall \langle a', b' \rangle \forall \alpha [\langle a', b' \rangle \in S_A \times S_B \wedge \alpha \in (\Sigma_A \cup \Sigma_B \cup syn_{A,B}) \Rightarrow \mu \| \lambda (\langle a', b' \rangle, \alpha) = \lambda \| \mu (\langle b', a' \rangle, \alpha)]$.*

Proof. The proof of this theorem is the simple illustration of the fact that the multiplication of two real numbers is communicative. Let $\langle a', b' \rangle \in S_A \times S_B$ be a tuple of states such that $\mu \| \lambda (\langle \langle a', b' \rangle, \tau_\alpha \rangle) = \frac{1}{2} \times \mu(\langle a', \alpha \rangle) \times \frac{1}{2} \times \lambda(\langle b', \alpha \rangle)$ exists for an input symbol $\tau_\alpha \in syn_{A,B}$ then $\lambda \| \mu (\langle \langle b', a' \rangle, \tau_\alpha \rangle) = \frac{1}{2} \times \lambda(\langle b', \alpha \rangle) \times \frac{1}{2} \times \mu(\langle a', \alpha \rangle)$ is also true by eq. 1; hence, $\mu \| \lambda (\langle \langle a', b' \rangle, \tau_\alpha \rangle) = \lambda \| \mu (\langle \langle b', a' \rangle, \tau_\alpha \rangle)$ because $\mu(\langle a', \alpha \rangle) \times \lambda(\langle b', \alpha \rangle)$ is communicative and $\langle a', b' \rangle \in S_A \times S_B \Rightarrow \langle b', a' \rangle \in S_B \times S_A$ is a tautology. Moreover, if $\mu \| \lambda (\langle \langle a', b \rangle, \beta \rangle) = \frac{1}{2} \times \mu(\langle a', \beta \rangle) \times \left(1 - \sum_{s \in S_A \times S_B \wedge \tau_\alpha \in syn_{A,B}} \mu \| \lambda (\langle s, \tau_\alpha \rangle) \right)$ for an input symbol $\beta \in \Sigma_A$ and $a' \in S_A$ then by eq. 2; $\lambda \| \mu (\langle \langle b, a' \rangle, \beta \rangle) = \left(1 - \sum_{s \in S_A \times S_B \wedge \tau_\alpha \in syn_{A,B}} \mu \| \lambda (\langle s, \tau_\alpha \rangle) \right) \frac{1}{2} \times \mu(\langle a', \beta \rangle)$; hence, $\mu \| \lambda (\langle \langle a', b \rangle, \beta \rangle) = \lambda \| \mu (\langle \langle b, a' \rangle, \beta \rangle)$ by the similar reasonings as above. Similar is the case for $\mu \| \lambda (\langle \langle a, b' \rangle, \beta \rangle)$, where $\beta \in \Sigma_B$ and $b' \in S_B$.   □

Proposition 2. *Let A and B be two CPRA such that $P = A ^\wedge B$, and $Q = B ^\wedge A$, then, for all $\langle \mu(\langle \langle a', b' \rangle, \gamma \rangle), \langle n', p' \rangle \rangle \in \partial_P(\langle a, b \rangle, cd, \langle n, p \rangle)$ iff $\langle \lambda(\langle \langle b', a' \rangle, \gamma \rangle), \langle p', n' \rangle \rangle \in \partial_Q(\langle b, a \rangle, cd, \langle p, n \rangle)$ and $\mu(\langle \langle a', b' \rangle, \gamma \rangle) = \lambda(\langle \langle b', a' \rangle, \gamma \rangle)$. Here, $\langle a, b \rangle, \langle a', b' \rangle \in S_P$; $\langle n, p \rangle, \langle n', p' \rangle \in conf_P$; $\gamma \in (\Sigma_C \cup \Sigma_D \cup syn_{C,D})$; and $cd \in \{\uparrow, \downarrow\}$.*

Proof. Proposition 1 argues $\mu(\langle \langle c', d' \rangle, \gamma \rangle) = \lambda(\langle \langle d', c' \rangle, \gamma \rangle)$. The definition of transition function ∂ states that after the transition, *memory* is modified by a tuple which contains the traces of the computations performed by both A and B, therefore, the changes in the memories of P and Q must be same after the transition. Hence, this proves the proposition.   □

Hence, it is proved that the *parallel joint* of two *CPRA* is communicative but the associativity is still an open question. Here, it is informed that p*arallel joint* of *CPRA* is not associative, therefore, having a limited utility. To overcome this limitation, the definition of operator $\|$ has been extended for n probability distributions; this extension allows *parallel joint* operator to work invariantly for any permutations of any numbers of *CPRA*. Although, the basic definition of *parallel joint* operator needs to be modified in order to reflect the belongings of compositing *CPRA* (states, *input symbols* and etc.) but these modifications are simple exercise of cross multiplication of n sets and left for the readers. Before, proceeding towards the extension of operator $\|$, an example has been framed to explain why operator $\|$ is not associative.

Example 2. Let C be another *CPRA* associated with probability distribution $\vartheta = \{\langle 9, \alpha \rangle \mapsto 1\}$ along with probability distributions of Example .1. The associativity is expressed by $D = ((\mu \| \lambda) \| \vartheta)$ and $E = (\mu \| (\lambda \| \vartheta))$. Now, consider the probabilities of reaching the state $\langle 2, 7, 9 \rangle$ by *synchronizing action* τ_α in both D and E. In case of D, it is possible only if $\langle 2, 7 \rangle$ is reached by the *synchronization action* τ_{alpha} and state 9 is retained, i.e. $D(\langle\langle\langle 2, 7 \rangle, 9 \rangle, \tau_\alpha \rangle) = \dfrac{937}{1024}$; whereas, in case E, state $\langle 7, 9 \rangle$ is reached by the asynchronous action α and then state $\langle 2, \langle 7, 9 \rangle \rangle$ is achieved by the *synchronization action* τ_α, i.e. $E(\langle\langle 2, \langle 7, 9 \rangle \rangle, \tau_\alpha \rangle) = \dfrac{7}{512}$; in this case, shared action α is a part of μ and $(\lambda \| \vartheta)$. The readers are appealed to cross check the calculations.

Definition 4. *For a $n \in \mathbb{N}$; let $\{A_i\}_{i \leq n}$ be the collection of CPRA n such that for all $i \leq n$ $\mu_i \in \delta_{A_i}(s_i)$ and $s_i \in S_{A_i}$ then $\mu = (\mu_1 \| \mu_2 \| \dots \mu_n)$ is a probability distribution given as follows:*

$$\mu(\langle s_1, \dots, s_i', \dots, s_j', \dots, s_n \rangle, \tau_\alpha)) = \frac{1}{n} \times \mu_i(\langle s_i', \alpha \rangle) \times \frac{1}{n} \times \lambda(\langle s_j', \alpha \rangle);$$

for all $i, j \leq n$ such that $\alpha \in \Sigma_{S_{A_i}} \cap \Sigma_{S_{A_j}}, s_i' \in S_{A_i},$ and $s_j' \in S_{A_j}$.

Let the sum of all the probablities given by the above is represented by p, i.e.

$$p = \left(\sum_{s \in\ S_{A_1} \times S_{A_2} \dots, \times S_{A_n} \wedge \tau_\alpha \in syn_{A_i, A_j}} \mu(\langle s, \tau_\alpha \rangle) \right), then$$

$$\mu(\langle s_1, \dots, s_i', \dots, s_n \rangle, \alpha)) = \frac{1}{n} \times \mu_i(\langle s_i', \alpha \rangle) \times (1 - p);$$

for all $i \leq n$ such that $\alpha \in \Sigma_{A_i}$ and $s_i' \in S_{A_i}$.

See, the difference between the original and extended version of $\|$ *operator*. In extended version, the original concept of distributing probabilities of two probability distributions has been extended for n probability distributions; remains are same. For more clarity in the understanding go through the Figure 3; it shows the probability distribution $\mu \| \lambda \| \vartheta$, where, μ and λ are presented in Example 1 and ϑ is described in Example 2.

4   Result and Discussion

The proposed automata models probabilistic reversible concurrent systems. The probabilistic characteristic of *CPRA* is implemented by defining δ function.

It takes a state in S and returns a finite set of probabilistic mass functions $\{\mu_i\}_{i \leq n}$ over subsets of $S \times \Sigma$, here n is a natural number. The choices over different μ are nondeterministic, such nondeterministic choices are the reflection of the fact of having incomplete information to define the exact probability distribution over $S \times \Sigma$. In some sense these choices are governed by the possibility (possibility theory) rather than probability. The non-determinism implemented by the $CPRA$ is of both types *external* and as well as *internal*. *External* non-determinism is guaranteed by the fact that δ maps each state in S to a set of probability distributions over subsets of $S \times \Sigma$. *Internal* non-determinism is supported by the argument that two different probability distributions over same subset of $S \times \Sigma$ are permitted by the function δ for any state in S. Hence, $CPRA$ implements full non-determinism. Full probabilistic analysis of $CPRA$ can also be performed by introducing the concept of the scheduler, it resolves the non-deterministic choices and results a full probabilistic automata. The definition of the scheduler along with the probabilistic analysis of the $CPRA$ is deferred for the future.

The reversibility is implemented by the $CPRA$ by associating the *memory* m^0 with the automata. m^0 is a sequence of 5-tuples and organized in the form of stack with *push* and *pop* operations defined on it. m^0 stores the sufficient information regarding past transitions of $CPRA$ which is necessary for back-tracking. The term "sufficient" here implies the least amount of the information necessary for reversing the ones computational step besides respecting the past synchronizations. This implication is much stronger than the consistency of the memories which argues only the non-accessibility of the states which were non-accessible in past. Both facts can be established formally by casual equivalence of traces and this is proposed as future work. For now, let assume $m_C = \langle *, \mu(\langle s', \alpha \rangle), \alpha, \mu - \mu(\langle s', \alpha \rangle), \delta_C(s) - \mu \rangle \circ \ldots$ and $m_D = \langle *, \lambda(\langle p', \gamma \rangle), \gamma, \lambda - \lambda(\langle p', \gamma \rangle), \delta_D(p) - \lambda \rangle \circ \ldots$ which are the configurations of the memories of the $CPRA$s C and D respectively at some instant. Now, C and D synchronizes on *input* symbol β then m_C and m_D becomes $m'_C = \langle m_D, \mu'(\langle s'', \beta \rangle), \beta, \mu - \mu'(\langle s'', \beta \rangle), \delta_C(s) - \mu' \rangle \circ \langle *, \mu(\langle s', \alpha \rangle), \alpha, \mu - \mu(\langle s', \alpha \rangle), \delta_C(s) - \mu \rangle \circ \ldots$ and $m_D = \langle m_C, \lambda'(\langle p'', \beta \rangle), \beta, \lambda' - \lambda'(\langle p'', \beta \rangle), \delta_D(p') - \lambda \rangle \circ \langle *, \lambda(\langle p', \gamma \rangle), \gamma, \lambda - \lambda(\langle s', \gamma \rangle), \delta_D(p) - \lambda \rangle \circ \ldots$, respectively. Lets assume system decides to backtrack at this moment but C and D cannot backtrack independently because they are locked (by eq.4) they must have to synchronize again in backward computation for backtracking. This example gives the intuition that *memory* implemented by the $CPRA$ is consistent and respects the past synchronizations. Although, the *memory* are consistence but at the same time it is maximally flexible. This is because the order of reversing the events doesnt depend on the exact ordering of the events in global time.

Parallel joint operator implements the concurrency and favors the *asynchronous* type of synchronization. When two $CPRA$ shares the same *input* symbol then they are independent to synchronize on the shared *input* symbol (by eq. 1) or act independently (by eq. 2 and eq. 3).

Although, Definition 2 makes a distinction among its input symbol: synchronized *input* symbol (say τ) and ordinary *input* symbol (say α) but this distinction is logical rather than technical in the sense that Definition 2 remains valid with slight modifications if one should not want to make such distinction. Previous formalisms (Section 2) made distinctions among actions (*input symbols*) to implement the appropriate probability distribution on the set of combined transitions of both automata. Here, the intensions to distinguish synchronized actions are to propose the theory of weak *bi-simulation* relation for the *CPRA*.

5   Conclusion

CPRA is capable of modelling concurrency as well as reversibility in a probabilistic environment. Furthermore, it provides the facility to model non-determinism. The level of non-determinism implemented by it can be seemed to be like *Pnueli-Zuck probabilistic automata* [6]. *Pnueli-Zuck probabilistic automata* suffers from having no suitable parallel composition operator [6]. Meanwhile, different parallel composition operators have been proposed; not intended mainly for *Pnueli-Zuck probabilistic automata* but can be compatible with it, but either they are *synchronous* or depend on bias factors for the *asynchronous* implementation. *CPRA* removes such limitations and provides the constructs of a *parallel joint* operator without introducing any bias factors. Moreover, like the *Segla probabilistic automata* [10], a probabilistic analysis of *CPRA* can be made by exploiting the concepts of the *measure theory*. The inclusion of *memory* in *CPRA* makes it distinct from the class *PA* in which the above mentioned automata lie. *CPRA* can be viewed as a means of formally specifying a system where verifications can be performed on building test cases on the states and *input symbols*; therefore, it partially rules out third party logics such as *LTL* [2] or *CTL* [15] for building test cases, which is a recent trend with process algebras.

References

1. Tanenbaum, A.: Computer Networks, 4th edn. Prentice Hall Professional Technical Reference (2002)
2. Shigong, L., Lijun, W.: Analysis of cryptographic protocols using ltl of knowledge. In: 2010 2nd International Conference on Networking and Digital Society (ICNDS), vol. 1, pp. 463–466 (2010)
3. Daws, C., Kwiatkowska, M., Norman, G.: Automatic verification of the ieee 1394 root contention protocol with kronos and prism. International Journal on Software Tools for Technology Transfer 5(2-3), 221–236 (2004)
4. Ma, J., Zhang, D., Xu, G., Yang, Y.: Model checking based security policy verification and validation. In: 2010 2nd International Workshop on Intelligent Systems and Applications (ISA), pp. 1–4 (2010)
5. Glabbeek, R.J.V., Smolka, S.A., Steffen, B.: Reactive, generative and stratified models of probabilistic processes. Information and Computation 121, 130–141 (1990)
6. Sokolova, A., de Vink, E.P.: Probabilistic automata: System types, parallel composition and comparison. In: Baier, C., Haverkort, B.R., Hermanns, H., Katoen, J.-P., Siegle, M. (eds.) Validation of Stochastic Systems. LNCS, vol. 2925, pp. 1–43. Springer, Heidelberg (2004)

7. Barendregt, H.P.: The Lambda Calculus, Its Syntax and Semantics, Revised Edition. Studies in Logic and the Foundations of Mathematics, vol. 103. North Holland (November 1985)
8. Milner, R.: Communication and Concurrency. Prentice-Hall, Inc., Upper Saddle River (1989)
9. De Alfaro, L.: Formal verification of probabilistic systems. PhD thesis, Stanford, CA, USA, AAI9837082 (1998)
10. Segala, R.: Modeling and verification of randomized distributed real-time systems. PhD thesis, Cambridge, MA, USA, Not available from Univ. Microfilms Int. (1995)
11. Delahaye, B., Katoen, J.-P., Larsen, K.G., Legay, A., Pedersen, M.L., Sher, F., Wąsowski, A.: Abstract probabilistic automata. In: Jhala, R., Schmidt, D. (eds.) VMCAI 2011. LNCS, vol. 6538, pp. 324–339. Springer, Heidelberg (2011)
12. Golovkins, M., Kravtsev, M.: Probabilistic reversible automata and quantum automata. In: Ibarra, O.H., Zhang, L. (eds.) COCOON 2002. LNCS, vol. 2387, pp. 574–583. Springer, Heidelberg (2002)
13. Golovkins, M., Kravtsev, M., Kravcevs, V.: On a class of languages recognizable by probabilistic reversible decide-and-halt automata. Theor. Comput. Sci. 410(20), 1942–1951 (2009)
14. Phillips, I., Ulidowski, I.: Reversibility and models for concurrency. Electron. Notes Theor. Comput. Sci. 192(1), 93–108 (2007)
15. Pnueli, A.: The temporal logic of programs. In: Proceedings of the 18th Annual Symposium on Foundations of Computer Science, SFCS 1977, pp. 46–57. IEEE Computer Society, Washington, DC (1977)

Finding Influential Nodes in Social Networks Using Minimum k-Hop Dominating Set

Partha Basuchowdhuri and Subhashis Majumder

Heritage Institute of Technology,
Department of Computer Science and Engineering,
Chowbaga Road, Anandapur, Kolkata 700107, WB, India
{parthabasu.chowdhuri,subhashis.majumder}@heritageit.edu

Abstract. Challenges in social interaction networks are often modelled as graph theoretic problems. One such problem is to find a group of influential individuals of minimum size or the initial seed set in a social network, so that all the nodes in the network can be reached with only one hop from the seeds. This problem is equivalent to finding a minimum dominating set for the network. In this paper, we address a problem which is similar to finding minimum dominating set but differs in terms of number of hops needed to reach all the nodes. We have generalized the problem as k-hop dominating set problem, where a maximum of k hops will be allowed to spread the information among all the nodes of the graph. We show that the decision version of the k-hop dominating set problem is NP-complete. Results show that, in order to reach the same percentage of nodes in the network, if one extra hop is allowed then the cardinality of the seed set i.e. the number of influential nodes needed, is considerably reduced. Also, the experimental results show that the influential nodes can be characterized by their high betweenness values.

Keywords: Social networks, Spread of influence, Viral Marketing, Dominating sets.

1   Introduction

Social interaction network can be interpreted as a network of communication between social entities. Such a network provides a backbone for information dissemination and spread of influence with the help of the entities participating in it. Online social networks have increasingly become an important part of our social setup.

Spread of influence in a network is widely used by many useful applications. For example, in a simple friendship network, someone wants to spread an information very quickly, using their influential friends. In other words, the objective is to find the minimum set of persons that should be chosen to start spreading an influence, so that the influence spreads to the whole network in minimum time. Increase in the initial set of persons, chosen as starting points for spread, will help reducing the time taken to spread the influence to the whole network and vice-versa. This indicates a trade-off between the cardinality of the seed set

P. Gupta and C. Zaroliagis (Eds.): ICAA 2014, LNCS 8321, pp. 137–151, 2014.

and the amount of time that is needed to reach the complete network. In case of viral marketing, a marketeer tries to influence the set of people who are the k most influential ones among all the nodes in the network.

If the budget for marketing is lesser, the cardinality of the seed set will be smaller and hence the time taken might be longer. If traversing one edge takes one unit of time and is referred to as a *hop*, then finding a minimum dominating set will give us the minimum number of people we need to target initially, in order to spread the influence to the whole network in one hop. In this paper, we discuss strategies to reach all the nodes in the network using a multiple hop variant of the solution for the minimum dominating set problem.

Based on the urgency of the marketing campaign, a marketing company can calculate the time (in *hops*) that can be allowed for the information to spread. Also, based on the budget, a proper seed set can be found that will limit the budget and simultaneously will not exceed the time period set by the company to spread the information to the whole network. In this paper, our objective is to find the initial seed sets for a network under both time and budget constraints.

2   Background

2.1   Social Networks

A social relationship network can be visualized as a graph denoted by $G(V, E)$ where V is defined as the vertex set or the set of entities present in that network and E is defined as the edge set or the set of relationships existing between the pairs of entities. Usually, cardinality of the edge set E is referred to as the *size* of the graph G and is given by $|E|=m$, similarly, cardinality of the vertex set V is referred to as the *order* of the graph G and is given by $|V|=n$.

Social networks are usually sparse graphs with features of a scale-free network. The basic centrality measures of a social network [1] are widely used in the network science community and hence are not described in this paper.

2.2   Graph Definitions

Definition 1. Dominating Set : *Given an undirected graph $G = (V, E)$, a dominating set is a subset $S \subset V$ of its vertex set such that any node $v \in V$ is either a neighbor of a node $s \in S$ or $v \in S$.*

Finding a dominating set of minimum size is an NP-hard problem. Therefore in practice approximation algorithms or heuristics are used to find solutions to dominating set problems that arise in various applications.

Figure 1 shows a minimum dominating set of a graph. Note that dominating set of a graph may not be unique. There are other kind of dominating sets defined in the literature.

Definition 2. k – Dominating Set : *Given an undirected graph $G = (V, E)$, a k-dominating set is a subset $S \subseteq V$ of its vertex set such that any node $v \in V \setminus S$ will be within the neighborhood of at least k nodes from S.*

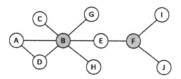

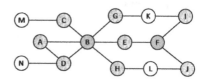

Fig. 1. Minimum dominating set for the given graph is {B,F}

Fig. 2. 2-hop minimum dominating set for the given graph is {B, F}

According to this definition, dominating set S can be considered as a 1-dominating set. However, the definition that we need for the work described in this paper is given in Definition 2.

In Figure 2, $\{B, F\}$ is the minimum 2-hop dominating set for the graph.

A node $v_k \in V$ is said to be at a k-hop distance from another node $v_0 \in V$, if there exists a shortest path from v_0 to v_k comprising of k edges. Say, the path from v_0 to v_k is denoted by $p(v_0, v_k)$ and it passes through a set of intermediate nodes $I(v_0, v_k) = \{v_1, v_2, v_3, ..., v_i, ...v_{k-1}\}$, v_i being in the neighborhood of v_{i-1} denoted by $N(v_{i-1})$, where $N(v) \subset V$ is the set of vertices adjacent to v. Here, $v_1, v_2, v_3, ..., v_i, ...v_{k-1}, v_k$ all are in the *k-hop neighborhood* of v_0, which is denoted by $N_k(v_0)$ as follows,

$$N_k(v_0) = \begin{cases} N(v_0) & \text{if } k = 1, \\ N_{k-1}(v_0) \cup \left(\bigcup_{\forall v \in N_{k-1}(v_0)} N_1(v) \right) & \text{if } k \geq 2. \end{cases}$$

We define *k-hop degree* of v_0 to be the cardinality of $N_k(v_0)$. The *k-hop neighborhood* of v_0 may consist of three types of nodes in terms of what role they are playing during the spread of influence in the network - the ones who have been influenced and have also spread the influence, the ones who have been influenced but did not get the chance to spread the influence yet and the last type are those who have not been influenced yet.

The subset of $N_k(v_0)$ consisting of all the nodes that have not been influenced yet and is devoid of the other two types of nodes, is said to be the *effective neighborhood* of v_0 and is denoted by $EN_k(v_0)$. The *effective degree* of v_0 is defined by the cardinality of $EN_k(v_0)$.

Definition 3. k − hop Dominating Set (kHDS) : *Given an undirected graph $G = (V, E)$, a k-hop dominating set is a subset $S \subseteq V$ of its vertex set such that any node $v \in V \setminus S$ will be within the k-hop neighborhood of s, denoted by $N_k(s)$, for at least one $s \in S$. If a k−hop dominating set of a graph G is given by S then,*

$$V(G) = S(G) \cup \left(\bigcup_{\forall s \in S} N_k(s) \right)$$

The set S is often called a seed set. A k-hop dominating set of minimum cardinality is called a minimum k-hop dominating set.

3   Prior Work

Finding *minimum dominating set* for a graph is one of the classical NP-complete problems [2]. It is approximable within $1 + \log|V|$ since the problem is a special instance of *minimum set cover* [3] but it is not approximable within $c\log|V|$, for some $c > 0$ [4]. Minimum dominating set problem admits a PTAS for planar graphs [5] and for unit disk graphs [6]. If the dominating set is restricted to be connected, the problem is called a connected dominating set problem and it is approximable within $\ln\Delta + 3$ where Δ is the maximum degree, and within $3\ln|V|$ for the vertex weighted version [7].

Dominating sets can be useful to reach all the nodes efficiently in social networks. Several studies reveal usefulness of dominating sets in social networks.

Bonneau et al. [8] studied Facebook user graphs and its samples to analyze its features. One of their findings reveal that minimum dominating set based seed sets spread information to all the nodes in the network faster than the seed sets selected based on purely degree. They also conclude that small dominating sets can be found that dominates a large part of the network. They chose a 100-node set and found out that around 65.2% of the nodes in the network can be dominated by that set of 100 nodes.

Borgatti [9] defined an *m-reach criterion* for reaching the nodes of a social network and showed it to be useful. Eubank et al. [10] has proven that the simple greedy algorithm gives a $1 + o(1)$ approximation with a small constant in $o(1)$ to the 1-dominating set problem in a power law graph.

Some variants of dominating sets have been used for social networks. Wang et al. [11,12] has defined a *positive influence* dominating set, which they have found to be selecting a larger seed set than in case of 1-dominating sets for power-law graphs. Also, based on experiments performed, they have observed that power law graphs produce empirically larger dominating sets than random graphs.

4   Problem Definition

Given an undirected, unweighted social network $G(V, E)$, an influence needs to be spread to all the nodes of the network within a reasonable time-frame, whereas the cost of marketing must also stay within the budget. It is assumed that an *active* node, which has already been influenced, will mandatorily influence its *inactive* neighbors that do not yet have the influence. In *independent cascade* model there is a propagation probability attached to every edge and based on that it is decided whether the edge will be able to succeed in influencing the neighbors. In our model, we consider the edge set to be consisting of only those edges for which the propagation probability exceeds a certain threshold value. Influence is passed from one *active* node u to one of its *inactive* neighbor v by using an edge $e(u, v)$ and not by any other alternate path.

We consider a typical word-of-mouth marketing scenario where the total budget constraint B is given for the problem, with P being the cost of influencing one person. Initially, a seed set (say, of cardinality β) will be chosen and they can be influenced with a cost βP, where $\beta P \leq B < (\beta + 1)P$. Traversal of an edge is related to the sequence of spread of influence and every edge traversal is considered to be taking unit time. Therefore, time taken for the marketing is also another constraint that needs to be taken into account. If the total time allowed for spread is T time units, our objective is to find the seed set of size $\leq \beta$ for which we can maximize the spread in the nodes in $V \setminus S$ within k hops, where $k \leq T$. If $k > T$, then the problem can not be solved simultaneously within the budget constraint of B and time constraint of T.

In the example given in Figure 2 the solutions for finding dominating sets would be different based on the time units allowed to spread the influence. If $T = 2$, where T is the total units of time stamps allowed for the spread from $T = 0$, then $k = 2$ and B, F would be the 2-hop minimum dominating set. The start of spread takes place at $T = 0$ and that is also when the seed set is chosen. If the marketing policy requires the spread to be completed in lesser time, we have to make $T_{new} < T$, therefore, in this example T_{new} can be assigned a value as low as 1 and hence the problem becomes same as finding the minimum dominating set problem. In that case, $\{C, D, F, G, H\}$ would be the dominating set and hence the seed set. It is evident that the cost for influencing the seed set at $T = 0$, increases from $2P$ to $5P$, if the restriction is being imposed on the time span for the spread. The speed and budget trade-off for viral marketing is thereby established by tuning the values of either T or B, which are inversely related to each other. The marketing policy will fix either of these parameters and the other will be tuned accordingly. Intuitively for large graphs, after a time threshold, say $T = t_{th}$, the growth of incremental spread will slow down. This time-stamp $T = t_{th}$ will signify a *critical time*, after which the number of *inactive* nodes left in the network becomes less because of the structure of the network and the rate of spread slows down drastically.

5   Finding Minimum k-Hop Dominating Set

We would like to find a minimum k-hop dominating set in the graph so that the time constraint on spreading can be relaxed from one time unit to k time units (assuming $k > 1$) and the budget can be reduced from nP to $n'P$ such that $n' < n$. We now formally state the problem P_k for which we present a solution procedure in this section.

Definition 4. P_k: *Find a kHDS of minimum size in a graph $G(V, E)$, such that, when used as a seed set for spreading the influence at time $T = 0$, all the nodes in the graph G can be reached within $T = k$.*

5.1   NP Completeness

We now show that the k-hop dominating set problem P_k is computationally hard. We actually consider the decision problem P'_k corresponding to P_k and show that it is NP-complete.

Definition 5. P'_k: *Given a graph $G(V, E)$, and an integer k, does there exist a set of vertices S, such that every vertex in V can be reached from some vertex $v \in S$ in at most k hops?*

To show that $P'_k \in NP$, we can consider each vertex once and take a decision nondeterministically whether it should belong to a k-hop dominating set or not in $O(n)$ time. Further, given a set S of vertices, we can check in polynomial time, whether it is a k-hop dominating set. First, flag all the vertices that are in S. Then in each step, flag all the unflagged neighbors of the vertices that are flagged before the start of that step. At the end of k steps, just check whether all the vertices are flagged. If yes, then the set S is a k-hop dominating set, otherwise not. The time taken is $O(k|E|)$ and hence polynomial. Hence $P'_k \in NP$. A polynomial time reduction of the Vertex Cover Problem, which is known to be NP-complete [2], to P'_k is established next.

Definition 6. Vertex Cover Problem: *Given a graph $G = (V, E)$, and an integer k, does G contain a vertex cover of size at most k?*

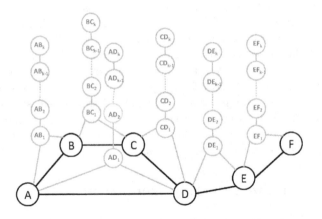

Fig. 3. The graph $G(V, E)$ has been drawn by using dark lines. V is given by $\{A, B, C, D, E, F\}$. $G' = (V', E')$ has been constructed on top of G by drawing nodes and edges in lighter shade.

Reduction : Let $G = (V, E)$ be a graph that has a vertex cover consisting of r vertices. From G, we generate an instance $G' = (V', E')$ of the k-hop dominating set problem, in the following way. We subdivide every edge $(v_i, v_j) \in E$ by adding a new vertex $v_{i,j}$, and then we attach a linear chain of k - 1 vertices to the vertex $v_{i,j}$, as shown in Figure 3. We then add an extra edge directly between v_i and v_j. The time required to construct G' from G is clearly $O(k|E|)$ and hence polynomial.

Claim 1 : If S is a vertex cover of size r in G, then the same set of vertices form a k-hop dominating set in G'.

Proof. All the edges of E are covered by S. So any vertex in V' that was originally in V, either belongs to S or has a neighbor in S. Also by the method of construction, any vertex that was added to subdivide the original edges of E, is at one-hop distance from some vertex of S. Hence any other vertex in V' that got added later is within k hops from some vertex of S. Thus S serves as a k-hop dominating set in G'.

Claim 2 : If S' is a k-hop dominating set in G' of size r, we can construct a vertex cover in G of size not more than r.

Proof. We need to take care of 2 cases. Case 1: All the vertices in S' are from V. In this case, exactly the same set of vertices in S' will serve as a vertex cover in G. This is because to reach the leaf, the last vertex of the added chain corresponding to every original edge (v_i, v_j) in E, within k hops, either v_i or v_j must belong to S'. Any other vertex from V will need at least $k + 1$ hops, to reach the leaf. Hence S' will be a vertex cover for G.

Case 2: Some of the vertices in S' are from $V' - V$. Note that by the argument of case 1, if neither v_i nor v_j belongs to S' for some edge (v_i, v_j) in E, then to cover the end vertex of the corresponding chain in k hops, at least one vertex from the chain has to be in S'. Then we can just replace that vertex by either v_i or v_j, without increasing the size of the set S'. Note that in k hops v_i or v_j will cover all the vertices (possibly more) that were covered by the vertex being replaced. Hence for every edge (v_i, v_j) in E, either v_i or v_j belonged to S' from the beginning or got added to it by replacement, showing that we can construct a vertex cover for G from S', of size not more than r.

As the instance can be created in polynomial time, we can now conclude that P'_k is NP-hard. As we have already shown that $P'_k \in NP$, we can conclude that problem P'_k is NP-complete.

5.2   Greedy Heuristics for Finding kHDS

In this section, we present a greedy heuristic to find the k-hop dominating sets, as described in Algorithm 1. The algorithm will return V', which will be the k-hop dominating set of the network $G(V, E)$. Lines 2-4 denote the initialization part. Coloring the nodes helps us in understanding the state of a node better, in the process of information spread. Initially all the nodes are colored white, which means that neither they have got the information nor they have spread the information. After a node receives information, it becomes grey and if it has spread the information to its neighbors, then it becomes black. A white node can turn grey or black, and a grey node can turn black but not otherwise. If at a certain stage, no node is white any more, that means information has reached to all the nodes of the network. In lines 2-4, the color flag for all nodes are set to white initially. Also, initially, the kHDS (V') is empty.

Lines 6-24 runs a while loop that stops when there exists no white node, i.e., the information has reached to all the nodes in the network. In lines 7-9, for all nodes we find the *effective* k-hop degrees. In the first iteration, all nodes are white, so for every node its *effective* k-hop degree is same as its k-hop degree. From the next step, not all nodes remain white and hence *effective* k-hop degree of a node v would be the number of white nodes it can reach to in k hops. Grey nodes already have the information, so getting information to them would be redundant and is not desired.

Algorithm 1. Finding kHDS

Input : Undirected, unweighted network $G(V, E)$
Output: $V' \subseteq V$, such that for any node $v \in V$, minimum distance from any
$v_i' \in V'$ is atmost k

```
1  begin
2  |   forall the v ∈ V do
3  |   |   flag[v] ← white
4  |   end
5  |   V' ← ∅
6  |   while TRUE do
7  |   |   forall the v ∈ V do
8  |   |   |   kdegree[v] ← effective k-hop degree of v
9  |   |   end
10 |   |   v'ᵢ = FIND-MAX(kdegree)
11 |   |   V' ← V' ∪ {v'ᵢ}
12 |   |   V ← V \ {v'ᵢ}
13 |   |   if flag[v'ᵢ] equals to white then
14 |   |   |   whiteCount ← whiteCount-1
15 |   |   end
16 |   |   flag[v'ᵢ] ← black
17 |   |   forall the u'ᵢ ∈ Nₖ(v'ᵢ) do
18 |   |   |   if flag[u'ᵢ] is white then
19 |   |   |   |   flag[u'ᵢ] ← grey
20 |   |   |   |   whiteCount ← whiteCount-1
21 |   |   |   end
22 |   |   end
23 |   |   if whiteCount equals to zero then  return V'
24 |   end
25 end
```

Breadth first traversal from a source node to up to k levels can be used for finding k-hop degree of a node. For calculating *effective* k-hop degree, an extra flag checking is needed, which will only count the number of the white nodes available within the k-hop neighborhood.

At lines 7-10, for all nodes in V the effective k-hop degree will be calculated and an array $k$degree is used for storing the k-hop degree values as its keys. A sequential search is executed in $k$degree, to identify the node v'_i, with the maximum *effective* k-hop degree at that stage. The sets V and V' are hence updated accordingly. If the selected node is presently a white node then whiteCount is decremented because it is turned to black afterwards in line 18.

In lines 17-22, all the white neighbors of the selected nodes are flagged grey and as the number of white nodes decrease, value of whiteCount is decremented. The grey nodes and the black nodes retain their colors. Line 23 keeps a check on the number of white nodes. When there is no more white node, it means the information has reached to all the nodes in the network, so the algorithm stops and returns the dominating set as represented by V'.

The run-time for the algorithm would depend on the parts 2-4 and 6-24. For lines 2-4, time required to execute is $O(|V|)$. Analysis of 6-24 can be further divided into subparts in order to make the estimation easier. In 7-9, we run the loop V times and use a breadth first traversal inside, which may take up to $O(|E|)$. So, time required for the lines 7-9 to execute is in $O(|V|.|E|)$.

FIND-MAX finds the maximum key from a list using a sequential search. Hence, in line 10, it would require $O(|V|)$ time to execute. Worst case run-time for lines 17-22 would be $O(|E|)$. If the cardinality of the dominating set is p, then the worst case time complexity would be $O(|V| + p(|V|.|E| + |V| + |E|))$. Using asymptotic notation, we can say that the run-time would be $O(p.|V|.|E|)$.

5.3   An Example of 2-Hop Spread

In this subsection, we illustrate with a small example how the greedy heuristic tries to find the 2HDS of minimum size. In Figure 4, we show a graph of 17 nodes. In the first step, we calculate the 2-hop degrees for all the nodes. At this

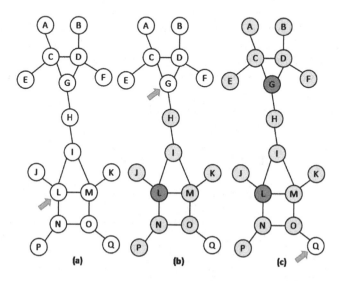

Fig. 4. Sequences for choosing 2HDS in a graph

stage, the maximum 2-hop degree found among all nodes is 8. In Figure 4 (a), we have 5 nodes (G, L, M), each of whose 2-hop degree is 8. Among those nodes, we randomly break the tie and pick one. Say, L is being picked in this case. Then the black and grey flags are put in place based on the choice of seed, as shown in Figure 4 (b). From the next step and onwards, maximum effective 2-hop degree will be used as the measure for the greedy choice.

So, we greedily choose the non-black node with the maximum effective 2-hop degree. In this case, it will be node G, which has an effective 2-hop degree of 6. After putting all the flags based on the choice of G, Q is the only node that remains to be influenced. So, our third choice becomes trivial and we choose Q as the last seed.

One important point here is, if we are trying to pick a seed node at some stage in the process of finding kHDS and run into a situation where there is a tie between a white and a grey node in terms of maximum effective k-hop degree, then the white node will be preferred because the white node itself is not included in its effective k-hop neighborhood and by picking the white node we are effectively reaching the information to one more node, which is the white node itself.

6   Experimental Results

In this section, we describe the experiments we have performed on some standard available datasets as well as a synthetic dataset to analyze the features and usefulness of kHDS. We have performed the experiments on a 2GHz Intel Xeon processor with 4MB cache, 16GB RAM and Red Hat Enterprise Edition 5.4 OS.

6.1   Datasets

We have used a total of four datasets for our experiments. Three of them are benchmark real-world social network data used by researchers for analysis of social networks. The synthetic data is an Erdös-Rényi random graph. Description of key features for the four datasets have been provided in Table 1.

For the fourth dataset, the parameters were chosen in such a way, so that a small-world network can be represented by this random network. The graph is connected but the low average clustering co-efficient signifies it to be extremely sparse. Two of the large real world networks show scale free feature as their degree distribution plots obey power law.

Table 1. Features of the Datasets

Name of Dataset	No. of Nodes ($|V|$)	No. of Edges ($|E|$)	Average Shortest Path Length	Diameter	Average Clustering Co-efficient
American College Football	115	613	2.5	4	0.4
Enron E-mail Data	33,696	180,811	4.025	13	0.509
Wiki-Vote Data	7,066	103,663	3.25	7	0.209
Erdös-Rényi Network	20,000	598,497	2.83	4	0.003

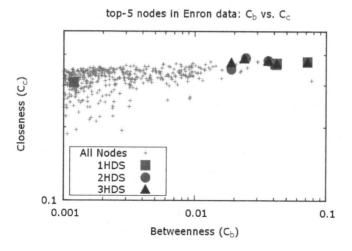

Fig. 5. Position of the top 5 influential nodes from 1HDS, 2HDS and 3HDS have been shown for the Enron e-mail network

6.2 Closeness vs. Betweenness

Closeness being a metric that takes into account shortest path distances of a node from other nodes, it is intuitive that the closeness values of the influential nodes compared to others may reveal some characteristics of the k-hop dominating sets. Similarly, when time or hop constraint is relaxed, the nodes that can reach to different groups quickly i.e., the *brokers* would be useful to observe rather than observing the nodes with high degrees. So, a correlation plot was used to observe the closeness values of the nodes against their betweenness values for comparing the influential nodes against the rest of the nodes in the network.

In Figures 5, 6 and 7 , we can see betweenness vs. closeness plot for all the vertices of the Football network, Enron e-mail network, Wiki-vote network and Erdös-Rényi network respectively. For all these datasets, the top 5 influential nodes for the 1HDS, 2HDS and 3HDS have been shown with legends. However, in case of football network, we have used top 4 influential nodes, as for 3HDS the network consists of 4 nodes only. For the Erdös-Rényi network, 3HDS consists of only one node that also belongs to the top 5 nodes of 2HDS and hence 3HDS was not plotted.

The results show us that higher the k value of k-HDS, the top influential nodes are more likely to have high betweenness value as well high closeness value than the other nodes. The top influential nodes for $k = \lfloor$ average shortest path distance $\rfloor$ are observed to have largest betweenness values. For some influential nodes, closeness values are not very high but high betweenness value is uniformly observed among all the influential nodes. Also, not all the nodes having high betweenness are chosen to be top influential nodes. This is because some of the nodes having high betweenness were skipped for not having a large enough incremental effective spread, right after an influential node with high

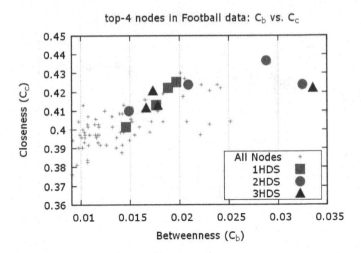

Fig. 6. Position of the top 4 influential nodes from 1HDS, 2HDS and 3HDS have been shown for the Football network

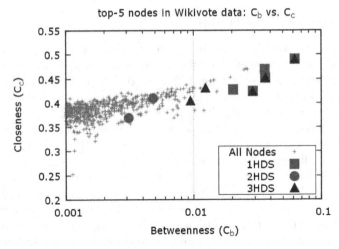

Fig. 7. Position of the top 5 influential nodes from 1HDS, 2HDS and 3HDS have been shown for the Wiki-Vote network

betweenness value has been chosen. Top influential nodes have some of the largest betweenness and closeness values.

Hence, we can say that, if we have betweenness and closeness values of all nodes in the network we can try to predict the top influentials from the network.

6.3   Growth in Spread with Top-Most Influential Nodes

The growth of the spread of influence in the networks were observed for a few consecutive number of time stamps. Top 5 node choices by the heuristic from

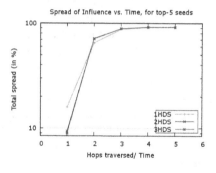
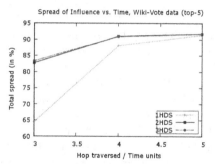

(a) Growth of Spread of Influence for top 5 nodes in Enron Data.

(b) Enhanced view of the performance of 1HDS, 2HDS and 3HDS for 3 to 5 hops in Enron data.

Fig. 8. Percentage of spread using top 5 influential nodes from 1HDS, 2HDS and 3HDS have been shown for the Enron E-mail network

the 1HDS, 2HDS and 3HDS are selected to observe their impact on how fast they help to reach the information to the whole network.

Real world social networks are usually small-world networks. The small world networks have small average shortest path distances. So, it is evident that beyond a value of k, cardinality of the kHDS for a small world network would become 1. So, that was the main reason for choosing to observe kHDS for k value up to 3. As expected, at time stamp k, top 5 nodes of kHDS provides spread to larger part of the network than top 5 nodes of other dominating sets. From the results, shown in Figures 8 and 9, we can conclude that the incremental calculation used for finding kHDS for increased value of k guarantees better performance.

The threshold time t_{th}, as discussed in Section 4, is said to be the time stamp for which the dominating set would be a considerably small one and by incrementing k (which is same as the value of t_{th}) at this stage, we may not be able to produce a set that would have any faster spread than the top nodes from kHDS would provide after k hops. In our experiments, we have found out the value of t_{th} to be around $\lfloor$ average shortest path distance $\rfloor$.

For the Football network and the Erdös-Rényi network, we have found up to 2HDS only because when $k=3$ is allowed, only one node can be used as a seed to reach all the nodes in three hops. It confirms the fact that for a graph with small average shortest path length, value of p, as described at the end of subsection 5.2, would be a small integer. For both the networks, the top 5 nodes in 2HDS spreads the information to a greater percentage of nodes than that of the top 5 nodes from their 1HDS in two hops.

6.4   Budget vs. Marketing Time Trade-Off

The main objective behind finding the kHDS is to find a compromise between the budget and the marketing time. If more time can be allowed for the word-of-mouth marketing campaign, a large part of the network can be reached starting from only a handful of nodes, hence reducing the budget to influence the initial seed set. The results obtained from our experiments, as shown in Table 2 and Figure 10, reinforces the drastic reduction of the size of seed set, with increased value of k.

For the large small-world graphs, the drop in the size of kHDS is considerable. In Enron data, size of 1HDS is about 15 times the size of 2HDS, which in turn is more than 70 times the size of 3HDS. In Wiki-vote data, size of 1HDS is about 20 times the size of 2HDS and the size of 2HDS is more than 11 times the size of 3HDS. So it is evident that with relaxation in one time unit for the spread process, the budget will get reduced by several times.

The experimental analysis can be reinforced by performing more extensive tests on more datasets and can be extended for finding kHDS in weighted graphs.

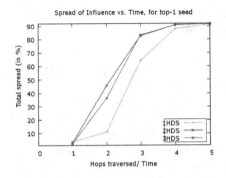
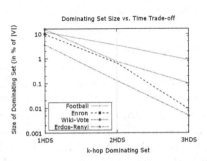

Fig. 9. Percentage of spread vs. time plot, using top 1 influential node from 1HDS, 2HDS and 3HDS, for the Enron E-mail network

Fig. 10. Change in size of dominating sets with increasing value of k for kHDS

Table 2. Cardinality of kHDS for all Datasets

Name of Dataset	|1HDS|	|2HDS|	|3HDS|
American College Football	14	4	1
Enron E-mail Data	3,317	227	3
Wiki-Vote Data	1,104	55	5
Erdös-Rényi Network	738	26	1

7   Conclusion

Experimental evaluation of the datasets reveals that if we want to find the optimized spread varying with time t, i.e., to maximize the spread at time $t = k$, finding kHDS is essential. We have shown that finding a kHDS of minimum cardinality is NP-hard, the corresponding decision version of the problem being NP-complete. From our experimental evaluation it follows that the top influential nodes in a social network, may be characterized by their high betweenness and closeness values. In order to accommodate the budget constraint in a typical word-of-mouth campaign, the time constraint for the marketing needs to be relaxed. Our experiments establish that with relaxation of the time constraint by one hop, the size of the dominating set may decrease considerably. The budget for the campaign being directly proportional to the cardinality of the dominating set will also decrease.

References

1. Newman, M.E.J.: Networks: An Introduction. Oxford University Press, Oxford (2010)
2. Garey, M.R., Johnson, D.S.: Computers and Intractability; A Guide to the Theory of NP-Completeness. W. H. Freeman & Co., New York (1990)
3. Johnson, D.S.: Approximation algorithms for combinatorial problems. J. Comput. Syst. Sci. 9(3), 256–278 (1974)
4. Raz, R., Safra, S.: A sub-constant error-probability low-degree test, and a sub-constant error-probability pcp characterization of np. In: Proceedings of the Twenty-Ninth Annual ACM Symposium on Theory of Computing, STOC 1997, pp. 475–484 (1997)
5. Baker, B.S.: Approximation algorithms for np-complete problems on planar graphs. In: Proceedings of the 24th Annual Symposium on Foundations of Computer Science, SFCS 1983, pp. 265–273. IEEE Computer Society, Washington, DC (1983)
6. Hunt III, H.B., Marathe, M.V., Radhakrishnan, V., Ravi, S.S., Rosenkrantz, D.J., Stearns, R.E.: Nc-approximation schemes for np- and pspace-hard problems for geometric graphs. J. Algorithms 26(2), 238–274 (1998)
7. Guha, S., Khuller, S.: Approximation algorithms for connected dominating sets. Algorithmica 20, 374–387 (1998)
8. Bonneau, J., Anderson, J., Anderson, R., Stajano, F.: Eight friends are enough: Social graph approximation via public listings. In: Proceedings of the Second ACM EuroSys Workshop on Social Network Systems, SNS 2009, pp. 13–18. ACM, New York (2009)
9. Borgatti, S.P.: Identifying sets of key players in a social network. Comput. Math. Organ. Theory 12(1) (2006)
10. Eubank, S., Anil Kumar, V.S., Marathe, M.V., Srinivasan, A., Wang, N.: Structural and algorithmic aspects of massive social networks. In: Proceedings of the Fifteenth Annual ACM-SIAM Symposium on Discrete Algorithms, SODA 2004 (2004)
11. Wang, F., Camacho, E., Xu, K.: Positive influence dominating set in online social networks. In: Du, D.-Z., Hu, X., Pardalos, P.M. (eds.) COCOA 2009. LNCS, vol. 5573, pp. 313–321. Springer, Heidelberg (2009)
12. Wang, F., Du, H., Camacho, E., Xu, K., Lee, W., Shi, Y., Shan, S.: On positive influence dominating sets in social networks. Theor. Comput. Sci. 412(3), 265–269 (2011)

Efficient Heuristics for the Time Dependent Team Orienteering Problem with Time Windows*

Damianos Gavalas[1,6], Charalampos Konstantopoulos[2,6],
Konstantinos Mastakas[3,6], Grammati Pantziou[4,6], and Nikolaos Vathis[5,6]

[1] Department of Cultural Technology and Communication,
University of the Aegean, Mytilene, Greece
dgavalas@aegean.gr
[2] Department of Informatics, University of Piraeus, Piraeus, Greece
konstant@unipi.gr
[3] Department of Mathematics, University of Athens, Athens, Greece
kmast@math.uoa.gr
[4] Department of Informatics, Technological Educational Institution of Athens,
Athens, Greece
pantziou@teiath.gr
[5] School of Electrical and Computer Engineering,
National Technical University of Athens, Athens, Greece
nvathis@softlab.ntua.gr
[6] Computer Technology Institute and Press "Diophantus" (CTI), Patras, Greece

Abstract. The Time Dependent Team Orienteering Problem with Time Windows (TDTOPTW) can be used to model several real life problems. Among them, the route planning problem for tourists interested in visiting multiple points of interest (POIs) using public transport. The main objective of this problem is to select POIs that match tourist preferences, while taking into account a multitude of parameters and constraints and respecting the time available for sightseeing in a daily basis. TDTOPTW is NP-hard while almost the whole body of the related literature addresses the non time dependent version of the problem. The only TDTOPTW heuristic proposed so far is based on the assumption of periodic service schedules. Herein, we propose two efficient cluster-based heuristics for the TDTOPTW which yield high quality solutions, take into account time dependency in calculating travel times between POIs and make no assumption on periodic service schedules. The validation scenario for our prototyped algorithms included the metropolitan transit network and real POI sets compiled from Athens (Greece).

1 Introduction

The aim of the Team Orienteering Problem with Time Windows (TOPTW) is to maximize the total profit collected by visiting a set of locations, each of which has

---

* This work was supported by the EU FP7/2007-2013 (DG CONNECT.H5-Smart Cities and Sustainability), under grant agreement no. 288094 (project eCOMPASS).

P. Gupta and C. Zaroliagis (Eds.): ICAA 2014, LNCS 8321, pp. 152–163, 2014.

a profit, a service time and a time window. The number of routes is limited, and each location can be visited at most once. The TOPTW has numerous real-life applications. In this paper, we consider the route planning application for tourists interested in visiting multiple POIs. The main objective is to select POIs that match tourist preferences, while taking into account a multitude of parameters and constraints (distances among POIs, visiting time required for each POI, POIs' opening hours) and respecting the time available for sightseeing in a daily basis. The problem is further complicated when considering the complexity of metropolitan transit networks commonly used by tourists to move from a POI to another. In this case, the tourist route planning problem can be modeled as a TDTOPTW. To our knowledge, the first TDTOPTW heuristic has been recently proposed by Garcia et al. [1]. However, the proposed algorithm is based on the simplified assumption of periodic service schedules which clearly, is not valid in realistic transportation networks, wherein arrival/departure frequencies typically vary within the services operational periods.

Herein, we propose two novel heuristic approaches, the Time Dependent CSCRoutes (TDCSCRoutes) and the SlackCSCRoutes, which address the above described shortcoming of the existing approach to TDTOPTW. The main incentive behind our approaches is to motivate visits to topology areas featuring high density of highly profitable candidate POIs, while taking into account time dependency (i.e. multimodality) in calculating travel times from one POI to another; the aim is to derive high quality routes (i.e. maximizing the total collected profit) while not sacrificing the time efficiency required for online applications. Our prototyped algorithms have been tested in terms of various performance parameters (solutions quality, execution time, number of transit transfers, etc) upon real test instances compiled from the wider area of Athens, Greece; the calculation of time dependent travel times has been carried out over the Athens metropolitan transit network. The performance of our algorithms has been compared against two variants that use precalculated average travel times (among the individual time dependent, real travel times) between POIs.

The remainder of this article is organized as follows: Section 2 overviews the related work while Section 3 presents our novel cluster-based heuristics. Section 4 discusses the experimental results and finally Section 5 concludes our work.

2   Related Work

The TOPTW is an extension of the orienteering problem (OP) Vansteenwegen et al. [2]. In the OP, several locations with an associated score have to be visited within a given time limit. Each location may be visited only once, while the aim is to maximize the overall score collected on a single tour. The team orienteering problem (TOP) extends the OP considering multiple routes while the TOP with time windows (TOPTW) considers visits to locations within a predefined time window. TOPTW is NP-hard (e.g. see [3]). Hence, exact solutions for TOPTW are feasible for instances with very restricted number of locations. As a result, the main body of TOPTW literature exclusively involves heuristic algorithms

([4], [5], [6], [7], [8], [9], [10]). ACS [8], Enhanced ACS [4] and the approach of
Tricoire et al. [9] are known to yield the highest quality solutions. The most
efficient known heuristic is based on Iterated Local Search (ILS) [10], offering
a fair compromise with respect to execution time versus deriving routes of reasonable quality [2]. However, ILS treats each POI separately, thereby commonly
overlooking highly profitable areas of POIs situated far from current location
considering them too time-expensive to visit. In [11] two cluster-based extensions to ILS have been proposed to address the aforementioned weakness by
grouping POIs on disjoint clusters, thereby making visits to such POIs more
attractive.

Time Dependent OP (TDOP) was introduced by Formin and Lingas [12].
TDOP is MAX-SNP-hard since a special case of TDOP, time-depenent maximum scheduling problem is MAX-SNP-hard [13]. Fomin and Lingas [12] give
a $(2 + \epsilon)$ approximation algorithm for rooted and unrooted TDOP. Abbaspour
et al. [14] investigated a variant of Time Dependent OP with Time Windows
(TDOPTW) in urban areas, and proposed a genetic algorithm for solving the
problem. The work of Garcia et al. [1] is the first to address algorithmically
the TDTOPTW. The authors presented two different approaches to solve TD-
TOPTW, both applied on real urban test instances (POIs and bus network of
San Sebastian, Spain). The first approach involves a pre-calculation step, computing the average travel times between all pairs of POIs, allowing reducing the
TDTOPTW to a regular TOPTW, solved using the insertion phase part of ILS.
In case that the derived TOPTW solution is infeasible (due to violating the time
windows of nodes included in the solution), a number of visits are removed. The
second approach uses time-dependent travel times but it based on the simplified assumption of periodic service schedules; this assumption, clearly, does not
hold in realistic urban transportation networks, especially on non fixed-rail services (e.g. buses). Herein, we propose an algorithmic approach that relaxes this
assumption and is applicable to realistic transit networks.

3   The Proposed TDTOPTW Heuristics

TDTOPTW is an extension of TOPTW integrating public transportation, i.e.,
time dependent travel costs among nodes. In TOPTW we are given a complete
directed graph $G = (V, E)$ where V denotes the set of locations with $N = |V|$; a
set $P = \{p_1, p_2, \ldots, p_{N_p}\} \subseteq V$ denoting the set of POIs; an integer m denoting
the number of days the trip shall last, and a time budget B. The main attributes
of each node $p_i \in P$ are: the service or visiting time ($visit_i$), the profit gained by
visiting p_i ($profit_i$), and each day's time window $[open_{ir}, close_{ir}]$, $r = 1, 2, \ldots, m$,
(a POI may have different time windows per day). Every link $(u, v) \in E$ denotes
the transportation link from u to v and is assigned a travel time. The objective is
to find m disjoint routes each starting from a starting location $s \in V$ and ending
at a location $t \in V$, each with overall duration limited by the time budget B, that
maximize the overall profit collected by visited POIs in all routes. TDTOPTW
is an extension of TOPTW where the travel time from a location $u \in V$ to a

location $v \in V$ (as well as the arrival time at v) depends on the leave time from u and the chosen transportation mode (e.g on foot or public transportation).

In TDTOPTW we assume that the starting and ending locations may be different for different routes. Therefore, $s_r, t_r \in V$ denote the starting, terminal location respectively of the r-th route, and st_r, et_r denote the starting, ending time respectively of the r-th route, $r = 1, 2, \ldots, m$.

The proposed TDCSCRoutes and SlackCSCRoutes algorithms modify the CSCRoutes algorithm for TOPTW [11] to handle time dependent travel times among different locations/POIs. CSCRoutes is a cluster-based heuristic that achieves best performance results with respect to execution time compared to the best known so far real-time TOPTW algorithm, ILS [10].

The algorithms introduced in this section, employ an insertion step which takes into account the fact that for each pair of locations u and v the travel time from u to v may vary (a tourist can choose between walking and using public transport), and the waiting time for public transport depends on the time the tourist arrives at u. In Subsection 3.1 we present the feasibility criterion for inserting a POI p in a route r in the case of time dependent travel costs.

3.1 Time Dependent Insertion Feasibility

In order to have the time dependent travel cost between all pairs of locations, for each (u, v), $u, v \in V$ we precalculate the walking time from u to v (might be ∞, when too far to walk) and a set S_{uv} containing schedule information of the public transportation system connecting u and v. Specifically, S_{uv} contains all the non-dominated pairs $(\text{dep}_i^{uv}, \text{trav}_i^{uv})$, $i = 1, 2, \ldots, |S_{uv}|$ in ascending order of dep_i^{uv}, where dep_i^{uv} is a departure time and trav_i^{uv} is the corresponding travel time of a service of public transport connecting u and v. We consider that a pair $(\text{dep}_i^{uv}, \text{trav}_i^{uv})$ dominates a pair $(\text{dep}_j^{uv}, \text{trav}_j^{uv})$ if $\text{dep}_i^{uv} + \text{trav}_i^{uv} \leq \text{dep}_j^{uv} + \text{trav}_j^{uv}$ and $\text{dep}_i^{uv} > \text{dep}_j^{uv}$. Note that departing from u at time t where $\text{dep}_i^{uv} < t \leq \text{dep}_{i+1}^{uv}$, will result in arriving at v either at the same time as if departing at dep_{i+1}^{uv}, or at time t plus the walking time from u to v. More specifically, the arrival time at v will be equal to the earliest of the times $\text{dep}_{i+1}^{uv} + \text{trav}_{i+1}^{uv}$ and $t + \text{walking}_{u,v}$, where $\text{walking}_{u,v}$ is the walking time from u to v.

For a specified time t, the departure time from u to v at t using public transport, $\text{deptime}_{u,v}(t)$, is defined as the earliest possible departure time from u to v, i.e.,

$$\text{deptime}_{u,v}(t) = \min_i \{\text{dep}_i^{uv} | (\text{dep}_i^{uv}, \text{trav}_i^{uv}) \in S_{uv} \text{ and } t \leq \text{dep}_i^{uv}\} \quad (1)$$

Then, the travel time from u to v at t using public transport, $\text{travtime}_{u,v}(t)$, is such that $(\text{deptime}_{u,v}(t), \text{travtime}_{u,v}(t)) \in S^{uv}$, and the departure delay at time t due to the use of public transport, is $\text{delay}_{u,v}(t) = \text{deptime}_{u,v}(t) - t$. Therefore, the total travelling cost from u to v at a specified time t, $\text{travelling}_{u,v}(t)$, is

$$\text{travelling}_{u,v}(t) = \min\{\text{walking}_{u,v}, \text{delay}_{u,v}(t) + \text{travtime}_{u,v}(t)\} \quad (2)$$

For a POI p_i in a route r the following variables are defined:

- $wait_i$, denoting the waiting time at p_i before its time window starts; $wait_i = \max(0, open_{i_r} - arrive_i)$.
- $start_i$, denoting the starting time of the visit at p_i; $start_i = arrive_i + wait_i$.
- $leave_i$, denoting the time the visit at p_i completes, i.e., the departure time from p_i; $leave_i = start_i + visit_i$.
- $arrive_i$, denoting the arrival time at p_i; $arrive_i = leave_{prev(i)} + travelling_{prev(i),i}(leave_{prev(i)})$, where $leave_{prev(i)}$ is the departure time from the previous node of p_i in route r ($prev(i)$). We assume that $arrive_{s_r} = st_r$.
- $maxStart_i$, denoting the latest time the visit at p_i can start without violating the time windows of the nodes following p_i; $maxStart_i = \min(close_{i_r}, \max\{t : t + travelling_{i,next(i)}(t) \leq maxStart_{next(i)}\} - visit_i)$, where $next(i)$ is the node following p_i in r. We assume that $maxStart_{t_r} = et_r$.

A POI p_k can be inserted in route r between POIs p_i and p_j if the arrival time at p_k does not violate p_k's time window and the arrival at p_j does not violate the time window of p_j as well as the time windows of the nodes following p_j in r. The total time cost for p_k's insertion is defined as $shift_k^{ij}$ (insertion cost) and is equal to the time the arrival at p_j will be delayed. In particular $shift_k^{ij}$ equals to the time required to travel from p_i to p_j having visited p_k in between minus the time taken for travelling directly from p_i to p_j.

$$shift_k^{ij} = (travelling_{i,k}(leave_i) + wait_k + visit_k + travelling_{k,j}(leave_k)) - travelling_{i,j}(leave_i) \tag{3}$$

Figure 1 illustrates an example of inserting p_k, between p_i and p_j shifting the visit at p_j later on time (in this figure, $wait_u^v$ denotes the waiting at u following a visit at v).

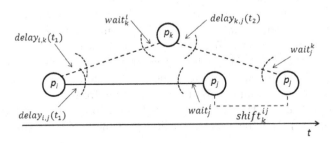

Fig. 1. Illustration of p_k insertion between p_i and p_j

Note that the insertion of p_k between p_i and p_j in route r is feasible when

$$arrive_k \leq close_{kr} \quad \text{and} \quad shift_k^{ij} \leq maxStart_j - arrive_j \tag{4}$$

A pseudo code implementation of the function $shift(k, i, j, r)$ which calculates the insertion cost $shift_k^{ij}$ in route r, in given in [15]. The function returns ∞ if the insertion of p_k is infeasible.

3.2   The Time Dependent CSCRoutes (TDCSCRoutes) Algorithm

TDCSCRoutes algorithm modifies the insertion step **CSCRoutes_Insert** of CSCRoutes algorithm to handle time dependent travel times among different locations/POIs. CSCRoutes uses the notion of *Cluster Route (CR)* defined as follows: Given a route r of a TOPTW solution, any maximal sub-route in r comprising a sequence of nodes within the same cluster C is called a *Cluster Route (CR)* of r *associated with cluster* C and denoted as CR_C^r. CSCRoutes algorithm is designed to construct routes that visit each cluster at most once, i.e. if a cluster C has been visited in a route r it cannot be revisited in the same route and therefore, for each cluster C there is only one cluster route in any route r associated with C. The only exception allowed is when the start and the terminal nodes of a route r belong to the same cluster C'. In this case, a route r may start and end with nodes of cluster C', i.e. C' may be visited twice in the route r and therefore, for a route r there might be two cluster routes $CR_{C'}^r$. The insertion step **CSCRoutes_Insert** of CSCRoutes does not allow the insertion of a POI p_k in a route r, if this insertion creates more than one cluster routes CR_C^r for some cluster C. Therefore, a POI cannot be inserted at any position in the route r [11].

In the sequel, the description of the insertion step of TDCSCRoutes (**TDCS Routes_Insert**) is given. It comprises a modification of **CSCRoutes_Insert** which takes into consideration the time dependent travel times among locations/POIs. Given a route r let CR_f^r be the first cluster route (starting at s_r) in r, and CR_l^r be the last cluster route (ends at t_r) in r. Let also clustersIn(r) be a set containing any cluster C for which there is a nonempty CR_C^r, and cluster(p) be the cluster where p belongs to. Given a candidate for insertion POI p_k **TDCSCRoutes_Insert** distinguishes among the following cases:

- cluster(s_r) = cluster(t_r)
   - if clustersIn(r) = {cluster(s_r)} then p_k can be inserted anywhere in the route.
   - if clustersIn(r) $\neq$ {cluster(s_r)} and cluster(p_k) = cluster(s_r) then p_k can be inserted in CR_f^r and CR_l^r
   - if clustersIn(r) $\neq$ {cluster(s_r)} and cluster(p_k) $\neq$ cluster(s_r) and cluster(p_k) $\notin$ clustersIn(r) then p_k can be inserted after every end of a CR except for CR_l^r
   - if clustersIn(r) $\neq$ {cluster(s_r)} and cluster(p_k) $\neq$ cluster(s_r) and cluster(p_k) $\in$ clustersIn(r) then p_k can be inserted anywhere in $CR_{\text{cluster}(p_k)}^r$
- cluster(s_r) $\neq$ cluster(t_r)
   - if cluster(p_k) = cluster(s_r) then p_k can be inserted everywhere in CR_f^r
   - if cluster(p_k) = cluster(t_r) then p_k can be inserted everywhere in CR_l^r
   - if cluster(p_k) $\in$ clustersIn(r) and cluster(p_k) is different from cluster(s_r) and cluster(t_r), then p_k can be inserted everywhere in $CR_{\text{cluster}(p)}^r$
   - if cluster(p_k) $\notin$ clustersIn(r) then p_k can be inserted at the end of any CR in r except for CR_l^r

For each POI p_k not included in a route, among all feasible insert positions (between POIs p_i, p_j) we select the one with the highest ratio

$$\text{ratio}_k^{ij} = \frac{\text{profit}_k^2}{\text{shift}_k^{ij}} (1 + a \cdot \frac{D_k^{ij} + 1}{D_k^{ij} + 2} + (1 - a) \cdot f(\text{shift}_k^{ij}, \text{wait}_j + \text{delay}_j)) \quad (5)$$

where $f(x, y) = 1$ if $x \leq y$ and 0 otherwise, and $D_k^{ij} = \text{delay}_{i,k}(\text{leave}_i) + \text{wait}_k + \text{delay}_{k,j}(\text{leave}_k) + \text{wait}_j$ where a takes the values of $1, \frac{1}{2}$ and 0, depending on the number of iterations executed by CSCRoutes. In particular, for the first $\frac{1}{3}$ iterations a is equal to 1, it decreases to $\frac{1}{2}$ in the second $\frac{1}{3}$ iterations and becomes 0 in the final iterations [11]. The incentive behind (5) is the following: $\frac{\text{profit}_k^2}{\text{shift}_k^{ij}}$ denotes preference for important (i.e. highly profitable) POIs associated with relatively short time to visit. In the first iterations (a=1), the operand $\frac{D_k^{ij} + 1}{D_k^{ij} + 2}$ dominates giving preference to insertion of POIs among pairs (p_i, p_j) creating prolonged 'empty' time periods (i.e. long aggregate waiting times and delays) to be utilized on later insertions. In the last iterations (a=0), $f(\text{shift}_k^{ij}, \text{wait}_j + \text{delay}_j)$ dominates favoring insertion of POIs that best take advantage of any left unexploited time (i.e. waiting and delays) remaining throughout the routes. Among all candidate POIs, TDCSCRoutes algorithm selects for insertion the one associated with the highest ratio.

Once a POI p_k is inserted between p_i and p_j in a route r, the variable values of all POIs in r need to be updated. Note that for each POI after p_k, the variables arrive, wait, start and leave should be updated while variable maxStart remains the same. For each POI p_l before p_k the value of maxStart$_l$ is the only one that should be updated . The pseudo code of **TDCSCRoutes_Insert** is given in [15].

3.3   The SlackCSCRoutes Algorithm

SlackCSCRoutes modifies the insertion step of TDCSCRoutes i.e., it follows a different approach for determining the POI p_k that will be selected for insertion in a route r. Specifically, while TDCSCRoutes algorithm's criterion for selecting a POI p_k in a route r is based on the insertion cost, SlackCSCRoutes involves a more global criterion as it takes into consideration the effect of this insertion in the whole route r.

SlackCSCRoutes uses an additional variable slack$_i$ defined for each node p_i in a tourist route r as follows:

$$\text{slack}_i = \text{maxStart}_i - \text{arrive}_i \quad (6)$$

Note that if the value of slack$_i$ is close to 0 then there is little hope in finding new POIs that can be inserted between POIs $p_{\text{prev}(i)}$ and p_i.

Let $p_1, p_2, \ldots, p_n$ be the successive POIs of a route r with $p_1 = s_r$ and $p_n = t_r$. Let p_k be a candidate POI for insertion between POIs p_i and p_{i+1} of r.

The insertion of the p_k will likely shift further the arrival time at p_j (arrive$_j$), for $j = i+1, \ldots, n$. That depends on the waiting time before the visit of each POI and the time dependent travelling time for moving between successive nodes along the route. Let arrive$_j^k$ be the new arrival time at POI p_j after the insertion of p_k, for $j = i+1, \ldots, n,$. The above insertion may shift the maximum time the visit at p_j can start (maxStart$_j$) ahead for $j = 1, \ldots, i$. Let maxStart$_j^k$ be the new latest time the visit at p_j can start after the insertion of p_k, for $j = 1, \ldots, i$.

Let also slack$_j^k$ = maxStart$_j$ − arrive$_j^k$, for $j = i+1, \ldots, n$, and slack$_j^k$ = maxStart$_j^k$ − arrive$_j$, for $j = 1, \ldots, i$, be the corresponding values of the "slack" variables. We define the quantity A_k^i as follows:

$$A_k^i = \frac{\sum_{j=1}^{i} \text{slack}_j^k + \text{slack}_k + \sum_{j=i+1}^{n} \text{slack}_j^k}{n+1}$$

Note that a large value of A_k^i implies that even after the insertion of p_k, there are many possibilities left for inserting new POIs along each leg of trip (that is, prior and after visiting p_k).

Then for each POI p_k, the maximum possible A_k^i is determined, i.e. the best possible insert position. Let the maximum value A_k^i over all possible insert positions be A_k. Then, in order to determine the POI that will be selected for insertion, the slackWeight for each POI p_k is calculated as

$$\text{slackWeight}_k = \text{profit}_k{}^2 * A_k$$

and the POI with the highest slackWeight is inserted.

The main issue with the above derivations is that for each POI p_k and for each possible insert position i within a route r we need to calculate A_k^i which involves the updated values of the maxStart and arrive variables for all POIs in r. This involves a global rather than a local decision perspective regarding possible insertion positions along the whole route. In order to develop a fast heuristic, a quick calculation of A_k^i is necessary. We may have a quick calculation of a good approximation of A_k^i, by making the assumption that the time windows at the POIs are fairly long spanning the most part of the day and therefore the waiting time before each POI is typically zero (Details will be given in the full version of the paper). Note this assumption is realistic for most tourist sites.

4   Experimental Results

4.1   Test Instances

While many different datasets exist for testing (T)OP(TW) problems, this is not the case for their time-dependent counterparts. Hence, relevant algorithmic solutions should unavoidably be tested upon real transit network data. In our experiments, we have used the GTFS (General Transit Feed Specification) data of the transit network deployed on the metropolitan area of Athens, Greece, provided by the Athens Urban Transport Organization. The network comprises

3 subway lines, 3 tram lines and 287 bus lines with an overall of 7825 transit stops. For our purposes, we require to know the pairwise quickest routes full (24h range) multimodal travel times between POIs, for all possible departure times of the day. This precomputation has been performed using the the algorithm of Dibbelt et al. [16] upon the Athens transit network. The overall shortest time dependent travel time information (either through transit or walking) is stored in a three-dimensional array of size $N \times N \times 1440$, where N is the number of specified locations/POIs and 1440 ($= 24 \times 60$) the time steps/minutes per day. This memory structure ensures instant access to time dependent travel times, given a specified pair of POIs (u, v), upon receiving a user query. We have also used a set of predefined start/end locations (100 hotels).

The POIs dataset used in our experiments features 113 sites (museums, archaeological sites, landmarks, streets & squares, neighborhoods, religious heritage, parks) mostly situated around Athens downtown and Piraeus areas. Profits have been set in a 1-100 scale and visiting times vary from 1 minute (e.g. for some outdoor statues) to 2 hours (e.g. for some not-miss museums and wide-area archaeological sites). The POIs have been grouped in $\lfloor \frac{N}{10} \rfloor = 11$ disjoint clusters.

The above described POIs dataset has been used to create three different 'topologies'. The real POIs coordinates have been maintained in all cases, however, their respective profits, visiting times and opening hours (i.e. time windows) have been 'shuffled', to remove any potential bias of a single topology.

Our algorithms have been tested using 100 different 'user preference' inputs per number of routes, each applied to all the three abovementioned topologies. Each 'preference' input is associated with a different start/end location, corresponding to a potential accommodation (hotel) option. Furthermore, for each 'preference' input a certain percentage of POIs is disregarded to 'simulate' preferences provided by real visitors, such as no interest on religious sites. The total time budget available for sightseeing in daily basis (B_r) has been set to 5 hours (10:00-15:00) in all experiments. All test instances-related files are accessible from: http://www2.aegean.gr/dgavalas/public/tdtoptw_instances/index.html

4.2   Results

We have implemented the following four algorithms: (a) TDCSCRoutes (see Section 3.2), (b) SlackCSCRoutes (see Section 3.3), (c) AvgCSCRoutes, and (d) Average ILS (AvgILS).

AvgILS refers to the average travel time approach proposed by Garcia et al. [1], wherein TDTOPTW is practically reduced to TOPTW and the standard ILS algorithm [10] is used to construct routes based on pre-computed average travel times. AvgILS exercises a repair procedure, introducing the real travel times between the POIs of the final TOPTW solution. If this causes a visit to become infeasible, the latter is removed from the route and the remainder of the route is shifted forward. Similarly to AvgILS, AvgCSCRoutes uses CSCRoutes to construct routes based on pre-computed average travel times. AvgCSCRoutes employs a repair step similar to AvgILS, followed by a 'gap filling' step the latter inserts new POIs into the routes, if feasible, thereby further improving the solution's quality (Details will be given in the full version of the paper).

All algorithms have been employed upon the test instances described in the previous subsection, deriving k daily personalized routes, $k = 1 \ldots 4$, each for every day of stay at the destination. All routes start and end at the tourist's accommodation location. Note that all the algorithms have been programmed in C++ and executed on a PC Intel Core i5, clocked at 2.80GHz, with 4GB RAM.

We use the standard profit criterion in our experimental results , i.e. we consider as best-found solution the one with the highest aggregate profit. Table 1 offers a comparative view on the performance of the four implemented algorithms. The analytical results may be found in [15]. The results shown are: the overall collected profit (over all routes); the execution time (in ms); the number of visited POIs; the overall number of public transit transfers (PT) over all routes; All the above results are averaged over all (= 100) the execution runs and the three 'shuffled' topologies. High quality solutions are those featuring high aggregate profit and relatively small number of transit transfers, derived in short execution time. Note that we normalize the actual performance parameter values assigning a value 100 to the highest recorded value and adapting the rest accordingly (this allows illustrating relative performance gaps among tested algorithms). Performance values shown in bold designate the best performing algorithm with respect to each performance parameter.

As shown in Table 1, AvgCSCRoutes executes considerably faster, since it disregards time dependency on the insertion decision, while also using a smaller memory structure to hold travel time information (hence, required travel times are retrieved more efficiently). Despite using precomputed average travel time values, AvgILS executes (on average) slower than the other three algorithms as it explores a larger search space on each POI insertion. It should be noted though that execution times are well beyond a second in all cases for all algorithms for the 113 POIs of Athens.

Interestingly, AvgCSCRoutes and AvgILS are competitive in terms of profit, with AvgCSCRoutes performing better than AvgILS, mainly due to the extra 'gap filling' step, which considerably improves the quality of its solutions and corrects potential suboptimal node insertion decisions made during the insertion phase. Nevertheless, we argue that the results obtained by AvgCSCRoutes and AvgILS could be worse when considering either less frequent transit services or timetables where transit frequencies changes considerably along the day or even when considering tourist visits in off-peak hours. In such scenarios, using the average travel time would not serve as a good approximation.

TDCSCRoutes performs marginally better than the three other algorithms with respect to the overall profit, while deriving solutions in comparable time with SlackCSCRoutes.

On the other hand, TDCSCRoutes performs worse in terms of public transit transfers, mainly due to its initialization phase which favors visits to clusters far located from the user's accommodation, hence, often requiring public transit rides to arrive there. AvgILS obtains best results with respect to that performance metric. Last, SlackCSCRoutes achieves higher number of POI visits (intuitively, due to its insertion criterion, the algorithm best exploits the available time budget, accommodating more POI visits).

Table 1. Comparative view on the performance of the implemented algorithms

# Routes		Profit	Time	Visits	Public Transport
1	TDCSCRoutes	**100**	89.88	97.57	100
	SlackCSCRoutes	99.99	100	**100**	92.92
	AvgCSCRoutes	98.38	**55.98**	96.41	88.78
	AvgILS	96.68	79.64	92.72	**85.84**
2	TDCSCRoutes	**100**	87.21	98.09	100
	SlackCSCRoutes	99.18	93.75	**100**	95.42
	AvgCSCRoutes	98.82	**51.07**	97.73	88.13
	AvgILS	97.64	100	95.14	**85**
3	TDCSCRoutes	**100**	92.05	97.1	100
	SlackCSCRoutes	98.15	89.01	**100**	90.48
	AvgCSCRoutes	99.05	**50.39**	97.39	80.26
	AvgILS	98.05	100	95.03	**78.77**
4	TDCSCRoutes	**100**	100	96.32	100
	SlackCSCRoutes	97.88	87.11	**100**	93.81
	AvgCSCRoutes	99.23	**52.34**	96.42	82.71
	AvgILS	98.21	88.72	94.03	**82.38**

5   Conclusions and Future Work

We introduced TDCSCRoutes and SlackCSCroutes, two new cluster-based heuristics for solving the TDTOPTW. The main design objectives of the two algorithms are to derive high quality TDTOPTW solutions (maximizing tourist satisfaction), while minimizing the number of transit transfers and executing fast enough to support online web and mobile applications.

With respect to the overall collected profit, TDCSCRoutes has been shown to perform marginally better. On the other hand, SlackCSCRoutes achieves a fair compromise among all the performance aspects. In practical applications, comprising very large datasets, AvgCSCRoutes could be the most suitable choice as it efficiently derives solutions of reasonably good quality (this conclusion agrees with that reported in [1], wherein a TDTOPTW algorithm has been evaluated against AvgILS). Nevertheless, its suitability largely depends on the high frequency of public transit services, so that average travel times represent a good guess.

In the future, we plan to test our algorithms on additional real datasets to remove potential bias introduced by the particularities of the Athens dataset and transit network. Besides, testing our algorithms over larger POI datasets will verify their scalability in terms of the required execution time. Along the same line, we plan to produce realistic synthesized multimodal timetabled data to serve as additional test benchmarks.

References

1. Garcia, A., Vansteenwegen, P., Arbelaitz, O., Souffriau, W., Linaza, M.T.: Integrating public transportation in personalised electronic tourist guides. Computers & Operations Research 40(3), 758–774 (2013)
2. Vansteenwegen, P., Souffriau, W., Van Oudheusden, D.: The orienteering problem: A survey. European Journal of Operational Research 209(1), 1–10 (2011)
3. Laporte, G., Martello, S.: The selective travelling salesman problem. Discrete Applied Mathematics 26(2-3), 193–207 (1990)
4. Gambardella, L., Montemanni, R., Weyland, D.: Coupling ant colony systems with strong local searches. European Journal of Operational Research 220(3), 831–843 (2012)
5. Labadi, N., Melechovský, J., Wolfler Calvo, R.: Hybridized evolutionary local search algorithm for the team orienteering problem with time windows. Journal of Heuristics 17, 729–753 (2011)
6. Labadi, N., Mansini, R., Melechovský, J., Wolfler Calvo, R.: The team orienteering problem with time windows: An lp-based granular variable neighborhood search. European Journal of Operational Research 220(1), 15–27 (2012)
7. Lin, S.W., Yu, V.F.: A simulated annealing heuristic for the team orienteering problem with time windows. European Journal of Operational Research 217(1), 94–107 (2012)
8. Montemanni, R., Gambardella, L.M.: An ant colony system for team orienteering problems with time windows. Foundations of Computing and Decision Sciences 34(4), 287–306 (2009)
9. Tricoire, F., Romauch, M., Doerner, K.F., Hartl, R.F.: Heuristics for the multi-period orienteering problem with multiple time windows. Computers & Operations Research 37(2), 351–367 (2010)
10. Vansteenwegen, P., Souffriau, W., Vanden Berghe, G., Van Oudheusden, D.: Iterated local search for the team orienteering problem with time windows. Computers & Operations Research 36, 3281–3290 (2009)
11. Gavalas, D., Konstantopoulos, C., Mastakas, K., Pantziou, G., Tasoulas, Y.: Cluster-based heuristics for the team orienteering problem with time windows. In: Bonifaci, V., Demetrescu, C., Marchetti-Spaccamela, A. (eds.) SEA 2013. LNCS, vol. 7933, pp. 390–401. Springer, Heidelberg (2013)
12. Fomin, F.V., Lingas, A.: Approximation algorithms for time-dependent orienteering. Information Processing Letters 83(2), 57–62 (2002)
13. Spieksma, F.C.R.: On the approximability of an interval scheduling problem. Journal of Scheduling 2, 215–227 (1999)
14. Abbaspour, R.A., Samadzadegan, F.: Time-dependent personal tour planning and scheduling in metropolises. Expert Systems and Applications 38, 12439–12452 (2011)
15. Gavalas, D., et al.: Appendix, http://www2.aegean.gr/dgavalas/public/tdtoptw_instances/icaa_appendix.pdf
16. Dibbelt, J., Pajor, T., Wagner, D.: User-constrained multi-modal route planning. In: Proceedings of the 14th Meeting on Algorithm Engineering and Experiments (ALENEX 2012), pp. 118–129 (2012)

Color Texture Image Segmentation Based on Neutrosophic Set and Nonsubsampled Contourlet Transformation

Jeethu Mary Mathew and Philomina Simon

Department of Computer Science
University of Kerala, Kariavattom
Thiruvananthapuram, Kerala, India
jeethu_mm@yahoo.co.in, philomina.simon@gmail.com

Abstract. In this paper, an automatic approach for image segmentation based on neutrosophic set and nonsubsampled contourlet transformation for natural images is proposed. This method uses both color and texture features for segmentation. Input image is transformed into LUV color model for extracting the color features. Texture features are extracted from the grayscale image. Image is then transformed into Neutrosophic domain. Finally, image segmentation is performed using Fuzzy C-means clustering. Clusters are adaptively calculated based on a cluster validity analysis. This method is tested in natural image database. The result analysis shows that the proposed method automatically segments image better than traditional methods.

Keywords: Neutrosophic set, Color Texture segmentation, Nonsubsampled Contourlet Transform, Fuzzy clustering.

1 Introduction

Image segmentation is an important task in pattern recognition. It is one of the difficult steps in image processing because many features such as intensity, blurring, etc affect segmentation quality. In segmentation, an image is divided into several regions based on some homogeneous properties such as color, texture, etc. Effective segmentation usually results in eventual success of the analysis. The goal of segmentation is to represent the image in a more meaningful way. The major applications of segmentation are in computer vision, object detection, medical imaging, recognition, content-based image retrieval etc. Segmentation algorithms can be basically divided into region based and edge based segmentation [1]. Region based segmentations are based on similarity metric according to a set of predefined criteria. Edge based segmentations are based on discontinuity or abrupt changes in intensity. Similarity may be due to color or texture properties. Several works have been developed based on either color [2] or texture [3] properties. Natural scenes contain the combination of both color and texture. So combining both properties helps in distinguishing regions having same color but different texture properties and vice versa. This gives accurate segmentation results.

P. Gupta and C. Zaroliagis (Eds.): ICAA 2014, LNCS 8321, pp. 164–173, 2014.

The rest of the paper is organized as follows. Section 2 describes literature review. Section 3 explains about Neutrosophic set. Section 4 discusses the traditional method. The proposed algorithm is described in Section 5. Section 6 demonstrates experimental results and analysis. Conclusion is given in Section 7.

2   Literature Review

Image segmentation separates individual objects in the image [1]. Many methods have been proposed for segmenting color images. Rosito Jung [4] proposed a multiresolution technique for color image segmentation. This method yields over-segmentation and is suited for noisy images. Ozden and Polat [5] developed a color image segmentation method based on color, texture and spatial information. This method does under-segmentation and most of the pixels are misclassified. Deng and Manjunath [6] proposed a JSEG method for unsupervised segmentation of color texture regions in images and video. This method consists of two steps-color quantization and spatial segmentation. However, it is often over-segmented into several regions and is affected by spatially varying illumination. Kothainachiar and Banu [7] developed an image segmentation approach based on adaptive clustering algorithm and complex wavelet transformation. But, it is computationally inefficient at the color feature extraction and semantic information alone is adequate for proper segmentation. Luis et al. [8] proposed an automatic image segmentation approach based on dynamic region growth and multiresolution merging. The limitation is that threshold is approximately calculated and which does not lead to accurate results. Anjikar and Shandilya [9] introduced an approach for color image segmentation based on region growing and region merging. Initial seed selection is required in this method. Ning and Pun [10] developed a new hybrid color image segmentation approach using adaptive color quantization and multiresolution texture characterization. But, this method is computationally complex. An approach for image segmentation based on neutrosophic set is introduced by Cheng and Y. Guo [11]. But, this method works only for gray scale images. Chen et al. [12] proposed a new approach for color texture image segmentation based on adaptive clustering algorithm. But, this method requires semantic information for proper image classification. Sengur and Guo [13] proposed a color texture image segmentation method based on neutrosophic set and wavelet transform. In this method, edges are not smooth and it results in over-segmentation.

3   Neutrosophic Set

Neutrosophic set is introduced by Florentin Smarandache in 1980s. It is a branch of philosophy which deals with the origin, nature and scope of neutralities as well as their interactions with different ideational spectra [14]. According to neutrosophic theory, every event has a degree of truth, falsity degree and an indeterminacy degree that have to be considered independently from each other

[14]. The indeterminacy originates from incomplete knowledge, acquisition errors, or stochasticity. For classifying the image pixels correctly, complete knowledge about the image is required. Indeterminate information of the image can be better described using neutrosophic set and which is reduced for better segmentation results. Neutrosophic components can be represented as T, I, F which are subsets of the hyperreal interval $]^-0, 1^+[$. The notation $X(T, I, F)$ means that it is t true $(t \in T)$, i indeterminate $(i \in I)$, f false $(f \in F)$, where t, i, f are real numbers in the sets T, I and F [14].

4   Traditional Method-NS and Wavelet Based Method

Sengur and Guo [13] developed a color texture image segmentation method based on neutrosophic set and wavelet transform. But this method causes over-segmentation, blurred edges and the accuracy of the segmentation can still be improved. Wavelet transform captures only limited directional information and it does not detect the smoothness along the edges. The salient features in source images cannot efficiently preserved by Wavelet transform. This will introduce some artifacts. In order to overcome the drawbacks of traditional method, we proposed an approach for color texture image segmentation based on neutrosophic set and nonsubsampled contourlet transform (NSCT). NSCT overcomes the limitations of wavelets and it represents edges sharper. The proposed method yields accurate segmentation compared to traditional methods.

5   Proposed Method-Color Texture Image Segmentation Based on Neutrosophic Set and NSCT

Image segmentation is an essential task in computer vision. For better segmentation results, indeterminacy of data needs to be reduced. Indeterminacy of the image may be due to some hidden or unknown parameters. Neutrosophic set is a powerful tool for quantizing indeterminacy of the image. In this paper, an automatic approach for image segmentation based on Neutrosophic set and Nonsubsampled Contourlet transformation is proposed. The proposed algorithm consists of following modules: Color transformation, Nonsubsampled Contourlet decomposition, Texture extraction, Neutrosophic set transformation, Clustering.

The algorithm is summarized as below:

Step 1 : Convert image from RGB to Luv color space.

Step 2 : Obtain gray scale image from RGB color space.

Step 3 : Use nonsubsampled contourlet transformation to decompose the gray image into sub-bands (LL, LH, HL, and HH).

Step 4 : Calculate the mean of LH and HL sub-bands using Eqs. (1) − (2).

Step 5 : Transform the L,u,v color channels and the mean values into NS domain independently using Eqs. (4) − (8).

Step 6 : Perform the indeterminacy reduction operation on the true subsets of L,u,v color channels and the mean values using Eqs. (9) − (10) .

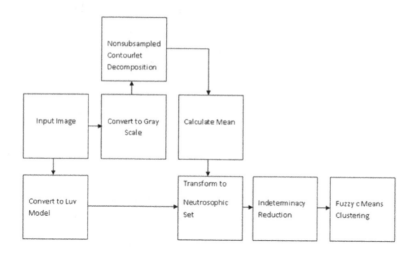

Fig. 1. Block diagram of the image segmentation algorithm

Step 7 : Apply Fuzzy C-means clustering to the true subset using Eq (11).
Step 8 : Segment the image according to the result in step 7.

The proposed method performs image segmentation based on Neutrosophic set [15] and Nonsubsampled contourlet transformation [16]. Both color and texture features are used for segmentation. In natural images, the combination of color and texture properties gives better segmentation results.

In the first step, input image is transformed into Luv color model [17]. Luv model is perceptually uniform which means that two colors that are equally distant in the color space are equally distant perceptually. The color information is extracted from the Luv transformed image. Luv model is suitable for measuring smaller color differences. So this model gives good results for color image segmentation.

For extracting the texture features, the input image is converted to grayscale image. Then, nonsubsampled contourlet transformation (NSCT) [16] is applied on the grayscale image. NSCT is a shift-invariant, multiscale and multidirection transformation. Edge information can be better described using nonsubsampled contourlet transform. NSCT decomposes the grayscale image to 4 subbands-LL, LH, HL and HH. Among these subbands, LH and HL are used for further processes. This is because most of the texture information is present in the LH and HL bands.

For texture characterization, mean of LH and HL subbands in a local window are calculated. After experimental analysis, window size is selected as 5 which are suitable for capturing the local texture features.

Mean of the image can be calculated using the following equation:

$$MLH\left(i,j\right) = \frac{1}{w \times w} \sum_{k=-\frac{w}{2}}^{\frac{w}{2}} \sum_{l=-\frac{w}{2}}^{\frac{w}{2}} LH(i+k,j+l) \tag{1}$$

$$MHL\left(i,j\right) = \frac{1}{w \times w} \sum_{k=-\frac{w}{2}}^{\frac{w}{2}} \sum_{l=-\frac{w}{2}}^{\frac{w}{2}} HL(i+k,j+l) \tag{2}$$

where w is the size of the sliding window. MLH and MHL are the mean values of LH, HL band respectively.

Then, the pixel $P\left(i,j\right)$ in the image domain for the color channels (L, u and v) and the mean values of LH and HL subbands are transformed into neutrosophic domain. Indeterminacy of the image can be quantified from the neutrosophic image.

$$P_{NS}\left(i,j\right) = \{T\left(i,j\right), I\left(i,j\right), F(i,j)\} \tag{3}$$

where $P_{NS}\left(i,j\right)$ is the neutrosophic image. $T\left(i,j\right), I\left(i,j\right)$ and $F(i,j)$ are the membership values belonging to the true set, indeterminate set and false set respectively.

$$T\left(i,j\right) = \frac{\bar{g}\left(i,j\right) - \bar{g}_{min}}{\bar{g}_{max} - \bar{g}_{min}} \tag{4}$$

$$\bar{g}\left(i,j\right) = \frac{1}{w \times w} \sum_{m=i-\frac{w}{2}}^{i+\frac{w}{2}} \sum_{n=j-\frac{w}{2}}^{j+\frac{w}{2}} g(m,n) \tag{5}$$

$$I\left(i,j\right) = \frac{\delta\left(i,j\right) - \delta_{min}}{\bar{\delta}_{max} - \bar{\delta}_{min}} \tag{6}$$

$$\delta\left(i,j\right) = abs\left(g\left(i,j\right) - \bar{g}\left(i,j\right)\right) \tag{7}$$

$$F\left(i,j\right) = 1 - T\left(i,j\right) \tag{8}$$

where $\bar{g}$(i,j) is the local mean value of the image. $\delta\left(i,j\right)$ is the absolute value of the difference between intensity $g\left(i,j\right)$ and its local mean value at.(i,j)

An indeterminacy reduction operation is applied on the true subset of the color channels and the mean values for reducing the indeterminacy of the image. More accurate segmentation results will be obtained if the indeterminacy or imprecise knowledge is reduced to a minimum.

Indeterminacy of the image can be reduced using the following equation.

$$T_{mod}\left(i,j\right) = \left\{ \begin{array}{ll} 2*T\left(i,j\right)\hat{}2 & \text{if } T\left(i,j\right) < 0.5 \\ 1 - 2*\left(1 - \bar{T}\left(i,j\right)\right)\hat{}2 & \text{if } T\left(i,j\right) \geq 0.5 \end{array} \right\} \tag{9}$$

$$\bar{T}\left(i,j\right) = \frac{1}{w \times w} \sum_{m=i-\frac{w}{2}}^{i+\frac{w}{2}} \sum_{n=j-\frac{w}{2}}^{j+\frac{w}{2}} T(m,n) \tag{10}$$

where $T_{mod}\left(i,j\right)$ is the modified true set after the indeterminacy reduction operation and $\bar{T}\left(i,j\right)$ is the mean of the true set.

After the indeterminacy reduction operation, the true set becomes more distinct and which is suitable for segmentation. A clustering is performed on the indeterminacy reduced data as the next step. Clustering is the process of classifying the elements with dissimilar characteristics into different classes.

The input to the clustering algorithm is a vector,

$$X = [T_{L_{NS}}, T_{u_{NS}}, T_{v_{NS}}, T_{MLH_{NS}}, T_{MHL_{NS}}]$$

where $T_{L_{NS}}, T_{u_{NS}}, T_{v_{NS}}, T_{MLH_{NS}}$ and $T_{MHL_{NS}}$ are the true subsets of the color channels (L, u, v) and the mean values of LH and HL bands.

Here, the classification is performed using Fuzzy C-means clustering [18]. Fuzzy C-means clustering is preferred because it allows pixels to belong to several classes with varying degrees of membership.

It is based on minimization of the following objective function:

$$J_m = \sum_{i=1}^{n} \sum_{j=1}^{K} u_{ij}^m \|x_i - c_j\|^2 \qquad , 1 \le m < \infty \qquad (11)$$

where m is any real number greater than 1, u_{ij} is the degree of membership of x_i in the cluster j, x_i is the ith of d-dimensional measured data, c_j is the d-dimension center of the cluster, and $\|*\|$ is any norm expressing the similarity between any measured data and the center.

The number of clusters is calculated automatically according to the validity index of Xie and Beni [19]. The validity criteria can be defined as:

$$N_X(K) = \frac{J_m}{n * min\|c_i - c_j\|^2} \qquad (12)$$

where n is the number of data to be clustered. An optimal $\acute{K}$ can be found out by solving the following equation.

$$\acute{K} = min_{2 \le K < k-1} N_X(K) \qquad , k = 10 \qquad (13)$$

gives the best clustering performance for the data set.X Finally, segmentation is performed on the clustered data.

6   Experimental Results and Analysis

The images tested are Berkeley database [20]. The proposed method is experimented on natural color texture images and the results are shown in Fig. 2. The original images are given in the first column, ground-truth segmentations are given in the second column, results of NS and wavelet based method [13] are given in third column, results of waveseg method [4] are given in fourth column and results of proposed method are given in fifth column respectively.

The proposed method gives almost exact results when compared to the ground-truth image. The performance of the proposed method is compared with NS and wavelet based method [13] and waveseg method [4] . This method gives better performance compared to other algorithms. From Fig. 2, it is clear that both

NS and wavelet based method [13] and waveseg method [4] produces many misclassifications.

In Fig .2(i), we obtained almost 100% correct segmentation when compared to the ground-truth image. The number of clusters obtained is 4. The NS and

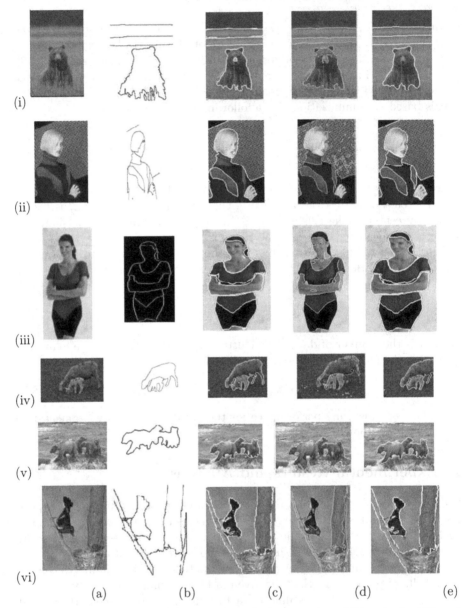

Fig. 2. (a) Original image. (b) Ground-truth segmentation. (c)Results by NS and wavelet based method [13]. (d) Results by Waveseg method [4] (e) Results by the proposed method.

wavelet based method [13] produces misclassification in the nose region. These misclassifications are not present in our method. Waveseg method [4] produces a worst segmentation result. The segment boundaries are smoothly located in the proposed method. In Fig .2(ii), a worst segmentation result is produced by both NS and wavelet based method [13] and waveseg method [4]. Our proposal gives better segmentation results compared to ground-truth. We obtained similar successful segmentation results for the rest of the images when compared to NS and wavelet based method [13] and waveseg method [4].

6.1   Performance Measures

The proposed method is evaluated using Pratt's figure of merit (FOM) [21] and F-measure [22].

FOM indicates the image quality. It is defined as:

$$FOM = \frac{1}{max\left\{I_I, I_A\right\}} \sum_{j=1}^{I_A} \frac{1}{1 + \alpha d^2(j)} \qquad (14)$$

where I_I and I_A are ideal and actual edge points. $d(j)$ is the pixel miss distance of the jth edge detected and α is a scaling constant which is selected as $1/9$ to provide a relative penalty between smeared edges and isolated, but, offset edges.

F-measure is based on precision and recall. Both precision and recall are combined into single measure called F-measure. It is defined as:

$$F = \frac{P \times R}{\epsilon \times P + (1 - \epsilon) \times R} \qquad (15)$$

where P and R represents precision and recall respectively. ϵ is a tradeoff between P and R and which is selected as $1/2$.

Table 1. FOM results of Fig 2(i)-(vi)

Image	Proposed Approach	NS and Wavelet Based Method	Waveseg
i	0.6509	0.5821	0.3971
ii	0.8477	0.5974	0.5619
iii	0.6065	0.6030	0.5237
iv	0.8388	0.5514	0.4494
v	0.5943	0.4790	0.3273
vi	0.7934	0.6398	0.5776

Table 1 represents the FOM values of Fig. 2(i)-(vi) for the proposed method, NS and wavelet based method and waveseg method respectively.

Table 2 represents the F-measure values of Fig. 2(i)-(vi) for the proposed method, NS and wavelet based method and waveseg method respectively. From the results, it is clear that our method gives better segmentation results compared to NS and wavelet based method [13] and waveseg method [4].

Table 2. F-Measure results of Fig 2(i)-(vi)

Image	Proposed Approach	NS and Wavelet Based Method	Waveseg
i	0.8363	0.8288	0.6739
ii	0.9383	0.9126	0.7612
iii	0.8981	0.8666	0.6532
iv	0.9388	0.8974	0.7989
v	0.7682	0.7634	0.3126
vi	0.8938	0.8817	0.7890

7   Conclusion

This paper presents an automatic approach for color image segmentation in natural images. The proposed method uses neutrosophic set and NSCT for image segmentation. Both color and texture features are used. Color and texture features are extracted from Luv and grayscale image respectively. Images are transformed into neutrosophic domain for better segmentation results. The proposed method is tested with natural color texture images. Experimental results show the superiority of the proposed method over traditional methods, both subjectively and quantitatively.

References

1. Gonzalez, R.C., Woods, R.E.: Digital image processing. Addison-Wesley (1992)
2. Cheng, H.-D., Jiang, X., Sun, Y., Wang, J.: Color image segmentation: advances and prospects. Pattern Recognition 34(12), 2259–2281 (2001)
3. Sengür, A.: Wavelet transform and adaptive neuro-fuzzy inference system for color texture classification. Expert Syst. Appl. 34(3), 2120–2128 (2008)
4. Jung, C.R.: Unsupervised multiscale segmentation of color images. Pattern Recognition Letters 28(4), 523–533 (2007)
5. Ozden, M., Polat, E.: A color image segmentation approach for content-based image retrieval. Pattern Recognition 40(4), 1318–1325 (2007)
6. Deng, Y., Manjunath, B.S.: Unsupervised segmentation of color-texture regions in images and video. IEEE Trans. Pattern Anal. Mach. Intell. 23(8), 800–810 (2001)
7. Kothainachiar, S., Wahita Banu, R.S.D.: A novel image segmentation based on a combination of colour and texture features. ICGST International Journal on Graphics, Vision and Image Processing, GVIP 07, 45–51 (2007)
8. Garcia-Ugarriza, L., Saber, E., Vantaram, S.R., Amuso, V., Shaw, M., Bhaskar, R.: Automatic image segmentation by dynamic region growth and multiresolution merging. IEEE Transactions on Image Processing 18(10), 2275–2288 (2009)
9. Li, S., Xu, J., Ren, J., Xu, T.: A color image segmentation algorithm by integrating watershed with region merging. In: Li, T., Nguyen, H.S., Wang, G., Grzymala-Busse, J., Janicki, R., Hassanien, A.E., Yu, H. (eds.) RSKT 2012. LNCS, vol. 7414, pp. 167–173. Springer, Heidelberg (2012)
10. An, N.-Y., Pun, C.-M.: Color image segmentation using adaptive color quantization and multiresolution texture characterization. Signal, Image and Video Processing, 1–12

11. Guo, Y., Cheng, H.D.: New neutrosophic approach to image segmentation. Pattern Recognition 42(5), 587–595 (2009)
12. Chen, J., Pappas, T.N., Mojsilovic, A., Rogowitz, B.: Image segmentation by spatially adaptive color and texture features. In: Proceedings of the 2003 International Conference on Image Processing, ICIP 2003, vol. 1, p. I-1005–8 (2003)
13. Sengür, A., Guo, Y.: Color texture image segmentation based on neutrosophic set and wavelet transformation. Computer Vision and Image Understanding 115(8), 1134–1144 (2011)
14. Smarandache, F.: A unifying field in logics: Neutrosophic logic. neutrosophy, neutrosophic set, neutrosophic probability and statistics, 4th edn. (2005)
15. Wang, H., Smarandache, F., Zhang, Y.-Q., Sunderraman, R.: Interval neutrosophic sets and logic: Theory and applications in computing. CoRR (2005)
16. Da Cunha, A.L., Zhou, J., Do, M.N.: The nonsubsampled contourlet transform: Theory, design, and applications. IEEE Transactions on Image Processing 15(10), 3089–3101 (2006)
17. Blesslin Elizabeth, C.P., Usha, K., Devi, K.: Spectral clustering of images in luv color space by spatial-color pixel classification
18. Bezdek, J.C., Ehrlich, R., Full, W.: Fcm: The fuzzy c-means clustering algorithm. Computers & Geosciences 10(2-3), 191–203 (1984)
19. Xie, X.L., Beni, G.: A validity measure for fuzzy clustering. IEEE Transactions on Pattern Analysis and Machine Intelligence 13(8), 841–847 (1991)
20. Martin, D., Fowlkes, C., Tal, D., Malik, J.: A database of human segmented natural images and its application to evaluating segmentation algorithms and measuring ecological statistics. In: Proc. 8th Int'l Conf. Computer Vision, vol. 2, pp. 416–423 (July 2001)
21. Abdou, I.E., Pratt, W.: Quantitative design and evaluation of enhancement/thresholding edge detectors. Proceedings of the IEEE 67(5), 753–763 (1979)
22. Martin, D.R., Fowlkes, C.C., Malik, J.: Learning to detect natural image boundaries using local brightness, color, and texture cues. IEEE Trans. Pattern Anal. Mach. Intell. 26(5), 530–549 (2004)

An Experimental Analysis of Vertex Coloring Algorithms on Sparse Random Graphs

Patrick Healy and Andrew Ju

Department of Computer Science and Information Systems
University of Limerick, Ireland
{patrick.healy,andrew.ju}@ul.ie

Abstract. The DSATUR algorithm for vertex coloring is popular both in its heuristic and exact (branch-and-bound) forms. Common to the known public implementations of the exact algorithm is the use of adjacency matrices to store the adjacency relations; this influences the algorithm's implementation and its running time. In this paper we investigate the benefits of the introduction of supporting data structures to improve its running time: in addition to replacing the adjacency matrix by adjacency lists, thus shifting the focus from vertices to edges, we also introduce a priority queue data structure to assist in vertex selection. Our goal is to explore under which circumstances additional supporting data structures can speed up (exact) DSATUR.

1 Introduction

Vertex coloring or graph coloring, as it is also known, is one of the most well-studied problems of computer science. In the optimization version of the problem given a graph $G = (V, E)$ we are asked to determine a "coloring" (labelling) of the vertices from the set $\{1, 2, \ldots, |V|\}$ that uses a minimum number of colors such that no two adjacent vertices receive the same color. The problem has a long history, dating back to the middle of the 19th century. The problem is also of practical importance with applications to – amongst many areas that appear in the literature – sports scheduling [15], numerical algorithms [11], course timetabling [3] and crew scheduling [8]. As further testament to its importance it was one of the subjects of the second DIMACS Implementation Challenge [12].

The decision problem is one of Karp's original list of *NP*-complete problems [13] and is even *NP*-complete for the case of graph 3-colorability[9]. This latter fact makes the search for a Fixed Parameter Tractable (FPT) algorithm parameterized by chromatic number futile. However FPT algorithms do exist for related problems such as testing the colorability of graphs with a parameterized number of edges (or vertices) added or removed [4].

Our interest is in solving the optimization version of the vertex coloring problem exactly. While mathematical programming techniques appear to be very successful [18,16,10] and solve many of the benchmark problems [23] they require access to an LP solver of industrial-strength. For reasons of cost, fewer external dependencies, and for their suitability to a related problem we focus on

P. Gupta and C. Zaroliagis (Eds.): ICAA 2014, LNCS 8321, pp. 174–186, 2014.

backtracking methods, and in particular we focus on the DSATUR algorithm initially proposed by Brélaz [1].

Two of the most widely-known and publicly available implementations of DSATUR, Trick's [22] and Culberson's [6] implement the algorithm centered on an adjacency-matrix representation of the graph. If the graph instance is dense then this choice can be reasonable, though it is our experience that practically occurring instances are usually quite sparse, having just a "handful" of edges per vertex on average.

Given the age of these implementations, when graph libraries such as LEDA or the Boost Graph Library were not mature, choosing to represent the graph with an adjacency-matrix internally was understandable. However, there is a price to pay for the ease of coding: when the graph instance is sparse and because of the representation, iterating over $N_G(v)$, the neighbors of a vertex v, tends to have running time $\Omega(n)$ rather than $\Omega(|N_G(v)|)$, $|N_G(v)| \ll n$. Thus, the initial aim of this investigation is to determine if an adjacency-list representation brings any discernible improvement to the DSATUR algorithm on sparse graphs.

The strategy of DSATUR (to be explained in the following section) is to select the most critical vertex for coloring as determined by the number of distinct colors adjacent to it. Selecting the vertex to color next ostensibly requires a further loop. Our second, and more important aim, is to investigate if the "next up" vertex selection phase can be improved through the use of supporting data structures. In addition to benefitting a standard implementation of DSATUR this would possibly be of even more benefit to the enhancements to the DSATUR next up vertex selection strategy. These have been proposed previously [21,20] and require more sophisticated (and compute-intensive) vertex selection strategies.

In the following section we review sequential coloring algorithms and the branch-and-bound, exact algorithms that derive from them. In Section 3 we describe our data structures to support the exact form of the DSATUR algorithms and the modified algorithm; in Section 4 we report on our experiments to measure the potential speedup that they yield.

2   Background

Given a graph $G = (V, E)$ with $|V| = n$ and $|E| = m$ we say that a coloring C of the vertices is a function $C : V \to \mathbb{N}$ where $C(u) \neq C(v), \forall (u, v) \in E$. A coloring C partitions V into subsets V_i so that $C(x) = C(y), \forall x, y \in V_i$. Over all such partitionings the *chromatic number*, $\chi(G)$, is the cardinality of the smallest one. We say that two colorings C_1 and C_2 are *equivalent* if they induce the same partitioning on V. For a vertex $u \in V$ we call $N_G(u) = \{v \in V : (u, v) \in E\}$ its *neighborhood* and $\delta_G(u) = |N_G(u)|$ the vertex's degree. Given a subset $U \subseteq V$ and a coloring defined on every vertex $u \in U$ we call $cc(U)$ the number (count) of colors used to color U.

In the next two sections we introduce general sequential coloring algorithms and backtracking algorithms.

2.1   Sequential Coloring Algorithms

A sequential coloring algorithm simply colors the vertices of G in some ordering $O = [v_{i_0}, v_{i_1}, \ldots, v_{i_{n-1}}]$ as follows: $C(v_{i_0}) = 1$; if $v_{i_0}, v_{i_1}, \ldots, v_{i_{k-1}}$, $k \geq 1$ have already been colored then vertex v_k is assigned the smallest valid color, namely, the smallest color not yet used in its neighborhood. Perhaps the simplest sequential coloring heuristic is *largest degree first* (LF) which colors the vertices in the order $O = [v_{i_0}, v_{i_1}, \ldots, v_{i_{n-1}}]$ where $\delta_G(v_{i_k}) \geq \delta_G(v_{i_{k+1}})$; ties are broken lexicographically. The running time complexity is (naïvely) $\mathcal{O}(|V|^2)$ or, if an upper bound C_u is known for the chromatic number, $\mathcal{O}(C_u|V|)$, ignoring the time to determine the ordering, O.

Brélaz's DSATUR algorithm [1] does not work with a fixed ordering but, rather, chooses the vertex to color next based on the most current information. The next up vertex is the one with the largest number of differently colored neighbors, which is called its *saturation degree*. A vertex with high saturation degree could be considered to be more critical than those of lower saturation degree and therefore should be colored sooner. Ties are broken by restricting the LF rule to the uncolored graph. A naïve implementation will require $\mathcal{O}(|V|^3)$ running time since the ordering O is no longer static.

2.2   Backtracking Algorithms

In the way described above DSATUR can provide good heuristic solutions [14]. However, we are interested in pursuing exact solutions. After briefly describing the general backtrack algorithm we will describe how the DSATUR decision can be incorporated, giving what we will call DSATUR-exact.

When developing a backtrack algorithm a crucial aspect is the elimination of equivalent colorings. Maintaining tight colorings plays an important role in this. We say a coloring is *tight* (with respect to a given ordering of the vertices) if $C(v_i) \leq cc(\{v_0, \ldots, v_{i-1}\}) + 1, 1 \leq i \leq n)$ with $C(v_0) = 1$. By proving that, for a given ordering of the vertices, every minimal coloring is equivalent to a tight coloring, Brown [2] argues that only tight solutions need be generated; therefore, many potential solutions that are as he calls them "redundant" can be avoided.

Borrowing from Brélaz's description of Brown's algorithm, let K_{pq} be a coloring of $v_0, \ldots, v_p$ with q colors; from K_{pq} we extend the solution by assigning (in turn) to v_{p+1} all of the colors $1, 2, \ldots, q + 1$ that maintain a valid coloring; then continue the same procedure with all new partial solutions. Thus every internal node of the search tree gives rise to $q + 1$ children.

Brélaz proposed a modified algorithm [1] by a) using the upper bound information that becomes available at leaf nodes of the tree and, b) using his DSATUR maximum saturation degree heuristic. The algorithm branches only if the upper bound has not been exceeded and dynamically determines which vertex to choose at iteration $p + 1$. If vertex v is chosen for consideration at iteration p as it is assigned (in turn) different colors, the vertex that should be colored on the next iteration may change also. This style of algorithm is known generally in the literature as branch-and-bound.

Two crucial pieces of information are required of a selected vertex: what is the set of valid colors to branch on and for each choice what is the next vertex to choose? How can those be found? In a time when memory costs were more than they are today it may have been reasonable to keep additional memory requirements to a minimum and rely on multiple iterations over the adjacency matrix. We now adopt the opposite approach: with memory no obstacle, what can we do to speed up DSATUR-exact? (We note that another publicly available code for graph coloring, GCP-v5.00[1] goes some way towards addressing our questions. However, this code still iterates over all uncolored vertices when selecting the next up vertex. Moreover, the implementation is limited to DSATUR-heuristic.)

3   Supporting Data Structures

We have identified two crucial questions that we must be able to answer quickly having selected a vertex for coloring. We need to maintain for every vertex the subset of feasible colors it may take, $C_F(v)$, if it is uncolored, and to assist with making the *next* selection we need to maintain the set of its uncolored neighbors, $N_U(v)$. When a vertex v is colored it must be removed from $N_U(u), u \in N_G(v)$ and if $C(v) = c$ then c must be removed from $C_F(u), u \in N_G(v)$. A linked list is a possible way of storing these two subsets but that makes expensive the query "is c a feasible color for u?" and the task of removing w from $N_U(u)$. What is common to the data being stored in both cases is that they can be represented by the integers (labels) $0, \ldots, n-1$.[2]

3.1   A Partitioned Set

We use, instead, a data structure that we call a pset, a partitioning of the set of integers $\{0, \ldots, n-1\}$. A pset comprises an array, v, of n integers which at all times represents a permutation of the integers $\{0, \ldots, n-1\}$. A marker, m, is maintained that specifies that the first m elements are in the partition while the remainder are not. A final array, called l, that is indexed by the data in v, (namely the values $\{0, \ldots, n-1\}$) indicates the *location*, or index, of a value in v. Since the domain and range of both arrays are the same, then from the definition of l clearly the two arrays act as inverses of each other: v[l[i]] = i and l[v[j]] = j. Given an element x of the set, x is then in the partition if and only if 0 <= l[x] < m, so membership can be tested in constant time. An element x can be removed from the partition by finding its location, i=l[x] in v, swapping elements i and m-1 of v (and l) and, finally, decreasing m by 1; insertions can be performed analogously. Thus, for a cost of $2n+1$ units of storage per vertex we can maintain a data structure that permits constant-time insertions, removals and membership tests as well as efficiently iterating over the

---

[1] Available at http://www.imada.sdu.dk/~marco/gcp-study/.

[2] Although earlier we talked about colors $1, \ldots, n$ they are represented internally as $0, \ldots, n-1$.

elements. (Although this is hardly new we have not been able to find a reference to a data structure of this type in the literature.)

This data structure can be used to maintain the (sub)set of feasible colors for a vertex or to maintain its uncolored neighborhood. As a generalisation of the latter it can also be used to simulate the adjacency list associated with a vertex.

3.2   The Priority Queue

The selection of the next up vertex suggests some type of ordered queue whereby we select the front element of the queue at each iteration. The *priority queue* abstract data type classically provides for the `insert()` and `delete_max()` functions, each achievable in $\mathcal{O}(\log n)$-time [5]. Thus, this appears to be an attractive alternative to an iteration over all uncolored vertices. Our situation makes further demands, however. After making a next up selection and assigning it a color the uncolored degree of its uncolored neighbors will decrease by 1 and the saturation degree of each may increase by 1. Thus, each neighbor needs to be repositioned in the priority queue. Prior to being recolored, at the backtracking step this vertex will need to be uncolored, requiring the undoing of the above. With the appropriate underlying data structure the priority adjusting operations `decrease_p()` and `increase_p()` are still achievable in $\mathcal{O}(\log n)$-time [5]. We do this by representing the priority queue as a *heap* [5] with an additional array that provides us with a *handle* to the index of any vertex similar to the look-up array, l, used in `pset`.

When a vertex is selected and assigned a color the priorities of all remaining uncolored vertices in the queue must be updated. It is clear that the set of vertices whose priorities might change is limited to those in $N_U(v)$, the uncolored neighborhood of the selected vertex, v. For sparse graphs it seems reasonable to make a separate call to `adjust_p()` for each $u \in N_U(v)$, adjusting its priority independently, for a total effort of $\mathcal{O}(|N_U(v)| \log n)$. However, it is possible to create an entire heap in $\mathcal{O}(n)$-time by making successive calls to the standard heap function `trickle_down()` on all of the non-leaf nodes of the heap. Therefore, assuming that the priority queue provides *some* benefit, a further question of interest is to investigate the interplay between updating in the priority queue only those vertices adjacent to the selected vertex and a full rebuild. We will return to this question in Section 4.

Note that as a consequence of a vertex being selected and assigned a color it is possible either for an uncolored neighbor's priority in the queue to increase or decrease. For example, if v is the next up vertex and it is assigned color c then if there is an uncolored neighbor w of v that did not have c in its neighborhood the saturation degree of w will increase, leading to an increase in its priority. If, on the other hand, w already had c in its neighborhood prior to v then there will be no change to its saturation degree; but since its uncolored neighborhood has been reduced its priority now decreases. However, the change in priority does not guarantee a change in its position in the queue.

3.3   The Algorithm

In order to compute a good starting point we obtain an initial lower bound by finding as large a clique as we can. This is done using the cliquer library[19]. For random graphs that adhere to the Erdös-Rényi model Matula [17] showed that with very high probability the expected clique number (the size of the maximum clique) is approximately equal to $2 \log_{\frac{1}{p}} n$ and this will be a lower bound, C_l, on $\chi(G)$.

Algorithm 1. DSATUR-exact

---

color()

```
 1: if (current_color ≥ BestColoring) or
 2:    (BestColoring == lb) or
 3:    (heap is empty) then
 4:      return
 5: end if
 6: select heap's root node vertex v as the next up vertex
 7: for each already used possible color i do
 8:    if vertex v can be assigned with color i then
 9:       color vertex v with color i
10:       update heap
11:       if color() < BestColoring then
12:          BestColoring = color()
13:       end if
14:       uncolor vertex v and update heap
15:       if BestColoring ≤ current_color then
16:          return
17:       end if
18:    end if
19: end for
20: if current_color + 1 ≤ BestColoring then
21:    color vertex v with color current_color+1
22:    update heap
23:    if color() < BestColoring then
24:       BestColoring = color()
25:    end if
26:    uncolor vertex v and update heap
27: end if
28: return
 1: read graph from input
 2: find a clique with size as large as possible and initialize variable lb;
 3: color the clique; update uncolored neighbors, feasible colors for all vertices;
 4: use heap's built-in function build_heap() to build the PQ with DSATUR rule;
 5: call color() function;
 6: print BestColoring
```

Following the coloring of the clique the algorithm then proceeds to select the most urgent vertex and, in turn, color it with each feasible and tight color. For each such assigned color the priority queue and associated data structures are updated and the process recurs on the remaining uncolored vertices. If the number of colors used exceeds that of a previous solution then the path is abandoned and another color possibility is examined. This is illustrated in Algorithm 1.

4   Experimental Evaluation

It is reasonable that for dense graphs the additions should not offer an obvious improvement over the straightforward implementation. One of the goals of this research was to investigate the range, if any, of edge densities where the additional data structure support was likely to be of benefit.

We investigated the run-time behaviour of four variants of DSATUR-exact. As a base point, we coded an implementation based on Trick's [22] branch-and-bound code. We call this first implementation simple to more clearly distinguish it from the others that follow. We then implemented a "middle ground" solution comprising a replacement of the adjacency matrix by adjacency lists, which takes an approach similar to the GCP-v5.00 project. We call this implementation simple+. The adjacency lists were implemented using the pset mechanism for consistency with our third and fourth implementations. These last two implementations are based around using a priority queue to assist in quickly determining the next up vertex; they differ in how the priority queue is updated: if only those neighbors of the selected vertex are targeted for update_p() then we call this algorithm PQ-p (partial update) whereas if the entire heap is rebuilt using successive calls to trickle_down() then we call the algorithm PQ-f (full update).

Since our suspicion is that these supporting data structures are most likely to be of benefit in the case of sparse instances, we generated random instances according to the $G(n, p)$ variant of the Erdös-Rényi model[7]. For fixed p the expected number of edges is $|E| = \binom{n}{2}p$. In a given graph, the edge density is $d = |E|/\binom{n}{2}$ and so d relates to the probability of an edge being present. We used those instances that our slowest algorithm was capable of solving.

In our experiments we generated data instances at a variety of vertex counts and densities. The first densities chosen were $d = \{0.01, 0.02, 0.025\}$. A denser pair of values were also used, $d = \{0.1, 0.2\}$. For each density value, 10 graph instances were generated for each value of $|V|$ in $[150, 750]$ in steps of 50. However, as will be seen later, the larger values of density did not permit us to solve such large graphs. For a choice of $|V|$ and d with $|E| = \binom{|V|}{2}d$ we could maintain exactly the same number of edges in each of the 10 instances. The edges were chosen by making $|E|$ random choices from the $\binom{|V|}{2}$ pairings.

All of our experiments were conducted on an Apple Macbook Pro running OS X version 10.8.2, 2.5GHz Intel Core i7 processor with 8Gb of DDR3 memory (clock speed 1333MHz). Our implementations were written in C++ and were compiled using g++-4.2.

Table 1. simple, simple+ vs. update-p on random instances of varying density

d	$|V|$	$|E|$	simple	(σ)	simple+	(σ)	PQ-p	(σ)
0.01	150	112	2.18e-04	(5.21e-06)	1.45e-04	(5.58e-06)	**1.40e-04**	(4.43e-06)
	200	119	3.68e-04	(1.50e-05)	2.40e-04	(8.43e-06)	**2.18e-04**	(7.69e-05)
	250	311	5.62e-04	(1.96e-05)	3.76e-04	(1.92e-05)	**3.09e-04**	(1.96e-05)
	300	449	7.96e-04	(2.36e-05)	5.45e-04	(2.16e-05)	**4.40e-04**	(2.08e-05)
	350	611	1.28e-03	(3.39e-04)	8.60e-04	(2.22e-04)	**6.87e-04**	(1.67e-04)
	400	798	2.23e-02	(5.71e-02)	1.53e-02	(3.92e-02)	**1.14e-02**	(2.94e-02)
	450	1010	9.95e-01	(9.67e-01)	6.81e-01	(6.68e-01)	**5.30e-01**	(5.10e-01)
	500	1248	4.89e+01	(6.92e+01)	3.41e+01	(4.85e+01)	**2.87e+01**	(4.00e+01)
	550	1510	4.63	(5.29)	3.15	(3.54)	**2.77**	(3.10)
	600	1797	1.32	(1.99)	9.02e-01	(1.36)	**7.99e-01**	(1.18)
	650	2109	6.92e-01	(6.84e-01)	4.73e-01	(4.67e-01)	**4.32e-01**	(4.27e-01)
	700	2447	1.41e-01	(1.16e-01)	9.72e-02	(7.99e-02)	**8.77e-02**	(7.20e-02)
	750	2809	1.65	(1.30)	1.21	(9.57e-01)	**7.37e-01**	(5.73e-01)
0.02	150	224	2.92e-03	(7.31e-05)	2.18e-03	(5.97e-05)	**2.29e-04**	(5.92e-05)
	200	398	7.51e-04	(1.46e-04)	5.98e-04	(1.15e-04)	**5.36e-04**	(1.36e-04)
	250	623	1.62e-02	(1.35e-02)	**1.28e-02**	(1.05e-02)	1.47e-02	(1.24e-02)
	300	897	6.92e-03	(8.00e-03)	**5.70e-03**	(6.50e-03)	6.73e-03	(7.60e-03)
	350	1222	8.96e-02	(2.56e-01)	6.92e-02	(1.97e-01)	**6.21e-02**	(1.75e-01)
	400	1596	1.43e+02	(1.52e+02)	1.16e+02	(1.24e+02)	**1.14e+02**	(1.17e+02)
0.025	150	279	5.66e-04	(4.25e-04)	**4.71e-04**	(4.09e-04)	5.40e-04	(3.89e-04)
	200	498	1.52e-02	(1.26e-02)	**1.20e-02**	(1.05e-02)	1.45e-02	(1.14e-02)
	250	778	2.56e-03	(1.63e-03)	**2.15e-03**	(1.35e-03)	2.74e-03	(1.94e-03)
	300	1121	1.27e-02	(1.12e-02)	**1.03e-02**	(9.09e-03)	1.06e-02	(8.90e-03)

4.1 Priority Queue Evaluation

Table 1 illustrates the performance of simple, simple+ and PQ-p on randomly generated instances of densities $d = 0.01, d = 0.02, d = 0.025$ respectively. Due to space restrictions we omit the presentation of our data in graphical form. For each of the three algorithms we report the average running time in seconds over the ten instances and the associated standard deviation, σ. The bolded entry in each row indicates the champion algorithm over the 10 instances at that graph size. While it was possible for a particular instance to have a different behaviour to the average behaviour over the three algorithms, in most cases the algorithms performed as the averages indicate. Table 2 illustrates the performance of the three algorithms on those instances where the running time is more than 1 second. It is clear that simple+ (adjacency lists to represent vertex neighborhoods) improves the running times throughout and that for the smaller values of density the addition of a priority queue further helps: for $d = 0.01$ the PQ-p algorithm provided the winner in all cases. As a result of using the priority queue with partial update the running time (over simple) is more than halved in the case of $|V| = 750$; generally the benefit is somewhat less than half its running time.

Table 2. simple, simple+ vs. update-p on random instances where running time is more than 1 *second*

d	$\|V\|$	$\|E\|$	simple	simple+	PQ-p
0.01	450	1010	2.54	1.79	**1.39**
	450	1010	2.77	1.95	**1.49**
	450	1010	1.14	0.81	**0.59**
	450	1010	1.77	1.05	**0.83**
	500	1248	5.03	3.68	**2.91**
	500	1248	5.53	3.91	**3.28**
	500	1248	244.70	171.41	**141.41**
	500	1248	39.55	27.64	**23.99**
	500	1248	9.80	6.96	**5.95**
	500	1248	20.13	14.10	**12.75**
	500	1248	26.70	18.34	**15.23**
	500	1248	73.07	51.14	**43.72**
	500	1248	61.68	41.69	**35.50**
	500	1248	3.20	2.13	**1.95**
	740	2734	5.26	3.85	**2.20**
	740	2734	23.00	17.01	**10.06**
	760	2884	8.06	5.85	**3.80**
	760	2884	89.38	52.85	**28.43**
	760	2884	2.94	2.14	**1.31**
0.02	400	1596	8.85	6.46	**5.91**
	400	1596	400.48	325.98	**311.53**
	400	1596	74.08	60.42	**57.53**

As density increased it was not possible for us to complete the required number of algorithm runs at each vertex size. All published data are on the basis of 10 runs with the exception of $d = 0.02, |V| = 400$, where only 4 instances completed. Another feature that becomes apparent is that PQ-p begins to lose its advantage. By $d = 0.025$ PQ-p has lost every round to simple+. With $|V| = 300$ and $d = 0.025$ this corresponds to each vertex having, on average, 7 - 8 edges. We suggest that $d = 0.025$ is an upper limit of density where providing this type of data structure support brings benefit; beyond this the overhead of maintaining the heap appears to cost too much. A further feature of the two tables is the widening spread of running times over the instances as evidenced by the increasing standard deviation, σ, in Table 1 and the larger deviations in running times amongst graphs of the same size in Table 2.

4.2   Further Evaluation of the Priority Queue

In view of the poor performance of PQ-p when the density increases, we considered whether the denser instances necessitated more work each time the priorities of the nodes in the priority queue had to be updated. Therefore, we replaced the calls to update_p() for each neighbour of the next up vertex by a blanket-wide build_heap(). For this strategy, we call it PQ-f. The manner of update does not account for the relative under-performance of the priority queue in this case.

Questioning if the update strategy should make a difference when PQ-p began to lose its dominance in Table 1 we revisited these cases. Table 3 below summarizes our results along this avenue of exploration. Note firstly that for $d = 0.1$ and $d = 0.2$ the range of instance size that we were able to complete is diminished: for $d = 0.2$ our data were collected in the ranges of $50 \leq |V| \leq 90$. It is clear from this table that rebuilding the heap at each step makes little sense; there are no cases – in the range $0.01 \leq d \leq 0.2$ – where the strategy pays off and the relative difference both is increasing with respect to $|V|$ in all cases. (Entry $|V| = 400, d = 0.02$ was generated from one instance and entry $|V| = 130, d = 0.1$ was generated from 6 instances.)

Table 3. PQ-f vs. PQ-p on random instances, for four choices of d.

$|V|$	d	PQ-f	(σ)	PQ-p	(σ)	d	PQ-f	(σ)	PQ-p	(σ)
150	0.01	5.23e-04	(1.18e-05)	**1.35e-04**	(3.33e-06)	0.02	6.70e-04	(1.90e-04)	**2.20e-04**	(6.40e-05)
200	0.01	8.68e-04	(1.34e-05)	**2.20e-04**	(8.06e-06)	0.02	1.70e-03	(4.20e-04)	**5.00e-04**	(1.20e-04)
250	0.01	1.31e-03	(2.96e-05)	**3.10e-04**	(1.46e-05)	0.02	5.85e-02	(4.93e-02)	**1.41e-02**	(1.15e-02)
300	0.01	1.85e-03	(1.92e-05)	**4.50e-04**	(1.33e-05)	0.02	2.63e-02	(3.16e-02)	**6.50e-03**	(7.40e-03)
350	0.01	2.80e-03	(6.49e-04)	**6.70e-04**	(1.52e-04)	0.02	2.27e-01	(6.38e-01)	**5.99e-02**	(1.69e-01)
400	0.01	6.24e-02	(1.63e-01)	**1.14e-02**	(2.94e-02)	0.02	2.26e+01	(0)	**5.44**	(0)
450	0.01	3.05	(3.05)	**0.51**	(0.51)	0.02	n/a		n/a	
500	0.01	1.52e+02	(2.13e+02)	**2.35e+01**	(3.27e+01)	0.02	n/a		n/a	
50	0.1	1.17e-04	(1.93e-05)	**8.29e-05**	(1.41e-05)	0.2	2.26e-04	(8.68e-05)	**1.96e-04**	(7.03e-05)
70	0.1	4.13e-04	(2.30e-04)	**2.57e-04**	(1.30e-04)	0.2	3.58e-03	(3.80e-03)	**2.74e-03**	(2.90e-03)
90	0.1	9.09e-03	(5.00e-03)	**5.08e-03**	(2.80e-03)	0.2	1.64	(1.84)	**1.24**	(1.41)
110	0.1	2.03e-02	(4.07e-02)	**1.21e-02**	(2.43e-02)	0.2	n/a		n/a	
130	0.1	8.81e+01	(8.81e+01)	**4.86e+01**	(4.86e+01)	0.2	n/a		n/a	

The story, however, is more complex than at first appears. Table 4 considers 4 typical instances (two from the DIMACS suite and two random) and counts the operations performed when updating the heap. For each of the four instances it will be seen that the number of swaps performed by the two competing heap update strategies is broadly similar. What differs hugely however is the number of comparisons performed. Heap priority comparisons are multi-way. In order to break ties firstly saturation degree is compared, then uncolored neighborhood size, and then lexicographic order. Further, trickling down a node involves comparing against both children.

Counting comparisons in this manner (and averaging over the four levels) we report those comparisons that did *not* result in a swap occurring. The large difference between the two algorithms was unexpected: we would have expected a large disparity between *swaps*. One possibility for reducing this work would be to save state on making a color assignment so that when undoing the assignment the previous state of the heap is *restored* rather than recomputed.

Table 4. Heap operation counts on 4 typical instances: full vs. partial update

name	$|V|$	$|E|$	d	PQ-f time	#swap	#comp	PQ-p time	#swap	#comp
anna.col	138	986	0.104	4.64e-04	1044	12444.5	2.33e-04	1698	1090.75
david.col	87	812	0.217	2.16e-04	507	4080	1.28e-04	845	658.5
random1	50	12	0.01	7.13e-05	209	2407	6.60e-05	387	293.75
random2	50	25	0.02	8.20e-05	268	2360.5	4.03e-05	440	337.5

4.3 Further Evaluation of PQ-f and PQ-p

From Table 4 we have noted that there is a large disparity in the count of heap comparisons between the PQ-f and PQ-p algorithms. Along with Table 3 it appears that PQ-f is the poorer of the two heap-based algorithms. To investigate this issue, we conducted extra experiments using DSATUR-*heuristic* to investigate when the full update strategy of PQ-f is worse than the partial heap update strategy, PD-p. (To extend the running times and magnify algorithm differences, we used large graphs which, consequently, made it impossible for DSATUR-*exact* to run to completion.) Table 5 illustrates a typical instance with $|V| = 2500$. It tells us that PQ-f algorithm is not to be dismissed, indicating that as *density* increases, it's better to use build_heap() to rebuild from the heap scratch.

Table 5. Fraction of runs when running time of full update beats partial

d	0.15	0.20	0.25	0.30	0.35	0.40	0.45
Full update best	5.7%	11.6%	25.1%	47.3%	72.2%	77.6%	85.8%

From the above results we suggest that a better approach for updating the priority queue is to choose between build_heap() and update_p() depending on the selected vertex's degree in the uncolored subgraph (though this analysis is beyond the scope of this paper); other parts of the algorithm may be improved by saving and (later) restoring the PQ's state. This appears to be replacing $\mathcal{O}(\log n) + \mathcal{O}(\log n)$ with $\mathcal{O}(\log n) + \mathcal{O}(n)$ but with the apparently high cost of heap operations perhaps this might be reasonable in some situations.

5   Conclusions

We have proposed additional support for the DSATUR-exact algorithm through the use of a priority queue. For sparse graphs (density $d \le 0.02$) the strategy has been demonstrated to be of significant benefit. Many large-instance networks have even lower density than this. Although we restricted our analysis to DSATUR-exact the benefits here can transfer to DSATUR-heuristic also.

Further algorithm tuning opportunities exist: when moving data within the heap full swaps are performed between successive levels. With a more careful writing of the `while`-loop one half of the swaps can be avoided. Thus, identifying other opportunities for code optimization, and applying our ideas to more constrained versions of graph coloring (e.g. list coloring) are our next priorities.

Acknowledgments. The research is jointly funded by *Irish Research Council* (previously known as *Irish Research Council for Science, Engineering and Technology*, RS/2011/5), and the *China Scholarship Council* (CSC). We are grateful to three anonymous referees for their careful reading and useful remarks which helped us in improving the paper.

References

1. Brélaz, D.: New methods to color the vertices of a graph. Communications of the ACM 22(4), 251–256 (1979)
2. Randall Brown, J.: Chromatic scheduling and the chromatic number problem. Management Science 19(4), 456–463 (1972)
3. Burke, E.K., Mareček, J., Parkes, A.J., Rudová, H.: On a clique-based integer programming formulation of vertex colouring with applications in course timetabling. Technical Report NOTTCS-TR-2007-10, The University of Nottingham, Nottingham (2007)
4. Cai, L.: Parameterized complexity of vertex colouring. Discrete Applied Mathematics 127(3), 415–429 (2003)
5. Cormen, T.H., Stein, C., Rivest, R.L., Leiserson, C.E.: Introduction to Algorithms, 2nd edn. McGraw-Hill Higher Education (2001)
6. Culberson, J.: Graph coloring programs (2001), http://webdocs.cs.ualberta.ca/~joe/Coloring/Colorsrc/index.html
7. Erdös, P., Rényi, A.: On the evolution of random graphs. Publication of the Mathematical Institute of the Hungarian Academy of Sciences, 17–61 (1960)
8. Gamache, M., Hertz, A., Ouellet, J.O.: A graph coloring model for a feasibility problem in monthly crew scheduling with preferential bidding. Computers & Operations Research 34(8), 2384–2395 (2007)
9. Garey, M.R., Johnson, D.S., Stockmeyer, L.: Some simplified NP-complete problems. In: Proceedings of the Sixth Annual ACM Symposium on Theory of Computing, STOC 1974, pp. 47–63. ACM, New York (1974)
10. Gualandi, S., Malucelli, F.: Exact solution of graph coloring problems via constraint programming and column generation. INFORMS Journal on Computing 24(1), 81–100 (2012)
11. Hossain, S., Steihaug, T.: Graph coloring in the estimation of sparse derivative matrices: Instances and applications. Discrete Applied Mathematics 156(2), 280–288 (2008)
12. Johnson, D.J., Trick, M.A. (eds.): Cliques, Coloring, and Satisfiability: Second DIMACS Implementation Challenge, Workshop, October 11-13, 1993. American Mathematical Society, Boston (1996)
13. Richard, M.: Karp. Reducibility among combinatorial problems. In: Miller, R.E., Thatcher, J.W. (eds.) Complexity of Computer Computations, pp. 85–103. Plenum, New York (1972)

14. Klotz, W.: Graph coloring algorithms. Technical Report Mathematik-Bericht 5, Clausthal University of Technology, Clausthal, Germany (2002)

15. Lewis, R., Thompson, J.: On the application of graph colouring techniques in round-robin sports scheduling. Computers & Operations Research 38(1), 190–204 (2011)

16. Malaguti, E., Monaci, M., Toth, P.: An exact approach for the vertex coloring problem. Discrete Optimization 8(2), 174–190 (2011)

17. Matula, D.W.: On the complete subgraphs of a random graph. In: Proceedings of the 2nd Chapel Hill Conference on Combinatorial Mathematics and its Applications, Chapel Hill, NC, pp. 356–369 (1970)

18. Méndez-Díaz, I., Zabala, P.: A cutting plane algorithm for graph coloring. Discrete Applied Mathematics 156(2), 159–179 (2008)

19. Östergård, P.R.J.: A new algorithm for the maximum-weight clique problem. Nordic Journal of Computing 8, 424–436 (2001)

20. Segundo, P.S.: A new DSATUR-based algorithm for exact vertex coloring. Computers & Operations Research 39(7), 1724–1733 (2012)

21. Sewell, E.C.: An improved algorithm for exact graph coloring. DIMACS Series in Discrete Mathematics and Theoretical Computer Science, pp. 359–373 (1996)

22. Trick, M.: Network resources for coloring a graph (1994), http://mat.gsia.cmu.edu/COLOR/color.html

23. Trick, M.: ROIS: Registry for optimization instances and solutions (2009), http://mat.tepper.cmu.edu/ROIS/solutions/coloring/display_sol.php

An Experimental Study of a Novel Move-to-Front-or-Middle (MFM) List Update Algorithm

Rakesh Mohanty[1], Tirtharaj Dash[2], Biswadeep Khan[2],
and Shiba Prasad Dash[2]

[1] Department of Computer Science and Engineering,
Indian Institute of Technology, Madras, Chennai-600036, India
[2] Department of Computer Science and Engineering,
Veer Surendra Sai University of Technology, Burla, Odisha-768018, India
{rakesh.iitmphd,tirtharajnist446,biswadeepkhan,titun.tiki}@gmail.com

Abstract. List Update Problem (LUP) or List Accessing Problem (LAP) is a well studied research problem in the area of online algorithms [5] and self organizing data structures [2] since the pioneering work of McCabe [7]. In this problem, the inputs are an unsorted list of distinct items and a sequence of requests where each request is an access operation on an item of the list. The objective of a list update algorithm is to reorganize the list after each access and minimize the total access and reorganization cost, while processing a request sequence of finite size on a fixed size list. LUP is one of the general memory accessing problem which was studied by Sleator and Tarjan [14] for the competitive analysis of online algorithms in their seminal paper. As offline list update has been proved to be NP-hard [3], there is no known trivial solution to the problem. Move-To-Front(MTF) has been proved to be the best online algorithm [12] in the literature. In this paper, we have proposed a novel variant of MTF algorithm, which we popularly call as Move-to-Front-or-Middle(MFM). We have performed an empirical study of MFM algorithm and comparative performance analysis with MTF algorithm using two dataset such as Calgary Corpus and Canterbury Corpus. Our experimental results show that MFM outperforms MTF for all request sequences in both the data set.

1 Introduction

LUP is a general memory access problem which uses linked list as the data structure due to its simplicity and dynamic memory allocation. It is one of the well studied problem in the area of online algorithms along with the paging problem by Sleator and Tarjan[14] in their seminal paper. The offline list update problem has been proved to be NP-hard in 2000[3], thereby posing greater challenges for the researchers to develop efficient list update algorithms. List update problem is widely used in data compression. Other applications of LUP are dictionary maintenance, collision resolution in hash table, storing identifiers in symbol table in compiler, and computing point maxima, convex hulls in computational geometry.

P. Gupta and C. Zaroliagis (Eds.): ICAA 2014, LNCS 8321, pp. 187–197, 2014.

List Update Problem (LUP) is a well studied computational problem in the area of self organizing data structures. Self organizing data structure is one in which the data structure is reorganized after each operation to make a future sequence of operations efficient. In the LUP, we are given an unsorted list L of items of size l and a request sequence of size n where each request is either an access or insert or delete operation on an item in the list. In an access operation, the list is scanned one by one from the front towards the end till the item is found in the list. In an insert operation, a new item is inserted at the end of the list, when the item is scanned and not found in the list. In the delete operation, the item is deleted from the list after it is accessed. As the insert and delete operations are special cases of access operation, we can consider only access operation in the list update problem for simplicity. Hence the list update problem is also known as list accessing problem. When an item is scanned from the request sequence and accessed in the list, a request is said to be served by incurring some access cost based on the position of the item in the list using some cost model. After accessing an item in the list, the list can be reorganized by incurring some reorganization cost. A list update algorithm is one which reorganizes the list to minimize the total access and reorganization cost when a request sequence is served on a list. In the LUP, our objective is to design efficient list update algorithms.

1.1 Primitive List Update Algorithms

There are three primitive list update algorithms such as Move-To-Front (MTF), Transpose (TRANS) and Frequency Count (FC), which are stated as follows[4].

- *MTF: Upon an access to an item x, move x to the front of the list without changing the relative order of other items in the list.*
- *TRANS: Upon an access to an item x, exchange x with the preceding item of the list.*
- *FC: Maintain a frequency counter for each item. Upon inserting an item, initialize its frequency counter to 0. After accessing an item, increment its counter by one and then reorganize the list so that items on the list are arranged in non-increasing order of their frequencies.*

Based on the amount of input information available, list update algorithms can be classified as *offline* and *online*. In the *offline algorithm*, the whole input request sequence is known in advance; whereas, in the online algorithm, the input request sequence is partially known and requests arrive one by one on the fly. *Competitive analysis* is a standard performance measure for analysis of online algorithms. In competitive analysis approach, the cost incurred by online algorithm for a request sequence is compared with the cost of optimal offline algorithm for the same request sequence. An *optimal offline algorithm* is one, which incurs minimum cost amongst all the offline algorithms. Let $ALG(\sigma)$ and $OPT(\sigma)$ be the cost of online algorithm and optimal offline algorithm respectively on request sequence σ. Then, $ALG(\sigma) \leq c.OPT(\sigma) + k$, where k is a constant and c is a positive real number. Here, c is called the competitive ratio of online algorithm ALG[5]. MTF has been proved to be the best online algorithm in the literature till date[6]. We present the MTF algorithm with an illustration for easy understanding of the reader. Sleator and Tarjan have developed the full cost model which is considered as a standard cost model for the LUP [14]. In the full cost model, the access cost is computed based on the position of the accessed item from the front of the list. *Free exchange* is one in which an accessed item is moved towards the front of the list without incurring any reorganization cost. *Paid exchange* is one in which an accessed item is exchanged with its preceding item in the list with unit cost. In this paper, we have assumed the full cost model for the LUP. As our study is focused on the MTF algorithm, we have illustrated this algorithm using full cost model with an example in the next section.

The computation of access cost by MTF algorithm has been illustrated in Fig. 1 as follows.

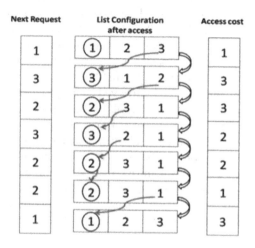

Fig. 1. Illustration of MTF algorithm for $L=<1\ 2\ 3>$ and $\sigma = <1\ 3\ 2\ 3\ 2\ 2\ 1>$

Let us consider a list $L =< 1, 2, 3 >$ of size 3 and request sequence $\sigma =< 1323221 >$ of size 7. The input σ_i be the ith item in σ. The first item $\sigma_1 = 1$ is to be accessed from the list. According to MTF algorithm, the requested item σ_1 is present in the position 1. So, the access cost of σ_1 is 1 and list configuration remains the same. Let $C_{MTF}(\sigma_i)$ be the cost of MTF algorithm on accessing request σ_i. Then $C_{MTF}(\sigma_1) = 1$ and the list configuration remains the same as the initial configuration. Similarly second request $\sigma_2 = 3$ is present in position 3 of the list. So $C_{MTF}(\sigma_2) = 3$. After accessing σ_2, it is moved to the front and the list configuration becomes$< 312 >$. The next requested item σ_3 is 2 at the position 3 of the current list configuration. So $C_{MTF}(\sigma_3) = 3$ and σ_3 is moved to the front of the list and so on. Similarly, other requests of the request sequence can be accessed in the list. Hence the total access cost is given by

$$C_{MTF}(\sigma) = \sum_{i=1}^{n} C_{MTF}(\sigma_i) = 1 + 3 + 3 + 2 + 2 + 1 + 3 = 15.$$

1.2   Literature Review

List update problem was first studied by McCabe[7] in 1965 with the concept of relocatable records in serial files. He also introduced two list update algorithms Move To Front(MTF) and Transpose(TRANS). Rivest[11] has examined a class of algorithms for maintaining the sequential list in optimal order with respect to the average time required to search for a specified item with an assumption of fixed probability of each search in his experimental study. He has shown that MTF and Transpose algorithms are optimal within a constant factor. Hester and Hirschberg have done a comprehensive survey of all permutation algorithms that modified the order of linear search lists with an emphasis on average case analysis [6]. Sleator and Tarjan[14] in their seminal paper, have formally introduced the concept of competitive analysis for online deterministic list update algorithms such as MTF, TRANS and FC using amortized analysis and potential function method. MTF has been proved to be $2 - competitive$ where as FC and TRANS are not $c - competitive$. Irani proposed the first randomized online list update algorithm, known as SPLIT, which is 1.932 -competitive[13]. Albers, Von-Stengel, and Werchner[15] proposed a simple randomized online algorithm-COMB that achieves a $1.6 - competitiveness$, which is the best competitive ratio for any randomized algorithm in the literature till date. Albers[1] introduced the concept of look ahead in the LUP and obtained improved competitive ratio for deterministic online algorithms. Reingold and Westbrook[10] have proposed an optimal offline algorithm which runs in time $O(2^l n!)$ where l is the size of the list and n is the size of request sequence. Bachrach et al. have provided an extensive theoretical and experimental study of online list update algorithms in 2002[9]. The study of locality of reference in LUP was initiated by Angelopoulos[12] in 2006, where he has proved that MTF is superior to all algorithms. Ambuhl in 2000[3] proved that off-line list update is NP-hard by showing a reduction from the Minimum Feedback Arc Set Problem. A recent survey on the LUP and related results can be found in [8].

1.3   Our Contribution

In this paper, we have proposed a novel variant of MTF algorithm, which we popularly call as Move to Front or Middle(MFM)algorithm. We have performed empirical study and comparative performance analysis of MFM with MTF using two dataset such as Calgary Corpus, Canterbury Corpus. We have computed the access cost of our proposed MFM algorithm and MTF algorithm through our experimental study. Our experimental results show that MFM outperforms MTF for all types request sequence for both the dataset-Calgary Corpus and Canterbury Corpus.

2   Proposed MFM Algorithm

It has been observed that when a request sequence contains distinct items of the list and the order of items in the request sequence is in the reverse order as that of the list, the performance of MTF algorithm is the worst. In this case, for serving each request, the last item of the list is accessed. Hence, to optimize the total access cost, we have to optimize access cost of individual request. We can save some future access cost if and only if the accessed item is present after the middle position and is expected to occur farthest in future in the request sequence. So, we have developed a novel idea of moving the accessed item to the middle position of the list immediately after access instead of moving it to the front of the list, when the item is present towards the end of the list. Based on the above idea, we have proposed a variant of MTF algorithm which we call as Move-to-Front- or-Middle (MFM). Now we formally state the MFM algorithm as follows.

MFM Algorithm: Upon an access to an item x in the list, move x to the front of the list if it is present either in the middle position or before that in the list, else move it to the middle position of the list.

2.1 Pseudo Code of MFM Algorithm

The pseudocode of our proposed MFM algorithm is presented in Fig. 2 as follows.

Inputs:
l: size of list L
n: size of request sequence σ

Notations:
$σ_j$: j^{th} scanned item in the request sequence, $1 \leq j \leq n$
P_m: position of middle element in L
$P_m = (l+1)/2$ if l is odd; l/2 if l is even
$C_{MFM}(σ_j)$: access cost of $σ_j$ in L; $σ_j \in σ$
$C_{MFM}(σ)$: total access cost of serving σ on L

Algorithm:
Initialize $C_{MFM}(σ) = 0$;
for j = 1 to n
{
    read request $σ_j$ in σ;
    scan $σ_j$ in L;
    $x = σ_j$;
    let p_i be the position of x in L
    $C(x) = p_i$;
    $C_{MFM}(σ) = C_{MFM}(σ) + C_{MFM}(x)$;
    if $p_i > P_m$
        move x to P_m;
    else
        move x to the front;
}

Fig. 2. Pseudo-code of our proposed MFM algorithm

2.2   Illustration of MFM Algorithm

The MFM algorithm for the above example has been illustrated in Fig. 3. Let us

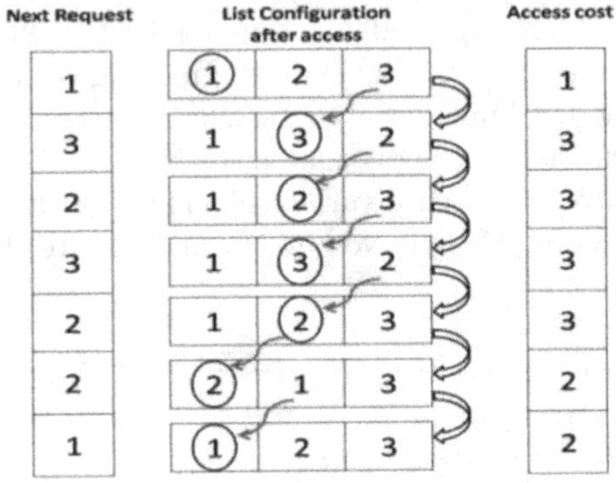

Next Request	List Configuration after access			Access cost
1	(1)	2	3	1
3	1	(3)	2	3
2	1	(2)	3	3
3	1	(3)	2	3
2	1	(2)	3	3
2	(2)	1	3	2
1	(1)	2	3	2

Fig. 3. Illustration of MFM algorithm for $L = < 1\ 2\ 3 >$ and $\sigma = < 1\ 3\ 2\ 3\ 2\ 2\ 1 >$

consider a list $L = < 123 >$ and request sequence$\sigma = < 1323221 >$. Let P_m be the middle position of the list. Here $l = 3$, $n = 7$ and $P_m = 2$. The first item $\sigma_1 = 1$ is to be accessed from the list. According to MFM algorithm, the requested item σ_1 is present in the position 1, which occurs before P_m in L. So, the access cost of σ_1 is 1 i.e. $C_{MFM}(\sigma_1) = 1$ and list configuration remains the same. Then second request $\sigma_2 = 3$ is present in position 3 of the list, which occurs after P_m. So $C_{MFM}(\sigma_2) = 3$. After accessing σ_2 in L, it is moved to the middle position of the list and the list configuration becomes$< 132 >$. Similarly, subsequents in σ can be accessed in the list as per MFM algorithm and access costs are computed. $C_{MFM}(\sigma_3) = 3$, $C_{MFM}(\sigma_4) = 3$, $C_{MFM}(\sigma_5) = 3$, $C_{MFM}(\sigma_6) = 2$ and $C_{MFM}(\sigma_7) = 2$. Hence the total access cost is given by

$$C_{MFM}(\sigma) = \sum_{i=1}^{n} C_{MFM}(\sigma_i) = 1 + 3 + 3 + 3 + 3 + 2 + 2 = 17.$$

3   Experimental Study

Our proposed MFM algorithm and MTF algorithm are tested with respect to two well known dataset such as Calgary Corpus and Canterbury Corpus, which are extensively used for data compression. These dataset contain various types of files which have been described in the next section.

3.1   Input Dataset

The Calgary Corpus and Canterbury Corpus are a collection of various types of files that serve as the popular benchmark for testing performance of list update algorithms. The Calgary Corpus contains nine different types of files making a total of 17 files. Particularly these are picture, text, book, program, numeric data, executable file etc. The Canterbury Corpus contains seven different types of files such as html, program, xls, text etc and a total of 11 files. We have used each file in the corpus to generate a request sequence. The sequence is generated by parsing the files byte by byte. But, for some executable files (like pic, geo), the method couldnt extract meaningful request sequence, so the results corresponding to such sequences are not considered. Table 1 and Table 2 in the next section specify for each file with the length of the request sequence(n), and the number of distinct requests (l). The access cost of MTF and MFM algorithms are represented as C_{MTF} and C_{MFM}. C_{MTF} and C_{MFM} with $gain(g)$ are computed for each file using byte parsing.

3.2 Experimental Setup

Both the MTF and MFM algorithms are implemented by consideringthe above mentioned dataset as the input request sequence. The total access costs are computed for various types of request sequence. The source codes for the implementation of both the algorithms are developed in C language in windows environment. The compiler is 32 -bit compiler (Dev C++ Version 4.9.9.2). RAM size is 2 GB and processor speed is 2 GHz. The program takes one file (dataset file) as input and creates the list by extracting distinct characters from the file.

3.3 Experimental Results

We have performed two different experiments for computing access cost of MTF and MFM algorithms using two input dataset. For both the two experiments we have defined *gain* (g) as follows.

$$g = \left(\frac{|C_{MTF} - C_{MFM}|}{C_{MTF}} \right) * 100$$

Performance of MFM algorithm is observed to be be better than MTF algorithm, if the gain is more.

In the first experiment, we have computed the access cost of MTF and MFM algorithms by considering Calgary Corpus as the input dataset. In the second experiment, we have computed the access cost incurred by MTF and MFM algorithm by taking Canterbury Corpus as the input dataset. For both the experiments we plot the total access cost incurred by MTF and MFM algorithms against the length of the request sequence (n). Here the length of the request sequence is the size of the file in byte.

Experiment-1: Calgary Corpus as Input Dataset. In this experiment, we have considered eleven different files of Calgary Corpus as the input dataset. We have computed the access cost of MTF and MFM algorithms as well as the gain as shown in Table 1.

Table 1. Access cost incurred by MTF and MFM for Calgary Corpus

File Name	n	l	C_{MTF}	C_{MFM}	Gain(μ)
paper5	11955	91	168691	167099	0.94374
paper4	13287	80	178312	173108	2.91848
geo	1986	208	109	109	0.00000
paper6	38106	93	522348	517379	0.95128
progc	39612	92	683826	658410	3.71673
progp	49380	89	716229	694915	2.97586
paper3	46527	84	614683	597542	2.78859
progl	71647	87	871904	866241	0.64950
paper2	82200	91	1063669	1048542	1.42215
trans	93696	99	24104	24741	2.64271
bib	111262	81	2197557	1999792	*8.99931*

Experiment-2: Canterbury Corpus as Input Dataset. In this experiment, we have considered six different files of Calgary Corpus as the input dataset. We have computed the access cost of *MTF* and *MFM* algorithms as well as the gain as shown in Table 2. For experiment-1 and experiment-2, we plot the

Table 2. Access cost incurred by MTF and MFM for Canterbury Corpus

File Name	n	l	C_{MTF}	C_{MFM}	Gain(μ)
asyoulik.txt	125180	68	1908415	1790904	*6.15752*
cp.html	24604	86	440326	417300	5.22931
fields.c	11151	90	170271	167408	1.68144
grammar.lsp	3722	76	46331	45309	2.20587
sum	50	15	23	23	0.00000
xargs.1	4228	74	60370	58500	3.09757

graphs by considering the length of the input request sequence in the X-axis and total access cost of MTF and MFM algorithms in the Y-axis which are shown in Fig. 4 and Fig. 6 respectively. We also plot graph the gain in experiment-1 and experiment-2 by considering length of the input request sequence in the X-axis and gain the Y-axis which are shown in Fig. 5 and Fig. 7 respectively.

It is observed that MTF and MFM algorithms incurred same access cost while executing the files geo and sum and hence, the gain is 0 for both the cases. This is because sum file contains executable codes and the geo file contains some unreadable characters. The MFM algorithm shows lowest gain of 0 for the sum file where as both MTF and MFM yield the same access cost. But, for the bib file the MFM algorithm has best performance with a gain of approximately 9 Observing the gain plots from Fig. 5 and Fig. 7, it is clear that the gain varies approximately from 1% to 9%. The mean gain of the proposed MFM algorithm

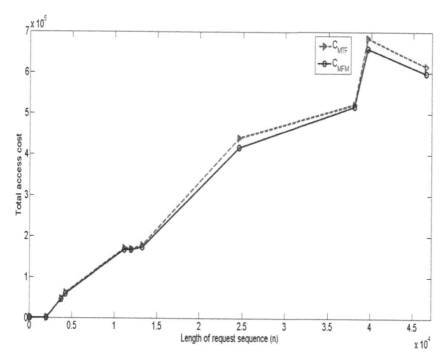

Fig. 4. Cost incurred by MTF and MFM for Calgary Corpus dataset

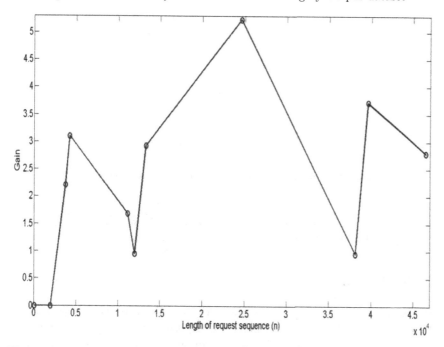

Fig. 5. Gain of MFM algorithm with respect to MTF for Calgary Corpus dataset

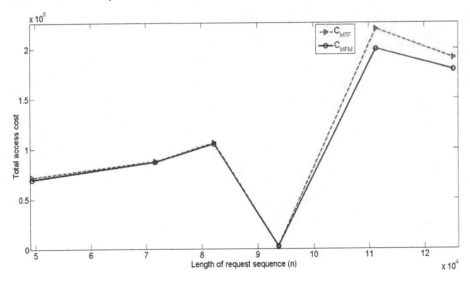

Fig. 6. Cost incurred by MTF and MFM for Canterbury Corpus

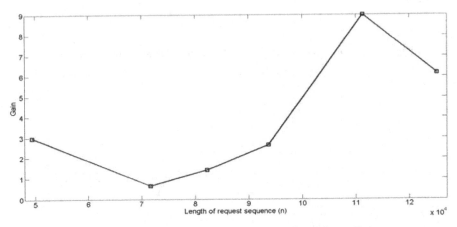

Fig. 7. Gain yield by MFM algorithm for Canterbury Corpus

over MTF algorithm is found to be approximately 3% which is one of the best gains over MTF algorithm computed by various algorithms in the literature.

4   Conclusion

In this work, we have proposed a novel Move-to-Front-or-Middle (MFM) list update algorithm. We have conducted an experimental study to evaluate the performance of our proposed MFM algorithm and Move-To-Front (MTF) algorithm by considering two input dataset such as Calgary Corpus and Canterbury

Corpus. Our experimental results show that MFM outperforms MTF for all request sequences generated from the above two dataset. In future, the MFM algorithm can be studied and analyzed using the look ahead and locality of reference in the input request sequence.

References

1. Albers, S.: A competitive analysis of the list update problem with lookahead. In: Privara, I., Ružička, P., Rovan, B. (eds.) MFCS 1994. LNCS, vol. 841, pp. 201–210. Springer, Heidelberg (1994)
2. Albers, S., Westbrook, J.: Self-organizing data structures. In: Fiat, A. (ed.) Online Algorithms 1996. LNCS, vol. 1442, pp. 13–51. Springer, Heidelberg (1998)
3. Ambühl, C.: Offline list update is NP-hard. In: Paterson, M. (ed.) ESA 2000. LNCS, vol. 1879, pp. 42–51. Springer, Heidelberg (2000)
4. Bachrach, R., El-Yaniv, R.: Online list accessing algorithms and their applications: recent empirical evidence, pp. 53–62. Society for Industrial and Applied Mathematics (1997)
5. Borodin, A., El-Yaniv, R.: Online computation and competitive analysis. Cambridge University Press (1998)
6. Hester, J.H., Hirschberg, D.S.: Self-organizing linear search. ACM Computing Surveys 17, 295–312 (1985)
7. McCabe, J.: On serial files with relocatable records. Operation Research 12, 609–618 (1965)
8. Mohanty, R., Narayanaswamy, N.S.: Online algorithms for self organizing sequential search – a survey. Electronic Colloquim on Computational Complexity (ECCC) TR-097, 1–13 (2009)
9. Bachrach, R., El-Yaniv, R., Reinstadtler, M.: On the competitive theory and practice of online list accessing algorithms. Algorithmica 32(2), 201–245 (2002)
10. Reingold, N., Westbrook, J.: Off-line algorithms for the list update problem. Information Processing Letters 60(2), 75–80 (1996)
11. Rivest, R.: On self-organizing sequential search heuristics. CACM 19(2), 63–67 (1976)
12. Angelopoulos, S., López-Ortiz, A., Dorrigiv, R.: List accessing with locality of reference: Mtf outperforms all other algorithms. School of Computer Science, University of Waterloo, TR CS-2006-46 (2006)
13. Irani, S.: Two results on the list update problem. Information Processing Letters 38, 301–306 (1991)
14. Sleator, D., Tarjan, R.E.: Amortized efficiency of list update and paging rules. CACM 28(2), 202–208 (1985)
15. Albers, S., von Stengel, B., Werchner, R.: A combined bit and timestamp algorithm for the list update problem. Information Processing Letters 56(3), 135–139 (1995)

Too Long-Didn't Read: A Practical Web Based Approach towards Text Summarization

Arjun Datt Sharma and Shaleen Deep

PEC University of Technology, Chandigarh, India- 160012
arjun_datt@yahoo.in,
shaleen.deep@gmail.com

Abstract. In today's digital epoch, people share and read a motley of never ending electronic information, thus either a lot of time is wasted in deciphering all this information, or only a tiny amount of it is actually read. Therefore, it is imperative to contrive a generic text summarization technique. In this paper, we propose a web based and domain independent automatic text summarization method. The method focuses on generating an arbitrary length summary by extracting and assigning scores to semantically important information from the document, by analyzing term frequencies and tagging certain parts of speech like proper nouns and signal words. Another important characteristic of our approach is that it also takes font semantics of the text (like headings and emphasized texts) into consideration while scoring different entities of the document.

Keywords: Generic text summarization, web based, proper noun tagging, scoring, font-semantics.

1 Introduction

With the digitization of knowledge around us, the amount of information being generated is huge. Summarizing texts can help users comprehend the information content quickly and efficiently. Even though, the proficiency of humans to summarize texts cant be replicated and incorporated into machines however, doing this task humanly is both costly and time-consuming. Automatic text summarization is a solution for dealing with this problem.

Perhaps the most difficult problem in designing an automatic text summarizer is to define what a summary is, and how to tell a summary from a non-summary, or a good summary from a bad one. We define a summary as a brief synopsis of the content of a larger document; an abstract recounting the main points while suppressing most details.

In this paper, we elucidate a methodology behind a web based application — *Abstractor*[1], which has been designed to generate a single-document generic summary of user defined length. The application is a practical demonstration of

---

[1] http://text-summarizer.appspot.com/

P. Gupta and C. Zaroliagis (Eds.): ICAA 2014, LNCS 8321, pp. 198–208, 2014.
© Springer International Publishing Switzerland 2014

how our algorithm does not suffer from any inherent implementational complexities as compared to some of the other, often more sophisticated, models that involve Markov Chains [1] which incur an additional cost over simple Bayesian classifier.

The algorithm which has been elucidated in the present paper, is an extractive summarization technique [2] which involves selection of important words, sentences or paragraphs from the original document and concatenating them into a summarized form. The decision of including a particular piece of text into the final summary depends on the aggregated output of the following four scores assigned to each sentence, namely — *Term-Oscillation score, Font semantic score, Proper Noun score* and *Signal word score.*

Each of the above four scores have been delineated in section 4. Further in section 5, we compare the results of our application to those of some existing text summarizers like the *AutoSummarize* in Microsoft Word [3] and *the Open Text Summarizer*(OTS) [4].

2   Related Work

Luhn [5] and Edmundson [6] proposed a simple approach to automatic text summarization. They used simple features of a texual document like number of sentences, word frequency, etc. Since then, this study has been the base of almost all further research on text summarization because of its simple yet effective methodology. However, this study ignores the structured analysis of the text, which can reveal a significant amount of information.

As an attempt to exploit the structural aspect of text, Marcu [7] provided an analysis when he created a tree, known as the Rhetorical Structure Theory (RST) Tree, for each segment in the text. Under this methodology, a tree is created for each document after which segments are ordered in accordance with their relative importance i.e. more important segments occupy the upper level of the tree nodes, whereas less important segments reside deeper in the tree. His approach, however, suffers from complexity issues as, every time a new document needs to be considered, the process for constructing its RST tree is very costly.

Goldstein et al [8]. pioneered the use of Machine learning techniques and SVM classifiers for the task of Text summarization. However, as discussed in [8] and [9], evaluating the quality of a summary often requires the use of a human reference summary. A detailed evaluation of summarizers was made at the TIPSTER Text Summarization Evaluation Conference (SUMMAC) [10] in order to standardize the process of summarizer evaluation and testing. In this case a reference summary collection was provided by a human panel to compare the direct performance of various summarizers. A reported problem is that even in the case of human panel summary, there is low agreement - 46% [11] [12]; and the summaries produced by the same human expert at different times were only 55% in concordance [13] [12].

There is another group of researchers who generated a summary by sentence extraction using the aforementioned non-structured features (e.g. title words) [14] [15]. Their significant contribution is that they made use of machine learning algorithms to determine the sentences to be extracted. However, since a sentence is the basic unit of their consideration, the resulting summary still be unnecessarily long. In addition, there is a lack of the features based on the structural aspects (e.g. rhetorical relations) of sentences.

Finally, studies like [2] which employ techniques like markov chaining and random indexing to generate summaries suffer from inherent complexity in summary generation. However, these studies provide state-of-the-art methods for finding sentence similarity using advanced algorithms that have formed the basis for a huge amount of research.

The present study tries to combine most of the aforementioned ideas into a single extraction based summarizer by extracting sentences, considering both structured as well as non structured aspects of the text and creating a summary that is concise and easy to construct. Another objective of the present study is to preserve and base the process of text summarization on the web semantics of the document including, but not limited to, font semantics, structured aspects of the document like bold text,underlined text, etc. and captions.

3   Information Retrieval

Using any technique for summary generation, one may be able to cater to the needs of particular users by generating query-specific summaries. Even though, query-driven summaries may suffice the demands of a particular user but they do not provide an overall sense of the document content and hence, are not appropriate for content overview [16]. Therefore, in this paper we focus on the creation of only generic text summaries. But before elucidating the summary generation technique, we first need to extract and decompose the document content into individual sentences, heading and sub-headings.

3.1   Retrieving Font Semantics: Why a Web-based Approach?

Being an extractive technique for summary generation our main focus should have been in evaluating a weighted term-frequency vector for each sentence [16]. But besides doing this, we also string along another key factor - font semantics of a document. In order to preserve and make use of font semantic information of a document, our application retrieves the textual content of the document directly from its HTML. For example, the following excerpt refers to the HTML content of a CNN news article [17].

```
<div class="cnn_storyarea" id="cnnContentContainer">
<h1 style="font-size=30px;font-weigth:bold;">Runners head to
London Marathon amid heightened security</h1><div class="cnn_
strycntntlft"><p class="cnn_storypgraphtxt cnn_storypgraph2"
style="font-size=13px;font-weigth:normal;">A 30-second silence is
being held to remember those killed and injured by the blasts near
the finish line of the Boston Marathon on Monday.</p></div></div>
```

Instead of merely retrieving the text of a document, like in the above example, our technique involves parsing the HTML DOM tree in order to filter out the textual content and also the meta-data of the content, and placing appropriate markers in the retrieved text to keep an account of the font properties, like font size and font weight, of the text. In this way, various headings ,sub-headings and emphasized entities of a document may be detected. Scoring of sentences based on font semantic information has been explained in section 4.2.

3.2   Tokenization

The process of demarcating and segmenting different sections of the input document into words or sentences is possibly one of the most challenging tasks in the process of information retrieval [18]. The process of tokenization of sentences is esp. difficult because detecting the *End of Sentence*(EOS) is a relatively ambiguous task. A sentence ends when a sentence-ending character (!, . or ?) is found which is not grouped with other characters into a token (such as for an abbreviation or number), though it may still include a few tokens that can follow a sentence ending character as part of the same sentence (such as quotes and brackets). Detection of EOS has been done by implementing a simple but efficient binary classifier [19] illustrated in Fig. 1.

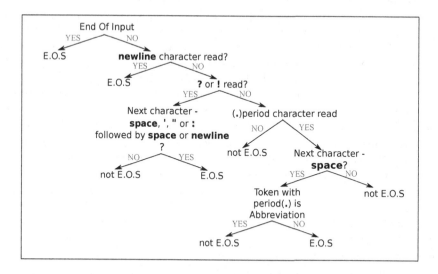

Fig. 1. Binary Classifier for determining End Of Sentence(E.O.S)

3.3   Handling Abbreviations/Acronyms:

In order not to misidentify a sentence-ending character, this sub-module considers abbreviations, acronyms, numbers with decimals or dates in numerical format. For this purpose, it makes use of a dictionary(referenced from the Oxford English Dictionary) consisting of 753 most commonly used abbreviation and acronyms, and a small set of rules to detect numbers and dates as described in Fig. 1.

4   Scoring Model

The summary vector $S = \{s_1, s_2, ..., s_k\}$ is a proper subset of the the document vector $S' = \{s_1, s_2, ..., s_n\}$, where $n > k$ and $\forall : s_j \in S'$ is a token(sentence) obtained by the sub-module explained in section 3.2. Here, each $s_j \in S$, has magnitude $g_j \in G$, where $G = \{g_1, g_2, ..., g_n\}$ represents the set of scores for each entity in S'. Addition of each entity s_j to the vector S depends on whether a s_j has the value $g_j > g_{threshold}$. This threshold value is dynamic and can be changed by the user. The overall score g_j, $\forall s_j \in S$ is an aggregated value of the following four scores:

4.1   Term Oscillation Score(S_O)

In order to prioritize the sentences based on term frequencies, we trace back to the summary generation theory proposed by Luhn [5], where the author justifies that measuring word significance by term frequency is based on the fact that a writer tends to repeat certain words as he elaborates on an aspect of a subject. These words are generally the key words of a document. However, it is important to note that the words with the highest frequency may not be certain *thematic words* but merely some *stop words*(the, is, a, etc.). Therefore, in order to do a more thorough analysis, these stop words have to be neglected. Our approach merely replicates and implements this theory. Further, it has been proposed in [5] that based on the term frequencies, a significance factor for each sentence can be calculated. We call this factor as the *Term Oscillation score(S_O)*, which is calculated by summing-up the docuement-frequency of every term in a sentence. For the purpose of a proper comparative analysis, the score metric S_O is normalized from 0-100.

For models generating extractive summaries, it can be argued that longer sentences generally also contain more number of words. Therefore, score of such sentences should be restricted based on sentence length. Although this may sound convincing, actual implementation of this theory suggests the opposite. Our implementation of sentence length score based model produced an inferior summary as compared to the model that does not use them. A simple explanation for this is that longer sentences contain higher density of thoughts and ideas.

4.2   Font Semantic Score(S_F)

Writers generally use certain corpus-specific heuristics to align passages at the document-structure granularity[21]. As a part of such heuristics, the text may contain certain labels like headings or subheadings, that are easily identified. Additionally, certain markup features like italicizing and underlining the text may also be adhibited, in order to emphasize certain portions of the document. Thus, the consideration of such font semantics in the process of summarizing a well-structured document may be very resourceful.

In order to prioritize the sentences based on font semantics, firstly retrieval of font-markup information is done, as elucidated in section 3.1. According to the applied methodology, after retrieval of text from its corresponding HTML corpus, we have the text [17] structure as demonstrated below.

```
#MARKER_fontSize_30_fontWeight_bold# Runners head to
London Marathon amid heightened security #MARKER_end#.
#MARKER_fontSize_13_fontWeight_normal#...#MARKER_end#.
```

Every token, which has a greater font size as compared to the neighbouring text, may be termed as a heading/sub-heading or a very important piece of text. Inclusion of such tokens into the summary has been made mandatory. Further, a bold, italicized or underlined text is considered as an emphasized text. It may be noted that the document-specific terms present in such tokens may bear more importance as compared to other document-specific terms. Thus, the Font Semantic Score(S_F) of such terms is evaluated as shown in Eq. 1.

$$S_F = \sum_{k=1}^{j}(f_F)_k/n_F \qquad (1)$$

here, $(f_F)_k$ refers to the frequency of that term as part of a heading or other markup features and n_F refers to the number of headings or markup terms in that document. Further S_F has been normalized from 0-10. This value of S_F for a particular term, augments the g_i value for a particular token(sentence) by adding up to the S_O value for that sentence.

4.3   Proper Noun Score(S_P)

Proper nouns are recognized as an important source of information for extracting contents from a text [20]. For instance, in a story the main character being introduced for the first time or in a news article mentioning Barack Obama, could be very important sections in their respective documents and therefore may be mentioned in the summary.

In order to evaluate Proper Noun Score(S_P), such terms are identied which begin with a capital letter and appear in non-ambiguous positions, i.e. in positions where if a word begins with a capital letter then it is a proper noun. For the purpose of identifying proper nouns at ambiguous positions, like beginning of a sentence, the term is compared with a dictionary of most commonly used words in English language. Our algorithm updates this dictionary with every new document passed into the application, checking for any new terms which have been used for parts of speech other than proper nouns. It is important to note that this procedure might not identify certain proper nouns(e.g., United States) at ambiguous positions because they may be a combination of two or more common nouns. Therefore, the algorithm also identifies Group Proper nouns [21] (e.g., Snow White).

The evaluation of S_P for every sentence is done similar to the evaluation of S_F as shown in Eq. 2.

$$S_P = \sum_{k=1}^{j} ((S_P)_{min} + (((S_P)_{max} - (S_P)_{min}) * (f_k - f_{min})/(f_{max} - f_{min}))) \quad (2)$$

here, j refers to the to the total number of proper nouns in a sentence and f_k refers to the term frequency of that proper noun in the entire document. Further S_P has been normalized from 0-10 i.e. minimum and maximum S_P values are 0 and 10 respectively. This value of S_P for a particular term, augments the g_i value for a particular token (sentence) by adding up to the S_O value for that sentence.

4.4   Signal Word Score(S_E)

In order to be able to lead a reader in a particular direction, writers generally use certain emphatic or signal terms in their writing. Knowledge of whether a word is emphatic or not could improve the quality of a summary drastically [22]. Therefore, an external dictionary of signal words, referenced from [23], is scanned for the presence of any signal word that might be present in some sentence. Frequency of such signal words is recorded and a Signal Word Score, as shown in Eq. 3, is assigned to each sentence in the document.

$$S_E = \sum_{k=1}^{j} (f_E)_k / n_E \quad (3)$$

here, $(f_E)_k$ refers to the frequency of the signal word and n_E refers to the number of signal terms in the document. Further S_E has been normalized from 0-10. This value of SE for a particular sentence, augments the g_i value for a particular token(sentence) by adding up to the S_O value for that sentence.

4.5   Calculating Weights of the Sentences and Generating Summary

In order to generate a summary of a user defined length, all the four aforementioned scores are summed up and normalized in the range 0-100. This results in the evaluation of the final g_i value for every sentence in the document. Further, the value of $g_{threshold}$ can be evaluated as shown in Eq. 4.

$$g_{thershold} = (l_{user-defined}/10) * ((g_i)_{max} - (g_i)_{min}) \quad (4)$$

here, $l_{user-defined}$ refers to the length metric of the summary defined by the user. This value ranges from 0-10. $(g_i)_{max}$ and $(g_i)_{min}$ refer to the maximum and minimum score out of all the sentences in the document.

5 Result

In order to evaluate our methodology, different sample texts were considered and extracts were computed at 10% and 30% of the entire document length. We compared the results with summaries created by humans[2] and also the summaries generated by Word [3] and Open Text Summarizer(OTS) [4]. Below we show a sample text[3] and its summary generated by *Abstractor* set at 50% of the original text. We also show the corresponding summary generated by [3]. Consider the text given below as our sample document, which is a ten-sentence long document.

Earthquake

An **earthquake** is the result of a sudden release of energy in the Earth's crust that creates seismic waves. The **seismicity, seismism** or **seismic** activity of an area refers to the frequency, type and size of earthquakes experienced over a period of time. Earthquake is measured using observations from **seismometers**. The moment magnitude is the most common scale on which earthquakes larger than approximately 5 are reported for the entire globe. The more numerous earthquakes smaller than magnitude 5 reported by national seismological observatories are measured mostly on the local magnitude scale, also referred to as the **Richter scale**. These two scales are numerically similar over their range of validity. Magnitude 3 or lower earthquakes are mostly almost imperceptible or weak and magnitude 7 and over potentially cause serious damage over larger areas, depending on their depth. The largest earthquakes in historic times have been of magnitude slightly over 9, although there is no limit to the possible magnitude. The most recent large earthquake of magnitude 9.0 or larger was a 9.0 magnitude earthquake in Japan in 2011 (as of October 2012), and it was the largest Japanese earthquake since records began. Intensity of shaking is measured on the modified Mercalli scale. The shallower an earthquake, the more damage to structures it causes, all else being equal.

The summary generated by our summarizer:

An **earthquake** is the result of a sudden release of energy in the Earth's crust that creates seismic waves. The **seismicity, seismism** or **seismic** activity of an area refers to the frequency, type and size of earthquakes experienced over a period of time. Earthquake is measured using observations from seismometers. The more numerous earthquakes smaller than magnitude 5 reported by national seismological observatories are measured mostly on the local magnitude scale, also referred to as the **Richter scale**. Magnitude 3 or lower earthquakes are mostly almost imperceptible or weak and magnitude 7 and over potentially cause serious damage over larger areas, depending on their depth .

The summary generated by Word (2007):

Earthquake is measured using observations from seismometers. The more numerous earthquakes smaller than magnitude 5 reported by national seismological observatories are measured mostly on the local magnitude scale, also referred to as the Richter scale. The most recent large earthquake of magnitude 9.0 or larger was a 9.0 magnitude earthquake in Japan in 2011 (as of October 2012), and it was the largest Japanese earthquake since records began.

---

[2] All the authors generated separate summaries and a consensus was arrived at for the final version.

[3] http://en.wikipedia.org/wiki/Earthquake

For evaluation of texts, we used *Precision* and *Recall*, extensively used in information retrieval [24] for evaluating our results. Human generated summary can be denoted by S_{ref}. If S_{gen} represents the generated summary [2] then

$$p = (S_{ref} \cup S_{gen})/S_{gen} \qquad (5)$$

$$r = (S_{ref} \cap S_{gen})/S_{ref} \qquad (6)$$

Using the aforementioned parameters, a metric F [2] is computed, as shown in Eq. 7, for each sample which represents the final points allocated to each summary. Here, F is an incremental metric i.e., higher is the F value, better is the result.

$$F = \begin{cases} 2pr/(p+r), & \text{if} \quad p+r \neq 0 \\ 0, & \text{Otherwise.} \end{cases} \qquad (7)$$

The results in Tab. 1 clearly indicate that summaries generated by our method-

Table 1. Comparitive Analysis

Excerpt No.	percentage of original	Abstractor			Word Summarizer			OTS		
		p	r	F	p	r	F	p	r	F
1	10%	0.666	0.333	0.444	0.666	0.5	0.571	0.5	0.333	0.399
	30%	1.000	0.75	0.857	0.571	0.666	0.614	0.666	0.333	0.444
2	10%	0.571	0.8	0.666	0.75	0.4	0.521	0.8	0.5	0.615
	30%	0.7	0.875	0.777	0.5	0.625	0.555	0.666	0.5	0.571
3	10%	0.714	0.833	0.768	0.60	0.333	0.428	0.625	0.75	0.681
	30%	0.555	1.000	0.713	0.4	0.666	0.499	0.5	0.5	0.5
4	10%	0.5	0.5	0.5	0.5	0.2	0.285	0.2	0.5	0.285
	30%	1.000	0.75	0.857	0.6	0.7	0.646	0.714	0.5	0.588
5	10%	0.75	1.000	0.857	0.1	0.1	0.1	0.666	0.286	0.4
	30%	0.80	0.80	0.8	0.5	0.250	0.333	0.666	0.333	0.444
6	10%	0.333	0.333	0.333	0.2	0.1	0.133	0.2	0.1	0.133
	30%	0.625	0.625	0.625	0.5	0.5	0.5	1.000	0.8	0.888
7	10%	0.75	0.666	0.705	0.666	0.125	0.210	0.666	0.625	0.644
	30%	1.000	0.8	0.888	0.8	0.333	0.470	0.75	0.333	0.461
8	10%	0.5	0.8	0.615	0.2	0.333	0.249	0.666	0.333	0.444
	30%	0.777	0.875	0.823	0.625	0.125	0.208	1.000	0.625	0.769
9	10%	1.000	1.000	1.000	1.000	0.5	0.666	1.000	1.000	1.000
	30%	0.7	0.777	0.736	0.625	0.4	0.487	0.5	0.714	0.588
10	10%	0.571	0.9	0.698	0.125	0.125	0.125	0.1	0.2	0.133
	30%	0.777	0.875	0.823	0.6	0.4	0.48	0.8	0.625	0.701

ology are closer to the human summaries, in atleast 90% of the cases, than OTS and Word summarizer in both 10% and 30% categories. However, the summaries generated by us at 50% and 75% are were much closer to Word Summarizer [3] and OTS [4] summaries, with both [3] and [4] yielding better results, occasionally. Limitation on space precludes us to show the actual figures for those experiments.

6   Conclusion and Future Work

This paper presents in detail a methodology for a web based text summarization tool called *Abstractor*. The methodology involves retrieval of data as well as meta-data (eg., structural details of the document) from the HTML content of the input text. Based on the retrieved information, we elucidate a fourfold scoring model, which incorporates assigning score to each sentence in different layers based on four different attributes, namely - term frequency, font semantics, proper nouns and signal words. In order to evaluate our methodology, we conducted a comparitive analysis of *Abstractor* with some well-established text summarization tools [3] [4]. We evaluated the results based on two parameter [24] - the amount of information which is relevant, out of the retrieved content and the amount of content retrieved out of the content which is actually relevant.

Although the model we propose is not the most rigorous or sophisticated technique for text summarization, but the benefit lies in the simple approach which is highly suitable for generating summaries with minimal overhead. It is thus apt for application in environments, such as the web, where speed is an important parameter.

For future work, we plan to extend this approach from a fourfold to an n-fold model, where we may be able to evaluate significance of a sentence based on certain other factors, in addition to the already existing ones, such as placement of a sentence in the document hierarchy and detection of frequently occurring n-grams instead of merely analysing unigram oscillations. In addition to this, mapping of terms (like pronouns, acronyms, etc.) to their corresponding parent terms, in the document, may also help ameliorate the results of this approach. Further, as this is a web-based approach, removal of external noise (like advertisements, etc.) from the input would help make the tool more robust and therefore, more research in this area would definitely yield more accuracy. But, antecedent to the aforementioned ideas, more improvements can be made in the current algorithm by making the detection of abbreviations and proper nouns more concrete and accurate.

References

1. Conroy, J.M., O'leary, D.P.: Text summarization via hidden markov models. In: Proceedings of the 24th Annual International ACM SIGIR Conference on Research and Development in Information Retrieval, pp. 406–407. ACM (2001)
2. Chatterjee, N., Mohan, S.: Extraction-based single-document summarization using random indexing. In: 19th IEEE International Conference on Tools with Artificial Intelligence, ICTAI 2007, vol. 2, pp. 448–455. IEEE (2007)
3. Fein, R.A., Dolan, W.B., Messerly, J., Fries, E.J., Thorpe, C.A., Cokus, S.J.: Document summarizer for word processors, US Patent 7,051,024 (May 23, 2006)
4. Rotem, N.: The open text summarizer (2003)
5. Luhn, H.P.: The automatic creation of literature abstracts. IBM Journal of Research and Development 2(2), 159–165 (1958)
6. Edmundson, H.P.: New methods in automatic extracting. Journal of the ACM (JACM) 16(2), 264–285 (1969)

7. Marcu, D.: Building up rhetorical structure trees. In: Proceedings of the National Conference on Artificial Intelligence, pp. 1069–1074 (1996)
8. Goldstein, J., Kantrowitz, M., Mittal, V., Carbonell, J.: Summarizing text documents: sentence selection and evaluation metrics. In: Proceedings of the 22nd Annual International ACM SIGIR Conference on Research and Development in Information Retrieval, pp. 121–128. ACM (1999)
9. McLellan, P., Tombros, A., Jose, J., Ounis, I., Whitehead, M.: Evaluating summarisation technologies: A task-oriented approach. In: Proc. 1st International Workshop on New Developments in Digital Libraries (NDDL 2001), International Conference on Enterprise Information Systems (ICEIS 2001), pp. 99–112 (2001)
10. Mani, I., House, D., Klein, G., Hirschman, L., Firmin, T., Sundheim, B.: The tipster summac text summarization evaluation. In: Proceedings of the Ninth Conference on European Chapter of the Association for Computational Linguistics, pp. 77–85. Association for Computational Linguistics (1999)
11. Mitra, M., Singhal, A., Buckley, C.: Automatic text summarization by paragraph extraction. Compare 22215(22215), 26 (1997)
12. Neto, J.L., Freitas, A.A., Kaestner, C.A.: Automatic text summarization using a machine learning approach. In: Bittencourt, G., Ramalho, G.L. (eds.) SBIA 2002. LNCS (LNAI), vol. 2507, pp. 205–215. Springer, Heidelberg (2002)
13. Rath, G., Resnick, A., Savage, T.: The formation of abstracts by the selection of sentences. Part i. Sentence selection by men and machines. American Documentation 12(2), 139–141 (1961)
14. Kupiec, J., Pedersen, J., Chen, F.: A trainable document summarizer. In: Proceedings of the 18th Annual International ACM SIGIR Conference on Research and Development in Information Retrieval, pp. 68–73. ACM (1995)
15. Teufel, S., Moens, M.: Sentence extraction and rhetorical classification for flexible abstracts. In: Spring AAAI Symposium on Intelligent Text Summarization, pp. 89–97 (1998)
16. Gong, Y., Liu, X.: Generic text summarization using relevance measure and latent semantic analysis. In: Proceedings of the 24th Annual International ACM SIGIR Conference on Research and Development in Information Retrieval, pp. 19–25. ACM (2001)
17. CNN: Runners start London marathon with moment of silence for Boston victims (April 2013), http://edition.cnn.com/ (cited: April 21, 2013)
18. Palmer, D.D.: Tokenisation and sentence segmentation. Marcel Dekker, Inc., New York (2000)
19. Coursera, Stanford University: Natural language processing, https://class.coursera.org/nlp/auth/welcome (cited: April 19, 2013)
20. Rau, L.F.: Extracting company names from text. In: Proceedings of the Seventh IEEE Conference on Artificial Intelligence Applications, vol. 1, pp. 29–32. IEEE (1991)
21. Paik, W., Liddy, E.D., Yu, E., McKenna, M.: Categorizing and standardizing proper nouns for efficient information retrieval. In: Corpus Processing for Lexical Acquisition, pp. 61–73 (1996)
22. Brenier, J.M., Cer, D., Jurafsky, D.: The detection of emphatic words using acoustic and lexical features. In: Proceedings of EUROSPEECH, pp. 3297–3300. Citeseer (2005)
23. Fry, E.B., Fountoukidis, D., Polk, J.K.: The new reading teacher's book of lists. Prentice-Hall, Englewood Cliffs (1985)
24. Ricardo, B.Y., et al.: Modern information retrieval. Pearson Education, India (1999)

A Comparative Study of Tag SNP Selection Using Clustering

Sujay Saha[1], Riddhiman Dasgupta[2], Anirban Ghose[1],
Koustav Mullick[2], and Kashi Nath Dey[3]

[1] Heritage Institute of Technology, Kolkata, India
sujay.saha@heritageit.edu, anighose25@gmail.com
[2] International Institute of Information Technology, Hyderabad, India
dasguptar@acm.org, koustav.mullick@yahoo.com
[3] University of Calcutta, Kolkata, India
kndey55@gmail.com

Abstract. The immense volume and rapid growth of human genomic data, especially single nucleotide polymorphisms (SNPs), present special challenges for both biomedical researchers and automatic algorithms. SNPs are confirmed as a major factor in human genome polymorphisms, and are found to be suitable as a genetic marker for disease characteristics. SNPs hold much promise as a basis for genome-wide disease-gene association. Determining the relationship between disease complexity and SNPs requires complex genotyping for large SNP data sets, and is thus very expensive and labor-intensive. In this paper, we attempt two novel approaches to solve the problem of tag SNP selection, one using self-organizing maps (SOM) for clustering the SNPs and the other using Fuzzy C Means clustering. Both the above methods have been shown to select a more optimal set of tag SNPs which capture the remaining SNPs more efficiently as compared to Haploview Tagger, thus satisfying the goal of tag SNP selection in a more suitable way.

Keywords: tag SNP selection, LD, self organising map, fuzzy c means.

1 Introduction

Single nucleotide polymorphisms (SNPs) are sequence variations observed across populations that are found at single points in the genome. Researchers are collecting information on every SNP in the human genome and use this data to find alleles that are associated with the increased risk of a disease. It has been found that a small number of SNPs, known as tag SNPs, are sufficient to capture the entire information conveyed in the entire SNP sequence, i.e. the entire genome can be represented by simply a sequence of SNPs, and the sequence of SNPs can in turn be represented by a set of tag SNPs. Naturally, this adds a layer of compression reducing the storage costs by a very large margin, and reduces complexity of algorithms in downstream applications that employ or use or need these SNP sequences. The problem of finding a set of tag SNPs that sufficiently

P. Gupta and C. Zaroliagis (Eds.): ICAA 2014, LNCS 8321, pp. 209–222, 2014.

capture the information stores in all the remanining SNPs is akin to the problem of finding the best possible clusters in a data distribution, such that each cluster can be represented by its representative point, to reduce the overall total number of points. Thus, the problem of finding tag SNPs can be reduced to a problem of clustering the SNPs into similar clusters, such that each cluster of SNPs can be repreented by a representative SNP, which will be a tag SNP. This forms the crux of this paper, and we present here two novel approaches to clusters SNPs using competitive learning based self organising maps and fuzzy C means clustering, both based on a similarity measure used in computational biology, known as linkage disequilibrium.The rest of the paper is organised as follows: Section 1 discusses some preliminary biological definitions related to genomics and SNPs as well as some basic concepts of the techniques used for clustering. Section 2 deals with the previous existing work done on this topic and discusses the available methods. Section 3 presents our proposed methods and provides the algorithm for the same. Section 4 has extensive results from experiments conducted on International HapMap Project genome datasets. Finally, Section 5 analyses our results and provides the future scope of this work.

A genome is an organisms complete set of DNA containing all the information required to build and maintain that organism. The biological information contained in a genome is encoded in its DNA and divided into discrete units called genes. Genes code for proteins that attach to the genome at the appropriate positions and switch on a series of reactions called gene expression. DNA sequence is made up of four basic nucleotides in every organism - Adenine, Guanine, Thymine, and Cytosine. DNA sequence variations occur when a single nucleotide A, T, C or G in the genome sequence is altered. A Single nucleotide polymorphism or SNP is a DNA sequence variation occurring when a single nucleotide - A, T, C or G in the genome differs between members of a species or between paired chromosomes in an individual.

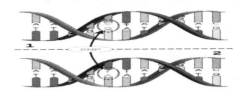

Fig. 1. Illustration of Single Nucleotide Polymorphisms

Alleles are alternative forms of a gene that is located at a specific position on a specific chromosome in two different individuals. For example, two sequenced DNA fragments from different individuals, AAGCCTA to AAGCTTA, contain a difference in a single nucleotide. In this case we say that there are two alleles: C and T. Almost all common SNPs have only two alleles. Within a population, SNPs can be assigned a minor allele frequency - the ratio of chromosomes in the population carrying the less common variant to those with the more common variant. It is important to note that there are variations between human populations, so a SNP allele that is common in one geographical or ethnic group may be much rarer in another. The genotype refers to the entire set of genes in a cell, an organism, or an individual. A gene for a particular character or trait (phenotype) may exist in two allelic forms. One is dominant (B) and the other is recessive (b). Based on this, there could be three possible genotypes for a particular character: BB (homozygous dominant), Bb (heterozygous), and bb (homozygous recessive).

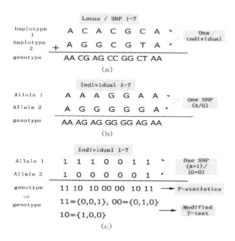

Fig. 2. Differences between haplotypes, genotypes, alleles and SNPs

A group of alleles of different genes on a single chromosome that are closely enough linked to be inherited usually as a unit. A haplotype can also be defined as a set of single-nucleotide polymorphisms (SNPs) on a single chromosome of a chromosome pair that are associated statistically. It is believed that these statistical associations, and the identification of a few alleles of a haplotype sequence, can unambiguously identify all other polymorphic sites in its region.

1.1   Linkage Disequilibrium

Genome wide association studies are done to find those alleles that are much more prevalent among sick individuals rather than between healthy ones. However, genome-wide SNP scans for disease association tests are infeasible owing to high genotyping costs. Therefore, it is desirable to reduce the number of SNPs to a small number of information representatives called tag SNPs. Alleles corresponding to tag SNPs must be sequenced and this information is used to predict alleles of remaining SNPs(target SNPs). This is essentially the Haplotype Tagging Problem, where given the full pattern of all haplotypes in a small population sample, we find the minimum number of tag SNPs and reconstruct each haplotype in the entire population from these tags [1]. Most of the current algorithms for locating tagging SNPs are based on the principle of the linkage disequilibrium (LD). If two SNPs are in LD, their values strongly depend on each other i.e. their alleles are strongly correlated. Thus, if allele A is in strong LD with allele B, it is possible to infer value of B using the value of A.

Two important measures of linkage disequilibrium are D and R2. Let there be the Haplotypes for two loci A and B with two alleles each. Then the frequency of each combination can be defined as:

Table 1. Haplotye Frequencies

Haplotype	Frequency
$A_1 B_1$	x_{11}
$A_1 B_2$	x_{12}
$A_2 B_1$	x_{21}
$A_2 B_2$	x_{21}

The above frequencies can be used to determine the allele frequencies:

Table 2. Allele Frequencies: Major and Minor

Haplotype	Frequency
A_1	$p_1 = x_{11} + x_{12}$
A_2	$p_2 = x_{21} + x_{22}$
B_1	$q_1 = x_{11} + x_{21}$
B_2	$q_2 = x_{12} + x_{22}$

The deviation of the observed frequency of a haplotype from the expected is a quantity called the linkage disequilibrium and is commonly denoted by D.

$$D = x_{11} - p_1 q_1 \tag{1}$$

Lewontin [2] suggested normalizing D by dividing it by the theoretical maximum for the observed allele frequencies. Thus:

$$D' = \frac{D}{D_{max}} \tag{2}$$

where, $D_{max} = \begin{cases} min(p_1 q_1, p_2 q_2), & \text{when } D < 0 \\ min(p_1 q_2, p_2 q_1), & \text{when } D > 0 \end{cases}$

Another measure of LD which is an alternative to D^2 is the correlation coefficient between pairs of loci, expressed as:

$$r = \frac{D}{\sqrt{p_1 p_2 q_1 q_2}}$$

However, squared coefficient of correlation (r^2) is often used to remove the arbitrary sign introduced.

1.2 Principal Component Analysis

One of the difficulties inherent in multivariate statistics is the problem of visualizing data that has many variables. Fortunately, in data sets with many variables, groups of variables often move together. One reason for this is that more than one variable might be measuring the same driving principle governing the behavior of the system. In many systems there are only a few such driving forces. But an abundance of instrumentation enables us to measure dozens of system variables. When this happens, we can take advantage of this redundancy of information. We can simplify the problem by replacing a group of variables with a single new variable.

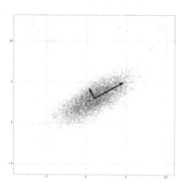

Fig. 3. A scatter plot of samples distributed according a bivariate Gaussian distribution. The directions represent the Principal Components (PC) associated with the sample

Principal component analysis is a quantitatively rigorous method for achieving this simplification [3]. The method generates a new set of variables, called principal components. Each principal component is a linear combination of the original variables. All the principal components are orthogonal to each other, so there is no redundant information. The principal components as a whole form an orthogonal basis for the space of the data.

1.3 Self Organising Map

Self-organizing maps are used for feature mapping processes which converts the patterns of arbitrary dimensionality into a response of one or two dimensional array of neurons [4]. Apart from its capability of reducing the dimensionality of vectors, SOMs also preserve the neighbourhood relations of the input patterns i.e. it preserves the topology of the input space. SOM is essentially a special type of neural network that uses an unsupervised learning algorithm and a neighbourhood function to preserve the topological properties of the training set. The goal of learning in the self-organizing map is to cause different parts of the network to respond similarly to certain input patterns. This is partly motivated by how

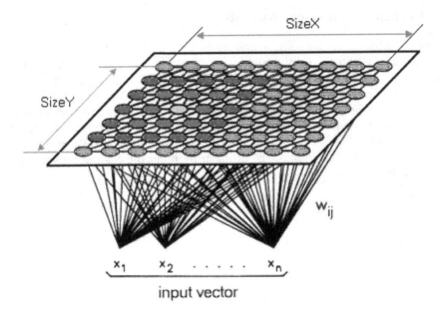

Fig. 4. Example illustration of a self-organising map with inputs and X*Y neurons

visual, auditory or other sensory information is handled in separate parts of the cerebral cortex in the human brain.

The SOM is composed of basically a grid of neurons (one-dimensional or two-dimensional). Each component of the input vector is connected to each of the neurons. SOM mapping starts by initializing the weight vectors. From the input space, a sample vector is selected randomly and the map of weight vectors is searched to find which weight best represents that sample. Each weight vector has neighbouring weights that are close to it. The weight that is chosen (Best Matching Unit) is rewarded by being able to become more like that randomly selected sample vector. The neighbours of the Best Matching Unit are also rewarded by being able to become more like the chosen sample vector. The number of neighbours associated with a BMU decreases over time. The closer a node is to the BMU, the more its weights get altered and the farther away the neighbour is from the BMU, the less it learns. The entire process is repeated over a large number of iterations.

1.4   Fuzzy C Means Clustering

Given a set of objects, $X = \{x_1, x_2, \ldots, x_n\}$, a fuzzy set S is defined as a subset of X that allows each object x_i to have a membership value between 0 & 1 [5]. Formally, a fuzzy set S can be modeled as a function $F_s : X \rightarrow [0, 1]$. Now its very much possible to apply the idea of fuzzy set on clusters. So, given a set of objects, a fuzzy cluster will be a fuzzy set of those objects.

Formally, if a set of n objects $o_1, o_2, \ldots, o_n$ are given, then a fuzzy clustering of k fuzzy clusters, $C_1, C_2, \ldots, C_k$, can be represented using a partition matrix,

$M = [w_{ij}](1 \leq i \leq n, 1 \leq j \leq k)$, where w_{ij} represents the membership value of object o_i in fuzzy cluster C_j. The partition matrix should satisfy the following three requirements:

- For each object o_i and cluster C_j, $0 \leq w_{ij} \leq 1$. This constraint confirms that a fuzzy cluster is really a fuzzy set.
- For each object o_i, $\sum_{j=1}^{k} w_{ij} = 1$. By this constraint, it can be surely said that every object participates in the clustering equivalently.
- For each cluster C_j, $0 < \sum_{i=1}^{n} w_{ij} < n$. Now this constraint ensures that for every cluster, there is at least one object for which the membership value is nonzero.

2 Literature Review

In the past decade many computational strategies have been developed for the efficient and accurate finding of haplotype tag SNPs (htSNPs) for particular chromosomal regions. Among those, following are the most predominant methods that emerged [6].

Patil, et. al. [7] reported the implementation of a greedy optimization algorithm in order to define a set of haplotype blocks, spanning chromosome 21. While this procedure is relatively simple and straightforward to implement, it has several disadvantages as a greedy algorithm. It gives an approximate solution, but it cannot guarantee that its solution is optimal.

Zhang, et. al. [8] implemented a dynamic programming algorithm to find a set of representative htSNPs using the same chromosomal sequence data as Patil, et. al. This algorithm recursively finds the minimal number of SNPs required to distinguish the set coverage percentage of haplotypes in each block, for the smallest number of blocks.

Stram, et. al. [9] proposed that the minimum set of htSNPs is not always the optimal one, and instead uses a statistic similar to the coefficient of determination to choose the optimal set of htSNPs.

Byng et al. [10] proposed the use of single and complete linkage hierarchical cluster analysis to select tag SNPs. Hierarchical clustering starts with a square matrix of pairwise distances between the objects to be clustered. For the problem of tag SNP selection, the objects to be clustered are the SNPs, and an appropriate measure of distance is $1R^2$, where R^2 is the squared correlation between two SNPs. The rationale is this: the required sample size for a tag SNP to detect an indirect association with a disease is inversely proportional to the R^2 between the tag SNP and the causal SNP.

S. I. Ao et al. [11] proposed a new definition of the distance between two clusters, as follows:

- For each SNP belonging to either cluster, find the maximum distance between it and all the other SNPs in the two clusters.

- The smallest of these maximum distances is defined as the distance between the two clusters.
- The corresponding SNP is defined as the tag SNP of the newly merged cluster.

This method is known as minimax clustering. There is a parallel in topology in which the distance between two compact sets can be measured by a sup-inf metric known as Hausdorff distance.

3 Proposed Algorithm

Computing a maximum informative set of tagging SNPs is a NP-hard problem. Fortunately, there are a number of algorithms that provide an approximate solution. Namely, they compute a set of tagging SNPs that can be used to predict values of remaining SNPs with some margin of error.

In this paper, we employ self- organising map (SOM) based unsupervised approach and fuzzy c means method (FCM) to cluster the SNPs based on the values of their linkage disequilibrium. In order to present our method, lets first formalise the problem.

The haplotype tagging problem that we are aiming to solve can be formally stated as: Given the full pattern of all haplotypes in a small population sample, find the minimum number of tag SNPs and the method for reconstructing each haplotype in the entire population from these tags.

The corresponding SNP prediction problem can be formulated as: Given the values of k tags of the individual x with unknown SNP s and n individuals with k tag SNP and known value of SNP s , find the value of s in x .

Let us consider a set of n SNPs and k genes. Each SNP is associated with two alleles out of four possible alleles-A, T, G, and C. Each gene has a certain value for the genotype at the corresponding locus for each of the n SNPs. The genotype may be a major homozygote, a minor homozygote or a heterozygote.

- Collect genotype data for m SNPs in n individuals, consisting of genotype information for each SNP for each individual
  - Calculate major and minor allele frequencies for each SNP.
  - Calculate genotype frequencies, both homozygote and heterozygote.
  - Calculate phase haplotype frequencies from unphased genotype information.
- Calculate LD metrics of D and r^2 using previously calculated genotype frequencies and haplotype frequencies
  - Construct LD matrix for pairwise linkage disequilibrium for each SNP.
- Perform hierarchical clustering on LD matrix with LD as the distance metric
  - Construct dendrogram for agglomerative clustering to estimate number of clusters.
- Perform Principal Component Analysis on LD matrix to identify principal components
  - Select components constituting a predetermined percentage of the total variance cumulatively.

- Initialise self-organising map with predetermined topology, distance function, and neuron map based on estimated number of clusters
  - Use selected components as input feature vectors to self-organising map.
- Train self-organising map and plot weight positions.
- Assign clusters by finding the nearest neuron to each SNP
  - Centroid of each such cluster is a tag SNP.
- Estimate number of clusters using subtractive clustering
  - Provide a vector containing as many elements as the number of dimensions, with each element between 0 and 1 and specifying a cluster center's range of influence in each of the data dimensions
- Perform clustering using Fuzzy C Means clustering approach
  - Use estimated number of clusters obtained from subtractive clustering
- Assign clusters by finding the nearest cluster center to each SNP
  - Centroid of each such cluster is a tag SNP

4   Results

The International HapMap Project [12] aims to develop a haplotype map (HapMap) of the human genome to describe the common patterns of human genetic variation. HapMap is a key resource for researchers to find genetic variants affecting health, disease and responses to drugs and environmental factors. Raw phased genomic data is considerably vast and difficult to process. We concentrate on specific ENCODE regions of a chromosome for a particular population as they are considerably smaller in size and easily analyzed. The Encyclopedia of DNA Elements (ENCODE) is a public research consortium which is dedicated in finding which parts of the DNA are biologically active and make an initial assessment of their functions, thereby reducing gigabytes of raw data. Haploview is a program available from the HapMap Project, designed to simplify and expedite the process of haplotype analysis by providing a common interface to several tasks relating to such analyses. We primarily use Haploview to compare the results of our methods with those of existing methods, since those existing methdos are already implemented optimally inside Haploview.

Table 3. Genetic regions experimented upon

Genetic Region	Number of SNPs
Sample data set provided in Haploview	29
ENCODE Region ENm010.7p15.2 of chromosome 7 of the individuals of CEU population	702
ENCODE Region Enm010.7p15.2 of chromosome 7 of the individuals of CHB population	518

We have used Haploview to estimate Haplotype frequency of the genotype data dumps and thus calculate LD R^2 values between pairs of SNPs. Haploview has been used since genotype data is widely available from the HapMap project, but haplotype data is not. Linkage disequilibrium calculations require haplotype frequencies which need to be estimated from genotype data using phase information and dynamic programming techniques. This is has been automated in Haploview to ease computation and downstream analysis. From this LD data we have constructed and LD matrix, which is a square matrix where each row and column represents the set of SNP marker ids and each element (i, j) represents the LD value between the ith and j^{th} SNPs.

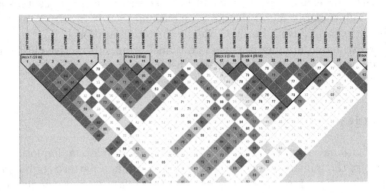

Fig. 5. Screenshot of Haploview showing estimated LD values from genotype data and haplotype estimation

We give a detailed analysis on the results obtained by performing clustering on the 29 X 29 LD matrix generated by the estimated LD data of the sample dataset provided in Haploview. We first perform hierarchical clustering to test whether tag SNPs can be detected using clustering. For the LD matrix of the Haploview dataset we obtain 7 clusters and we shall use this as an estimate or a basis for the minimum number of clusters future use.

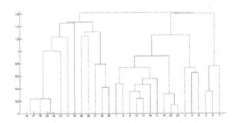

Fig. 6. Dendrogram formed after hierarchical clustering

Then we perform principal component analysis on the LD matrix generated from the Haploview dataset. It is observed that the first 5 components make up 90% of the variance cumulatively, and hence, these 5 components are chosen to be the input feature vectors to the self-organising map in the next stage.

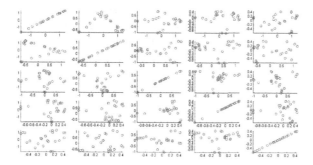

Fig. 7. Plots of first five principal components versus each other

We then employ a one dimensional Self Organizing Map of five neurons and perform 500 epochs of the learning method on the sample dataset and obtain the following cluster units. The corresponding tag SNPs and some of the alleles predicted by the tags are shown in the following figure.

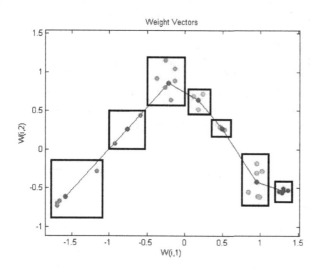

Fig. 8. Neuron weight positions along with actual data points of first two principal components. Colours show different clusters based on distance to nearest neuron

Subtractive Clustering is used to estimate a number of clusters before experimenting with fuzzy C means clustering. A vector of size equal to the number of dimensions is provided, with each element lying between 0 and 1, and providing a radius of influence in each dimension. The radius specifies the maximum distance in which the elements can lie if all the elements were in a unit hyperbox. When applied on the data matrix obtained from the first five principal components, the number of clusters are to be 15, 9, 7 when the radius of influence is set to be .25, .5 and .75 respectively. Since 7 is also the number of clusters obtained with self organising maps, we use the same number for fuzzy C means clustering, and obtain the tag SNP clusters. The tag SNPs along with clusters formed by fuzzy C means are shown in the following figure.

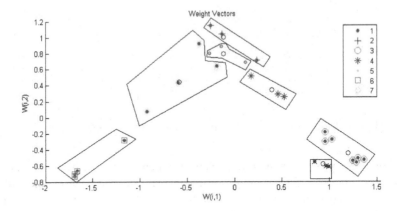

Fig. 9. Clusters obtained using fuzzy C means clustering. Colours show different clusters based on distance and membership to nearest cluster center

To test the accuracy measure of our prediction method we shall run the Tagger program of Haploview which is based on the tag SNP selection program developed by Paul Baker [13] on the sample dataset. We set the R2 threshold to 0.5, i.e. SNPs with LD values greater than or equal to 0.5 will be able to predict one another. After running the Tagger Program we obtain 9 SNPs which correctly predict all the 29 SNPs of the dataset.

Table 4. Comparison of tag SNP selection using Tagger, SOM and FCM

Algorithm	Number of Tag SNPs	Average Cluster Size
Haploview Tagger	9	3.44
Self Organising Map	7	4.14
Fuzzy C Means	7	4.14

An important observation here is the fact that even though there is no significant reduction in the number of tag SNPs, each tag SNP that has been chosen from each cluster of the self-organising map and fuzzy clustering approaches captures several SNPs. In contrast, using Haploviews Tagger, we get several tag SNPs that capture only themselves. Since the ultimate goal is data compression by storing only a small subset of SNPs instead of all of them so that the others can be predicted by the tagging SNPs, the tag SNPs selected by Tagger are inefficient. The tag SNPs chosen by both the proposed methods, however, are much more efficient since each of them captures multiple SNPs other than themselves, thereby being better predictors of the entire genome. The above table shows a summary of the number of clusters and average cluster size of all three methods.

Three tables are presented below, each of which gives the results for each of the proposed methods as well as for Tagger, which serves as a baseline comparison. In each case, the tag SNP is given, along with a list of SNPs that are tagged by it, i.e. in the same cluster. Each tag SNP is the center of each cluster of SNPs. The number of clusters is not vastly reduced, but the average cluster size increases, and there are almost no tag SNPs that tag only themselves. This provides evidence that clustering using the proposed methods tends to result in a more efficient clustering with an increased average cluster size.

Table 5. Tag SNPs and Alleles Captured by Haploview Tagger

TAG SNP	ALLELES CAPTURED
rs1943699	6952211,6592202,7121845,1943707,957438,1943707,957438, 1943705, 1943699,1940094, 1943715,1943696,1943701
rs1943710	1943710,952201,876695,1943733,1227671,1943725
rs6592199	1789175,1940092,6592199
rs7108021	1073987,7108021,2155413
rs472857	555867,47287
rs7111775	7111775
rs4370960	4370960
rs3802893	3802893
rs1940125	1940125

Table 6. Tag SNP and Alleles Captured by SOM

TAG SNP	ALLELES CAPTURED
rs7108021	7108021,1073987,7111775
rs1940125	1940125,2155413,3802893
rs1227671	1227671,1943725,,1943733,876695,952201,1943710
rs4307690	4307690,1943715,6592211,957438,7121845
rs1943705	1943705,1943696,1943707
rs1940072	1940072,1789175
rs6592202	6592202,472587,555867,1943699,1940094,1943701,6592199

Table 7. Tag SNP and Alleles Captured by FCM Clustering

TAG SNP	ALLELES CAPTURED
rs876695	876695, 952201,1943725, 1227671, 1943733, 1943710
rs1943715	1943715, 957438, 6592211
rs1943699	1943699, 1943696, 1943705, 6592202, 1943701, 7121845, 1943707
rs555867	555867, 1940094, 472587
rs7108021	7108021, 1073987, 2155413
rs1940092	1940092, 1789175, 6592199
rs3802893	3802893, 1940125, 7111775, 4370960

5   Conclusion

From the results, it is quite clear that selecting tag SNPs by clustering them based on their linkage disequilibrium values using either SOM or FCM clustering methods give a more efficient set of tag SNPs as compared to existing established techniques. There are no tag SNPs that predict only themselves, and hence all tag SNPs are efficient and useful. This is of utmost importance, since the entire purpose of selecting tag SNPs is to reduce the number of SNPs required to predict the entire genotype of a gene.Due to the usage of dimensionality reduction, the number of clusters can be tweaked according to need as determined from the dendrogram of hierarchical and/or subtractive clustering.

However, the work on this method is far from over. A number of interesting extensions can be made. SNP prediction, using tag SNP prediction, which is done to validate tag SNPs and gauge the accuracy and quality of tagging SNPs, needs to be automated instead of having to rely on Tagger in Haploview. Different topologies, distance functions, and initial weights for the self-organising maps and different membership functions for fuzzy C means clustering can be tried. Feature vectors consisting of allele and genotype frequencies could be used instead of LD values.

Genome wide associate studies would widely benefit from improved methods of selecting tag SNPs, since that would in turn provide cheaper and faster methods to genotype whole genome sequences, which would help in classifying patients and identifying symptoms, and in effect, associate the two. Clustering is indeed a better way of selecting tag SNPs as we have shown and our method of selecting tag SNPs using self-organising maps and fuzzy C means Clustering is a step in that right direction.

References

1. Jingwu, et al.: Haplotype Tagging using Support Vector Machines. In: IEEE International Conference on Granular Computing, pp. 758–761 (2006), doi:10.1109/GRC.2006.1635911
2. Lewontin: The interaction of selection and linkage. I. General considerations; heterotic models. Genetics 49(1), 49–67 (1964), PMC 1210557. PMID 17248194
3. Pearson: On Lines and Planes of Closest Fit to Systems of Points in Space. Philosophical Magazine 2(11), 559–572 (1901)
4. Kohonen, Honkela: Kohonen Network. Scholarpedia 2(1), 7421 (2007)
5. Han, Kamber, Pei: Data Mining: Concepts and Techniques, 3rd edn. Elsevier
6. Lee, R.: A Critical Review of Strategies for Selecting Haplotype Tag SNPs (2011)
7. Patil, et al.: Blocks of Limited Haplotype Diversity Revealed by High-Resolution Scanning of Human Chromosome 21. Science 294, 1719–1723 (2001)
8. Zhang, et al.: A dynamic programming algorithm for haplotype block partitioning. PNAS 99, 7335–7339 (2002)
9. Stram, et al.: Choosing Haplotype Tagging SNPS Based on Unphased Genotype Data Using a Preliminary Sample of Unrelated Subjects with an Example from the Multiethnic Cohort Study. Hum. Hered. 55, 27–36 (2003)
10. Byng, et al.: SNP subset selection for genetic association studies. Ann. Hum. Genet. 67, 543–556 (2003)
11. Ao, et al.: CLUSTAG: hierarchical clustering and graph methods for selecting tag SNPs. Bioinformatics 21(8), 1735–1736 (2005)
12. The International HapMap Consortium, The International HapMap Project Nature 426, 789–796 (2003)
13. Bakker, et al.: Efficiency and power in genetic association studies (2005), doi:10.1038/ng1669

Application of Spectral Unmixing Algorithm on Hyperspectral Data for Mangrove Species Classification

Somdatta Chakravortty, Ekta Shah, and Arpita Saha Chowdhury

Govt. College of Engineering & Ceramic Technology, Kolkata, India
csomdatta@rediffmail.com

Abstract. This study makes use of non-linear unmixing model to unmix pixels of hyperspectral imagery in a heterogenous mangrove forest. This model takes into account the multi-path effects of radiation between endmember spectra that may occur before final interception by the sensor. Non linear models represent naturally occurring situations more accurately such as that commonly found within the mangrove forests where a variety of species co-exist as a mixed stand. This paper analyses the classification accuracy of linear and non-linear unmixing models for discrimination of mangrove species in the Sunderban Delta, India. On analysis, it has been found that linear unmixing has successfully identified mangrove species which exist as a pure patch whereas the non-linear model has been able to discriminate between species more accurately in a heterogenous patch. 10 dominant mangrove species have been identified in the study area and the results validated through field visits and RMSE values.

Keywords: non linear unmixing, multi-path interaction, bilinear model, linear mixing model, mangrove species , fractional abundance, N-FINDR.

1 Introduction

The combined use of hyperspectral remote sensing with digital image processing has enabled efficient mapping of the spatial extent and distribution pattern of mangrove species present in the tropical mangrove forests throughout the world [18]. Sub pixel classification for mangrove identification, Linear Mixture Modelling (LMM) in particular, has been attempted by researchers with multispectral imagery [12] The LMM approach has been a useful technique for converting spectral information into data products that can be related to the physical abundance of materials on the surface [21]. This is strictly valid for the situation where the endmembers are arranged in discrete, segregated patches on the surface. However, this condition is almost never met in nature. Many constituents of interest for earth science investigations exist in forests, soils, or at smaller scales, in intimate association with one another [1,2,5]. The drawback of LMM is that it takes into account only first order interactions between photons neglecting multiple path interactions which are quite likely in a tropical

P. Gupta and C. Zaroliagis (Eds.): ICAA 2014, LNCS 8321, pp. 223–236, 2014.

dense mangrove forest with mixed patches of mangrove species. To overcome the limitations of LMM, non linear unmixing has been proposed which takes into account multiple interactions between end members and is hence expected to give good classification results in a mixed mangrove stand. Non-linear models [14] takes into consideration the interaction amongst different endmembers (mangrove species) present in close proximity that cannot be ignored [5,8]. Multiple scattering of light occurs when light is incident on a region that is composed of mixtures in a heterogenous manner. The amount of light falling on an object has a part of it reflected back to the sensor directly and some part of it strikes the neighboring endmembers. This reflected light after interacting with the other endmembers is then reflected to the sensor. This is said to be the second-order interaction among endmembers. There are higher levels of interaction, but they can be ignored [16]. Nonlinear mixture models best describe the mixed spectra for certain end member distributions occurring naturally in the mixed patches of mangrove species in mangrove forests. In Guilfoyle et al. [8] and Plaza et al. [17], the authors designed neural networks for unmixing nonlinearly mixed pixels. However, these methods require their networks to be trained by training data and the quality of training data may affect the performance notably. Kernel-based nonlinear unmixing approaches have also been investigated [4,3,20], by deriving nonlinear algorithms based on linear ones thanks to the kernel trick. Kernels are however applied to the spectral signature of each pure component, as a whole, and independently of interactions between materials, thus operating as nonlinear distortion functions. This paper makes use of the potential of hyperspectral imagery for species level classification of mangroves through applicat ion of Fan's Bilinear model [7] for unmixing hyperspectral images. This non-linear model takes into account multiple photon bounces by introducing additional interaction terms in the linear mixture model. This paper also compares the classification accuracy of the non-linear models with that of LMM. The end members (mangrove species) have been detected by the unsupervised end member detection algorithm, NFINDR [6,10], which extracts pure pixels from the hyperspectral imagery of the study area. It is of worth to mention that the application of non-linear spectral unmixing is a unique attempt in mangrove forest areas and the Sunderban Deltaic region of West Bengal, India in particular.

2   Spectral Mixing Models

2.1   Linear Mixture Model

The model [13] is based on the assumption that a photon of light incident on an object is reflected back into the atmosphere directly and does not interact with the neighboring endmembers, this reflected light is captured by the sensors. The resultant spectrum can be expressed as,

$$y = m\alpha + n, \tag{1}$$

where,y is a $L \times 1$ matrix containing the reflectance of every pixel in the image for all the L spectral bands, $m = [m1, m2, ..., mR]$, is a $L \times R$ mixing matrix, with R being the number of different endmembers detected and mj is a $L \times 1$ matrix of the reflectance values for endmember j. Here, $\alpha = [\alpha, \alpha, ...\alpha]T$ is the matrix containing the fractional abundances of the different endmembers and n is the additive noise. To be physically meaningful, the equation must satisfy the non-negativity and sum-to-one constraints.

2.2   Non-linear Mixture Model

This model takes into account the effects of multiple scattering effect of light. The nonlinear model is basically an improvement over the linear mixing model, as it adds on some new terms and a few more parameters to it, thus taking into account the second order interaction between endmembers. The generalized nonlinear model can be written as,

$$y = f(m, \alpha) + n, \tag{2}$$

where f is the nonlinear function [8,15]. In this study we have used a Bilinear model to study fractional abundance of each endmember. This model is a generalized version of the linear spectral unmixing.

Fan's Bilinear Mixing Model

The uniqueness of this model [1] is that it assumes that the amplitudes of end member interactions depend on the component fractions involved in the mixture [7]. This model is described by the following equation

$$y = \sum_{r=1}^{R} \alpha_r m_r + \sum_{i=1}^{R-1} \sum_{j=i+1}^{R} \alpha_i \alpha_j m_i \odot m_j + n. \tag{3}$$

Here, y is a matrix that contains the reflectance of every pixel in the image; mr is a matrix containing the reflectance values of pixels that contain pure patches of an endmember [7]. These endmembers have been detected using the N-FINDR algorithm. $m_i \odot m_j$ represents the hadamard product, i.e. term-by-term product of the i-th and j-th spectra.

$$m_i \odot m_j = (m_{1,i} m_{1,j} \quad \vdots \quad m_{L,i} m_{L,j}) \tag{4}$$

The Hadamard product basically represents the second order contribution by the endmembers. It can also be rewritten as $\text{diag}(m_i * m_T)$, where diag (A) represents the column vector containing the diagonal elements of the matrix A. It represents the fractional abundances of different endmembers. Here, $\alpha_i * \alpha_j$, is the amplitude of interaction between end members and depends on the product of the fractional abundances of the species present in a pixel. The constraints imposed on Fan's model are:

$$\sum_{k=1}^{R} \alpha_k = 1 \qquad \beta_{i,j} = \alpha_i \alpha_j. \tag{5}$$

The first constraint means that the fractional abundances of the different components present in a pixel must sum up to 1 . This is a very obvious assumption because each pixel comprises of mixture of different species and the area that is represented by a single pixel is completely occupied by those species on the whole. Thus if we consider the total area represented by a pixel to be 1, then the part occupied by each species must be a fractional value, the sum of which shall be 1.

3 Study Area

As a case study, the pristine mangrove habitats of Henry island (approximately 10 sq.km. in area, extending between 21^0 36' 00"N to 21^0 34' 00"N latitude and 86^0 18' 30"E to 88^0 18' 30"E longitude) of the Sunderban Biosphere Reserve of West Bengal,India has been selected for the present study. The selection of the study area (Fig 1) is based considering the fact that this island harbours a rich and bio-diverse mangrove community in pure and mixed patches that are rare and also endangered.

Fig. 1. Location of Study area

4 Spectral Unmixing of Hyperspectral Data

The hyperspectral imagery of the study area has been procured by the EO-1 Hyperion sensor on the 27th of May, 2011. The imagery has a spatial and spectral resolution of 30m and 10nm respectively. The 242 bands of the imagery have been reduced to 155 bands after removal of absorption bands and bands with no information. The non mangrove areas has been masked out from the mangrove areas by Normalised Differential Vegetation Index with a threshold of 0.5.

4.1   End Member Detection

This step is to estimate the set of distinct spectra (endmembers) [11] that constitute the mixed pixels in t he scene. In situations, when no priori knowledge is available about the end members that may be present in the study area, an unsupervised target detection algorithm, N-FINDR [19], has been applied on the imagery. The idea of the original N-FINDR algorithm is to find the pixels that can construct a maximum volume simplex, and these pixels will be considered end members. For the study, 10 pure end members have been extracted by NFINDR and are shown in Fig 2. The spectral library of the end members are shown in Fig2.

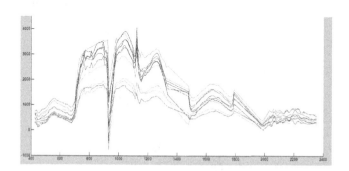

Fig. 2. Spectral Library of Mangrove Species extracted from NFINDR

4.2   Linear Mixture Model

The LMM model uses the endmembers identified in the previous step to estimate the fractional abundances of each mixed pixel from its spectrum. Sub pixels which show high abundance value (60% and above) are less likely to be mixed pixels with more degree of certainty towards being pure pixels i.e. representing a homogeneous patch of mangrove species. On the contrary, the sub pi xels with lower abundance fractions are more likely to be labeled as mixed pixels. The main objective of this step is to classify and identify pure pixels from the hyperspectral imagery of the study area. Fig 3 shows the classified image generated after integrating the fractional abundances showing species with abundance of 60% and above.

4.3   Non-Linear Mixture Model

Due to moderate spatial resolution of Hyperion data, most of the pixels contain a combination of several species present in c lose proximity. We have assumed that the light falling on each endmember interacts with all the other species present in close neighbourhood. Thus, we can say that the light falling on a particular species may strike and get reflected by the remaining 9 species. Thus, for the R different endmembers we are supposed to have, $R * (R + 1)/2$ interactions. Every such interaction will have amplitude that is represented by $m_i * m_j$.

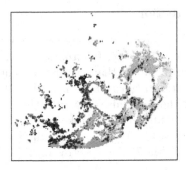

Fig. 3. Classified Output of Constrained Linear Spectral Unmixing

Fig. 4. Classified Output of Constrained Non-Linear Spectral Unmixing

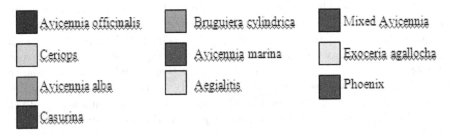

Avicennia officinalis	Bruguiera cylindrica	Mixed Avicennia
Ceriops	Avicennia marina	Exoceria agallocha
Avicennia alba	Aegialitis	Phoenix
Casurina		

Fig. 5. Legend

The amplitude of interaction basically represents the extent of interaction between the two end members. If two species are present as a very intimate mixture then $m_i * m_j$ in such cases will have a higher value within the range 0 to 1. The reflected light from the first end member is the again reflected by the second end member, and is then captured by the sensor. From this point it suffers another reflection and then reaches the sensor. This is second order interaction between endmembers. The levels of interaction can be higher but they yield negligible values hence can be ignored. In this way, for 10 endmembers we get 110 different interaction values between the endmembers. The classified image obtained from non-linear unmixing is shown in Fig 4.

4.4   Comparison of Linear and Non-Linear Model

To validate the results obtained using the nonlinear spectral unmixing approach, the fractional abundances of the end members (mangrove species) identified have been calculated using the linear and nonlinear unmixing models. The absolute error in frac tional abundance of each endmember has been defined as the absolute difference between the fraction obtained by the linear or nonlinear unmixing model and that by the actual ground data of a particular area. The relative error is defined as the ratio of the absolute error and the fraction obtained by actual ground observation. The absolute and relative Root Mean Square Errors (RMSE) has been calculated as follows:

$$RMSE(\%) = (((1/N)/(\Sigma|f_{ck} - f_{mk}|^2))^{1/2} * 100\%)/f_{cav}, \qquad (6)$$

where f_{ck} is the actual ground data fraction results and f_{mk} is the linear/non-linear model result; f_{cav} is the average of the ground data results.

Table 1.

Geographic Location on image	Algorithm Used	Avicennia officinalis	Ceriops	Avicennia marina	Exoceria agallocha	Avicennia alba	Aegialitis	Phoenix	Average RMSE
(21.5770⁰N, 88.2750⁰E) Image Co-ordinate (107,96)	LSU (Cons trained)	0.2482	0.0555	0.3131	0	0.2732	0	0	0.2444
	Fan's re-sult NLSU (Con-strained)	0.0822	0.0517	0.3783	0.1384	0.1335	0.0319	0	0.2627
	Ground truth value	0.60	0	0	0.30	0.10	0	0	0
Image Co-ordinate (107,97) (21.5769⁰N, 88.2752⁰E)	LSU (Con-strained)	0.2591	0.1045	0.2895	0	0.247	0	0	0.2418
	Fan's re-sult NLSU (Con-strained)	0.0787	0.0994	0.3735	0.1578	0.1047	0	0	0.2673
	Ground truth value	0.600	0	0	0.250	0.100	0	0	0

Table 1. (*continued*)

Geographic Location on image	Algorithm Used	Avicennia officinalis	Ceriops	Avicennia marina	Exoceria agallocha	Avicennia alba	Aegialitis	Phoenix	Average RMSE
Aegialitis (Mixed patch) Image Co-ordinate (109,116) (21.5763°N, 88.2807°E)	LSU (Cons trained)	0.1813	0.2672	0.0663	0	0.2803	0.0825	0.084	0.2041
	Fan's result NLSU (Con-strained)	0	0.2218	0.1073	0.103	0.1769	0.1851	0.1012	0.1673
	Ground truth value	0	0.200	0.300	0	0.100	0.300	0.100	0
(21.5771°N, 88.2748°E) Image Co-ordinate (106,96)	LSU (Con-strained)	0.3548	0.0503	0.2545	0.0597	0.2542	0	0.0264	0.2232
	Fan's result NLSU (Con-strained)	0.1833	0.0803	0.3284	0.2159	0.0616	0.0892	0.0013	0.2548
	Ground truth value	0.727	0	0	0.182	0.091	0	0	0
Ceriops + Exocaria agallocha Image Co-ordinate (121,171)	LSU (Con-strained)	0.2097	0.4161	0	0	0	0.0942	0.2505	0
	Fan's result NLSU (Con-strained)	0.1140	0.2975	0	0.1760	0	0.0360	0.2652	0.1746
	Ground truth value	0.1	0.5	0	0.3	0	0	0.1	0

Table 1. (*continued*)

Geographic Location on image	Algorithm Used	Avicennia officinalis	Ceriops	Avicennia marina	Exoceria agallocha	Avicennia alba	Aegialitis	Phoenix	Average RMSE
Avicennia var aquitisima Image Co-ordinate (106,114) (21.5771°N, 88.2801°E)	LSU (Con-strained)	0.1076	0.1009	0.3465	0.0625	0.2682	0	0	0.1796
	Fan's re-sult NLSU (Con-strained)	0.0170	0.0960	0.3640	0.1414	0.1945	0.0438	0	0.1739
	Ground truth value	0	0	0.500	0	0.350	0.150	0	0
Avicennia var aquitisima Image Co-ordinate (105,113) (21.5775°N, 88.2798°E)	LSU (Con-strained)	0.0768	0.3052	0.3522	0	0.1203	0	0	0.2159
	Fan's re-sult NLSU (Const rained)	0	0.2321	0.3749	0.1201	0.1026	0	0	0.2106
	Ground truth value	0	0	0.500	0	0.350	0.150	0	0

5   Results and Analysis

As the main objective of this study is to discriminate mangrove species, we have masked the non-mangrove zones such as clouds, agricultural land, mud flat and water bodies from the mangrove forest area to concentrate only on the mangrove vegetation for further processing. After atmospheric and geometric correction of data Minimum Noise Fraction has been applied and output and has been used for end member detection and mangrove classification. Matlab(Matrix Laboratory) has been used as a platform for programming the linear and non-linear models. The main objective of this study is to compare the accuracy of linear and non-linear mixture models for identification of mangrove species in a mixed mangrove stand. Ground data during field survey has been used for validating the results of the mixing models. A field survey of a patch in the study area represented by coordinates $X : 96, Y : 106$ in the imagery is seen to be a dominant patch of Avicennia Officinalis with very small abundance of Avicennia Marina, Excoecaria Agallocha and Avicennia Alba. The fractional abundance values generated by LMM (Table 1) at $X : 96, Y : 106$ reveals that Avicennia Officinalis shows 35.48% abundance at that pixel location whereas non-linear model shows an abundance of 18.33% for that species. The mangrove species of lesser abundance present in the patch are Avicennia Marina, Excoecaria Agallocha and Avicennia Alba and show fractional abundances of 25.45%, 5.97% and 25.42% respectively with LMM and 32.84%, 21.59% and 6.16% respectively for NLMM. The RMSE values (Table 1) of LMM (0.2232) are lower than the NLMM (0.2548) for the pure Officinalis patch. Another field survey of a patch in the study area represented by coordinates $X : 105, Y : 113$ in the imagery is seen to be a mixed patch of mangrove species namely Avicennia Marina var Aquitesima dominant with smaller abundances of Officinalis and Alba. LMM (Table 1.0) results show that Avicennia Marina var Aquitesima is the most abundant species (35.22%) in the patch followed by Avicennia Officinalis (30.52%) and Avicennia Alba (12.03%). Non-linear model gives a representation with Avicennia Marina var Aquitesima being most abundant species (37.49%) in the patch followed by Avicennia Officinalis (23.21%) and Avicennia Alba (10.26%). When compared with the ground truth data, LMM shows a higher RMSE value (0.2159) than non-linear (0.2106) which helps us conclude that mixed patches are accurately represented with non-linear models than the commonly used Linear Models. Fig 2 shows the spectral library of end members extracted using NFINDR which have been fed into the linear and non-linear mixing model for sub-pixel classification and mixed mangrove mapping. Fig 3 and 4 shows the classified image of linear and non-linear mixing models respectively which has been generated after integration of the individual fractional abundance maps of the respective mangrove species. The fractional abundance map of Non-Linear Mixing Model (NLMM) (Fig.(6-15) shows a larger distribution of species than that of LMM as it also identifies end members that are present in very small abundances in the study area. The island is seen to be dominated by Avicennia Marina and mixed patches of Ceriops - Excoecaria Agallocha and Avicennia Marina var Aquitesima-Aegialitis. The other mangrove species which have been identified in Henry's Island after classification are Avicennia Officinalis, Avicennia Alba, Bruguiera Cylindrica, Phoenix Paludosa and Casurina.Fig.5 shows legend of mangrove species identified.

Fig. 6. Fractional Abundance of Avicennia officinalis with LMM and NLMM

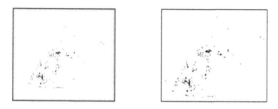

Fig. 7. Fractional Abundance of Bruguiera Cylindrica with LMM and NLMM

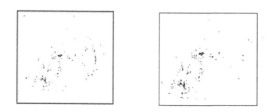

Fig. 8. Fractional Abundance of Mixed Avicennia with LMM and NLMM

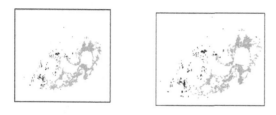

Fig. 9. Fractional Abundance of Ceriops with LMM and NLMM

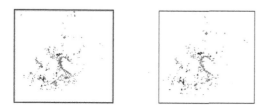

Fig. 10. Fractional Abundance of Avicennia marina with LMM and NLMM

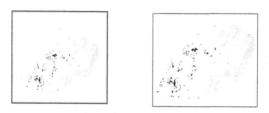

Fig. 11. Fractional Abundance of Exocaria agallocha with LMM and NLMM

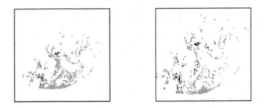

Fig. 12. Fractional Abundance of Avicennia alba with LMM and NLMM

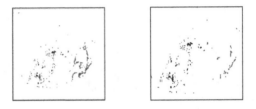

Fig. 13. Fractional Abundance of Aegialitis with LMM and NLMM

Fig. 14. Fractional Abundance of Phoenix with LMM and NLMM

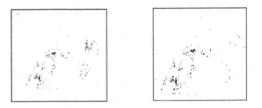

Fig. 15. Fractional Abundance of Casurina with LMM and NLMM

6   Conclusion

The linear approach has been a useful technique for converting spectral information into data products that can be related to the physical abundance of materials on the surface. Nevertheless, it is only strictly valid for the situation where the endmembers are arranged in discrete, segregated patches on the surface. From our results we can conclude that the locations with homogeneous mangrove patches show better identification results with linear spectral unmixing algorithm as in case of pure Avicennia Officinalis patch and pure Excoecaria Agallocha patch. The RMSE values generated for pure patches are much lower when LSU is used. The linear condition is almost never met in nature, and many components of interest for earth science investigations exist in forests, soils, or at smaller scales, in intimate association with one another. In such cases nonlinear unmixing processes is assumed to be more useful. After analyzing both the models we realize that Fan's non-linear algorithm gives much better results in cases of mixed mangrove patches. The mixed mangrove species are much better identified using Fan's algorithm as compared to Linear spectral unmixing algorithm. The RMSE generated is much lower on application of non-linear algorithm (Fan's model) in mixed patches as in case of mixed Ceriops-Excoecaria patch, mixed Alba-Officinalis patch and Ceriops-Avicennia Alba-Aegialitis mixtures as compared with that of linear spectral unmixing results. Fan's algorithm has assumptions which are much more relevant in natural condition s and thus show better target detection results. Hence we may conclude, in our study, mangrove species in a mixed stand gives better results with use of non-linear spectral unmixing and pure stands are identified more accurately with use of linear spectral unmixing.

Acknowledgments. The corresponding author expresses her sincerest thanks to Department of Science & Technology, Govt. of India, New Delhi, India for extending financial support in the form of a Major Research Project on the above study problem.

References

1. Altmann, Y., Dobigeon, N., Tourneret, J.Y.: Bilinear models for nonlinear unmixing of hyperspectral images. In: Hyperspectral Image and Signal Processing: Evolution in Remote Sensing (WHISPERS), pp. 1–4 (2011)
2. Borel, C.C., Gerstl, S.A.: Nonlinear spectral mixing models for vegetative and soils surface. Rem. Sens. of the Environ. 47(2), 403–416 (1994)
3. Broadwater, J., Banerjee, A.: A comparison of kernel functions for intimate mixture models. In: Proceedings of Workshop on Hyperspectral Image and Signal Processing, Evolution in Remote Sensing, Grenoble, France, pp. 1–4 (2009)
4. Broadwater, J., Chellappa, R., Banerjee, A., Burlina, P.: Kernel fully constrained least squares abundance estimates. In: Proceedings of IEEE International Geoscience and Remote Sensing Symposium, Barcelona, Spain, pp. 4041–4044 (2007)
5. Dobigeon, N., Tourneret, J.Y.: Spectral unmixing of hyperspectral images using a hierarchical bayesian model (2011)
6. Du, Q., Raksuntorn, N., Younan, N.H., King, R.: Variants of N-FINDR Algorithm for Endmember Extraction. In: Image and Signal Processing for Remote Sensing XIV, Proc. of SPIE, vol. 7109, p. 71090 G-1 (2008)
7. Fan, W., Hu, B., Miller, J., Li, M.: Comparative study between a new nonlinear model and common linear model for analysing laboratory simulated-forest hyperspectral data. Remote Sensing of Environment 30(11), 2951–2962 (2009)

8. Guilfoyle, K.J., Althouse, M.L., Chang, C.-I.: A quantitative and comparative analysis of linear and nonlinear spectral mixture models using radial basis function neural networks. IEEE Geoscience and Remote Sensing Letters 39(8), 2314–2318 (2001)

9. Halimi, A., Altmann, Y., Dobigeon, N., Tourneret, J.Y.: Nonlinear Unmixing of Hyperspectral Images Using a Generalized Bilinear Model. IEEE Transactions on Geoscience and Remote Sensing 49(11) (2011)

10. Hsuang, R., Chang, C.: Automatic Spectral Target Recognition in Hyperspectral Imagery. IEEE Transactions on Aerospace and Electronic Systems 39(4) (2003)

11. Javier, P., Plaza, A., Martin's, G.: A Fast Sequential Endmember Extraction Algorithm Based on Unconstrained Linear Spectral Unmixing. In: Bruzzone, L., Notarnicola, C., Posa, F. (eds.) Image and Signal Processing for Remote Sensing XV. Proc. of SPIE, vol. 7477, p. 74770L (2009)

12. Kanniah, K., Wai, N., Shin, A., Rasib, A.: Per-pixel and sub-pixel classifications of high-resolution satellite data for mangrove species mapping. Applied GIS 3(8), 1–22 (2007)

13. Keshava, N., Mustard, J.: Spectral Unmixing. IEEE Signal Processing Magazine (2002)

14. Liu, W., Wu, E.: Comparison of non-linear mixture models: sub-pixel classification. Remote Sensing of Environment 94, 145–154 (2005)

15. Nascimento, J.M.P., Bioucas-Dias, J.M.: Nonlinear mixture model for hyperspectral unmixing. In: Bruzzone, L., Notarnicola, C., Posa, F. (eds.) Proc. SPIE Image and Signal Processing for Remote Sensing XV, vol. 7477, pp. 74 770I-1–74 770I-8. SPIE, Berlin (2012)

16. Plaza, J., Plaza, A., Mart'inez, R., Mart'inez, P.: Joint Linear/Nonlinear Spectral Unmixing of Hyperspectral Image Data. I-4244-1212-9/07/25.00c2007IEEE (2007)

17. Plaza, J., Mart'inez, P., P'erez, R., Plaza, A.: Nonlinear neural network mixture models for fractional abundance estimation in AVIRIS hyperspectral images. In: Proceedings of XIII JPL Airborne Earth Science Workshop, Pasadena, CA (2004)

18. Vaiphasa, C., Ongsomwang, S.: Tropical mangrove species discrimination using Hyperspectral data: A Laboratory Study. Estuarine, Coastal and Shelf Science 65, 371–379 (2005)

19. Winter, M.: Fast autonomous spectral end-member determination in hyperspectral data. In: Proc. 13th Int. Conf. on Applied Geologic Remote Sensing, Vancouver, vol. 2, pp. 337–344 (1999)

20. Wu, X., Li, X., Zhao, L.: A kernel spatial complexity-based nonlinear unmixing method of hyperspectral imagery. In: Li, K., Jia, L., Sun, X., Fei, M., Irwin, G.W. (eds.) LSMS/ICSEE 2010. LNCS, vol. 6330, pp. 451–458. Springer, Heidelberg (2010)

21. Yang, C., Everitt, J.H., Bradford, J.M.: Using multispectral imagery and linear spectral unmixing Techniques for estimating crop yield variability. Transactions of the ASABE, Vol 50(2), 667–674 (2007) ISSN 0001-2351

Automatic Extraction of Headlines from Punjabi Newspapers

Vishal Gupta*

Computer Science & Engineering,
University Institute of Engineering & Technology,
Panjab University Chandigarh, India
vishal@pu.ac.in

Abstract. For any language in the world, headlines of newspapers are always important and by reading headlines we can have idea of whole news without completely reading the news articles. Moreover there are many websites whose task is to extract the news headlines from online newspapers and display those headlines on their websites for information to their users. One other important application of headlines extraction is in text summarization where headline-sentences are given more importance than other sentences for including in final summary. This paper concentrates on automatic headlines extraction from Punjabi newspapers. Punjabi is the official language for state of Punjab. But Punjabi is under resource language. There are very less number of computational-linguistic resources available for Punjabi. But a lot of research is going on for developing NLP applications in Punjabi language. It is first time that automatic headlines extraction from Punjabi newspapers has been developed with four features of headlines: 1) Punctuation mark feature 2) Font feature 3) Number of words feature and 4) Title keywords feature. Weights of these four features are calculated by applying mathematical regression as machine learning approach. For extracting headlines, final scores of sentences are obtained using feature weight equation as: $w_1f_1 + w_2f_2 + w_3f_3 + w_4f_4$ where f_1, f_2, f_3 and f_4 are feature-scores of four features and w_1, w_2, w_3 and w_4 are learned weights of these features. The accuracy of Punjabi headline extraction system is 98.39% which is tested over fifty Punjabi single/multi news documents. A part of Punjabi headlines extraction system with Punctuation mark feature has been integrated with Punjabi Text Summarization system which is available online.

Keywords: Punjabi headlines, Headlines Extraction, Newspaper Headlines Extraction.

1 Introduction to Automatic Extraction of Headlines

For any language in the world, headlines of newspapers are always important and by reading headlines we can have idea of whole news without completely

---

* Assistant Professor.

P. Gupta and C. Zaroliagis (Eds.): ICAA 2014, LNCS 8321, pp. 237–244, 2014.

reading the news articles. Moreover there are many websites whose task is to extract the news headlines from online newspapers and display those headlines on their websites for information to their users. For example News blaster [1] is a system that helps users find the news that is of the most interest to them. The system automatically collects, clusters, categorizes, and summarizes news from several sites on the web (CNN, Reuters, Fox News, etc.) on a daily basis, and it provides users a user-friendly interface to browse the results. Articles on the same story from various sources are presented together and summarized using state-of-the-art techniques. The Newsblaster system has already caught the attention of the press and public. One other important application of headlines extraction is in text summarization [2,3] where headline-sentences are given more importance than other sentences for including in final summary.

This paper concentrates on automatic headlines extraction from Punjabi newspapers. Punjabi is the official language for state of Punjab. But Punjabi is under resource language. There are very less number of computational-linguistic resources available for Punjabi. But a lot of research is going on for developing NLP applications in Punjabi language. It is first time that automatic headlines extraction from Punjabi newspapers has been developed with four features of headlines: 1) Punctuation mark feature 2) Font feature 3) Number of words feature and 4) Title Keywords feature. Weights of these four features are calculated by applying mathematical regression as machine learning approach. In regression, feature parameters of many manually extracted headlines from text documents are used as independent input variables and corresponding dependent outputs are specified in training phase. In the training phase, headlines are manually extracted from fifty Punjabi multi news documents by assigning scores to the sentences of these documents (i.e. score= 1 for headlines and score= 0 for other sentences) and then mathematical regression has been used to estimate the text features weights and then average weights are taken.

For extracting headlines, final scores of sentences are obtained using feature weight equation as: $w_1 f_1 + w_2 f_2 + w_3 f_3 + w_4 f_4$. Where f_1, f_2, f_3 and f_4 are feature-scores of four features and w_1, w_2, w_3 and w_4 are learned weights of these features. The accuracy of Punjabi headline extraction system is 98.39% which is tested over fifty Punjabi single/multi news documents. A part of Punjabi headlines extraction system with Punctuation mark feature has been integrated with Punjabi Text Summarization system [6,9] which is available online.

2   Automatic Extraction of Headlines from Punjabi Newspapers

In single/multi news documents, headlines are most important and usually contain lot of information. In Punjabi news corpus [4] of 11.29 million words with 957553 sentences, the frequency count of these headlines is 32861 lines which cover 3.43% of the corpus. Features for automatic headlines extraction from Punjabi newspapers are:

2.1   Punctuation Mark Feature

In Punjabi news papers, headlines usually end with punctuation mark characters like new line character, enter key, question mark (?) or exclamation sign (!) etc. If current sentence ends with any of above mentioned punctuation mark characters then flag for punctuation mark feature is set to true for that sentence.

2.2   Font Feature

Headlines in Punjabi news papers are usually in bold font with more font size than rest of the text. This feature is enough to distinguish between headlines and rest of the text in newspapers. If current sentence is in bold font or has more font size than rest of text then set the flag for font feature to true for that sentence.

2.3   Number of Words Feature

Headlines are usually short in Punjabi news papers. After thorough analysis of Punjabi news corpus, it is found that most of Punjabi headlines contain around 05 to 15 words. Out of 32,861 headlines from Punjabi news corpus, the frequency count of headlines with 05 to 15 words is 30,674 which cover 3.20% of Punjabi corpus. If number of words in current Punjabi sentence are between 05 to 15 then set the number flag feature to true for that sentence.

2.4   Features Weight Learning and Final Score Calculation

Mathematical regression [7,8] has been used as model to estimate the weights of four text features for automatic headlines extraction from Punjabi newspapers. In this model, a mathematical function can relate output to input. The feature parameters of many manually extracted headlines from text documents are used as independent input variables and corresponding dependent outputs are specified in training phase. In the training phase, headlines are manually extracted from fifty Punjabi multi news documents by assigning scores to the sentences of these documents (i.e. score=1 for headlines and score=0 for other sentences) and then mathematical regression has been used to estimate the text features weights and then average weights are taken. A relation between inputs and outputs is established. Regression can be represented in matrix notation as:

$$\begin{bmatrix} Y_0 \\ Y_1 \\ . \\ Y_m \end{bmatrix} = \begin{bmatrix} X_{01} & X_{02} & \cdots & X_{04} \\ . & . & \cdots & . \\ . & . & \cdots & . \\ X_{m1} & X_{m2} & \cdots & X_{m04} \end{bmatrix} \begin{bmatrix} w_0 \\ w_1 \\ . \\ w_m \end{bmatrix}$$

Where
$[Y]$ is output vector having values either 0 or 1 based on headlines manually extracted from fifty documents.

$[X]$ is the input matrix (feature parameters) for different features having values either 0 or 1.

$[w]$ is linear statistical model of system (the weights $w_1, w_2 \ldots w_4$ in the equation)

m is total number of sentences in the training corpus.

Weight w of a particular feature k ($k = 1$ to 4) with input matrix x and fuzzy output matrix y can be calculated as follows:

$$w = \sum_{i=01}^{m1} \frac{\left(x_i - \text{mean}(x)\right)\left(y_i - \text{mean}(y)\right)}{\sum_{i=01}^{m1}\left(x_i - \text{mean}(x)\right)^2}$$

From the above equation, weights of each of four features of Punjabi headlines extraction have been calculated.

Results of weight learning for four features are shown in Table 1.

Table 1. Weight Learning Results Using Mathematical Regression

Features	Learned weights
Punctuation mark feature	1.53
Font feature	0.96
Number of words feature	0.78
Title keywords feature	0.82

From the above table, we can conclude that, the two most important features for automatic extraction of headlines from Punjabi newspapers are punctuation mark feature and font feature.

In automatic headlines extraction from Punjabi newspapers, final scores of sentences are obtained using feature weight equation as: $w_1 f_1 + w_2 f_2 + w_3 f_3 + w_4 f_4$ where f_1, f_2, f_3 and f_4 are values of four features and w_1, w_2, w_3 and w_4 are learned weights of these four features.

2.5   Algorithm for Automatic Extraction of Punjabi Headlines

Step1: Input the Punjabi newspaper which contains multi news articles

Step2: Segment the input Punjabi text in to sentences and words.

Step3: If current Punjabi sentence ends with any punctuation mark characters like: new line character, enter key, question mark (?) or exclamation sign (!) etc. then flag for punctuation mark feature is set to true for that sentence.

Step4: If current Punjabi sentence is in bold font or has more font size than rest of text then set the flag of font feature to true for that sentence.

Step5: If number of words in current Punjabi sentence lie between 05 to 15 words, then set the number flag feature to true for that sentence.

Step6: Calculate term frequency of each word in a sentence. Term frequency of each word in a sentence is calculated as number of times that word appears in the whole news.

Step7: If the current Punjabi sentence is subset of any other sentences in the given news and contains the keywords with maximum term frequency then set the flag for title keyword feature to true for that sentence.

Step8: Calculate weights of four features using mathematical regression in which a mathematical function can relate output to input. The feature parameters of many manually extracted headlines from text documents are used as independent input variables and corresponding dependent outputs are specified in training phase.

Step9: Calculate final scores of sentences by using feature weight equation as: $w_1 f_1 + w_2 f_2 + w_3 f_3 + w_4 f_4$ where f_1, f_2, f_3 and f_4 are values of four features and w_1, w_2, w_3 and w_4 are learned weights of these four features.

Step10: Top scored sentences from step9 are extracted as headlines from this step.

After analysis of Punjabi corpus, we have discovered that, if a given sentence possesses at least any of two features out of four features mentioned above then that sentence is candidate of headline and is part of output.

Algorithm input (Punjabi multi news input):

ਘੁੰਨਸ ਦੀ ਅਗਵਾਈ 'ਚ ਵਿਕਾਸ ਕਾਰਜਾਂ 'ਚ ਬੇਹੱਦ ਤੇਜੀ ਆਈ-ਭਾਨਾ

ਸ਼ਹਿਣਾ, 8 ਜਨਵਰੀ (ਪੱਤਰ ਪ੍ਰੇਰਕ)-ਹਲਕਾ ਵਿਧਾਇਕ ਸੰਤ ਬਲਵੀਰ ਸਿੰਘ ਘੁੰਨਸ ਦੀ ਅਗਵਾਈ ਹੇਠ ਹਲਕੇ ਦੇ ਵਿਕਾਸ ਕਾਰਜਾਂ ਵਿਚ ਬੇਹੱਦ ਤੇਜੀ ਆਈ ਹੈ। ਇਹ ਸ਼ਬਦ ਭਗਵਾਨ ਸਿੰਘ ਭਾਨਾ ਯੂਥ ਆਗੂ ਤੇ ਸੰਮਤੀ ਮੈਂਬਰ ਨੇ ਪਿੰਡ ਨਾਨਕਪੁਰਾ ਵਿਖੇ ਸ਼ਗਨ ਸਕੀਮ ਦੇ ਚੈਕ ਦੇਣ ਸਮੇਂ ਸੰਬੋਧਨ ਕਰਦਿਆਂ ਆਖੇ। ਭਗਵਾਨ ਸਿੰਘ ਨੇ ਕਿਹਾ ਕਿ ਸ਼ਗਨ ਸਕੀਮ ਲਈ ਰਹਿੰਦੇ ਪਰਿਵਾਰਾਂ ਲਈ ਛੇਤੀ ਹੀ ਬਾਕੀ ਦੀ ਰਾਸ਼ੀ ਜਾਰੀ ਕੀਤੇ ਜਾਣ ਦੀ ਹਲਕਾ ਵਿਧਾਇਕ ਨੇ ਹਾਮੀ ਭਰੀ ਹੈ ਅਤੇ ਸੰਮਤੀ ਰਾਹੀਂ ਵੀ ਪਿੰਡਾਂ ਲਈ ਸਬਮਰਸੀਬਲ ਪੰਪ ਤੇ ਗਰਾਂਟਾਂ ਦਿੱਤੀਆਂ ਜਾ ਰਹੀਆਂ ਹਨ। ਇਸ ਸਮੇਂ ਸੁਖਦੇਵ ਸਿੰਘ ਸਰਪੰਚ ਨਾਨਕਪੁਰਾ, ਪਵਨ ਕੁਮਾਰ, ਗੁਰਚਰਨ ਸਿੰਘ ਜ਼ੈਲਦਾਰ, ਕੇਰ ਸਿੰਘ ਪੱਖੋਕੇ, ਗੁਰਤੇਜ ਸਿੰਘ ਘੋਨਾ, ਜੰਗ ਸਿੰਘ ਪ੍ਰਧਾਨ ਟੈਕਸੀ ਯੂਨੀਅਨ, ਜਗਸੀਰ ਸਿੰਘ, ਕਰਤਾਰ ਸਿੰਘ ਪੱਖੋਕੇ ਆਦਿ ਆਗੂ ਵੀ ਹਾਜ਼ਰ ਸਨ।

ਸਾਹਿਤ ਚਰਚਾ ਮੰਚ ਬਰਨਾਲਾ ਦੀ ਚੋਣ ਹੋਈ

ਬਰਨਾਲਾ, 8 ਜਨਵਰੀ (ਸਟਾਫ਼ ਰਿਪੋਰਟਰ)-ਸਾਹਿਤ ਚਰਚਾ ਮੰਚ ਬਰਨਾਲਾ ਦੀ ਚੋਣ ਗਰੀਨ ਐਵੀਨਿਊ ਦੇ ਪਾਰਕ ਨੇੜੇ ਨਾਨਕਸਰ ਗੁਰਦੁਆਰਾ ਵਿਖੇ ਹੋਈ, ਜਿਸ ਵਿਚ ਸਰਬ ਸੰਮਤੀ ਨਾਲ ਬੂਟਾ ਸਿੰਘ ਚੰਹਾਨ ਅਤੇ ਸੁਰਜੀਤ ਸਿੰਘ ਦਿਹੜ ਸਰਪੁਸਤ, ਡਾ: ਉਜਾਗਰ ਸਿੰਘ ਮਾਨ ਪ੍ਰਧਾਨ, ਡਾ: ਅਮਨਦੀਪ ਸਿੰਘ ਟੱਲੇਵਾਲੀਆ ਅਤੇ ਕੁਲਵੰਤ ਸਿੰਘ ਧਿਂਗੜ ਮੀਤ ਪ੍ਰਧਾਨ, ਜਨਰਲ ਸਕੱਤਰ ਪਾਲ ਸਿੰਘ ਲਹਿਰੀ, ਸਹਾਇਕ ਜਨਰਲ ਸਕੱਤਰ ਲੈਕਚਰਾਰ ਸੁਖਮਿੰਦਰ ਸਿੰਘ ਸ਼ਹਿਣਾ, ਜਥੇਬੰਦਕ ਸਕੱਤਰ ਬਿੰਦਰ ਖੁੱਡੀ ਕਲਾਂ, ਸੁਦਰਸ਼ਨ ਗੁੱਠੂ ਤੇ ਅਵਤਾਰ ਸਿੰਘ ਸੰਧੂ, ਪ੍ਰਚਾਰ ਸਕੱਤਰ ਅਸ਼ੋਕ ਭਾਰਤੀ ਅਤੇ ਬੰਤ ਸਿੰਘ ਬਰਨਾਲਾ, ਵਿੱਤ ਸਕੱਤਰ ਲਛਮਣ ਦਾਸ ਮੁਸਾਫ਼ਿਰ ਤੇ ਸਹਾਇਕ ਵਿੱਤ ਸਕੱਤਰ ਬਲਵਿੰਦਰ ਸਿੰਘ ਠੀਕਰੀਵਾਲਾ ਚੁਣੇ ਗਏ। ਚੋਣ ਉਪਰੰਤ ਡਾ: ਉਜਾਗਰ ਸਿੰਘ ਮਾਨ ਨੇ ਦੱਸਿਆ ਕਿ ਇੱਕੀ ਮੈਂਬਰੀ ਕਾਰਜਕਾਰਨੀ ਦਾ ਐਲਾਨ ਅਗਲੀ ਸੂਚੀ ਵਿਚ ਕੀਤਾ ਜਾਵੇਗਾ।

Under leadership of Ghunnas development activities are highly accelerated-Bhana

Shhina, 8 January (motivational letters) Under the leadership of local MLA Sant Balbir Singh Ghunnas development activities in the constituency are highly accelerated. These words are spoken by Bhagwan Singh Bhana youth leader and Committee member in the village Nankpura while distributing the cheques of shagun scheme. Bhagwan Singh said that local MLA has agreed to release the remaining amount soon to rest of families for shagun scheme and submersible pumps & grants are also given to the villages through Committee. On this occasion the Nankpura Sarpanch Sukhdev Singh, Pawan Kumar, Gurcharan Singh jaildar, Kaur Singh Pakhoke, Gurtej Singh Ghona, Jang Singh head taxi union, Jagsir Singh, Kartar Singh pakhoke etc. leaders were also present.

Election held for literature discussion forum Barnala

Barnala, January 8 (Staff Reporter)—Election of literature discussion forum held at Gurdwara Nanksar near the park of Green Avenue, in which unanimously Buta Singh Chauhan and Surjit Singh Dehd patron, Dr Ujagar Singh Mann head, Dr: Amandeep Singh Tallewalia, Kulwant Singh Dhingad circle head, General Secretary Pal Singh Lahiri, assistant general secretary lecturer Sukminder Singh Shhina, organisational secretary Binder Khuddi kalan, Sudarshan Guddu, Avtar Singh Sandhu, publicity secretary Ashok Bharti, Bant Singh Barnala, finance secretary Lakshman Das Musafir and assistant financial Secretary Balwinder Singh Thikriwala were elected. After election Dr Ujagar Singh Mann said that executive list of twenty one members will be announced in the next list.

Algorithm output:

ਘੁੰਨਸ ਦੀ ਅਗਵਾਈ ਚ ਵਿਕਾਸ ਕਾਰਜਾਂ ਚ ਬੇਹੱਦ ਤੇਜੀ ਆਈ-ਭਾਨਾ

ਸਾਹਿਤ ਚਰਚਾ ਮੰਚ ਬਰਨਾਲਾ ਦੀ ਚੋਣ ਹੋਈ

Under leadership of Ghunnas development activities are highly accelerated-Bhana Election held for literature discussion forum Barnala

3   Implementation and Analysis of Results

Automatic headlines extraction system for Punjabi has been implemented in VB.NET at front end and MS ACCESS at back end. The accuracy of Punjabi headline extraction system is 98.39% which is tested over fifty Punjabi single/multi news documents.

$$\text{Accuracy} = \frac{\text{Number of correct headlines identified by our system}}{\text{Total number of headlines extracted}}$$

Figure 1 shows accuracy and errors %age for automatic Punjabi headlines extraction system. Errors of 1.61% are due to the reason that some times name of author and location name are written in second line after the headline with

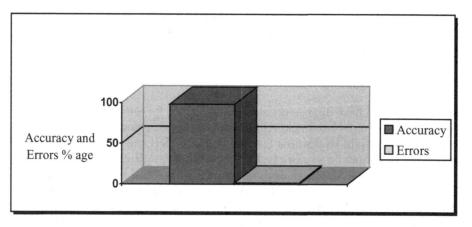

Fig. 1. Accuracy and errors % age for automatic Punjabi extraction system

enter key as last character in bold font, so it may be wrongly picked as second headline because it possesses first two features of headlines extraction. But actually it is not headline. For example consider the single news document as input:

ਅੱਸੀ ਲੜਕੀਆਂ ਨੂੰ ਸਿਲਾਈ ਦਾ ਕੰਮ ਸਿਖਾਇਆ

ਉਜਾਗਰ ਸਿੰਘ (ਬਰਨਾਲਾ)

8 ਜਨਵਰੀ ਨੂੰ ਮਾਲਵਾ ਸੱਭਿਆਚਾਰਕ ਅਤੇ ਵੈਲਫੇਅਰ ਕਲੱਬ ਬਰਨਾਲਾ ਵੱਲੋਂ ਚਲਾਏ ਜਾ ਰਹੇ ਸਿਲਾਈ ਸੈਂਟਰ ਦੀਆਂ ਦਸ ਵਿਦਿਆਰਥਣਾਂ ਨੂੰ ਸਿਖਲਾਈ ਸਰਟੀਫਿਕੇਟ ਵੰਡੇ ਗਏ।

Eighty girls were taught the sewing work

Ujagar Singh (Barnala)

"On 8 January the sewing centre run by Malwa cultural and welfare club Barnala distributed the training certificates to ten students."

In the above news, second line **ਉਜਾਗਰ ਸਿੰਘ (ਬਰਨਾਲਾ)** "Ujagar Singh (Barnala)" will also be treated as headline along with first line because it possesses first two features of headlines extraction but other two features are missing in this case. So it will be wrongly picked as another headline which is not true as this line is not important.

Moreover a part of automatic headlines extraction system with first feature (i.e. Punctuation Mark Feature) has been integrated with Punjabi Text Summarization system [6,7] because headlines are given highest importance in summary. Punjabi text system has been tested over fifty Punjabi single/multi news documents and it has been discovered that if headline extraction feature is omitted then efficiency of Punjabi summarizer is reduced by 10.23%, 6.23% and 2.34% at 10%, 30% and 50% compression ratios respectively. The reasons are that at 10% compression ratio, if headlines feature is omitted then headlines may be missing from summary because other lines may get more scores due to the presence of other features like nouns feature, proper names feature and cue phrases feature etc. At 30% and 50% compression ratios, if headlines identification feature is missing then the efficiency of Punjabi text summarization is affected by

6.23% and 2.34% respectively because at 30% and 50% compression ratios, sufficient lines are retrieved for summary which may also contain head lines due to presence of certain other features in the headlines.

4   Conclusions

In this paper, we have discussed the various features for automatic extraction of headlines from Punjabi news papers. Most of the lexical resources used in the system such as Punjabi stop words list and Punjabi dictionary etc. had to be developed from scratch as no work had been done in that direction. For developing these resources an in depth analysis of Punjabi corpus had to be carried out using manual and automatic tools. It is the first time that automatic headlines extraction from Punjabi news papers has been developed and a part of it has been integrated with Punjabi summarization system [9] to give importance to those sentences which belong to headlines. In future it could also be integrated with different Punjabi websites to highlight the headlines of different Punjabi newspapers. It could be very much beneficial for people of Punjab to know about the latest headlines of Punjabi newspapers without actually opening the websites of those news papers. After analysis of Punjabi corpus, we have discovered that If a given sentence possesses at least any of two features out of four features mentioned above then that sentence is candidate of headline and is part of output.

References

1. McKeown, K., Barzilay, R., Chen, J., Elson, D., Evans, D., Klavans, J., Nenkova, A., Schiffman, B., Igelman, S.: Columbia's NewsBlaster: New Features and Future Directions. In: Proceedings of NAACL-HLT 2003 (2003)
2. Berry, M.W.: Survey of Text Mining: Clustering, Classification and Retrieval. Springer Verlag, LLC, New York (2004)
3. Kyoomarsi, F., Khosravi, H., Eslami, E., Dehkordy, P.K.: Optimizing Text Summarization Based on Fuzzy Logic. In: Proceedings of Seventh IEEE/ACIS International Conference on Computer and Information Science, pp. 347–352. IEEE, University of Shahid Bahonar Kerman, UK (2008)
4. Punjabi Ajit News Corpus
5. Neto, J.L., Santos, A.D., Kaestner, C.A.A., Alexandre, N., Santos, D., Celso, A.A., Alex, K., Freitas, A.A., Parana, C.: Document Clustering and Text Summarization. In: Proceedings of 4th International Conference on Practical Applications of Knowledge Discovery and Data Mining, London, pp. 41–55 (2000)
6. Gupta, V., Lehal, G.S.: Automatic Punjabi Text Extractive Summarization System. In: Proceedings of COLING, pp. 191–198 (2012)
7. Gupta, V., Lehal, G.S.: Feature Selection and Weight Learning for Punjabi Text Summarization. Proceedings of International Journal of Engineering Trends and Technology, 45–48 (2011)
8. Fattah, M.A., Ren, F.: Automatic Text Summarization. Proceedings of Journal of World Academy of Science, Engineering and Technology, 192–195 (2008)
9. Gupta, V., Lehal, G.S.: Automatic Text Summarization System for Punjabi Language. International Journal of Emerging Technologies in Web Intelligence 5, 257–271 (2013)

A Similarity Measure for Clustering Gene Expression Data

Ram Charan Baishya, Rosy Sarmah, Dhruba Kumar Bhattacharyya,
and Malay Ananda Dutta

Dept. of CSE, Tezpur University, Tezpur, Assam, India
{rosy8,dkb,malay}@tezu.ernet.in

Abstract. A similarity measure for gene expression data should give
the shapes of the patterns of the gene expression data and should be less
susceptible to outliers. In this paper, we present a similarity measure
for clustering gene expression time series data. Our similarity measure,
PWCTM, uses the pairwise changing tendency measure of every pair
of conditions. We have compared our measure with several proximity
measures using k-means clustering algorithm in terms of Silhouette index, z-score and p-value. Our experimental results indicate that the gene
clusters obtained with PWCTM as the similarity measure are biologically
significant in the respective clusters due to their low p-values and high
z-values.

Keywords: Gene expression data, proximity measure, clustering, p-
value.

1 Introduction

Distance or similarity measures, also known as proximity measures, are essential
to solve many pattern recognition problems such as classification, clustering, and
retrieval. Various distance (similarity) measures have been reported in the literature. However, choosing an appropriate measure for a specific problem depends
on the problem domain as well as data domain. Clustering is based on proximity
measures that help in detecting clusters based on proximity among different objects. Clustering of gene expression data [1, 2] is highly sensitive to the proximity
measure used [2–5]. Choosing an appropriate dissimilarity measure is of utmost
importance [6].

In this paper, an effective similarity measure, Pair Wise Changing Tendency
Measure (PWCTM)[1], is proposed for effective clustering of gene expression data.
The PWCTM measure retains the up- down- regulation information inherent in
gene expression data and is robust in the presence of outliers.

---

[1] This work is an outcome of a research project supported by DST, Govt. of India in
collaboration with CSCR, ISI, Kolkata.

P. Gupta and C. Zaroliagis (Eds.): ICAA 2014, LNCS 8321, pp. 245–256, 2014.

1.1   Different Proximity Measures

A microarray experiment compares genes from an organism under different development time points, conditions or treatments. For an n condition experiment, a single gene has an n-dimensional observation vector known as its gene expression profile. A similarity (or dissimilarity) measure is a real-valued function that assigns a positive real number as a dissimilarity value between any two expression vectors. Therefore, to identify genes or samples that have similar expression profiles, appropriate similarity (or dissimilarity) measures are required. Next, we discuss some of the commonly used distance metrics.

Euclidean distance [7] (Equation 1) expressed in terms of the Pythagorean theorem is one of the most popular distance measures in use today. For two n-dimensional objects, $x = x_1, x_2, ..., x_n$ and $y = y_1, y_2, ..., y_n$, the Euclidean distance is defined as,

$$Euclidean(x, y) = \sqrt{\sum_{i=1}^{n} |x_i - y_i|^2} \tag{1}$$

Pearson's correlation coefficient [7] is a widely used similarity measure. Using the means (μ_x, μ_y), standard deviations (σ_x, σ_y) and covariance (cov_{xy}), the Pearson's correlation $(corr(x, y))$ is defined as the ratio of covariance to the standard deviations:

$$\mu_x = \frac{1}{n}\sum_{i=1}^{n} x_i, \quad \mu_y = \frac{1}{n}\sum_{i=1}^{n} y_i$$

$$\sigma_x = \sqrt{\frac{1}{n-1}\sum_{i=1}^{n}(x_i - \mu_x)^2}, \quad \sigma_y = \sqrt{\frac{1}{n-1}\sum_{i=1}^{n}(y_i - \mu_y)^2},$$

$$cov_{xy} = \frac{1}{n-1}\sum_{i=1}^{n}(x_i - \mu_x)(y_i - \mu_y)$$

$$corr(x, y) = \frac{covariance(x,y)}{standard\_deviation(x)*standard\_deviation(y)}$$
$$= \frac{cov_{xy}}{\sigma_x \sigma_y}$$

Pearson's correlation is always in the range [-1, 1]. Correlation and Euclidean distance are useful for dense data such as time series or two-dimensional points.

Spearman's rank-order correlation coefficient [7] is a similarity measure that works on ranked data. It is derived by replacing the data x_{ij} with its rank r_{ij} among all conditions. For example, $r_{ij} = 3$ if x_{ij} is the third highest value among x_{ik} , where $1 \le k \le n$. Spearman's correlation coefficient does not require the assumption of Gaussian distribution and is more robust against outliers than Pearson's correlation coefficient. However, as a consequence of ranking, a significant amount of information present in the data is lost.

BioSim Measure [8] models the coexpression of a gene pair using the sample-by-sample angular deviations within the expression vectors. This measure is calculated as follows. Given an expression vector $x = x_1, x_2, ..., x_n$, the deviation vector of x is computed as, $\Delta x = x \backslash x_i - x \backslash x_n$. The angular deviation vector for the n-conditions can be derived from the real-valued deviation vector x, as $\alpha'(t) = (tan^{-1}(\Delta x)) mod\ 2\pi$. The individual components of an angular deviation vector is present in only the first or third quadrant. The tan^{-1} function forces the range to be $[0, 2\pi]$. To preserve the correct angular deviation, the α' is converted to the new vector α as follows.

$$\alpha(t) = \alpha'(t), \qquad \alpha'(t) \in [0, \tfrac{\pi}{2}]$$
$$= \alpha'(t) - 2\pi, \alpha'(t) \in [\tfrac{3\pi}{2}, 2\pi]$$

The similarity between two modified angular deviation samples $\alpha_1(t)$ and $\alpha_2(t)$ is given by,

$$BioSim = \frac{1}{n-1} \sum_{t=1}^{n-1} \left(\frac{\alpha_1(t)\alpha_2(t)}{|\alpha_1(t)\alpha_2(t)|} \cdot \frac{cos(|\alpha_1(t)| - |\alpha_2(t)|)}{1 + cos(min(|\alpha_1(t)|, |\alpha_2(t)|))} \right) \quad (2)$$

Euclidean distance imposes a fixed geometrical structure [6] and finds clusters of that shape even if they are not present. It is scale variant and cannot detect negative correlation. Euclidean distance gives the distance between two genes but does not focus on the correlation between them. Pearson's Correlation, on the other hand, retains the correlation information between two genes as well as the regulation information. However, since it uses the mean values while computing the correlation between genes, a single outlier can aberrantly affect the result. Spearman's rank correlation is not affected by outliers; however, there is information loss w.r.t. regulation since it works on ranked data. BioSim uses includes trigonometric functions that are prone to rounding and approximation errors [8]. Thus, it can understood that choosing an appropriate distance measure for gene expression data is a difficult task.

2 Pair Wise Changing Tendency Measure (PWCTM)

One of the crucial tasks of any gene expression clustering algorithm is choosing the similarity measure to assess the similarity between pairs of expression profiles of genes. According to literature, the most popular measure that has been employed widely is the Pearson Correlation coefficient. However, this measure is susceptible to being skewed by outliers: a single data point can result in two genes appearing to be correlated even when all of the other data points suggest that they are not.

In this work, we propose an effective similarity measure, PWCTM, to assess the similarity of two gene expression profiles. In this measure we compare the pair wise changing tendency of the two expression profiles. A gene expression profile g is an n-dimensional vector, with each dimension representing a condition or time point. This n-dimensional vector is transformed into an order type vector which we call the changing tendency of the gene profile. For a given pair of conditions (c_i, c_j) the changing tendency can be evaluated as,

If $exp(c_i) > exp(c_j)$, changing tendency is represented by D
If $exp(c_i) < exp(c_j)$, changing tendency is represented by U
If $exp(c_i) = exp(c_j)$, changing tendency is represented by E
where $exp(c_i)$ denotes the expression value at condition c_i and $i < j$.

Thus given an expression profile g of n time points (conditions) we can compute the changing tendency of all the $q = n \times (n-1)/2$ possible pairs of conditions

which gives us the overall changing tendency (represented by CT_g here onwards) of the expression profile g. CT_g is now an order type vector of dimensionality q. For example given an expression profile of 4 conditions as follows $g < 3, 1, 4, 3 >$ its overall changing tendency can be written as Condition pair: (1,2) (1,3) (1,4) (2,3) (2,4) (3,4) Changing tendency: D U E U U D Hence the changing tendency of the expression profile is $CT_g = DUEUUD$. For two given expression profiles, we first compute the changing tendency for both of them, and then we compare them to find their similarity. The basic idea is that a match in a consecutive condition pair contributes more to similarity than a match in non- consecutive condition pair. Also, further the conditions are less will be the effect rendered by them. To incorporate this idea we assign some weights to each pair of conditions. For consecutive pairs in CT_g (for example (1,2), (2,3) and (3,4)) we assign the highest weight, then less weight to condition pairs which are one condition apart (eg. (1,3), (2,4)), lesser weight to condition pairs which are two conditions apart (eg. (1,4)) and so on. We can assign the weights as follows,
$w_k = \frac{1}{j-i}$, $k = 1, 2, \cdots q; i = 1, 2, \cdots, n - 1; j = i + 1, i + 2, \cdots, n$ and $i < j$. Thus given two gene profiles the following two steps are required to find their similarity.

  i. Construct their changing tendency sequence.
  ii. Compare the sequences.

When comparing the changing tendencies of two expression profiles, g, g', for each match in the corresponding positions of CT_g and $CT_{g'}$, weights associated with those positions will be added as score. Higher the value of the final score, higher is the similarity between the expression profiles. If the changing tendencies of both the expression profile matches in all condition pairs, then the final score will be the sum of all the weights. On the other hand if they dont match even in a single pair of condition then the score will be zero.

Thus for any two given expression profiles the similarity score will be with in zero and sum of all the weights. i.e $0 \leq score \leq sum\ of\ all\ weights$.

2.1   Basics of PWCTM

A gene sequence g is a sequence $g = (g(1), g(2), \cdots, g(n))$ of length n. Suppose, $k = 1, 2, \cdots, q$ represent the set of pairs (i, j) such that $1 \leq i < j \leq n$. Let $w_1, w_2, \cdots, w_q$ be a set of positive weights where, $w_k = \frac{1}{j-i}$, $k = 1, 2, \cdots q; i = 1, 2, \cdots, n - 1; j = i + 1, i + 2, \cdots, n$.

Thus we define a similarity function, $s(g, g')$, which gives a measure of the similarity of g and g' as follows:

$$\chi_k^{g,g'} = \begin{cases} 1 \text{ if } CT_g(k) = CT_{g'}(k), k = 1, \cdots, q \\ 0 \text{ otherwise.} \end{cases}$$

Then, $score(g, g') = \sum_{k=1}^{q} w_k \times \chi_k^{g,g'}$ and $s(g, g') = \frac{score(g,g')}{\sum_{k=1}^{q} w_k}$.

$s(g, g')$ is 1 (which is the maximum value) iff g, g' are identical and 0 (minimum value) iff g, g' are completely different i.e., $CT_g(k) \neq CT_{g'}(k)$ for every k.

2.2   Similarity to Distance Conversion

We can convert our similarity measure into a distance measure as $(d(g, g') = 1 - s(g, g'))$. Now, we shall show that $(d(g, g')$ gives a distance function for the genes. i.e., $(d(g, g')$ should satisfy the properties of a distance metric. Next, we show that our measure follow the distance properties.

1. Non-negativity: $d(g, g') \geq 0$
   Proof: We know that $0 \leq s(g, g') \leq 1$. Therefore, $0 \leq d(g, g') \leq 1$
2. Identity: $d(g, g') = 0$ iff $g = g'$
   Proof: $s(g, g') = 1$ iff $g = g'$. Therefore, $d(g, g') = 1 - 1 = 0$ and hence the proof.
3. Symmetricity: $d(g, g')$ should be equal to $d(g', g)$, i.e., $d(g, g') = d(g', g)$.

   Proof. :

$$d(g, g') = 1 - s(g, g') = 1 - \frac{\sum_{k=1}^{q}(w_k \times \chi_k^{g,g'})}{\sum_{k=1}^{q} w_k} \tag{3}$$

$$d(g, g) = 1 - s(g', g) = 1 - \frac{\sum_{k=1}^{q}(w_k \times \chi_k^{g',g})}{\sum_{k=1}^{q} w_k} \tag{4}$$

where, w_k is weight at k^{th} condition and q is the total number of possible pairs of conditions as explained in section 4. We know,

$$\chi_k^{g,g'} = \chi_k^{g',g} = \begin{cases} 1 \text{ if } CT_g(k) = CT_{g'}(k), \ k = 1, \cdots, q \\ 0 \text{ otherwise.} \end{cases}$$

Then, from equation 3 and 4, we get, $d(g, g') = d(g', g)$ (Denominator of both equations are same) and hence the proof.

4. Triangle inequality: $d(g_1, g_2) \leq d(g_1, g_3) + d(g_3, g_2)$
   Proof: Let,

$$\chi_k^{i,j} = \begin{cases} 1 \text{ if } CT_{g_i}(k) = CT_{g_j}(k), \ k = 1, \cdots, q \\ 0 \text{ otherwise.} \end{cases}$$

We shall prove that,

$$1 + \chi_k^{1,2} \geq \chi_k^{1,3} + \chi_k^{3,2} \text{ for } k = 1, \cdots, q \tag{5}$$

if $CT_{g_1}(k) \neq CT_{g_2}(k), \chi_k^{1,2} = 0$ and either $CT_{g_3}(k) \neq CT_{g_1}(k)$ or $CT_{g_3}(k) \neq CT_{g_2}(k)$.
   Hence, either $\chi_k^{1,3} = 0$ or $\chi_k^{2,3} = 0$. Thus equation 5 is satisfied. Otherwise, if $CT_{g_1}(k) = CT_{g_2}(k), \chi_k^{1,2} = 1$.
   Therefore, $1 + 1 = 2 \geq \chi_k^{1,3} + \chi_k^{2,3}$, i.e., equation 5 is satisfied in this case also equation 5 is satisfied in all cases.
   Multiplying equation 5 by w_k and summing over k we have,

$$\sum_{k=1}^{q} w_k + \sum_{k=1}^{q} w_k \times \chi_k^{1,2} \geq \sum_{k=1}^{q} w_k \times \chi_k^{1,3} + \sum_{k=1}^{q} w_k \times \chi_k^{3,2} \tag{6}$$

But, $\sum_{k=1}^{q} w_k \times \chi_k^{1,2} = \sum_{k=1}^{q} w_k \times s(g_1, g_2)$, $\sum_{k=1}^{q} w_k \times \chi_k^{1,3} = \sum_{k=1}^{q} w_k \times s(g_1, g_3)$ and $\sum_{k=1}^{q} w_k \times \chi_k^{3,2} = \sum_{k=1}^{q} w_k \times s(g_3, g_2)$.
Therefore, from equation 6 we have,

$$\sum_{k=1}^{q} w_k(1 + s(g_1, g_2)) \geq (\sum_{k=1}^{q} w_k)(s(g_1, g_3) + s(g_3, g_2))$$

Hence,

$$1 - s(g_1, g_2)) \leq (1 - s(g_1, g_3)) + (1 - s(g_3, g_2))$$

Therefore, $d(g_1, g_2) \leq d(g_1, g_3) + d(g_3, g_2)$ and hence the triangle inequality is proved.

Thus, $d(g, g')$ defines a distance function and the similarity function $s(g, g') = 1 - d(g, g')$ is based on this underlying distance function.

We have represented the similarity value in % form for ease of setting the threshold. Thus $s\%(g, g) = s(g, g') \times 100$ i.e if two expression profiles are exactly same in their changing tendencies, then according to PWCTM they are 100% similar. On the other hand if their changing tendencies are completely different then PWCTM will evaluate them as 0% similar. Instead of accumulating the weights in corresponding matches, if we add up the weights for the positions where there is a U in one expression and the other have a D in the corresponding position and vice versa then the final score will give us how much negatively correlated the two expression profiles are.

3 Performance Evaluation

As explained in the previous section PWCTM between two genes say g_i and g_j given by $s(g_i, g_j)$, can be used as a measure of how systematic is the change of their expression values with respect to (w.r.t.) each other. The more the value of $s(g_i, g_j)$, more systematic is their changes w.r.t. each other.

We used the k-means algorithm using the CVAP3.7 tool for validating clusters [9] and to test the effectiveness of PWCTM we tested it on the microarray datasets mentioned in Table 1 and compared the results with Pearson's correlation, Spearman's correlation, Biosim [8] measure and Euclidean distance. The PWCTM measure was implemented in MATLAB and the test platform was an HP workstation with Intel(R) Core(TM) i3 CPU @2.40 GHz processor and 2 GB memory running Windows 7 operating system.

For validity evaluation of the clustering solutions, we designed three procedures for (i) internal validation using Silhouette index [7], (ii) Biological validation using z-score [13] and (iii) statistical validation using z-score and p-value [14].

3.1 Internal Validation

Silhouette index reflects the compactness and separation of clusters; a larger average Silhouette index indicates a better overall quality of the clustering result,

Table 1. Datasets used for evaluating PWCTM

Serial No.	Dataset	No. of genes	No of conditions	Source
1	Yeast CDC28-13 [11]	6214	17	http://yscdp. stanford.edu/yeast_cell _cycle/full_data.html
2	Subset of Yeast Cell Cycle [11]	384	17	http://faculty. washington.edu/kayee /cluster
3	Yeast Diauxic Shift [12]	6089	7	http://www.ncbi.nlm. nih.gov/geo/query

so the optimal number of clusters is the one that gives the largest average Silhouette value. The k-means algorithm was executed for various values of k starting from 2 to 16 and their corresponding Silhouette index was computed using different proximity measures such as Euclidean distance, Pearson correlation (PCC), Spearman correlation, BioSim and PWCTM. The results of this comparison for Dataset 2 is given in Figure 1. From the figure, we observe that $k = 4$ gives the optimal number of clusters according to Silhouette index (a larger value indicates better quality of the clustering result). From the figure we conclude that our PWCTM gives good comparable Silhouette values in comparison with the other proximity measures. For the yeast dataset, Dataset 2, K-means obtained the best result for k=4 based on the Silhouette index because K-means has the largest Silhouette value 0.5 at k= 4 (see Figure 1). Then the optimal number of clusters for the clustering solutions of K-means is estimated to be 4, where the Silhouette value is the largest for K-mean. The optimal clustering solution by K-means is obtained by repeating the clustering 10 times and returning the solution with the minimum mean-square-error.

3.2   Z-Score Validation

The ClusterJudge tool [13] can evaluate clusterings by calculating correlation with functional annotations in the Gene Ontology (GO) database. This tool computes a z-score; higher z-scores indicate superior clustering. We used the tool to evaluate the results of k-means clustering (k=4) on Dataset 2 using different similarity measures. Table 2 lists the mean z-scores over 10 runs. We see from the table that Pearson and PWCTM performed best.

The result of k-means clustering using PWCTM and Pearson's correlation for Dataset 2 with k=4, taking the best of 50 repetitions of the algorithm are illustrated in Fig. 2 and 3 and for Dataset 3 is reported in Fig. 4 and 5.

3.3   P-Value

In order to give the biological relevance of our work we have used the statistical analysis tool FuncAssociate [14] tool to find out the p-values. The functional enrichment of each GO category in each of the clusters is calculated by its p-value.

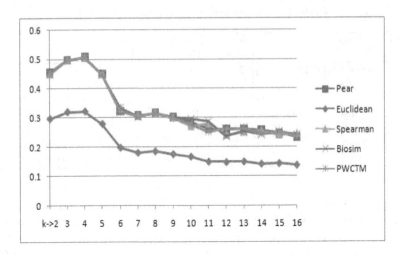

Fig. 1. Performance comparison among various proximity measures based on Silhouette index and using k-means clustering over Dataset 2 for k=2 to 16. The vertical axes represents the Silhouette values and the horizontal axes represents the k values. More the Silhouette value better is the clustering. At k=4, the Silhouette value is maximum. (Pear refers to Pearson's correlation).

Table 2. Comparative Z-scores of k-means clustering using various proximity measures for k=10 over Dataset 2

Similarity/Distance measure	z-score
Euclidean distance	7.29
Biosim	8.02
Spearman's rank correlation	8.23
Pearson correlation coefficient	8.26
PWCTM	**8.82**

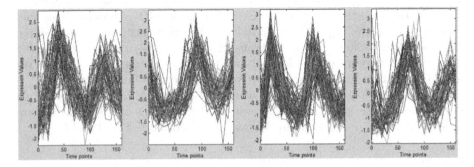

Fig. 2. The clusters detected using k-means with PWCTM as the similarity measure for k=4 for Dataset 2. The vertical axes denotes expression values of the genes and horizontal axes denotes the seventeen time points during the yeast cell cycle dataset.

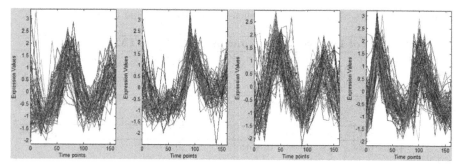

Fig. 3. The clusters detected using k-means with Pearson correlation as the similarity measure for k=4 for Dataset 2. The vertical axes denotes expression values of the genes and horizontal axes denotes the seventeen time points during the yeast cell cycle dataset.

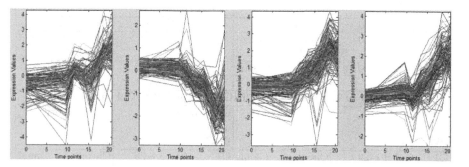

Fig. 4. The clusters detected using k-means with PWCTM as the similarity measure for Dataset 3 at k=4. The vertical axes denotes expression values of the genes and horizontal axes denotes the seven time points during the diauxic shift.

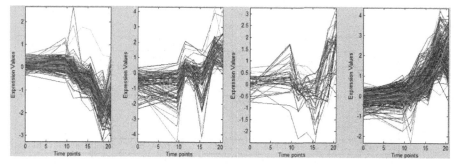

Fig. 5. The clusters detected using k-means with PCC as the similarity measure for Dataset 3 at k=4. The vertical axes denotes expression values of the genes and horizontal axes denotes the seven time points during the diauxic shift.

Table 3. P-values of Dataset 2 for k-means and CLICK using PWCTM and PCC

P-values of Dataset 2 for k-means using PWCTM and PCC					
Clusters using PWCTM	P-value	GO category	Clusters using PCC	P-value	GO category
C1	3.6 e-31	MCM complex	C1	7.0 e-28	Chromosomal part
	8.2 e-31	Cell cycle		7.3 e-28	Cell cycle process
	3.09 e-24	S phase mitotic cycle		5.0 e-23	Cell cycle
	5.3 e-24	S phase		9.7 e-23	Nuclear chromosomal part
	2.5 e-22	Cell cycle phase		1.0 e-20	DNA metabolic process
C2	1.2 e-12	Cell cycle process	C2	4.3 e-13	Cell cycle
	5.6 e-11	Chromos omal part		7.5 e-11	Cellular bud neck
	5.5 e-10	Cell cycle		1.8 e-9	MCM complex
	5.5 e-10	Nuclear chromosomal part		3.2 e-9	Site of polarized growth
	9.6 e-10	DNA metabolic process		1.139 e-8	Cell cycle process
P-values of Dataset 2 for CLICK using PWCTM and PCC					
Clusters using PWCTM	P-value	GO category	Clusters using PCC	P-value	GO category
C1	3.1 e-29	Chromo some part DNA Metabolic process	C1	8.63 e-26	Chromos omal part
	2.3 e-25	Cell cycle process		5.92 e-24	DNA Metabolic process
	1.4 e-22	Nuclear chromosome part		6.43 e-21	Cell cycle process
	8.5 e-21	DNA Metabolic process		1.90 e-20	DNA repair
	1.7 e-19	DNA repair		3.71 e-20	DNA Replication
C2	6.2 e-15	Cell cycle	C2	1.95 e-11	Cell cycle
	1.8 e-13	chromo some segregation		8.66 e-10	NCN Complex
	3.2 e-13	Mitotic Sister chromatid segregation		1.57 e-8	Cell cycle phase
	1.7 e-12	Cell division		2.67 e-8	Cellular bud neck
	3.6 e-12	Sister chromatid segregation		2.99 e-8	Cell cycle process
	3.3 e-12	Cell cycle process		6.38 e-8	S phase of mitotic cell cycle

Lower the p-value better is the clustering. The enriched functional categories for two of the clusters obtained by k-means algorithm using PWCTM and Pearson's correlation (PCC) measures on Dataset 2 are listed in Table 3. We report functional categories with p-values $< e - 18$ for cluster 1 and p-value $< e - 07$ for cluster 2 in order to restrict the size of the article. The values shown in Table 3 indicate that the genes categorized in the corresponding clusters through this algorithm are biologically significant in the respective clusters due to their low p-values. From the table, we see that PWCTM gave better result than Pearson correlation coefficient, most of the times. In cluster C1 we see that our PWCTM obtained as higher p-value of 3.6 e-31 for the highly enriched functional category of MCM complex while using PCC this same GO category had a p-value of 1.8 e-9 in C2. The lowest p-value obtained by k-means with PCC is 7.0 e-28 for GO category Chromosomal part.

Further experimentation of our measure was done using another clustering algorithm, CLICK [10]. Table 3 also reports the p-values when CLICK algorithm was used with PWCTM and PCC as the similarity measure. We see that CLICK using our PWCTM obtained a higher enrichment of functional categories in comparison with PCC. The lowest p-value of our PWCTM being 3.1 e-29 of GO category Chromosome part DNA Metabolic process and for PCC the lowest p-value is 8.6 e-26 for GO category Chromosomal part. In cluster c2, we see that for the GO category Cell cycle the p-value obtained by our measure is 6.2 e-15 and for PCC it is 1.9 e-11. We would again like to mention that the results have been truncated to restrict the size of the paper. The values shown in Table 3 indicates that the genes categorized in the corresponding clusters through the algorithms with PWCTM as the similarity measure are biologically significant in the respective clusters due to their low p-values.

4   Conclusion

This paper presents a similarity measure for clustering gene expression time series data. The similarity measure gives the shapes of the patterns of the gene expression data and is less susceptible to outliers as we are using the pairwise changing tendency measure of every pair of conditions. We have experimented our measure with k-means clustering technique and compared it with the widely used Euclidean distance, Pearson's correlation, Spearman's correlation and BioSim measures in terms of Silhouette index, z-score and p-value. Our experimental results show that the clusters obtained by PWCTM are of better quality than those obtained by Euclidean distance, Spearman's correlation and BioSim measures in terms of Silhouette index, z-score and p-value. Pearson's correlation however shows better result in Silhouette index but it is susceptible to outliers. Moreover in terms of biological relevance PWCTM showed a better clustering. Biosim measure as well as our PWCTM measure neglects the significance of the pattern for very high deviations. However, both measures localizes the computation by computing the value between a gene pair by unit time steps. Also PWCTM tries to find the relation between various time steps which is not there in BioSim. A variant of PWCTM can be developed incorporating the varying degrees of deviations in the patterns.

References

1. Sarmah, R.: Gene Expression Data Clustering using a Fuzzy Link based Approach. International Journal of Computer Information Systems and Industrial Management 5, 532–541 (2013) ISSN No. 2150-7988
2. Das, R., Bhattacharyya, D.K., Kalita, J.K.: A new approach for clustering gene expression time series data. International Journal of Bioinformatics Reasearch and Applications 5(3), 310–328 (2009)
3. Das, R., Bhattacharyya, D.K., Kalita, J.K.: Clustering Gene Expression Data using an Effective Dissimilarity Measure. International Journal of Computational BioScience (Special Issue) 1(1), 55–68 (2010)
4. Choudhury, N., Sarmah, R., Sarma, S.: A Modified QT-Clustering Algorithm over Gene Expression Data. In: Proc. of International Conference on Recent Advances in Information Technology, pp. 542–547 (2012) ISBN: 978-1-4577-0694-3
5. Sarmah, S., Bhattacharyya, D.K.: An Effective Technique for Clustering Incremental Gene Expression data. International Journal of Computer Science Issues 7(3) (2010)
6. Stekel, D.: Microarray Bioinformatics. Cambridge University Press, Cambridge (2003)
7. Jiang, D., Tang, C., Zhang, A.: Cluster Analysis for Gene Expression Data: A Survey (2003),
   http://www.cse.buffalo.edu/DBGROUP/bioinformatics/papers/survey.pdf
   (accessed April 2008)
8. Bandyopadhyay, S., Bhattacharyya, M.: A Biologically Inspired Measure for Coexpression Analysis. IEEE/ACM Transactions on Computational Biology and Bioinformatics 8(4) (2011)
9. Wang, K., Wang, B., Peng, L.: CVAP: Validation for Cluster Analyses. Data Science Journal 8, 88–93 (2009)
10. Sharan, R., Shamir, R.: CLICK: A clustering algorithm with applications to gene expression analysis. In: Proc. of Eighth Int. Conf. on Intelligent Systems for Molecular Biology. AAAI Press (2000)
11. Cho, R.J., Campbell, M., Winzeler, E., Steinmetz, L., et al.: A genome-wide transcriptional analysis of the mitotic cell cycle. Mol. Cell 2(1), 65–73 (1998)
12. Iyer, V.R., DeRisi, J.L., Brown, P.O.: Exploring the metabolic and genetic control of gene expression on a genomic scale. Science 24, 278(5338), 680–686 (1997)
13. Gibbons, F.D., Roth, F.P.: udging the Quality of Gene Expression-Based Clustering Methods Using Gene Annotation. Genome Research 12, 1574–1581 (2002)
14. Berriz, F.G., et al.: Characterizing gene sets with funcassociate. Bioinformatics 19, 2502–2504 (2003)

A Huffman Code Based Image Steganography Technique

Amitava Nag[1], Jyoti Prakash Singh[2], Sushanta Biswas[3], Debasree Sarkar[3],
and Partha Pratim Sarkar[3]

[1] Academy of Technology, West Bengal, India
[2] National Institute of Technology, Patna, Bihar, India
[3] University of Kalyani, West Bengal, India

Abstract. We present here a novel steganographic method based on
Huffman coding and the least significant bit substitution in order to
provide high embedding capacity, a strong security and imperceptible
visual quality to secret message. Every eight bits of the secret image
are first encoded by building a Huffman tree. After that those encoded
bits of secret image are divided into 4 groups. Each part has a decimal
value between 0 to 3. These decimal values determine the location where
to embed the message in a particular pixel of cover image. To embed
the message we just put a one in the corresponding location in a pixel
of the cover image which identified by the decimal values of the secret
image. Since Huffman Table reduces the size of the original image, an
attacker cannot easily recover from the stego image those fine details of
the original image that would enable him to mount a reliable attack. We
have got comparable visual quality as the Peak Signal to Noise Ratio
values lie between 30 dB to 31 dB.

Keywords: Steganography, Huffman Code, LSB Technique, Information Hiding, Image Processing.

1 Introduction

The internet has proved to be an excellent distribution system for the digital
media because of its inexpensiveness and efficiency. Due to widespread use of internet, the sharing and transmission of images in digital form has become quite
easy. However, the transmitted data can be very easily copied or modified by
unauthorized persons in cyberspace. Therefore, finding ways to transmit data
secretly through internet has become an important issue. Encryption is a one of
the ancient way to provide a safe way by transforming data into a cipher text via
cipher algorithms. Encryption techniques scrambles the message so that it cannot be understood by unauthorized users. However, this can naturally raise the
curiosity level of an eavesdropper. It would be rather more prudence if the secret
message is cleverly embedded in another media such that the secret message is
concealed to everyone. This idea forms the basis for steganography [1], which is
a branch of information hiding by camouflaging secret information within other

P. Gupta and C. Zaroliagis (Eds.): ICAA 2014, LNCS 8321, pp. 257–265, 2014.
© Springer International Publishing Switzerland 2014

information. The word steganography in Greek means "covered writing" [1]. In context of steganography, a message represents the information that can be embedded into a bit stream. The cover medium is an image, video, or audio signal that conceals the message. The stego-medium is the result of embedding the message in cover-medium. Images provide excellent carriers for hidden information. Many different techniques have been introduced to embed messages in images [1]. The most common approaches for message hiding in images are Least Significant Bit (LSB) modification, frequency domain techniques [2,3] and spread spectrum techniques. An extensive recent survey of steganography is given in [1].

In this article, we have proposed a novel steganographic procedure based on Huffman code and LSB replacement. Instead of substituting the exact message in the cover image, we encode the secret message based on their weight and put on or off some bits of pixel of the cover image. We also encode the message using Huffman coding prior to embedding the message. Due to this encoding, even if someone detects and retrieves the message from the stego image, he or she gets an encoded version of the message. The decoding can be done by parties who hold the correct Huffman Table.

The rest of the article is organized as follows. In section 2, we briefly discuss the related work done in the area of LSB substitution steganography. We present our proposed algorithm of encoding and steganography in section 3. Section 4 presents our the experimental results and security analysis. We conclude the paper in Section 5 pointing to some future directions.

2   Related Works

By far the most popular and frequently used steganographic method is the LSB embedding. It works by embedding message bits in the LSBs of sequentially or randomly selected pixels. The selection of pixels depends upon the secret stego key shared by the communicating parties. The popularity of the LSB embedding is due to its simplicity. The LSB substitution embeds secret data by replacing k LSBs of a pixel with k secret bits directly [4]. Mathematically, the pixel value $c_{i,j}$ of the chosen pixel of cover image for storing the k-bit message $m_{i,j}$ is modified to form the stego-pixel $s_{i,j}$ as follows:

$$s_{i,j} = c_{i,j} - c_{i,j} \odot 2^k + m_{i,j} \tag{1}$$

where $\odot$ represent modulus operation. Many optimized LSB methods have been proposed to improve this work [5]. The human visual system has a property that it is sensitive to some changes in the pixels of the smooth areas, while it is not sensitive to changes in the edge areas. Not all pixels in a cover image can tolerate equal amount of changes without causing noticeable distortion. Hence, to improve the quality of stego images, several adaptive methods have been proposed in which the amount of bits to be embedded in each pixel is variable [6,7]. In 2003, Wu and Tsai proposed a novel steganographic method that uses the difference value between two neighboring pixels to determine how many secret bits should be embedded [8]. Chang and Tseng proposed a side match approach to embed secret data, where the number of bits to be embedded in a pixel is decided by the difference between the pixel and its upper and left side pixels [9]. In 2005, Wu et al. presented a novel steganographic method, which combined pixel-value differencing and LSB substitution [6]. Park et al. proposed a new method based on the difference value between two pixels adjacent to the target pixel [7]. In 2008, Wang et al. presented a steganographic method that utilizes the remainder of two consecutive pixels to record the information of secret data [10]. Yang et al. proposed an adaptive LSB steganographic method using the difference value of two consecutive pixels to distinguish between edge areas and smooth areas [11]. All pixels are embedded by the k-bit modified LSB substitution method, where k is decided by the range which the difference value belongs to [11]. Liao et. al. [12] proposed a steganographic method based on four-pixel differencing and modified LSB substitution to improve the embedding capacity. A Nag et al. used transform domain technique along with Huffman coding for image steganography. In [2], they used discrete cosine transform and in [3], discrete wavelet transform to achieve quite better results in terms of security and visual quality.

3 Proposed Steganography Algorithm

Through out the article, the following notations are used.

◇ C represents a cover image with $c_{i,j}$ representing the value at location (i, j) of that image.

◇ B represents a block of the cover image with $B_{l,k}$ representing the block number (l, k)

◇ M represent the message with $m_{i,j}$ representing the value at location (i, j) of that message.

◇ F represent the Huffman encoded message with f_i representing the 8-bit value at location (i) of that encoded message.

◇ S represent the stego image with $s_{i,j}$ representing the value at location (i, j) of that stego image.

◇ F' represent the encoded recovered message with f'_i representing the 8-bit value at location (i) of that message.

◇ M' represent the recovered message with $m'_{i,j}$ representing the value at location (i, j) of that message.

◇ B' represents a block of the stego image with $b'_{l,k}$ representing the block number (l, k).

Our steganography procedure consists of two phases. In first phase, we encode the message using Huffman coding [13,14]. Huffman codes are optimal codes that map one symbol to one code word. For an image Huffman coding assigns a binary code to each intensity value of the image. To apply the Huffman coding a 2-D image with size $h \times w$ is converted to a 1-D bits stream with length

$L_H \leq h \times w$. A Huffman Table is build based on the encoding of the given bit stream. The same Huffman Table is needed to get back the original bit stream from encoded bit stream. Huffman encoding performs a lossless compression on the secret image which reduces the size of that image. Host image can now embed more encoded secret data as Huffman encoding decreases the size of secret image. It also provides extra security to the secret message by means of encoding because Huffman encoded bit stream cannot reveals anything. To get back the original secret image, one needs to decode the Huffman encoded bit stream using the same Huffman Table which was used for encoding. It provides one type of authentication as a single change in bit stream i.e. any tempering with the message will make it unrecoverable as Huffman Table is unable to decode message even with a single bit error. The Huffman Table is encrypted with RSA algorithm [15] using 1024 bits sized key. The key size is taken as 1024 as a 1024-bit key using asymmetric RSA is considered approximately equal in security to an 80-bit key in a symmetric algorithm like DES [16]. The 4 LSBs of the cover image is used to embed the Huffman encoded secret message. In order to do that 4 LSBs of the cover image is replaced with 0 by performing the operation.

$$c_{i,j} = c_{i,j} - c_{i,j} \odot 2^4 \qquad (2)$$

where $c_{i,j}$ represents the $(i,j)^{th}$ pixel of the cover image and $\odot$ represent modulus operation. The encoded secret message F is concatenation of the length of encoded message L_H, the encoded message H, the length of Huffman Table L_{T^e}, and the RSA encrypted Huffman Table T^e. The final encoded message F is then divided into $\frac{L_F}{8} + 3$ blocks of 8 bit each. Each blocks of 8-bit are further divided into 4 groups of 2 bit each. The decimal value of each group decides the location where to put the message in the cover image. The the cover image is also divided into blocks of 4 pixels to embed the encoded secret message. Depending on the value of each group of pixel in encoded secret message F, a 1 is put in corresponding pixel of the block of the cover image. The mapping of 4 groups of secret message to 4 blocks of cover image is explained with an block. An example of of a 2×2 block of a cover image is given in Table 1.

Table 1. A 2×2 block of the cover image

10100110	11100011
00111111	10110111

We replace the 4-LSB of each pixel of this block with zero by performing equation 2. The resulting resulting block with four least significant bits put to zero is given in Table 2. If a 8-bit group of encoded secret message F is 10010011, then they are divided into 4 groups as 10, 01, 00 and 11. For bit group 10, the decimal value is 2. We put a 1 in 2nd position of pixel (1,1) of given block. Similarly, for group 2, 3 and 4, we put 1 in 1st position of pixel (1,2), 1 in 0th position of pixel (2,1) and 1 in 3rd position of pixel (2,2) respectively. The block after the changed pixels values are shown in Table 3 with changed bit are underlined.

Table 2. A 2×2 block of the cover image with 4-LSB replaced by 0's

10100000	11100000
00110000	10110000

Table 3. A block of the cover image after insertion of secret image

10100<u>1</u>00	111000<u>1</u>0
0011000<u>1</u>	1011<u>1</u>000

During extraction, 1 in 2nd location of pixel (1,1) gives 10, 1 in 1st location of pixel (1,2) gives 01, 1 in 0th location of pixel (2,2) gives 00 and 1 in 3rd location of pixel (2,2) gives 11. When these values are put in order, they form the bit patterns 10010011 of recovered image.

The complete process of obtaining the stego image from secret and cover images is given in detail in algorithm 1.

3.1   The Embedding Algorithm

Algorithm 1:The embedding algorithm
Input: A gray-level cover image C of size $h \times w$, a 8 bit gray-level secret image M of size $\frac{h}{2} \times \frac{w}{2}$ and a private keys K.
Output: An stego image of size $h \times w$
Steps

1. for each pixel $c_{i,j}$ of cover image C
   (a) perform $c_{i,j} = c_{i,j} - c_{i,j}\%2^4$
2. Obtain Huffman Table T of the secret message/image M.
3. Find the Huffman encoded binary bit stream H of secret message/image M using Huffman Table obtained in step 2.
4. Encrypt the Huffman Table T using RSA algorithm using private key K.
5. Calculate the length L_H and L_T of the encoded bit stream H and encrypted Huffman Table T^e respectively in bits (16 bit representation)
6. The final message F to be embedded is $L_H + H + L_{T^e} + T^e$ where + represents concatenation.
7. Divide binary bit stream F into 8 bit sequence from $0 \cdots \frac{L_F}{8} + 3$ where L_F represents length of final message
8. Decompose C into $\frac{h}{2} \times \frac{w}{2}$ number of 2×2 blocks
9. if($\frac{L_F}{8} < \frac{h}{2} \times \frac{w}{2}$)
10. For each 8 bit value f_i of F do
    (a) Divide 8 bit value f_i as follows
       $(b_7 b_6)_3 (b_5 b_4)_2 (b_3 b_2)_1 (b_1 b_0)_0$.
    (b) place a 1 at $(b_7 b_6)_3^{th}$ location in pixel (1,1) of $B_{i,j}$ block
    (c) place a 1 at $(b_5 b_4)_2^{th}$ location in pixel (1,2) of $B_{i,j}$ block

(d) place a 1 at $(b_3 b_2)_1^{th}$ location in pixel (2,1) of $B_{i,j}$ block
(e) place a 1 at $(b_1 b_0)_0^{th}$ location in pixel (2,2) of $B_{i,j}$ block
11. else
12. The secret size exceed cover image.
13. END.

The extraction algorithm works in the reverse way by first making the recovered secret image F' which includes the length of encoded message L_H, the encoded message H, the length of Huffman Table L_{T^e}, and the RSA encrypted Huffman Table T^e. The extraction process divides the stego image into blocks of 2×2. All 4 pixels of a block is read to get a pixel for recovered secret image F'. From recovered secret message, the encoded message H and RSA encrypted Huffman Table T^e is extracted to proceed further. The RSA encrypted Huffman Table T^e is decrypted to get actual Huffman Table T. The Huffman Table T is then used to decode the secret message H yielding M. The complete process of recovering the secret image is given in algorithm 2.

3.2   The Extracting Algorithm

Algorithm 2:The extracting algorithm
Input: An stego image S of size $h \times w$ and one public key K'
Output: The recovered image M' of size $\frac{h}{2} \times \frac{w}{2}$
Steps

1. Decompose stego image S into $\frac{h}{2} \times \frac{w}{2}$ number of 2×2 blocks
2. For each block $B'_{i,j}$ of the stego image S do
   (a) Read the 4 LSB of each pixel of block $B'_{i,j}$
   (b) For 1 in location L_i of pixel (1,1), write $(b_7 b_6)$ binary equivalent of location L_i.
   (c) For 1 in location L_i of pixel (1,2), write $(b_5 b_4)$ binary equivalent of location L_i.
   (d) For 1 in location L_i of pixel (2,1), write $(b_3 b_2)$ binary equivalent of location L_i.
   (e) For 1 in location L_i of pixel (2,2), write $(b_1 b_0)$ binary equivalent of location L_i.
   (f) write $(b_7 b_6)(b_5 b_4)(b_3 b_2)(b_1 b_0)$ into pixel f'_i of recovered encrypted secret image F'.
3. Extract first two 8-bit block to determine the length L_H of encoded secret messageF'
4. Extract block number $\frac{L_F}{8}, \frac{L_F}{8} + 1$ to determine the length L_{T^e} of Huffman Table T
5. Read block numbers $\frac{L_F}{8} + 2 \cdots \frac{L_F}{8} + L_T + 2$ to get encrypted Huffman Table.
6. Decrypt the RSA encoded Huffman Table T^e using public key K' to get Huffman Table T
7. Read block numbers $2 \cdots \frac{L_F}{8} - 1$ to get the Huffman coded message.
8. Decode the Huffman encoded message H using the Huffman Table recovered in step 6 to get the actual secret M.
9. END

4   Experimental Results

In this Section, some experimental results are given to show the effectiveness of our proposed method. Experimentation is done for several images as cover and secret images. For illustration purpose, we are going to show the result obtained by Lena image only. We have selected 256×256 gray level Lena image as the host image which is shown in Fig. 2. The secret image F is a visually recognizable 8-bit gray level image of "Ship" of size 128×128 is shown in Fig. 1. The stego image generated by embedding the encoded secret image F shown in Fig. 3. The criterion for the visual quality of the output images is the peak-signal-to-noise ratio (PSNR) which is defined as

$$PSNR = 10 \times log \frac{255^2}{MSE} \tag{3}$$

where

$$MSE = \frac{1}{M \times N} \sum_{i=1}^{M} \sum_{j=1}^{N} (h_{i,j} - h'_{i,j})^2, \tag{4}$$

where $h_{i,j}$ is the pixel value of the original image and the $h'_{i,j}$ is the pixel value of the recovered image. MSE is the Mean Squared Error.

Fig. 1. The secret image

The larger PSNR indicates that the difference between the cover image and the stego image is very small and this is what is desirable by steganographic algorithms. We have got PSNR value of 30 dB or more for all test images. The PSNR values for different images are shown in Table 4. The PSNR values as well as the visual appearance of the stego image shown in Fig. 3 suggests that the distortion level in our stego image is very less and insensitivity to human eye. Our method improves the embedding capacity by compressing the secret image and provides strong security to the message. We have also got a very good visual quality of stego image. Since, we do not store the actual data from the secret message which makes it robust to steganalysis. Even if attackers are able to know that LSB techniques are used, normal LSB steganalysis will not suffice to get the secret image from cover image. Even if an attackers recovers the secret image by using some improved steganalysis method, what he will get

Fig. 2. The cover image   **Fig. 3.** The stego image

Table 4. Capacity and PSNR for different Images

Images	Size of cover image	Capacity of embedding	PSNR
Name	Pixel	Pixel	dB
Lena	256	128	30.48
Baboon	256	128	30.28
Airplane	256	128	30.91
Boat	256	128	30.36

will be an encoded message which will be useless to them. The attacker needs to find out the public key and Huffman Table in order to decrypt that message and get the actual content.

5   Conclusion

In this paper, we have proposed a novel steganographic method based on Huffman code and location based LSB substitution. Secret data are encoded into each pixel of cover image by 4-bit LSB modification method. We do not embed the actual data instead we change the bit values of certain position in LSB of the cover image. Along with this encoding, we also perform encoding of the secret message using Huffman code which makes it more secure than existing steganographic techniques. Experiments show that the stego-image of our method are almost identical to the cover image. The stego image generated by our method has got just one 1 in 4 LSB of the stego image which can be a point of attack by steganalyzers. The authors are currently engaged into finding ways to mitigate this limitation and make a more robust signature free stego image.

References

1. Cheddad, A., Condell, J., Curran, K., McKevitt, P.: Digital image steganography: Survey and analysis of current methods. Signal Processing 90, 727–752 (2010)
2. Nag, A., Biswas, S., Sarkar, D., Sarkar, P.P.: A novel technique for image steganography based on block-DCT and Huffman encoding. International Journal of Computer Science and Information Technology 2(3), 103–111 (2010)
3. Nag, A., Biswas, S., Sarkar, D., Sarkar, P.P.: A novel technique for image steganography based on DWT and Huffman encoding. International Journal of Computer Science and Security 4(5), 561–570 (2010)
4. Bender, D.W., Gruhl, N.M., Lu, A.: Techniques for data hiding. IBM Systems Journal 35, 313–316 (1996)
5. Wang, R.Z., Lin, C.F., Lin, J.C.: Image hiding by optimal LSB substitution and genetic algorithm. Pattern Recognition 34(3), 671–683 (2001)
6. Wu, H.C., Wu, N.I., Tsai, C.S., Hwang, M.S.: Image steganographic scheme based on pixel-value differencing and lsb replacement methods. Images Signal Processing 152(5), 611–615 (2005)
7. Park, Y.-R., Kang, H.-H., Shin, S.-U., Kwon, K.-R.: A steganographic scheme in digital images using information of neighboring pixels. In: Wang, L., Chen, K., Ong, Y.S. (eds.) ICNC 2005. LNCS, vol. 3612, pp. 962–967. Springer, Heidelberg (2005)
8. Wu, D.C., Tsai, W.H.: A steganographic method for images by pixel-value differencing. Pattern Recognition Letters 24(9-10), 1613–1626 (2003)
9. Chang, C.C., Tseng, H.W.: A steganographic method for digital images using side match. Pattern Recognition Letters 25(12), 1431–1437 (2004)
10. Wang, C.-M., Wu, N.-I., Tsai, C.-S., Hwang, M.-S.: A high quality steganographic method with pixel-value differencing and modulus function. Journal of System Software 81, 150–158 (2008)
11. Yang, C.-H., Weng, C.-Y., Wang, S.-J., Sun, H.-M.: Adaptive data hiding in edge areas of images with spatial LSB domain systems. IEEE Transactions on Information Forensics and Security 3(3), 488–497 (2008)
12. Liao, X., Wen, Q.-Y., Zhang, J.: A steganographic method for digital images with four-pixel differencing and modified lsb substitution. Journal Visual Communication and Image Representation 22, 1–8 (2011)
13. McIntyre, D.R., Pechura, M.A.: Data compression using static Huffman code-decode tables. Communications of ACM 28, 612–616 (1985)
14. Jeong, J.C., Jo, J.M.: Adaptive huffman coding of 2-d dct coefficients for image sequence compression. SP:IC 7(1), 1–11 (1995)
15. Rivest, R., Shamir, A., Adleman, L.: A method for obtaining digital signatures and public-key crypto-systems. Communications of the ACM 21(2), 120–126 (1978)
16. Stallings, W.: Cryptography and Network Security: Principles and Practices, 4th edn. Pearson Education Pvt. Ltd., India (2004)

Expression-Invariant 3D Face Recognition Using K-SVD Method

Somsukla Maiti[1,2], Dhiraj Sangwan[2], and Jagdish Lal Raheja[1,2]

[1] Academy of Scientific and Innovative Research
[2] CSIR-Central Electronics Engineering Research Institute, Pilani, Rajasthan, India
somsuklamaiti@gmail.com,
{dhiraj,jagdish}@ceeri.ernet.in

Abstract. This paper proposes a method to perform expression invariant face recognition using dictionary learning approach. The proposed method performs the operation in the following stages: the T-region extraction from the face to get the facial region having minimum variation with expression, determination of the wavelet coefficients of the extracted region, dictionary learning using K-SVD and matching. The experiment has been performed on a database that contains 40 persons with 9 expressions each under different illumination conditions. The recognition performed has shown a good accuracy rate as compared to the mostly used PCA-SVM approach. Our system uses label-consistent K-SVD algorithm for dictionary learning to learn a set of dictionaries that represents 3D information of the face. This method fulfills the purpose of sparse coding and classification.

Keywords: Label-Consistent KSVD, Sparse Coding, Expression Invariant, T-Region, Dictionary Learning.

1 Introduction

Most of the recent security issues have brought up the attention of mankind about the serious drawbacks in most of the sophisticated security systems. To solve these issues, the security systems are heading towards the use of biometric technologies for verification and identification of individuals. Biometrics refers to the identification of humans by their physical traits. The biometric system, in general, processes the raw data captured from camera, scanner, RFID Tag etc. Certain features are then extracted from the data followed by the extraction of templates which are easier to process and store, but carries most of the important information needed about the person. There are several biometric traits that are used commonly for the recognition of individuals. Face recognition is one of the most acceptable and popular method, as it is a good tradeoff between reliability and social acceptance due to its non-intrusive nature; and balances security and privacy at the same time [1]. However, the face recognition suffers from some significant challenges due to variations in illumination, viewing angle, facial expressions, occlusion, and changes over time, etc.

P. Gupta and C. Zaroliagis (Eds.): ICAA 2014, LNCS 8321, pp. 266–276, 2014.

In the past two decades, most of the works were focused on 2D facial images. But the current 2D face recognition systems are greatly affected by differences in pose, illumination, expressions, and other characteristics that can vary between the captures of a human face. This issue becomes more significant when the subject has incentives of not to be recognized. There are very few 2D algorithms which handle variations in pose and illumination. There exists Principal Component Analysis (PCA), Linear Discriminant Analysis (LDA) and Independent Component Analysis (ICA) based algorithms for 2D face recognition. All these statistical methods do not consider the effects of facial expressions and very large variations in pose.

To achieve significantly higher accuracy 3D face recognition methods have been adopted. The 3D facial data can provide a promising way to understand the feature of the human face in 3D space and has potential possibility to improve the performance of the system. There are some distinct advantages in using 3D information: sufficient geometrical information, invariance of measured features relative to transformation and capture process by laser scanners being immune to illumination variation.

Several studies have been performed in 3D face recognition. Early face recognition algorithms advocated the invariant approach by finding a set of fiducial points such as eyes, nose, mouth, etc. and comparing their geometric relations (feature-based recognition) or comparing the face with a whole facial template (template-based recognition). Xu et al suggested an automatic face recognition method combining the global geometric features with the local shape variation information of the face [2]. The method represents the face using a scattered 3D point cloud with a regular mesh by using the hierarchical mesh fitting. For the purpose of recognition, the mesh data and the shape information had been passed to dimensionality reduction chamber using principal component analysis (PCA) [3, 4] to obtain a lower-dimensional vector followed by nearest neighbor classifier (NN) for classification. The method does not provide a good degree of accuracy in recognition and the parameters varies drastically with the different sets of faces. Another approach of 3D face recognition was suggested by Bronstein et al that concentrated on the computation of the geodesic distances over the facial surfaces, given only the metric tensor of the surface [5]. To determine the face features the method of Fast Marching (FMM) had been used. The method though provides a good result, but leads to lot of computations to be performed in finding the geodesic distances over individual face surfaces.

The expression and pose invariant face recognition has captured the major atten-tion in the recent researches of face recognition. This is to provide more robustness to the system and to make it view independent. The 3D model-based pose invariant face recognition method estimated the pose from the face view available and then tried to adapt a 3D face model [6]. Thus the frontal view face images were synthesized using the estimated 3D models and the discriminant features were further extracted from these synthesized frontal view images. In this paper, the wavelets are used as the features and are classified using nearest feature space classifier. The algorithm provides a robust recognition and can recognize faces under variable poses with good accuracy.

Berretti et al presented a novel approach in the recent time (2010) to 3D face matching that showed high effectiveness in distinguishing the facial differences be-tween distinct individuals from differences induced by non-neutral expressions within the same individual [7]. The face is partitioned into iso-geodesic stripes that provide an approximate representation of the local morphology of faces that exhibits smooth variations for changes induced by facial expressions. The approach takes into account the geometrical information of the 3D face and encodes the relevant information in the form of a graph.

1.1 Proposed Method

The method proposed here is based on the idea of dictionary learning using the Label-Consistent KSVD. As the facial expressions have a large impact on the mouth region of the face so the T-region of the face has been extracted from the face. The T-region is least affected and contains the most important information in the face. T-region specifies the region starting from the top of the eyebrows to the nose end. The wavelets of the T-region have been calculated to find the characteristics/features of the face. The method allows memory efficient representation of the face with the maximum information content in it. The process then uses label-consistent K-SVD algorithm for dictionary learning to learn a set of dictionaries to perform sparse cod-ing and classification of the 3D information of the faces from the database.

2 Label Consistent K-SVD

The face data is obtained as high dimension large size matrix. The underlying features that can be used to recognize the face are large in number and often contain multiple correlated versions of the same feature. The relevant informa-tion about the faces is generally of much smaller dimensionality and so the first aim is to reduce the redundancy in data and get the relevant information.

Dictionary learning [8][9] is a method to determine the proper representation of data sets by means of reduced dimensionality subspaces, which are adaptive to both the characteristics of the input signals and the processing task at hand. These representations are based on the principle that our observations can be described by a sparse subset of atoms taken from a redundant dictionary that features the main difference among the faces in the database.

Let us consider $Y = y_i, i = 1, 2, \ldots\ldots, N$ as a set of n dimensional N input signals $y_i \in R_{nXN}$. Learning a reconstructive dictionary with K items for sparse representation of Y (where $N >> K$) can be accomplished by solving (1).

$$< D, X > = \arg \min_{D,X} ||Y - DX||_2^2 \text{ subject to } \forall i, ||x_i||_0 <= T_0 \qquad (1)$$

where D is the dictionary and X is the sparse code matrix that generates thye signal Y.

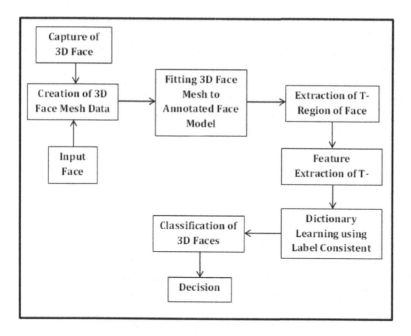

Fig. 1. Block Diagram of the Proposed Method

Jiang et al. proposed a label consistent K-SVD (LC-KSVD) method to learn a discriminative dictionary for sparse coding [10]. It is a supervised algorithm to learn a compact, reconstructive and discriminative dictionary for sparse coding. Here they introduce a label consistent constraint called discriminative sparse-code error and combine it with the reconstruction error and the classification error to form a unified objective function and then it is optimized using the KSVD algorithm. The learned dictionary provides discriminative sparse representations of signals and thus a good accuracy on object classification is achieved even with a simple multiclass linear classifier in contrast to other existing sparse coding approaches.

Each dictionary item $d_k \in D$ is so chosen that it represents a subset of the training signals ideally from a single class, so each dictionary item d_k can be associated with a particular label. Then the signals are classified and the performance of the linear classifier depends on the discriminability of the input sparse codes x. For obtaining discriminative sparse codes x with the learned dictionary D, an objective function for dictionary construction is defined in (2).

$$< D, A, X >= \arg \min_{D,A,X} ||Y - DX||_2^2 + \alpha ||Q - AX||_2^2 \qquad (2)$$

where α is the parameter that controls the relative contribution between the reconstruction (the first term) and the label consistent regularization(the second term). The term $||Y - DX||_2^2$ is the reconstruction error and the term $||Q - AX||_2^2$ represents the discriminative sparse code error and the term Q is called the label consistent matrix that enforces dictionary items from the same label as the input signals to be used in the reconstruction of such signal. It is defined as $Q = q_1, q_2, \ldots\ldots, q_N \in R_{NXK}$ those are the discriminative sparse codes of input signals Y for classification.

To make the dictionary optimal for classification, the classification error is considered as a term in the objective function as mentioned earlier. Thus the objective function for learning a dictionary D having both reconstructive and discriminative nature has been defined in (3).

$$< D, W, A, X > = \arg \min_{D,W,A,X} ||Y - DX||_2{}^2 + \alpha||Q - AX||_2{}^2 + \beta||H - WX||_2{}^2$$

$$\text{subject to } \forall i, ||x_i||_0 <= T_0$$

$$(3)$$

The term $||H - WX||_2{}^2$ represents the classification error where the matrix W represents the classifier parameter and the matrix H is defined as $H = h_1, h_2, , h_N \in R_{mXN}$ that defines class labels of the input signal Y and h_i represents a label vector corresponding to an input signal y_i and is the contribution factor.

Now if we assume the sparse codes as $X' = AX$ where the matrix $A \in R_{KXK}$ is invertible, then the modified dictionaries and modified classifier parameters are given as $D' = DA^{-1}$ and $W' = WA^{-1}$. The objective function then can be defined as (4).

$$< D', W', X' > = \arg \min_{D',W',X'} ||Y - D'X'||_2{}^2 + \alpha||Q - X'||_2{}^2 + \beta||H - W'X'||_2{}^2$$

$$\text{subject to } \forall i, ||x_i||_0 <= T_0$$

$$(4)$$

The first term $||Y - DX||_2{}^2$ in (4) represents the reconstruction error, the second term $\alpha||Q - X'||_2{}^2$ is the discriminative sparse-code error and the third term $\beta||H - W'X'||_2{}^2$ is the classification error. The second term can make the sparse codes discriminative between classes while the third term supports learning an optimal classifier.

The optimal solution for the parameters can be found by rewriting (3) in the basic solution form of the KSVD algorithm.

$$< D, W, A, X > = \arg \min_{D,W,A,X} || \begin{pmatrix} Y \\ \sqrt{\alpha}Q \\ \sqrt{\beta}H \end{pmatrix} - \begin{pmatrix} D \\ \sqrt{\alpha}A \\ \sqrt{\beta}W \end{pmatrix} X||_2{}^2$$

$$\text{subject to } \forall i, ||x_i||_0 <= T_0 \qquad (5)$$

3   Proposed Approach

The method proposed here performs the face recognition in the subsequent steps. The first step is to find the 3D mesh data for the face and then fitting the mesh data to the annotated face model to scale the faces properly. The second step is to extract the T-region of the face to obtain the portion of the face that is having the least effect of the facial expressions as well as the facial hairs. The Haar wavelet features are to be extracted subsequently to find the features of the face. The process then uses label-consistent K-SVD algorithm for dictionary learning to learn a set of redundant dictionaries to perform sparse coding to attain the goal of reduced dimensionality and classification of the 3D faces.

3.1 Fitting the Face to Annotated Face Model

The first step of the algorithm is to create the 3D mesh using the Annotated Face Model (AFM) [11]. The face image captured by the 3D sensor is considered and then it is fitted to an AFM. This creates the generation of the proper fitting of the x, y, z coordinates of the 3D face points in a same scale of the AFM for each person. The fitted 3D mesh has been shown in Fig. 2 using the interface of MeshLab. The frontal and tilted views are shown in (a) and (b) of Fig. 2 respectively.

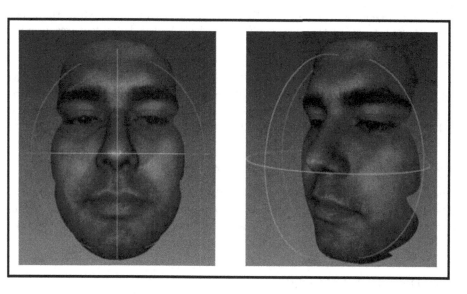

Fig. 2. 3D Face data in MeshLab

3.2 Extraction of Haar Features of Face

We need to find out T-region of the face that has been generated in Sect. 3.1. The T-region is found out by selecting a calculated region from the face. As all the faces are fitted to the same scaled AFM, so it gives only the T-region for the respective face. Fig. 3 shows the extracted T-region of the above selected face

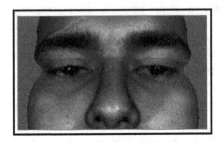

Fig. 3. T-Region of the Face

as shown in Fig. 2. The selection of the T-region removes the effect of the facial hairs, e.g. moustache and beard. It also helps in considering and processing the part of the face that is least affected by the non-neutral expressions.

3.3   Extraction of the T-Region

The Haar wavelet features of the 3D mesh are determined to reduce the space re-quirement to store the face coefficients [12]. As the Haar features provide knowledge of the vertical, horizontal and the diagonal details of the image. It provides all the required information of the face with the reduced memory requirement. The Haar features of the T-region are shown in Fig. 4, in which (a) represents the approximated version of the face image, (b) represents the horizontal details of the image, (c) repre-sents the vertical details of the image and (d) represents the diagonal details of the image.

3.4   Initialization of the Dictionaries

The dictionaries are initialized by taking the face coefficients from the database. The dictionaries are formed by taking the 9 meshes corresponding to each person and each of the rows in Fig. 5 represents a dictionary corresponding to every subject. Thus initially we are having 40 dictionaries in our hand.

3.5   Dictionary Learning

Using the method of Label consistent K-SVD, we learnt a set of dictionaries that can be used to classify the faces. The method of matching pursuit [13] has been employed in order to find out the most optimal dictionary for reconstruction in each step. The work flow of the dictionary learning has been shown in Fig. 6.

3.6   Classification of the Faces Using Label Consistent K-SVD

The face coefficients are generated by calculating the Haar wavelet transform of the test face. The learned dictionaries as obtained from the Sect. 3.5 are used

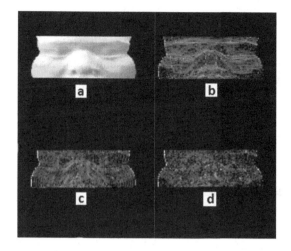

Fig. 4. Haar Wavelets of the face image

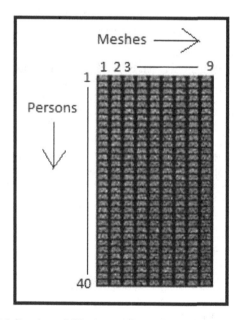

Fig. 5. Initialization of Dictionary from Extracted Face Coefficients

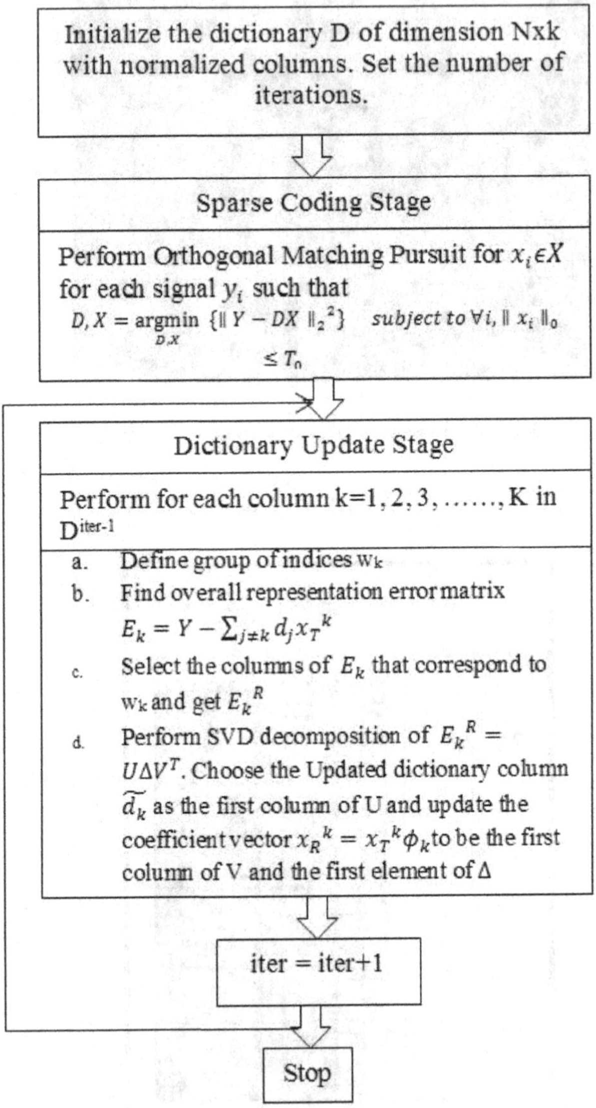

Initialize the dictionary D of dimension Nxk with normalized columns. Set the number of iterations.

Sparse Coding Stage

Perform Orthogonal Matching Pursuit for $x_i \epsilon X$ for each signal y_i such that

$$D, X = \underset{D,X}{\arg\min} \ \{\| Y - DX \|_2{}^2\} \quad subject \ to \ \forall i, \| x_i \|_0$$

$$\leq T_0$$

Dictionary Update Stage

Perform for each column k=1, 2, 3, ..., K in D^{iter-1}

a. Define group of indices w_k

b. Find overall representation error matrix
    $E_k = Y - \sum_{j \neq k} d_j x_T{}^k$

c. Select the columns of E_k that correspond to w_k and get $E_k{}^R$

d. Perform SVD decomposition of $E_k{}^R = U \Delta V^T$. Choose the Updated dictionary column $\widetilde{d_k}$ as the first column of U and update the coefficient vector $x_R{}^k = x_T{}^k \phi_k$ to be the first column of V and the first element of Δ

iter = iter+1

Stop

Fig. 6. Dictionary Learning Stage

and the classification of the test face is performed by using the Label consistent K-SVD approach. This provides the parallelization of the training of the learned dictionaries as well as the classification of the test faces.

4 Results

The result of the proposed algorithm has been compared with the PCA-SVM and the method proposed by Kakadiaris [11]. The experiment has been performed on a data-base created using 40 subjects under 11 illumination conditions. The proposed algo-rithm and its testing for the 3D face dataset has been implemented in MATLAB 2011b on a PC with 3 GB RAM. It has been found that the storage required for the dictionaries is quite small in our case, as for each dictionary we need only a few MB (5 MB approx.) of the disk space. The testing time for each of the 3D mesh is 8-10 seconds. The Table 1 shows a comparative chart of the accuracy of the different methods along with the proposed method.

Table 1. Comparison of the Proposed Method with the Existing Methods

Methods	Recognition Rate	Recognition Time	Storage
Proposed Method (LC-KSVD)	91%	8-10 sec	Very small(5 MB)
PCA-SVM	95%	28-30 sec	Large storage($\sim$ 400 MB)
Kakadiaris Method	93%	10-12 sec	Small(32 MB)

As per the results shown in Table 1, it is clear that the proposed method gives the best result in terms of the storage requirement for dictionaries. The recognition time is small (8-10 sec) as compared to the PCA-SVM (28-30 sec) and Kakadiaris method (10-12 sec).

5 Conclusion

The proposed method of expression invariant 3D face recognition gives a very prom-ising result as it performs a good optimization between the recognition rate, recognition time as well as the storage requirement of the features. The method provides good result in the cases of persons with beard or moustache as the T-region of the face is only considered for the further recognition operation. The limitation of such tech-niques is that the training of new data requires the dictionaries to be learnt from the initial stage and thus takes a lot of time to include a new data. It can be reduced by proposing a Semantic Network Model [14] using Hidden Markov model by using the factorization of state transition probabilities to reduce training requirements. The advantage of the proposed method is that it incurs less storage requirement per training input and it does not increase abruptly with the increase in the size of the database. For example if the dictionaries are being formed using the 200 faces of the database, the storage required in order to store the dictionaries is 4.8 MB whereas if the number of faces in the database is increased to 360, the storage requirement becomes 5 MB. This implies that the storage requirement increases only by 0.2 MB. Thus the proposed method gives quite a good result in terms of storage optimization whereas the storage requirement for the PCA-SVM increases in a linear fashion.

References

1. Michele, N., Riccio, D., Sabatino, G., Abate, A.F.: 2D and 3D face recognition: A survey. Pattern Recognition Letters 28(14), 1885–1906 (2007)
2. Wang, Y., Tan, T., Quan, L., Xu, C.: Automatic 3D Face Recognition Combining Global Geometric Features with Local Shape Variation Information. In: 6th IEEE Iinternational Conference on Automatic Face and Gesture Recognition, pp. 308–313. IEEE Press (2004)
3. Shah Zainudin, M.N., Radi, H.R., Muniroh Abdullah, S., Rahim, R.A., Muzafar Ismail, M., Idzdihar Idris, M., Sulaiman, H.A., Jaafar, A.: Face Recognition using Principle Com-ponent Analysis (PCA) and Linear Discriminant Analysis (LDA). International Journal of Electrical and Computer Sciences 12, 50–55 (2012)
4. Chris, B., Tanya, P., Trina, R.: 3D Face Recognition Using 3D Alignment for PCA. In: IEEE Computer Society Conference on Computer Vision and Pattern Recognition, pp. 1391–1398. IEEE Press (2006)
5. Bronstein, A.M., Bronstein, M.M., Kimmel, R.: Three-Dimensional Face Recognition. International Journal of Computer Vision 64, 5–30 (2005)
6. Jiang, Z., Lin, Z., Davis, L.S.: Learning A Discriminative Dictionary for Sparse Coding via Label Consistent K-SVD. In: IEEE Conference on Computer Vision and Pattern Recognition. IEEE Press (2011)
7. Del Bimbo, A., Pala, P., Berretti, S.: 3D Face Recognition Using Isogeodesic Stripes. IEEE Transactions on Pattern Analysis and Machine Intelligence 32, 2162–2177 (2010)
8. Zhou, Z., Zhang, H.-J., Chen, T., Huang, F.J.: Pose Invariant Face Recognition. In: 4th IEEE International Conference on Automatic Face and Gesture Recognition, p. 245. IEEE Press (2000)
9. Frossard, P., Tošić, I.: Dictionary Learning. IEEE Signal Processing Magazine, 27–38 (2011)
10. Aharon, M.: Overcomplete Dictionaries for Sparse Representation of Signals, Haifa (Novemeber 2006)
11. Passalis, G., Toderici, G., Murtuza, M.N., Lu, Y., Karam-Patziakis, N., Theoharis, T., Kakadiaris, I.A.: Three-Dimensional Face Recognition in the Presence of Facial Expressions: An Annotated Deformable Model Approach. IEEE Transactions on Pattern Analysis and Machine Intelligence 29, 640–649 (2007)
12. Perlibakas, V.: Face Recognition Using Principal Component Analysis and Wavelet Packet Decomposition. Informatica 15, 243–250 (2004)
13. Kwon, S., Shim, B., Wang, J.: Generalized Orthogonal Matching Pursuit. IEEE Transactions on Signal Processing 60, 6202–6216 (2012)
14. Rajko, S., Qian, G., Ingalls, T., James, J.: Real-time Gesture Recognition with Minimal Training Requirements and On-line Learning. In: Proc. of Computer Vision and Pattern Recognition, CVPR, pp. 1–8 (2007)

An Efficient Face Recognition Method by Fusing Spatial Discriminant Facial Features

Aniruddha Dey[1], Shiladitya Chowdhury[2], Jamuna Kanta Sing[1],
Dipak Kumar Basu[1], and Mita Nasipuri[1]

[1] Department of Computer Science & Engineering, Jadavpur University,
Kolkata, India
[2] Department of Master of Computer Application, Techno India, Kolkata, India
{anidey007,dipakkbasu}@gmail.com, {dityashila,mitanasipuri}@yahoo.com,
jksing@ieee.org

Abstract. Feature level fusion is a very well known technique for improving the performance of a face recognition system. This paper presents an approach of fusion of directional spatial discriminant features for face recognition. The key idea of the proposed method is to fuse the facial features lying along the horizontal, vertical and diagonal directions, so that this fused feature vector can contain more discriminant information than the individual facial feature of single direction only. However due to the fusion of features the size of fused feature vector becomes larger, which may increase complexity of the classifier to be used for recognition. To optimize this lower dimensional discriminant features are again extracted from this large fused feature vector. In our experiment we have applied G-2DFLD method on the original images to extract the discriminant features. Then original images are converted into diagonal images and another set of discriminant features, representing the diagonal information, are extracted by using the G-2DFLD method. The original and diagonal feature matrices are then fused to form a large feature matrix. The dimension of this large fused matrix is then further reduced by G-2DFLD method and this resultant matrix is used for classification and recognition by Radial Basis Function-Neural Networks (RBF-NN). Experiments on the *AT&T* (formally known as ORL database) face database indicate the competitive performance of the proposed method, as compared to some existing subspaces-based methods.

1 Introduction

Face recognition is one of the most challenging areas in computer vision and biometrics. There are a number of face recognition algorithms which work well in constrained environments [2]. Face recognition is still an open and very challenging problem in real applications. It has been seen that due to variability of many parameters like facial expression, pose, scale, lighting, and other environmental parameters, many problems arise in face recognition [3,4].

P. Gupta and C. Zaroliagis (Eds.): ICAA 2014, LNCS 8321, pp. 277–286, 2014.
© Springer International Publishing Switzerland 2014

The concept of data fusion has arrived with the search for practical methods of merging images from various sensors to provide a composite image which could be used to better identify of natural objects. Data fusion is a formal framework in which data originates from different sources. It aims at obtaining information of greater quality; the exact definition of "greater quality" will depend upon the application. Information from multiple sources can be consolidated in three different levels; i) feature level, ii) image level, and iii) decision level [8].

Fusion at feature level involves the integration of feature sets corresponding to multiple or same modalities. Since the feature set contains richer information about the raw biometric data than the match score or final decision, integration at this level is expected to provide better recognition results.

In this paper, we propose a fusion method of directional spatial discriminate features for face recognition. The G-2DFLD method [11] is applied on the original image matrix to extract most discriminant features representing the information along the row and column directions. A face can be recognized by human cognition system by observing only the diagonal vector of the image matrix. Therefore, diagonal vectors of an image also play an important role for providing sufficient discriminant information. To realize this, we convert the original image matrix to corresponding diagonal image matrix and G-2DFLD method is applied on this diagonal image matrix to extract discriminant features [10]. Now the feature matrix extracted from the original image and its corresponding diagonal image are fused to get a large feature matrix. To reduce the dimension of the fused feature matrix and complexity of the classifier, G-2DFLD method is applied again on the appended feature matrix. It is to be noted that we use G-2DFLD method due to its superiority over many other feature extraction methods [11]. The hidden layer neurons of the Radial Basis Function-Neural Networks (RBF-NN) have been modelled by considering intra-class discriminating characteristics of the training images. In our experiment the final feature matrices are applied on Radial Basis Function-Neural Networks (RBF-NN) for classification and recognition. The experimental results on AT& T face database [7] (formally known as ORL database) indicate the competitive performance of the proposed method as compared to some conventional methods.

The remaining part of the paper is organized as follows. Section 2 describes the G-2DFLD method for feature extraction. Our proposed method is described in section 3. The experimental results on the AT& T face database are presented in Section 4. Finally, Section 5 draws the concluding remarks.

2   Generalized Two-Dimensional FLD (G-2DFLD) Method for Feature Extraction

Generalized two-dimensional FLD (G-2DFLD) method [11] is based on two-dimensional image matrix. It maximizes class separability not only from row wise direction, but also from column wise direction simultaneously, using the following linear transformation:

$$Z = U^T X V \tag{1}$$

where, $\mathbf{X}$ is image matrix, an m*n random matrix, U and V are two projection matrices of dimensions $m*p$ ($p <= m$) and $n*q$ ($q <= n$), respectively and T denotes the transpose of a matrix. This method finds the optimal projection directions $\mathbf{U}$ and $\mathbf{V}$ so that the projected vector in the $(p*q)$ dimensional space reaches its maximum class separability.

The *image row between-class scatter matrix* G_{br} and *image row within-class scatter matrix* G_{wr} are defined as follows[11]:

$$G_{br} = \sum_{c}^{C} N_c(\mu_c - \mu)(\mu_c - \mu)^T \tag{2}$$

$$G_{wr} = \sum_{c}^{C} \sum_{i\epsilon c}^{N} N_c(X_i - \mu_c)(X_i - \mu_c)^T \tag{3}$$

The image column between-class scatter matrix Gbc and image column within-class scatter matrix Gwc are defined as follows [11]:

$$G_{bc} = \sum_{c}^{C} N_c(\mu_c - \mu)^T(\mu_c - \mu) \tag{4}$$

$$G_{wc} = \sum_{c}^{C} \sum_{i\epsilon c}^{N} N_c(X_i - \mu_c)(X_i - \mu_c)^T \tag{5}$$

where, N is the number of total training images, each one is denoted by $m*n$ image matrix X_i (i=1, 2, , N), C is the number of classes (subjects), C_c is the cth class, N_c is the number of samples in cth class, satisfying ($\sum_{c=1}^{C} N_c = N$, μ is the mean of all the training images and μ_c is the mean training image of the cth class.

The size of the scatter matrices G_{br} and G_{wr} is $m*m$, whereas, for G_{bc} and G_{wc} the size is $n*n$. The sizes of these scatter matrices are much smaller than that of the conventional FLD algorithm, whose scatter matrices are $mn*mn$ in size.

In G-2DFLD method there are two alternative Fishers criteria $J(U)$ and $J(V)$ corresponding to row and column-wise projection directions, respectively. $J(U)$ is defined as follows:

$$J(U) = \frac{|U^T G_{br} U|}{|U^T G_{wr} U|} \tag{6}$$

and $J(V)$ is defined as follows:

$$J(V) = \frac{|V^T G_{bc} V|}{|V^T G_{wc} U|} \tag{7}$$

Column vectors of the projection matrices U and V, are the eigenvectors of $G_{br} G_{wr}^{-1}$ and $G_{bc} G_{wc}^{-1}$ respectively. The optimal projection (eigenvector) matrix U_{opt} and V_{opt} are defined as follows [11]:

$$U_{opt} = \arg \max_{U} |G_{br} G_{wr}^{-1}|$$

$$= [u_1, u_2, ..., u_p] \tag{8}$$

$$V_{opt} = \arg \max_{V} |G_{bc} G_{wc}^{-1}|$$

$$= [v_1, v_2, ..., v_q] \tag{9}$$

where, $\{u_i | i = 1, 2, ..., p\}$ is the set of normalized eigenvectors of $G_{br} G_{wr}^{-1}$ corresponding to p largest eigenvalues $\{\lambda_i | i = 1, 2, ..., p\}$ and $\{v_j | j = 1, 2, ..., q\}$ is the set of normalized eigenvectors of $G_{bc} G_{wc}^{-1}$ corresponding to q largest eigenvalues $\{\alpha_j | j = 1, 2, ..., q\}$.

The optimal projection matrices U_{opt} and V_{opt} are used for feature extraction. For a given image sample X, following linear projection produces an image feature;

$$Z_{ij} = u_i^T X v_j, i = 1, 2, ..., p; j = 1, 2, ..., q \tag{10}$$

where, $z_{ij}(i = 1, 2, , p; j = 1, 2, , q)$ is known as the principal component of the sample image **X**. The principal components of the G-2DFLD method are scalar and are used to form a G-2DFLD-based image feature matrix **Z** of dimension $p*q$ ($p <= m, q <= n$). Therefore, in G-2DFLD method, an image matrix is reduced considerably not only in row wise direction, but also in column were direction simultaneously.

3 Proposed Method for Feature Extraction by Fusing Features

In this paper our proposed method is based on the feature level fusion. Feature level fusion involves the integration of feature sets corresponding to multiple or same modalities. Since the feature set contains richer information about the raw biometric data than the match score or final decision, integration at this level expected to provide better recognition results [7]. It has been observed that human cognition process can recognize a face by looking into the diagonal vectors of the image matrix. So, like row and column vectors, the diagonal vectors of an image also play an important role for providing sufficient discriminating information.

The key idea of the proposed method is to fuse the facial features lying along the horizontal, vertical and diagonal directions, so that this fused feature vector can contain more discriminant information than the individual facial feature lying along a single direction. However due to fusion the size of fused feature vector is becoming larger, which may increase complexity of the classifier.

To optimize this, lower dimensional discriminant features are again extracted from this large fused feature vector with the help of G-2DFLD method. In our experiment the G-2DFLD method [11] is applied on the original image matrix to extract most discriminant features representing the information along the row and column directions. The original image matrix is also converted to corresponding diagonal image matrix and G-2DFLD method is applied on this diagonal image matrix to extract discriminant features [10]. Now the feature matrix extracted from the original image and its corresponding diagonal image are fused to get a large feature matrix. To reduce the dimension of the fused feature matrix and complexity of the classifier, G-2DFLD method is applied again on this large fused feature matrix. This reduced feature matrix is then applied on RBF-NN for classification and recognition. Fig. 1 shows the schematic diagram of the proposed method.

Let N be the number of total training images, each one is denoted by $m*n$ image matrix X_i (i=1, 2,..., N), where usually mn and n should be odd. C be the number of classes (subjects), C_c be the cth class, and N_c be the number of samples in cth class satisfying$\sum_{c=1}^{C} N_c = N$.

Let X be an original image matrix of dimension $m*n$. G-2DFLD method is applied on the original image matrix X to produce feature matrix of dimension $p*q$, where $p < m$ and $q < n$. The original image matrix is also converted to a corresponding diagonal image matrix [10], as shown in Fig.2. To get diagonal image from an original image, the original image matrix Table 1 is scanned from the upper left-corner pixel, along the diagonals from left to right, towards the lower right-corner pixel. Place pixel(s) of the major and minor diagonals into rows of the diagonal image starting from the top row. Make sure that the pixel(s) of the minor diagonals are placed in the middle of the corresponding row as shown in Table2 . It is to be noted that the dimension of the resultant diagonal image matrix will be $(m+n-1)*MIN(m,n)$. The G-2DFLD method is also applied on the converted diagonal image matrix to produce feature matrix of the same size i.e. $p*q$.

Let Z_1 be the feature matrix of dimension $p*q$ which we get after applying G-2DFLD method on the original image matrix and Z_2 be the feature matrix of dimension $p*q$ which we get after applying G-2DFLD method on the corresponding diagonal image matrix. Let F be the feature matrix which we get after fusing the feature matrix Z_1 and Z_2. F can be defined as follows:

$$F = (Z_1, Z_2)^T \tag{11}$$

It is to be noted that the size of these fused feature matrix F will be $2p*q$. To reduce the dimension of the fused feature matrix F and complexity of the classifier, G-2DFLD method is applied again on this fused feature matrix. Let R be the resultant matrix of dimension $k*l$ which we get after applying G-2DFLD method on the fused feature matrix F, where $k < 2p$ and $l < q$. This reduced feature matrix R is then applied on Radial Basis Function-Neural Networks $(RBF$-$NN)$ for recognition and classification.

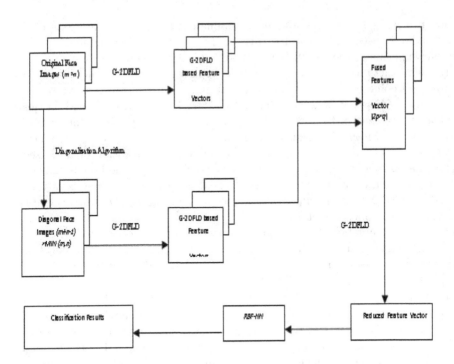

Fig. 1. Schematic diagram of the proposed method

Table 1.

A_{11}	A_{12}	A_{13}	A_{14}	A_{15}
A_{21}	A_{22}	A_{23}	A_{24}	A_{25}
A_{31}	A_{32}	A_{33}	A_{34}	A_{35}
A_{41}	A_{42}	A_{43}	A_{44}	A_{45}
A_{51}	A_{52}	A_{53}	A_{54}	A_{55}
A_{61}	A_{62}	A_{63}	A_{64}	A_{65}

4   Experimental Results

The performance of the proposed method has been evaluated on the AT & T Laboratories Cambridge database (formerly ORL database) [7]. The AT & T database contains quite a high degree of variability in lighting, facial expression (open/closed eyes, smiling/non smiling etc.), pose (upright, frontal position etc.), and facial details (glasses/no glasses). All images were taken against a dark homogeneous background with the subjects in an upright, frontal position, with tolerance for some tilting and rotation of up to 20 degree.The AT & T database contains images of 40 people (subject). Each subject has 10 images having a resolution of 112 * 92 pixels. So, the AT & T database contains total of 400

Table 2.

		A_{11}		
	A_{21}	A_{12}		
	A_{31}	A_{22}	A_{13}	
A_{41}	A_{32}	A_{23}	A_{14}	
A_{51}	A_{42}	A_{33}	A_{24}	A_{15}
A_{61}	A_{52}	A_{43}	A_{34}	A_{25}
	A_{62}	A_{53}	A_{44}	A_{35}
	A_{63}	A_{54}	A_{45}	
		A_{64}	A_{55}	
		A_{65}		

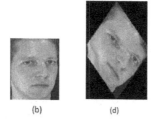

(b)   (d)

Fig. 2. Generation of diagonal image from original image. Table1 and (b): original images; Table2 and (d): resultant diagonal images corresponding to original images.

Fig. 3. Schematic diagram of the proposed method

grey-scale images. The variation in scale is up to about 10.Sample face images of a person are shown in Fig. 3.

In our experiment on the AT & T database, s images are selected randomly from each subject to form the training set and the remaining images are included in the test set. To ensure sufficient training and to test the effectiveness of the proposed method for different sizes of the training sets, we choose the value of s as $3, 4, 5, 6 and 7$. To reduce the influence of performance on the training and test sets, for each value of s, experiment is repeated 10 times with different training

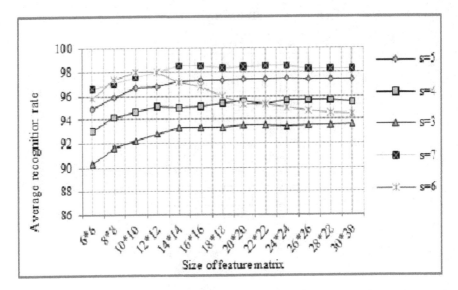

Fig. 4. Average recognition rates of the proposed method on the AT& T database for different values of s by varying the values of k and l

and test sets. Since the number of projection vectors k, l have a considerable impact on the performance of the proposed method, we have performed several experiments by varying the values of k, and l.

Fig. 4 shows the recognition rates of the proposed method using *RBF-NN*. For each value of s, average recognition rates are plotted by varying the values of k and l. For $s=3$, 4, 5, 6 and 7 the best average recognition rates are found to be 93.57, 95.62, 97.45, 98.00 and 98.58, respectively and the dimension $(k*l)$ of the corresponding image feature matrices are $(30 * 30)$, $(24 * 24)$, $(24 * 24)$, $(12 * 12)$ and $(22 * 22)$, respectively.

For a fair comparison, we have implemented the PCA [1],2DPCA [3],PCA + FLD [5],2DFLD [6],Dia-FLD [9] and G-Dia2DFLD [10] algorithms and used the

Table 3. Comparison of different methods in terms of average recognition rate on the AT &T database, Figures within the parentheses denote the number of features

Method	Average Recognition Rates				
	S = 3	S = 4	S = 5	S = 6	S = 7
Our Proposed Method	**93.57**	**95.62**	**97.45**	**98**	**98.58**
G-Dia2DFLD	89.00	93.27	95.05	96.48	97.13
Dia FLD	88.66	92.73	94.88	96.31	96.71
PCA	85.58	89.42	93.10	95.28	96.01
2DPCA	91.27	94.33	96.83	97.72	97.79
PCA+FLD	83.65	88.65	92.60	95.30	95.83
2DFLD	92.30	95.08	97.50	98.26	97.88

same *RBF-NN* classifier and parameters for classification. The comparisons of the best average recognition rates of the above mentioned methods along with the proposed method for s= 3, 4, 5, 6 and 7 are shown in Table 3. It may be noted that in all the cases excepting for s=5 and s=6, the performance of the proposed method is better than other methods in terms of face recognition.

5 Conclusion

This paper presents a feature fusion method for face recognition. Feature level fusion involves the integration of feature sets corresponding to multiple or same modalities. Since the feature set contains richer information about the raw biometric data than the match score or final decision, integration at this level is expected to provide better recognition results. Human cognition process can recognize a face by looking into the diagonal vectors of the image matrix. So, like row and column vectors, the diagonal vectors of an image also play an important role for providing sufficient discriminating information. To realize this, aim of this paper is to integrate the discriminant features lying along the horizontal, vertical and diagonal directions. The diagonal images are constructed from the original images. Then the G-2DFLD method is applied on both original and diagonal images for feature extraction. The extracted features are then fused to get a large feature matrix. Then G-2DFLD method is again applied on the large fused matrix for dimensional reduction. The finally extracted features by G-2DFLD method leads to the application of the *RBF-NN* for classification. The hidden layer neurons of the *RBF-NN* have been modelled by considering intra-class discriminating characteristics of the training images. This helps the *RBF-NN* to acquire wide variations in the lower-dimensional input space. The experimental results on the AT & T (formerly ORL) database have been found to be superior to some of the subspace-based methods.

Acknowledgement. This work was partially supported by the UGC major research project (F. No.: 37-218/2009(SR), dated: 12-01-2010), CMATER and the SRUVM projects of the Department of Computer Science & Engineering, Jadavpur University, Kolkata, India. The author, Shiladitya Chowdhury would like to thank Techno India, Kolkata for providing computing facilities and allowing time for conducting research works.

References

1. Sirovich, L., Kirby, M.: Low-dimensional procedure for the characterization of human faces. Journal of Optical Society of America 4, 519–524 (1987)
2. Sirovich, L., Kirby, M.: Multi-directional two dimensional PCA with matching score level fusion for face recognition. Neural Comput. & Applic. 23, 169–174 (2013)
3. Yang, J., Zhang, D., Frangi, A.F., Yang, J.Y.: Two-dimensional PCA: A new approach to appearance-based face representation and recognition. IEEE Trans. Pattern Anal. Mach. Intell. 26, 131–137 (2004)

4. Belhumeur, P.N., Hespanha, J.P., Kriegman, D.J.: Eigenfaces versus fisherfaces: Recognition using class specific linear projection. IEEE Trans. Pattern Anal. Mach. Intell. 19, 711–720 (1997)
5. Er, M.J., Wu, S., Lu, J., Toh, H.L.: Face recognition with radial basis function (RBF) neural networks. IEEE Trans. Neural Networks 13, 697–710 (2002)
6. Xiong, H., Swamy, M.N.S., Ahmad, M.O.: Two-dimensional FLD for face recognition. Pattern Recognition 38, 1121–1124 (2005)
7. AT&T face database, AT&T Laboratories, Cambridge, U.K., http://www.uk.research.att.com/facedatabase.html
8. Su, C., Deng, J., Yang, Y., Wang, G.: Expression Recognition Methods Based on Feature Fusion. In: Yao, Y., Sun, R., Poggio, T., Liu, J., Zhong, N., Huang, J. (eds.) BI 2010. LNCS, vol. 6334, pp. 346–356. Springer, Heidelberg (2010)
9. Noushatha, S., Hemantha Kumara, G., Shivakumara, P.: Diagonal Fisher linear discriminant analysis for efficient face recognition. Neurocomputing 69, 1711–1716 (2006)
10. Sing, J.K., Roy, D., Basu, D.K., Nasipuri, M.: Generalized Diagonal 2D FLDA for Efficient Face Recognition. In: Proceeding of the CODIS 2012, pp. 101–112 (2012)
11. Chowdhury, S., Sing, J.K., Basu, D.K., Nasipuri, M.: Face recognition by generalized two-dimensional FLD method and multi-class support vector machines. Applied Soft Computing 11, 4282–4292 (2011)

Author Index